ART
in the
Elementary
School

fifth edition

Marlene Gharbo Linderman

Boston, Massachusetts   Burr Ridge, Illinios   Dubuque, Iowa
Madison, Wisconsin   New York, New York   San Francisco, California   St. Louis, Missouri

Book Team

Developmental Editor *Joey Retzler*
Production Editor *Ann Fuerste*
Proofreading Coordinator *Carrie Barker*
Art Editor *Rita Hingtgen*
Photo Editor *Amber Bettcher*
Production Manager *Beth Kundert*
Production/Costing Manager *Sherry Padden*
Design and New Media Development Manager *Linda Meehan Avenarius*
Visuals/Design Freelance Specialist *Mary L. Christianson*
Marketing Manager *Kirk Moen*
Copywriter *Sandy Hyde*
Proofreader/Production Assistant *Ann Morgan*

Basal Text *10/12 Times Roman*
Display Type *Futura*
Typesetting System *Macintosh™ QuarkXPress™*
Paper Stock *50# Spinnaker*

McGraw·Hill

A Division of The **McGraw·Hill** *Companies*

Executive Vice President and General Manager *Bob McLaughlin*
Vice President, Business Manager *Russ Domeyer*
Vice President of Production and New Media Development *Victoria Putman*
National Sales Manager *Phil Rudder*
National Telesales Director *John Finn*

Cover and interior design by Elise Lansdon

Cover art by Keith William Conners, first grade, Maddox Elementary School, Englewood, CO. Mary Lynn Ulrich Baird, teacher

Copyedited by Mary Monner; proofread by Rose R. Kramer

Library of Congress Catalog Card Number: 96–86033

ISBN 0–697–12500–9

Printed in the United States of America

10 9

This book is dedicated to ART and ART STUDENTS

contents

part
3

Art Appreciation:
*Looking at and
Responding to Art—
History, Analysis,
Aesthetics* **179**

chapter 10
Art History   181

chapter 11
Art Analysis: Looking at and Responding to Art   215

part
4

Elementary Art Fundamentals:
*Planning and
Assessment, Organizing,
and Questions* **229**

chapter 12
Lesson Planning and Assessment   231

chapter 13
Organizing the Art Room and Materials   238

chapter 14
Good Questions Teachers Often Ask   246

preface

A young student once said to me, "Art is the only learning area where I can be totally me. In math, often the answer's in the book. In spelling, the same thing—the words are spelled correctly. Even music has the right melodies and notes to follow. In art, I am only me and my own ideas."

Our information superhighways have shrunk our globe into one large community. Communication across the planet is instantaneous—filling our minds with facts and information gleaned from television, newspaper, and computers. Just fifty years ago, we had few of these. Now, perhaps more than ever, we need focusing stations to contemplate, investigate, feel, experience, discover, and perceive the aesthetic values crucial to our lives.

Art is universal. It reaches out beyond the boundaries of time, history, language, and space. It overlaps into every area. We can visit the histories and cultures of the world through artistic imagery that helps us understand peoples of the past and present. Art is a natural expression for everyone. It begins even before communication with words.

Individually, art offers ways to visualize from our inner minds, both intellectually and spiritually. To create art requires a combination of our mind, eyes, and hands. Art is introspective; it provides us with avenues for intuitive, creative, divergent thinking—to discover and explore with artistic freedom. We can then communicate with others through this imagery.

Today, more than at any other time in history, we live in communities that are abundant in the fine arts, such as architecture, books, film, television, photography, graphic design, interior spaces, computer imagery, clothing, and product design, as well as the visual arts. From all of these sources, we form critical judgments and opinions. These judgment skills are important for everyone in order to arrive at personal aesthetic choices during a lifetime.

Much of the information in this fifth edition has been retained and continues to remain valid. You will also find several exciting additions to the text that will be significant in your approach to teaching. Highlights of the fifth edition include:

- Reorganization, updating, and clarification of information
- Addition of color and colorful student art examples
- Greater aesthetic quality of book design
- Broad curriculum content and objectives for identifying student progress at various age levels
- Information on art for the gifted and talented and on art therapy
- Many new ideas and motivations for both two- and three-dimensional artworks
- Vocabulary terms for various art areas, such as photography, computers, art education
- New photographs throughout the text
- Ideas for and information on how to create murals
- A new section on art and technology (slides, video, photography, film, projectors, computers)
- Multicultural motivations for teaching with art examples
- Interdisciplinary motivations and teaching examples in art and science, math, language, social studies, and others
- Over a hundred specific teaching examples on teaching about and through art
- Specific drawing and painting techniques to apply in the classroom
- New quotes by noted artists, philosophers, business people, and educators
- A comprehensive glossary of art terms at the end of the book
- The images and philosophies of a variety of artists (many of them women)
- Questions to ask when looking at and responding to artworks
- How to plan lessons and measure achievement in student progress
- A new historical time line of art

- The most popular questions that students and teachers ask in three areas: art thinking, teaching methods, and student behavior in art
- Appendix listings of the most prominent artists in history (easy teacher resource material)
- Appendix listings of the major art museums in the United States, as well as art learning resources

All of the art concepts, instructional procedures, and teaching examples have been researched and practiced with all levels of students by practicing art teachers and elementary teachers. They were gathered from personal teaching experiences, from visiting classrooms, galleries, and museums all over the world, and from generous sharing of students' artworks.

The two primary functions of this text are (1) learning about art and (2) creating—the making of art. This book is intended to answer the needs of the prospective elementary and art teacher, the practicing teacher, administrators, school board members, and parents—all who wish to strive and achieve in art. The information illustrates how to plan and motivate students for art experiences that will stress individual direction and encourage and build upon personal uniqueness and talent. This book is a direct, practical approach that explains how to teach art to students.

This fifth edition is divided into four major parts. Part 1 focuses on the art curriculum foundation. Chapter 1 explores art in our world as seen in history and various cultures. Central to all is how art is an integral part of our lives. We experience it through our perceptions and express it through our creativity, imagination, and minds. Chapter 2 zeros in on art as curriculum content and lists objectives for a sequential curriculum, along with developmental stages for each grade level. Also included are art experiences, achievements to strive for, and materials to use at each grade level. The chapter concludes with discussions of art for the gifted and talented and for exceptional students (those with mental or physical disabilities).

Part 2 is the most extensive and includes seven chapters devoted to the content study of art and design and the tools involved in art production. These chapters list specific skills to teach, such as line, shape, space, color, pattern, texture, and design (putting it all together). Each concept includes significant vocabulary, specific ideas and motivations for developing skills, and information on how students understand and use such skills at various grade levels. Additional ideas and motivations, as well as lists of artists to study, are provided at the end of most chapters.

Chapter 8 is an extensive chapter focused on art production—the creative making. It includes many ideas and motivations for portraits, figures, still lifes, landscapes, drawing and painting, printmaking, puppets, clay, fibers, and for using technology to create art.

Chapter 9, another important chapter, provides specific teaching examples for multicultural and interdisciplinary art learning. Art can be an integral part of and overlap into all learning.

Part 3 spotlights art appreciation—looking at and responding to art. This section has been expanded and includes a time line of art history, along with the images and philosophies of many contemporary artists. A number of teaching examples are also presented.

Part 4 stresses teaching methods and focuses on lesson plans, teaching examples, measuring achievement, and assessment of student progress. Art room organization and suggested art materials for a basic art program are also covered. The final chapter of the book—perhaps the most popular—answers questions that students and teachers ask most frequently about the day-to-day experience of teaching art.

There are many ways for you to grow through art. You, the teacher, student, or parent, can determine the best avenue suited to achieve your individual goals. Each of you has unique and creative artistic talent. Only you can unleash this spirit and tap into your artistic energies. The instructions, ideas, motivations, art topics, and techniques within these pages will help you to develop this expressive power.

ABOUT THE AUTHOR

Marlene Linderman has taught elementary-age students, as well as university students and practicing teachers at Arizona State University. She is an exhibiting artist/teacher, lecturer, and television courtroom news artist. Most recently, she has painted several murals in the Phoenix area.

ACKNOWLEDGMENTS

The author wishes to thank the following individuals and organizations for supplying statements and excellent photographs relating to the teaching of art: Earl Linderman, Mrs. Milton Avery, Arizona State University Art Collection, The Art Institute of Chicago, California Palace of the Legion of Honor, M. H. De Young Memorial Museum, The Fine Arts Gallery of San Diego, The Museum of Contemporary Art–Los Angeles (MOCA), Adele Bednarz Galleries, Richard Feigen Gallery, Sidney Janis Gallery, The J. Paul Getty Trust, Marlborough Gallery, Inc., Gallerie Ann, Houston, Texas, Phoenix Art Museum, Dr. Jon Sharer, Marilyn Butler Fine Arts, Fritz Scholder, Dr. Anne Taylor, Dr. Muriel Magenta, Scottsdale School District, Scott Harris, Miriam Chynoweth, Hazel Scott, Dr. Dwayne Greer, Joan Hall, Leo Castelli Gallery, Houghton Mifflin Company, Andrea Bartlett, Dr. William E. Arnold, Leigh Hann,

Connie Ellis, Pat Jones-Hunt, Pat Koepp, Cartwright School District, Scottsdale Center for the Arts, the city of Scottsdale, Jack Stuler, The Hand and the Spirit Craft Gallery, Scottsdale, Andre Duetsch Limited, London, for the quotations from *The Natural Way to Draw* by Kimon Nicholaides, Destina Vigil, Tempe School District, Heather Davenport, Roger Davenport, Dr. Bernard Young, Dr. Mary Erickson, Albright-Knox Art Museum, Flo Patrenos, James Cowlin, Barbara Hartman, Maria Luisa Ruiz/Malintzin, Linda Ingraham, Esmeralda Delaney, Sue Raymond, Robert Miller Gallery, Ruth Weisberg, The National Art Education Association, The Phoenix Zoo, Dick George, Jackie Bondie, and Barbara Nessim, America West Sports Arena.

My deepest gratitude to Cheryl, Heather, Gwen, Bill and Mark Linderman and to the many outstanding students, teachers, and artists who helped make this book a reality.

I would also like to thank the following reviewers for their valuable feedback: Cynthia Cetlin, Ohio Wesleyan University; Kathleen E. Connors, Ph.D., Southern Connecticut State University; Kathy Danko-McGhee, Tennessee Tech University; Charles M. Dorn, Florida State University; Bonnie L. Khavaran, Cuyahoga Community College; Joanne Kurz Guilfoil, Eastern Kentucky University; Dr. Donald A. Parks, Delaware State University; and Marvin Spomer, University of Nebraska–Lincoln.

All photographs not credited were taken by the author.

The Art Curriculum Foundation

chapter

1

Art
Its Meaning and Significance in Our World

When I examine myself and my method of thought, I come to the conclusion that the gift of fantasy has meant more to me than my talent for absorbing knowledge.

Albert Einstein

If ever there was a time when we need to reawaken our intellectual and creative spirit, that time is now. To prepare ourselves for the future, we need to understand ourselves as a state and a nation and as part of the global community. The arts, humanities, and sciences are the foundation on which we will build that understanding.

Robert P. Casey, Governor of Pennsylvania

As a chief executive of a technology company that thrives on creativity, I want to work with people whose imaginations have been unleashed and who tackle problems as challenges rather than as obstacles. An education enriched by the creative arts should be considered essential for everyone.

John Scully, Chairman and CEO Apple Computer, Inc.

Albert Einstein's great aspiration was to capture a beam of light. He conceived the theory of general relativity after imagining a person taking a ride in a box through space. He believed that imagination is more important than knowledge. Yet, as adults, we sometimes close our imaginations and forget how to dream. The current global arena of electronic imagery, satellites, mass communication, and computers bombards us with multiple options with regard to thinking, feeling, and experiencing.

Our busy lifestyles seldom encourage us to contemplate, investigate, and discover the fullness of experience that is all around us. We need to establish focusing stations where our mind's eye can perceive the aesthetics crucial to our existence.

Art speaks to our creative spirits, allowing us to be both creators and/or appreciators. Personal forms of artistic expression—whether in the visual arts, music, the performing arts, literature, dance, drama, architecture—allow us to search the sensory, intuitive aspects of our experiences, to explore our responses to thinking, perceiving, and being. Art helps us to discover our individual identities and potentials. It reminds us how to dream.

ART AS A UNIVERSAL VISUAL LANGUAGE

Art reaches beyond the boundaries of language, time, and space to become a nonverbal and universal visual language. It is the creative and aesthetic merging of the eye, hand, and mind. Art symbolically expresses our ideas and feelings about ourselves and others.

Artistic expression is like putting words together to represent human thought in a visual dimension. As such, it is an effective system of communication through which artists speak to us across the boundaries of time, language, and civilizations (fig. 1.1). Some of the earliest records of humankind are the creative images from aboriginal societies of 32,000 years ago and the 20,000-year-old paintings on cave walls in Lascaux, France. The study of art can lead us to an understanding of both past and present societies (fig. 1.2).

Figure 1.1 Artifacts reflect the beliefs and attitudes cherished and expressed by a particular culture. Masks—artifacts found in even the earliest cultures—are used to change the wearer's identity.

Many cultures throughout history considered art an integral part of everyday living. In today's highly technological society, art has often been placed in museums or exhibition halls. As such, it has tended to become something magical and extraordinary, a special subject for special people.

Today, art is increasingly a feature of quality educational programs, city and state arts commissions, alternative art spaces, corporation collections, public spaces (such as parks), recreational programs, billboards, graffiti, and architectural spaces. Art knowledge and art expression are and should be basic fundamental aspects of our lives.

The visual and cultural arts include, but are not limited to, the categories that follow in the next section. New terms continually emerge as cultural values change. For example, the technological arts play an increasingly important part in today's art production. In addition, keep in mind that categories of art forms often overlap. For example, artists sometimes paint on sculpture, pottery, and fibers. And while watching television, we also often observe graphics, costumes, and stage designs. These same categories could be considered when discussing art careers with students. See also chart 2.1 in chapter 2 for a selected glossary of visual arts terms.

Figure 1.2 Art can be a reflection of humankind throughout history. During a study of Egypt, students created a papier-maché mummy.

CATEGORIES OF VISUAL AND CULTURAL ARTS

Visual arts: A broad category, including drawing, painting, printmaking, sculpture, and communication and design arts, such as film, television, and graphic arts.

Technological arts: Photography, Polaroid photography, film, video, computer-generated images, videodiscs, video cameras and tapes, laser disks, television, holography, copy machines, color copiers. All of these art forms use technology and can be used in the art room. Music videos are popular examples of newer media techniques.

Environmental arts: Architecture, landscape design, community design, interior and furniture design, clothing and items of adornment, product design.

Figure 1.3 The study of cultures includes artistic expression. This kachina sculpture represents a spiritual being to the Hopi Native Americans.

Figure 1.4 Navajo students treasure traditional weaving techniques handed down for centuries and still practiced today.

Cultural arts: Traditional expressions of ethnic groups of peoples, such as Native American forms of weaving and basketry, African masks, American quilts and handcrafted toys, and the Mexican "tree of life" sculpture. Sometimes referred to as "folk arts."

Two-dimensional art: Painting, drawing, printmaking, bookmaking, collage making.

Three-dimensional art: Sculptures of clay, metal, wood; mobiles; assemblages; neon light sculptures; installation arts (art exhibitions using materials and objects to convey ideas); and earthworks (artworks consisting of a portion of land modified by an artist).

Crafts: Ceramics, fibers, jewelry, enamel, wood, leather, paper, plastic, and other media.

Popular art: Clothing and items of adornment, graphic design in videos, magazines, book illustrations.

ART AS HISTORY AND CULTURE

Art is a creation and extension of the individual self. As such, it provides a record of people and their cultural achievements—their ideas, feelings, beliefs, attitudes, values, social concerns, ethnicity, customs, traditions, and sometimes, gender. Study of a culture's unique art forms reveals whatever that culture felt significant enough to communicate to others. A culture's paintings, sculptures, architecture, religious artifacts, technology, utensils, clothing, items of adornment, masks, and tools are reflections of the beliefs and attitudes that are cherished and expressed by that culture (fig. 1.3).

Today, we live in a complex, multicultural world. Cross-cultural concerns are apparent in music videos, television, films, books and other publications, murals, religious art and architecture, cityscape architecture, and propaganda art, such as billboards, political posters, and ethnic department stores. Art is one bridge that helps us to span our multicultural differences and to learn about and value each other. From creating, studying, and discussing works of art, we better understand ourselves and the world we live in.

Art helps us to span our multicultural differences, to express and preserve our cultural uniqueness (fig. 1.4). Increasingly, technology, communication networks, and the electronic media are leveling individual differences in cultures. We are becoming a global society. And as a result, art is becoming international in scope. This meshing of cultures eliminates the inherent qualities that comprise our differences and create our uniqueness. We need to cherish our differences, nourish our inherent artistic gifts, and respect our individual artistic uniqueness to gain insight into and to share the traditions of others (fig. 1.5).

Figure 1.5   A painted mural by sixth-graders increases their knowledge of the traditions, architecture, and customs of another culture.

ART IN THE COMMUNITY AND SCHOOL

A community requires the collective participation of all of its members. Today's communities are complex, as indicated by the diversity of their members. An important educational goal is to facilitate the involvement of young people in their communities so that they will be active contributors as adults.

A variety of community organizations provide, encourage, and maintain the visual arts traditions. Some of these public settings include libraries, art museums, commercial galleries, public parks, places of worship, commercial industrial art collections, banks, informal artist groups, artist studios, art classes, and theaters. Collections and exhibition arenas provide rich resources for the school art curriculum and offer resource opportunities and art experiences. Students learn when community art programs are invited into the school and also when they visit art spaces outside the school.

Innovative arts involvement programs being established across the country include community programs that receive aid from parent-teacher associations, the National Endowment for the Arts, local school districts, state and city arts commissions, Percent for Art programs, state funds, and community resources, such as banks. Many of these programs are designed to integrate professional and visiting artists into the educational program, where they work alongside teachers in the classroom. Artists may demonstrate their art form to students and/or offer students firsthand technical assistance while overseeing student projects and products. Often, slide lectures are presented on art fundamentals and techniques.

Another community art opportunity is the art museum and the art educators associated with them. Educators, as well as museum volunteer docents, visit schools to generate excitement about what students might experience in a museum visit. They often bring texts, slide shows, and videotapes in advance of a museum visit so that students can become more familiar with what they will see and experience. For example, if students have never been to a museum, the docent or educator can explain what a museum is, how it decides what to acquire and preserve for exhibition, how museums prepare for exhibitions, how museums differ from each other, and what to expect from a museum experience.

For the actual museum visit, educators strive to plan an experience that is sensitive to students' age, class level, art experience, and cultural backgrounds, as well as to the class curriculum and to what the students' teacher wishes to accomplish. A return visit to the classroom by the educator after the museum experience is helpful for questions about and discussion of the works seen and how the experience relates to students' classroom studies. See appendix B for a more detailed discussion of museums.

THE ARTIST

From artists' point of view, art is a total life commitment—a way of life. It is a way artists perceive, are aware of, and interpret experience. It is how they use knowledge and imagery, how they develop and expand their imaginations. Art influences their flexibility to situations and concepts, how they go about searching for unique ideas, and how they are sensitive to the needs of others. Artists strive to improve the aesthetic environment.

Art influences artists' choices, such as what art films, concerts, museums, schools, and studios they attend, how they organize their thoughts and ideas, and with whom they share these ideas. By practicing, improving, and expanding in the arts, they develop aesthetic criteria for making these choices.

We are all art practicers and art viewers, to one extent or another, and regardless of our age or level of ability, we can strive to increase and broaden our art scope. Art development and art skills also aid us in understanding such related arts as music, dance, theater, literature, and architecture.

ART AND THE INDIVIDUAL STUDENT

An education of excellence includes quality art education opportunities and experiences for all students. Art experiences encourage both verbal and nonverbal forms of communication, sometimes allowing student artists to express ideas that they are otherwise unable to verbalize. Art reflects students' emotional, physiological, and intellectual development and serves as an arena for problem solving. Students with problems, such as disabilities, drug and alcohol abuse, sexual and emotional abuse, homelessness, or disease, can often express their unique characteristics and situations through art. Art also offers ways for students to relate to one another through involvement, demonstration of abilities, and expression of feelings.

Actively involving parents in school art programs ensures that students will be encouraged in their art exploration at home. Ask parents to attend and/or assist at artist demonstrations, to donate surplus materials, to act as art aides, to demonstrate their personal art expertise, and to help organize student art exhibits. Encourage your local parent-teacher association to purchase art objects, artifacts, or art supplies.

Sometimes, parents ask how they can encourage their individual child to engage in the arts. Suggest that they become actively supportive of the school art program and that they also provide their child with high-quality art materials to work with at home. Many of the concepts discussed in this book are helpful to the parent who wishes to know more about children's art and ways to support children's art interests.

For many children, elementary art classes may be the only educational experiences they will have in the visual arts. As a teacher, you can provide the artistic, creative energy that will help your students to reap maximum benefits from this potentially short exposure. Art experiences will help to instill in your students the ingenuity, inventiveness, flexibility, and originality in thinking that will be required of them in the twenty-first century (fig. 1.6).

In recent years, research and scientific testing have indicated that the human brain has two hemispheres, which interlock in a series of networks to perform different functions. The left hemisphere analyzes; differentiates; is deductive; influences language, logic, and rationality; and deals with

Figure 1.6   Teacher Sue Raymond discusses art and the individual by looking and talking about artists and works of art.

information. In contrast, the right hemisphere dominates integration (relating parts of an experience to a large whole), imagination, intuition, free association, wisdom, and spatial realizations, and is responsible for emotional responses and also for skills that relate more to drawing and painting, dance, music, acting, and creating with one's hands—in short, more with the spiritual literacy of our lives.

In right-handed people, the left hemisphere operates rationally and the right hemisphere intuitively. The right hemisphere appears to have control over creative behavior. Both right and left hemispheres control motor behavior, but the left hemisphere's control exceeds the right. Each hemisphere learns independently and has memory. One side can work on one task while the other works on another, and both have communication with each other.

A problem in many schools today is the emphasis on left-hemisphere activities—the focus on scientific, realistic, and verbal modes of thinking. Meanwhile, right-hemisphere activities that provide opportunities for free organization, such as fantasy, dreaming, and discussion of open-ended ideas, are neglected.

The arts, and specifically the visual arts, help to develop right-hemisphere capabilities and give impetus to such learning that deals with intuition, innovation, flexibility, and creativity. Thus, art education provides opportunities for students to use creative and intuitive approaches to problem solving and is critical to balancing the development of the whole brain and, thereby, the whole person.

PERCEPTUAL EXPERIENCES AND CREATIVE THINKING

By focusing and reflecting on perceptual experiences and creative thinking, and by providing educational strategies that focus on right-hemisphere activities, you can help students to fuse and meld the various streams of learning and to integrate the skills of art production, history, and analysis.

Perceptual Experiences

Perceptual experiences involve taking in information, learning through the senses, and exploring internal imagery. Through sight, touch, hearing, taste, and smell, we participate in a myriad of experiences and interact with our environment (figs. 1.7, 1.8, and 1.9).

Infants first learn about the world around them through perceptual experiences. Shortly after birth, infants respond to voices and open their eyes for the first time. At two weeks of age, they are able to follow a moving shape with their eyes. In the first six months, their hands point to objects. They make bubbles and other mouth movements in imitation of adult speech movements. When parents stop talking, they respond and fill in gaps with sounds and body movements. During a conversation between two adults, babies often move to the rhythm of the human speech in terms of the syllable sounds and the high and low pitches. Thus, babies rely heavily on perceptual contact prior to language development.

To toddlers, everything in the world is new. They laugh with delight at new experiences and look for and welcome new challenges, new unveilings. Toddlers run *toward* new happenings, not away from them. When given a new toy, toddlers look at it, feel it, taste it, squeeze it, hit it, pinch it, smell it, throw it, sit on it, jump on it, move it back and forth, up and down, and in and out. They explore and discover this new object in as many ways as they can think of. When they are done "playing" with the toy—after they have taken from it all the information they can—they throw it down and move on to something new, to begin all over again (fig. 1.10).

All of us sort out from various sensory experiences the information and knowledge that has meaning to us and store this knowledge in our brains. From the billions of stored items of information, we form associations, synthesize, and build understanding, meaning, and concepts (or theories) about our world. This is a complex process, involving for each of us a unique succession of isolated events. Yet, we are constantly aware of the relations of these separate events to the larger context. Our past experiences relate to our present ones and influence our future ones. As philosopher and educator John Dewey noted:

> Where there is form, there is a sense of qualitative unity; each color, line, plane, etc. is related to its neighbors in such a way that a sequential whole is built up in the act of perception.[1]

In short, everything we see, hear, touch, smell, and taste contributes to making us who we are.

Creative Thinking

The spirit of the creative imagination exists in each of us and should be a top priority in our lives and in art. Are some people born more creative than others? How can creative thinking in an individual be identified? Researchers

Figure 1.7   The eye is an important tool in sensory experiencing. Looking through a magnifying glass brings the microscopic world into focus.

Figure 1.8   What does a child see when she looks into a puddle? What do you see? Children learn to see by opening their senses and their minds.

Figure 1.9   When children explore the world around them, they often use their imaginations.

Figure 1.10   Discovery is an important part of the creative process.

have investigated such questions as the ratio of creativity to intellectual ability, the part of humor in creative people, the relationship between environment and aesthetic response, and the importance of classroom environment on productive thinking.

Perhaps the best approach to understanding creative thinking is to explore the various characteristics that others have applied to the concept. The list that follows notes characteristics that a variety of sources have identified as "creative." If creative characteristics can be identified, then teaching goals can be aimed at supporting such characteristics.

Creative people have been described as:

Fluent (can generate a large number of ideas within a
   given time period)
Flexible (can suggest unusual uses for objects)
Able to provide elaboration (complexity of detail in
   verbal or visual tasks)
Original (able to come up with new and unusual ideas)
Discerning
Curious
Receptive
Reflective
Eager to experience
Secure
Spontaneous
Natural
Uninhibited
Individuals who do not rely on the familiar
Attracted and responsive to the mysterious and
   puzzling
Independent in ideas and judgment
Able to use free association
Not interested in "quick" solutions; resistant to
   premature closing
Open to new ideas and possibilities
Responsive to constructive criticism
Willing to take risks
Able to find relationships in unrelated ideas
Challengers of established ideas
Eager to share discoveries with others
Individuals who ask penetrating questions
Energetic
Persistent
Intuitive
Sensitive to the outside world
Resolved to alter reality
Individuals who continue creative activity beyond
   scheduled time

Noted philosopher and educator John Dewey wrote that the creative process has two aspects: First, it arises from a domain of knowledge or skill, and second, it has a marked quality of freshness or novelty.[2] Thus, creative individuals in various areas, such as in science, mathematics, and the arts, are able to take their knowledge or skills in these areas and apply them in new, imaginative ways.

Figure 1.11 Everyone has the capacity for creative imagination.

Well-known art educator Viktor Lowenfeld believes that:

> Creativity is an instinct which all people possess, an instinct with which we were born. It is the instinct which we primarily use to solve and express life's problems. . . . Creativity, the ability to explore and investigate, belongs to one of the Basic Drives, a drive without which man cannot exist.[3]

Psychologist, educator, and professor of graduate studies at Tufts University, David Henry Feldman stated that one of three basic parts of creativity is the person's resolve to alter reality—not just by seeing things differently but by transforming them into something new altogether.[4]

Margaret DiBlasio, the head of art education at the University of Minnesota, wrote:

> We have learned to be suspicious of any claim that creativity springs full-blown from the undisciplined, unprepared mind. Rule-bound, rigorous learning is the soil in which creativity grows. Even such prototypically creative people as Einstein, Freud, and Leonardo Da Vinci had teachers from whom— before they made their creative departures—they acquired a rich context of images and meanings drawn from their cultures and from disciplinary traditions.[5]

The National Art Education Association defines **creativity** as the flexible and fluent generation of unique, complex, or elaborate ideas.[6]

Regardless of how it is defined, creative, imaginative behavior does not appear to be a one-time reaction to a situation, but a continual, ongoing response that involves relationships and grows as a pattern (fig. 1.11).

Avenues to Creative Art Thinking

Art stresses all of the ingredients attributed to creativity. Included are ideas that deal with originality, uniqueness of response, and inventive, independent solutions. For example, art teachers can motivate students with subject areas (an object, theme, or place) that require imaginative interpretations, such as "A Visit to Saturn." Such a theme demands an inventive solution because no one knows what Saturn is like. Therefore, one step to creativity is selecting an inventive theme.

Creative people search for unique ways to communicate ideas. For example, they may use relationships in a new way in an artwork. Artists often get their inventive themes from self-stimulus. That is, they may come up with ideas that are pure fantasy from their imaginations, or they may be inspired by objects, places, or persons, which they then interpret in a unique way.

Once an inventive theme is selected, the subconscious mind explores and plays with the idea. Time for contemplating ideas; for reflection, daydreaming, visualization; and for experimenting with inventions is another critical step in creativity, which is why it is also an important component of any art curriculum. John Ashbery exemplified this when he described his writing style:

> I sort of collect words that suddenly seem to have a new meaning for me, in contexts I have never thought of before. I don't plan my writing. What comes out is usually quite surprising. I write to find out what I'm thinking.[7]

The actual production of any idea, such as in an art form, is another step in creativity. The concrete form of the product allows the inventor to advance, to step back from and then further into the idea, and to consider it more objectively in order to make conscious adjustments. According to Harvard professor Howard Gardner:

> Perception means learning to see better, to hear better, to make finer discriminations, to see connections between things. Reflection means to be able to step back from both your production and your perceptions, and say, 'What am I doing? Why am I doing it? What am I learning? What am I trying to achieve? Am I being successful? How can I revise my performance in a desirable way?'[8]

Creativity is a dominant force in art, transferring an experience into an expressive artwork. Limited only by the power of their imaginations, artists attempt to create new meanings.

Ways to Encourage Art Perception and Creativity in the Classroom

An elementary art program should attempt to provide mind-opening, perceptive experiences and to embrace creative attitudes and characteristics. When students' perceptions, creative thinking, self-expression, and discovery are nurtured through art experiences, the benefits of that nurturing can then be applied to other learning areas, such as mathematics and the sciences.

One way to expand students' perceptual and creative potentials is to construct unique environments and situations for your classroom that encourage students to discover—to enter openly with the senses. Discovery learning occurs when students are guided to "discover" information—when they can manipulate objects, have boundless freedom to experiment, can ask relevant questions, are encouraged to act on their intuitive and spontaneous responses, and have time to contemplate, discriminate, and form conclusions and judgments (fig. 1.12). To encourage creative discovery learning, provide art situations and environments that:

- Encourage unique ways to communicate ideas.
- Use relationships in new ways in artworks.
- Deal with the abstract, the mind's inventive world.
- Invite inquiry and exploration.
- Require original and imaginative solutions.
- Offer challenges.
- Display cause and effect.
- Develop initiative.
- Deepen sensory involvement through sensory experiences.
- Require analysis as well as synthesis of new ideas.
- Offer numerous solutions that do not require approval.
- Instill feelings of confidence, enthusiasm, self-satisfaction, and achievement.

Adventure Environment

For an "adventure environment," take students out and explore, as fully as you can, a beach, a desert, a river, a skyscraper, a church, a mountaintop, a television station, or an amusement park (fig. 1.13). Record students' impressions with a tape recorder, on note pads, in photographs, and/or on videotape. Invent sounds, poems, and movements "on the spot." Then, back in the classroom, you and the students can interpret your impressions and perceptions into total environmental art sensory experiences.

Your props will be lights and materials that add suspense, excitement, and imaginative involvement. They might include:

- Tactile sensitizers
- Sound and listening sensitizers
- Taste and smell sensitizers
- Elastic bandage (pretend "spider web") strips that students can push, pull, stretch, and move
- Cloth sheets or an old parachute that moves and changes with air currents and with holes for walking through
- Structures that students can build or stack and that are painted or that reflect lights cast on them
- Large boxes that are different on the inside as well as on the outside, that can be worn or hidden behind, and that can divide spaces
- Sheets and other reflective surfaces that can be worn or that can reflect slides of exciting images
- Tree trunks, stuffed animals, forms from nature, and other "extras" that you have collected

Your classroom is a stage and can become anything your imagination can invent. Improvise and change the spaces within the room as the ideas develop and progress. Tailor your creative environments to students' abilities and growth. This enables students to learn by doing.

Figure 1.12 Unique classroom environments encourage students to manipulate objects, to experiment, to ask questions, to act on their intuitive and spontaneous responses, and to contemplate, discriminate, and form conclusions and judgments.

Do your school spaces meet the students' physical needs with regard to size, scale, and levels? Does your curriculum determine space needs? Is the space flexible? Does it reflect students' interests and skills?

Follow up your creative environments by recording students' sensory impressions through interpretations with words, drawings, paintings, structured body movements, invented music, and sounds.

Be sure to provide a creativity space in the classroom—a table or corner where students can go to invent, explore, manipulate, create, and paint. The time spent in the creative space should not be considered "art" time. Plan a daily theme, such as (1) "Can you invent a math game that we can play in teams?" (2) "Can you build some furniture out of paper that we can use for our playhouse?" (3) "Paint a picture of what you think Jennifer will find when she visits the Hopi reservation." (4) "Here is a 'mystery' painting. See if you can guess the subject of the painting, the artist, and the technique the artist used."

Ask students to relate unusual words to pictures, to compose animals from various animal parts, to create space imaginations, and to look at the world through the eyes of an elephant, an ant, a bird. A trip to the bottom of the sea, a ride on a windstorm, the adventure of a raindrop, or the travels of a butterfly are just a few of the endless possibilities that engage the imagination in new ways of seeing the world.

Encourage creative art behavior by experimenting with tools and media (fig. 1.14). Have unusual, exciting, stimulating materials available. Challenge students to look at objects in the environment from many viewpoints and attitudes, to analyze objects in detail, to bring together new ideas, and to be inventive with many solutions for a single art idea.

(a)

(b)

Figure 1.13 (*a*) Environments can be artworks in themselves. Interior of San Xavier del Bac, Arizona. (*b*) Exploring an "adventure environment," such as an amusement park ride, can be a total environmental sensory experience.

Expand on these creativity lessons by emphasizing creative behaviors—fluency (coming up with many ideas), inventiveness, looking for differences and similarities, flexibility, originality, curiosity, imagination, more elaborate and complex thinking, and risk taking—in art and all classroom subjects. Establish a classroom environment in which far-out questioning; speculative, anything-goes approaches; and open inquiry methods without judgment are the rule. When students are encouraged to work independently, to be resourceful and self-expressive, to solve their own problems (instead of letting adults solve problems for them), and to eliminate stereotyped solutions in art, they begin to work independently in other areas of study as well.

Chart 1.1 is a list of creativity sparkers—tools and stimuli that will help students to develop greater sensitivity to and awareness of perception and creativity.

Figure 1.14   New and unusual materials can spark creative responses.

chart 1.1
Creativity Sparkers

Themes and subject matter for artworks:

Real or imaginary flowers, animals, birds, insects, plants, and trees
Fantasy subjects, such as a ride on a windstorm, the travels of a hummingbird
Objects at the beach; seascapes
Buildings: schools, homes, farms, shopping malls, cities
Transportation: trains, planes, buses, space shuttles
Water activities: boating, surfing, sailing, swimming, waterskiing
Sports: football, baseball, basketball, tennis, golf
Historical themes: governments, peoples, historical events
Events: circuses, rodeos, county fairs
Holidays, celebrations
Foods, fruits, and vegetables (inside and outside, touch, taste, and smell)
Magnification
Precision instruments, clocks, radios, televisions
Optical illusions
Geometric shapes and forms in nature and in human-made objects
Flat and rounded forms
Plays, stories, myths, fables, improvisation, make-believe
Clothing, costumes, stage sets, masks
Other cultures, lands, peoples, traditions, artifacts
Social themes: pollution, nutrition, family relationships, poverty, crime, war, drugs
Themes like recycling wastes, how food changes, how artists have used foods in artworks
Landscapes, skyscapes, cityscapes, clouds
Skeletal frameworks: fish, people, animals, bridges, architecture, dinosaurs, bones

Visits to airports, grocery stores, restaurants, movies, television studios, malls, factories, photography studios, city and government buildings, greenhouses
Visual, tactile, sound and listening, space, movement, taste, and smell sensitizers
Creativity walks
Smells: flowers, bread factories, cigars, spices, cars, artists' studios, houses, herbs, cafeterias, candles, perfumes

Supplies for motivating creative artworks:

Magnifying devices
Telephone wire for sculpting
Blocks, boxes, wood scraps
Scraps of yarn, leather, string, cloth, wrapping papers
Popsicle sticks, toothpicks
Cuisenaire rods
Cookie cutters, bottle caps, buttons
Magnets, iron filings
Masks, fake mustaches and noses, eyeglasses
Spoons, strainers, corks, plastic bottles
Packing materials for sculpturing and building
Puppets, stages, and scenery; chalkboards
Cameras, video recorders, typewriters, computers
Materials for printmaking and rubbings
Foods from other cultures for holidays and certain seasons
Secret tactile boxes, old jewelry
Listening devices, such as tape recorders, stethoscopes, microphones, bells, kazoos, musical instruments, radios, clocks, motors, people's voices, birds, animals, drums, creaking doors

NOTES

1. John Dewey, *Art As Experience* (New York: Putnam, 1958).
2. John Dewey, *Art As Experience* (New York: Putnam, 1958).
3. Viktor Lowenfeld, *Creative and Mental Growth* (New York: Macmillan, 1960).
4. "Discipline-Based Art Education: What Forms Will It Take?" Proceedings of a National Invitational Conference sponsored by the Getty Center for Education in the Arts, Los Angeles, California, January 1987 (p. 84).
5. "Discipline-Based Art Education: What Forms Will It Take?" Proceedings of a National Invitational Conference sponsored by the Getty Center for Education in the Arts, Los Angeles, California, January 1987 (pp. 84–85).
6. *National Art Education Association News* 36, no. 3 (1994): 10–11.
7. John Ashbery, "The Puzzle of Genius," *Newsweek,* 28 June 1993, p. 50.
8. R. Brandt, "On Assessment in the Arts: A Conversation with Howard Gardner," *Educational Leadership* 45, no. 4 (1987): 30–34.

2

Curriculum Components and Identifying Student Art Progress

Art establishes the basic human truths which must serve as the touchstone of our judgment.

John F. Kennedy, thirty-fifth president of the United States

No longer can we consider what the artist does to be a self-contained activity, mysteriously inspired from above, unrelated and unrelatable to other human activities. . . . Instead, we recognize the exalted kind of seeing that leads to the creation of great art as an outgrowth of the humbler and more common activity of the eyes in everyday life. . . . There was a wholesome lesson in the discovery that vision is not a mechanical recording of elements but rather the apprehension of significant structural patterns. . . . The mind functions as a whole, all perceiving is also thinking, all reasoning is also intuition, all observation is also invention.

R. Arnheim, *Art and Visual Perception*

In effective art programs, student learning about art and through art is the central focus to everything else. Art teachers are the first to realize that there are no perfect solutions to art, no prescribed artistic formulas, and no sure methods or guarantees for producing art. But that is part of the excitement, the surprise, the unknown possibilities inherent in art. In art, there is no "right" way or "wrong" way; there is only the artist's freedom to do it his or her way. Art expresses the artist's intellectual, emotional self.

Art experiences are a unique and indispensable component of a child's entire development. They help children to express creative and unique personal ideas, to develop many potential solutions to a problem, to be flexible in their ideas, to enhance their reasoning and intuitive thinking, to develop initiative, and to cultivate attitudes of success and achievement (fig. 2.1). There are many reasons why art is invaluable to the school curriculum.

ART OBJECTIVES

Art . . .

- is a natural form of expression and offers opportunities to investigate, express, and respond.
- is a separate learning subject consisting of content and skill development.
- is a curriculum cohort related to other literary and performing arts as well as to integrated studies.
- helps to develop each individual's unique potential through imagination, creative behavior, art production, and aesthetic responses.
- is an arena for creative problem solving and thinking, new ideas, invention, originality, unexpected responses, independence, discovery, experimentation, open attitudes, idea interactions, imagination, flexibility, self-expression, personal imagery, risk taking, trial and error, self-evaluation, decision making, and decision justification.
- stresses sensory experiencing, thereby increasing perception.
- enhances creative problem solving that can be applied to thinking skills across the curriculum.
- increases skills of observation, perception, memory, imagination, innovation, manipulating materials (knowing materials' differences and uses), reflection on life experiences.

Figure 2.1   Art experiences are unique and indispensable in a child's development. Elementary students studied the artist Henri Matisse and then created their own wall mural.
Teacher: Heather Davenport

- increases skills in integrating, organizing, creating, and evaluating aesthetic responses.
- is a form of communication and a way to share ideas verbally and nonverbally.
- provides opportunities to identify, describe, analyze, interpret, and evaluate artworks.
- increases aesthetic literacy (What is good? What is beautiful? Why?) and art vocabulary.
- provides opportunities for increasing artistic skills and for learning about specific art processes and techniques, art movements, artists and their works, and art forms and styles.
- is a way to study today's society and how art is an integral part of the life and environment of that society.
- can be applied to all aspects of life, from personal living choices (architecture, interiors, clothing, and so on) to art and society.
- develops attitudes of appreciation, positive reinforcement, self-worth, success, and achievement.
- helps the individual to realize the joy of art creation.
- is a humanizing endeavor in that it is self-fulfilling, gratifying, and a lifelong attitude.
- is a study of history and cultures, a way to appreciate differences.

This chapter focuses first on the standards and components of a quality visual arts curriculum and then examines in detail and by grade level how art growth in elementary children can be recognized.

STANDARDS FOR A VISUAL ARTS CURRICULUM

The National Visual Arts Standards were prepared by the National Art Education Association (NAEA) in response to the Goals 2000: Educate America Act. The NAEA,

founded in 1947 and the largest professional art education association in the world, has stated the following educational goals for art education and the art curriculum:

> Art education benefits the *student* because it cultivates the whole child, gradually building many kinds of literacy while developing intuition, reasoning, imagination, and dexterity into unique forms of expression and communication. This process requires not merely an active mind but a trained one. An education in the arts benefits *society* because students of the arts gain powerful tools for understanding human experiences, both past and present. They learn to respect the often very different ways others have of thinking, working, and expressing themselves. They learn to make decisions in situations where there are no standard answers. By studying the arts, students stimulate their natural creativity and learn to develop it to meet the needs of a complex and competitive society. And, as study and competence in the arts reinforce one another, the joy of learning becomes real, tangible, and powerful.[1]

The Visual Arts Standards ask that students should know and be able to do the following by the time they have completed secondary school:

1. Understand and apply visual arts media, techniques, and processes.
2. Use knowledge of visual arts structures and functions.
3. Choose and evaluate a range of subject matter, symbols, and ideas.
4. Understand the visual arts in relation to history and cultures.
5. Reflect upon and assess the characteristics and merits of their work and the work of others.
6. Make connections between visual arts and other disciplines.

MEETING THE OBJECTIVES AND STANDARDS

To meet the National Visual Arts Standards, students must learn vocabularies and concepts associated with various types of work in the visual arts and must exhibit their competence at various levels in visual, oral, and written form.

In kindergarten through grade 4, young children experiment enthusiastically with art materials and investigate ideas through visual arts instruction. A sense of joy and excitement is exhibited as they make and share their artwork with others. To create is at the heart of this learning with various tools, process, and media. They learn to coordinate their hands and minds in explorations of the visual world and to make choices that enhance communication of their ideas. Their natural inquisitiveness is encouraged.

From kindergarten through the early grades, students develop skills of observation, and they learn to examine the objects and events of their lives. They grow in their ability to describe, interpret, evaluate, and respond to work in the visual arts. With examination of their own work and that of other people, times, and places, students learn the essence of artwork and how to appraise its purpose and value. Through these experiences, students begin to understand the meaning and impact of the visual world in which they live.

In the upper grades, students grow ever more sophisticated in their need to use the visual arts to reflect their feelings and emotions and in their abilities to evaluate the merits of their efforts. As students gain this knowledge and these skills, they gain in their ability to apply the knowledge and skills in the visual arts to their widening personal worlds. As they develop increasing fluency in visual, oral, and written communication, they exhibit their greater artistic competence through all of these avenues. Students' visual expressions become more individualistic and imaginative. The problem-solving activities inherent in art making help them develop cognitive, affective, and psychomotor skills. They select and transform ideas, discriminate, synthesize and appraise, and they apply these skills to their expanding knowledge of the visual arts and to their own creative work. Students understand that making and responding to works of visual art are inextricably interwoven and that perception, analysis, and critical judgment are inherent to both.

Students should be able to develop and present basic analysis of works of art from structural, historical, and cultural perspectives, and from combinations of those perspectives. They should have an informed acquaintance with exemplary works of art from a variety of cultures and historical periods and a basic understanding of historical development in the arts disciplines, across the arts as a whole, and within cultures.

A SEQUENTIAL CURRICULUM

A sequential curriculum structure for art requires defining broad student objectives and behaviors—that is, what students will learn, produce, and achieve—for each grade level. The objectives can specify the experiences, the concepts to be learned, and the skills that amplify these concepts and that are appropriate to students' level of development. Evaluative and assessment procedures that relate to artistic and perceptual skills, art production skills, and art history and analysis skills can be developed for each objective. Each classroom should still function with an independent, flexible format while also meeting established goals within a framework.

High school and middle school art curriculum personnel should consult with their counterparts in the elementary school so that, throughout their school years, students are provided with an ongoing art curriculum sequence that is structured to their general as well as unique needs. By defining such needs, art teachers are able to inform administrators, parents, and students of their objectives.

FOUR COMPONENTS OF A QUALITY ART CURRICULUM

The four primary areas of art experiencing in a quality art curriculum are:

1. Artistic and perceptual skills
2. Art production
3. Art history
4. Art analysis

These areas work together to reinforce and broaden students' response to art and self-expression, knowledge, and understanding of art. Each area may be experienced individually or may overlap another, but the curriculum should provide a good balance of experiences in all four areas at all grade levels.

The sections that follow present an overall picture of the concepts to teach and of students' capabilities in each of these areas from kindergarten through sixth grade. Keep in mind that art growth is continuous and that many stated objectives overlap. Remember also that no particular student is typical of any defined skill level. Students may indicate varying level abilities and characteristics at any one time. What follows are broad generalizations that imply certain growth and that will help you to identify attainable goals for your students. If any of the art terms or processes referred to in these next sections is unfamiliar, please consult chart 2.1, the glossary at the end of the book, and/or the index.

Artistic and Perceptual Skills

Development of artistic and perceptual skills involves a heightened awareness of and greater sensitivity to the self, the visual arts, and the visual environment in which we live. The more intensely that students see and involve all the senses, the more that they feel, understand, experience, and respond to art.

Students at different grade levels have different artistic/perceptual capabilities. Students in kindergarten through third grade are imaginative, inquisitive, and eager to learn. They are aware of self, people, and objects in the environment, but tend to relate to self-centered interests. They like to classify objects and enjoy both the real and the make-believe. They tend to be impatient with themselves, and their attention spans increase with age. Students in kindergarten and first grade tend to select color emotionally. By third grade, they use color symbolically, draw more realistic proportions, work for predetermined effects, and have a greater awareness of differences in people.

Fourth-graders are interested in boy-girl relationships. Fifth-graders show interest in the real and in details. Sixth-graders like group activities, are loyal to peers, tend to analyze the world, and have the longest attention spans.

chart 2.1

Vocabulary of Visual Arts Terms

The content in art education includes terms that encourage students to communicate ideas through their artworks and to be able to look at, respond to, and give meaning to their work and the work of others.

Aesthetics A branch of philosophy that focuses on the nature of beauty, the nature and value of art, and the inquiry processes and human responses associated with those topics.

Art analysis Identifying and examining separate parts as they function independently and together in creative works and studies of the visual arts.

Art content What the artwork is about, the idea or intended meaning.

Art criticism Describing and evaluating the media, processes, ideas, history, subject matter, symbols, themes, and meanings of works of visual art, and making comparative judgments. (See *art analysis*.)

Art elements The visual arts components of line, value, shape, space, color, pattern, and texture.

Art history A record of the visual arts, incorporating information, interpretations, and judgments about art objects, artists, and conceptual influences on developments in the visual arts.

Art materials Resources used in the creation and study of visual art, such as paint, clay, cardboard, canvas, film, videotape, models, watercolors, wood, and plastic.

Art media Broad categories for grouping works of visual art according to the art materials used.

Assess To analyze and determine the nature and quality of achievement through means appropriate to the subject.

Context A set of interrelated conditions (such as time, place, purpose, influence, function, style, and social, economic, and political conditions) in the visual arts that influence and give meaning to the development of thoughts, ideas, or concepts and that define specific cultures and eras.

Create To produce works of visual art using materials, techniques, processes, elements, and analysis. The flexible and fluent generation of unique, complex, or elaborate ideas.

Description Facts about the subject and who, when, where, and how the artwork was created. This includes the time and place, climate, resources, ability to communicate ideas of the times, themes, symbols used, and technology. It also includes knowledge of the media, techniques, and processes and what makes them effective or not in expressing the intent of the artwork.

Design principles The underlying organizational characteristics in the visual arts: balance, dominance, rhythm, contrast, harmony, variety, unity.

Evaluation Reflecting on and forming a judgment, and then validating reasons for choices regarding a work of art.

Expression A process of conveying ideas, feelings, and meanings through selective use of the communicative possibilities of the visual arts.

Expressive qualities Elements evoking affects such as joy, sadness, or anger. There are sensory, formal, and individual stylistic qualities.

Ideas A formulated thought, opinion, or concept that can be represented in visual or verbal form.

Interpretation Ways to understand the artworks, either the student's own or others. This includes responding to an artwork in many ways and identifying with and reflecting on the artwork's meaning, function, purpose, and value.

Perception Visual and sensory awareness, discrimination, and integration of impressions, conditions, and relationships with regard to objects, images, and feelings.

Process A complex operation involving a number of methods or techniques, such as the addition and subtraction processes in sculpture, the etching and intaglio processes in printmaking, or the casting or constructing processes in making jewelry.

Structures Means of organizing the components of a work into a cohesive and meaningful whole, such as sensory qualities, organizational [design] principles, expressive qualities, and functions of art.

Synesthesia A mental image that corresponds to something that is entirely different; that is, when one hears a certain sound, it induces the visualization of a particular color.

Techniques Specific methods or approaches used in a larger process. For example, graduation of value or hue in painting or conveying linear perspective through overlapping, shading, or varying size or color.

Technologies Complex machines used in the study and creation of art, such as lathes, presses, computers, lasers, and video equipment.

Tools Instruments and equipment used to create and learn about art, such as brushes, scissors, brayers, easels, knives, kilns, and cameras.

Visual arts A broad category that includes the traditional fine arts, such as drawing, painting, printmaking, and sculpture; communication and design arts, such as film, television, graphics, and product design; architecture and environmental arts, such as urban, interior, and landscape design; folk arts; and works of art, such as ceramics, fibers, jewelry, and works in wood, paper, and other materials.

Source: Adapted from *National Art Education Association News* 36, no. 3 (June 1994): 10–11.

To develop students' artistic and perceptual abilities, instruct students, according to grade level and student proficiency, in art content and art skills, including the formal elements of art and how each interacts with and depends on the whole. Emphasize the attitudes that artistic skills are essential for expression and that all persons are creative and productive. The following are some general guidelines for developing elementary students' artistic and perceptual growth:

- Encourage perceptual experiencing with techniques that emphasize seeing, touching, hearing, tasting, smelling, movement, and space awareness.
- Urge students to reach beyond the senses to their imaginations, intellects, and feelings.
- Encourage students to show imaginative, original, and expressive responses in their drawings, paintings, and creations.
- Develop the figure concept—from geometric lines in kindergarten to group figures in action in the environment in third grade.
- Expand the art concept of "art and me" in kindergarten and first grade to "art and the world" in third grade.
- Use objects, scenes, situations, the imagination, inventions, materials, tools, museums, artists' studios, the electronic media, and all the related arts as art stimulators.
- Have students observe and practice the art elements—line, shape, value, color, space, texture, and pattern—so that they begin to understand how these elements relate to balance, dominance, rhythm, and contrast.
- Promote art as an experience of the spirit and as therefore a humanizing endeavor.
- Help students to develop a heightened awareness of and greater sensitivity to the self, the visual arts, and the visual environment.
- Show students how to apply art knowledge directly to personal living.
- Cultivate students' attitude of joy in the creation of personal artworks.
- Develop students' appreciation for the artworks of others.
- Discuss the relevance of the visual arts in relation to the literary and performing arts.
- Suggest that students keep sketchbooks, idea books, and journals.
- Discuss space concepts—what we know, feel, and see in space—and the use of spatial perspective.
- Discuss and practice size relationships and proportions.
- Demonstrate how line, form, and color can be used to express mood.
- Engage students in a dialogue about how art—whether a political cartoon, a commercial illustration, or public art—is a means of communicating ideas and feelings, a way of telling others of our thoughts and dreams.
- Discuss where artists get their inspiration—from nature, objects, events, imaginations.

- Observe how other artists have interpreted the figure, portrait, landscape, seascape and still life in realistic and imaginative ways.
- Have students analyze art in their environment—from design, to architecture, to city structure.
- Discuss art careers, such as in advertising, graphics, printing, crafts, and architecture.
- Take field trips to art exhibits, museums, arts festivals, and art classes and demonstrations.
- Have students compare arts in other cultures with those in their own culture.
- Discuss how artists have enriched the world.
- Emphasize the importance of art in communication media—film, graphics, video, and so on.

Art Production

To produce art is to engage in using exciting two- and three-dimensional art media, various tools, processes, and techniques. Students of all ages require in-depth art production experiences that involve both visual and tactile thinking.

In three-dimensional media, students benefit from a working knowledge of design, as well as of subject and content. As students improve in working with tools and materials, they develop various skills that can be used in personally expressive and creative ways.

Some sculpture and craft processes require that students sketch ideas beforehand, which allows students to change and improve the design, rather than the actual art product. Older students, who are more critically aware of their work, do not necessarily want a representational image from which to work. This permits greater freedom with ideas.

With some crafts, the media often dictate what happens in the design. The design can be inherent in the form of the object produced, as well as in the design applied to the object.

The following are some general classroom guidelines for developing elementary students' art production skills:

- Have students practice their drawing, painting, and design skills with a variety of media: charcoal, felt-tip pens, crayons, chalks, oil pastels, pencils, and watercolor and tempera paints.
- Explore color mixing, from simple to complex, with students.
- Have students experiment with new and varied tools and materials and with from simple to more complex procedures that require developed motor skills and control.
- Continue encouraging students to display expressive skills in printmaking, three-dimensional design, mixed media, and crafts.
- Build, sculpt, and construct with three-dimensional media, creating weavings (fig. 2.2), soft sculptures, yarn designs, puppets, and masks out of papers, wood, clay, fibers, and papier-maché.

Figure 2.2   Weaving requires manipulative skills.

- Involve students in such varied projects as dioramas, yarn baskets, banners, simple stitching, and appliqué.
- Discuss the possibilities and limitations of the chosen medium and how the medium influences form, idea, and structure.
- Discuss how design affects the function of manufactured products and structures in the environment.
- Practice with communication media, such as cameras, video, graphics, and murals.

Art History

The study of art history involves thoughtful viewing and discussion of objects and artworks of past and present cultures. Because these two- and three-dimensional art forms record the feelings, ideas, and events of the cultures they came from, art history is a reflection of humanity throughout history and helps us to understand how we have come to be who we are.

Some general classroom guidelines and discussion ideas for developing students' abilities in art history at all grade levels follow. Tailor these guidelines to the needs and abilities of students.

- Discuss artists and their artworks.
- Discuss the role of the artist within society. How has one influenced the other?
- Identify and discuss how art has been expressed and is important in societies—in architecture, environments, religious beliefs, celebrations, social customs, festivals, ornament decoration, record keeping, and communication. Point out similarities and differences among cultures.
- Discuss art movements, styles, and various art forms.
- Describe and contrast the folk and craft arts of various cultures around the world.
- Encourage students to learn about past and present American artists.
- Develop students' appreciation of the various ethnic art contributions to the American culture.
- Discuss and evaluate current artworks in terms of the interrelationship of the individual, the community, and the environment.
- Discuss the cultural value of art in terms of the art's purpose—for example, was the art made for social, political, or traditional reasons?
- Investigate and discuss the importance of artists as architects, illustrators, industrial designers, fabric designers, interior designers, and product designers. Consider artists' roles with electronic media.
- Identify and discuss art concepts in music, literature, dance, and theater.
- Discuss art as a cross-cultural language.
- Discuss how art has changed the world.

Art Analysis (Criticism and Aesthetics)

Art analysis involves identifying the aspects of an artwork that follow. Tailor experiences and discussions to the understanding level of students.

Description

Subject. Ask students: What is the image? What is the theme? What do you see? What is happening? What is the most important idea or experience in this artwork? Does the subject relate to a place or event in your own life? Does it show emotions or other ideas, such as social or political ideas? Is it mysterious? Does it tell a story, legend, or myth? What mood does it reflect? What is the meaning here?

Materials used. Ask students to identify the technique or process used by the artist. Students learn to differentiate and describe such media as watercolor paint, tempera paint, oil paint, clay, fibers, and prints, and such art forms as drawing, painting, sculpture, construction, architecture, ceramics, textile design, environmental design, collage, printmaking, types of illustration, cartooning, advertising art, industrial design, photography, filmmaking, computer art, and television art.

Analysis

Visual structure. Ask students to identify and describe the art elements and design principles—line, shape, value, color, space, pattern, texture, balance, dominance, rhythm, and contrast—exemplified in the artwork and to explain how these are brought together in a composition.

Historical importance. Ask students: What do you know about the artist, the time period in which the artist lived, and the art movements of that particular time? How does this artwork compare to other artworks of its historical time? Has the importance of this artwork changed over time? How did culture influence the artist's work?

Interpretation

An artwork is just one solution (one manipulation of an idea) that the artist has chosen to solve an art problem to his or her satisfaction. Students will all have different interpretations of artworks because of their various levels of understanding and their different insights into an artwork's meaning.

Aesthetics. For students to aesthetically appreciate an artwork, they must go beyond merely looking at it and describing its visual characteristics. Aesthetic inquiry involves determining what is personally significant and of value about the artwork. Ask students interpretive and philosophical questions to develop their aesthetic appreciation: What is art? What makes something beautiful? Why? By what standards do we appraise art? What makes an artwork "great" or "not great"? What is being said in this artwork? Why is it made to look like this? Does the artwork have personality? How do you interpret its meaning? What is happening? What is the artist's intent? How do you feel about the artwork? Why? Does this work remind you of something?

Judgment

Over time, students develop personal aesthetic criteria for judging artworks and for how the quality of design affects function. They can then apply these criteria to personal lifetime choices, such as architecture, interiors, furniture design, clothing, utensils, photography, and commercial objects.

IDENTIFYING ART PROGRESS IN STUDENTS (K–6)

PRESCHOOL OBJECTIVES

According to Benjamin S. Bloom of the University of Chicago, there are characteristic growth curves. For instance, half of a child's future height is reached by age two and a half. Half of a child's general intelligence is formed by approximately age four. By the time children enter school at approximately age six, they will have developed up to two-thirds of their mature intelligence. In terms of pure academic achievement, one-third of development at age eighteen is reached before the child even enters first grade.

Therefore, according to Bloom, the environment will have greatest impact on a specific trait during that trait's period of greatest growth. In other words, if we ignore this period of rapid growth of the intellect during these early preschool years, we may never be able to make up for this loss of growth. For the preschooler, this means we must provide the most stimulating, challenging, meaningful, and perceptive experiences that we can during this accelerated growth period.

Because preschoolers are just learning all about life, everything in their environment is new to them. Nothing is structured. They are open to all experiences. They welcome, run toward, enjoy, take in, even laugh at new kinds of experiences. All of life is an adventure! They are turned on to discovery and living.

Their greatest learning happens through their senses—where they see, feel, smell, hear, taste, and how they move through space. Listen to their conversation. Very much of what they say relates to the way they perceive their environment.

Scribbling is the first step in growing. Scribbling is an important kinetic, developmental, expressive form. Do not ask questions, make suggestions, or interfere while the young child is scribbling. Provide materials that encourage large, free movements and big motions, such as lots of paper and crayons or other marking tools. Watch for different developmental steps in scribbling:

1. **Disorderly scribbling.** Haphazard lines go in many directions. Children use large movements of the arm—big kinetic motions.
2. **Controlled scribbling.** Children develop motor coordination in the discovery of the relation of arm movements to circular, longitudinal, horizontal, and diagonal marks and lines on the paper.
3. **Naming of scribbling.** Children's scribbles become objects or "things" to them. The drawings do not *look like* the object or thing. They are still a scribble. This is an important development because the children begin to think in terms of images. They connect themselves to the world around them. They think in imaginative terms. They may begin to include some geometric forms that suggest people or objects. For example, the concept of "Daddy" might be a circle with extended lines for legs growing directly from the circle.

Do not introduce stereotypes, such as coloring books, which offer adult concepts and adult solutions. These are crutches and do not encourage independent solutions and thinking. Encourage painting and exploration of colors. Do not present representational objects to be painted or drawn. Encourage varied, deeply involving experiences that emphasize perceptual development in looking, smelling, hearing, touching, tasting, and moving. Color and proportions have no realistic meaning for children during this period.

Children may continue to scribble as they grow. Children are ego-centered and think of themselves as the center of their world. They are concerned with concepts that relate mainly to the bodily parts of the self and the self in relation to other things in the environment. Challenge children with action stories, films, field trips, discussions, dramatics, action, and perceptual activities.

Encourage sensory experiences. For example, explore many ways of seeing—as through a microscope, magnifying glass, prisms, water, colored glass, cameras, slides, octoscopes. Help children learn about art and artists; look at art reproductions. Have discussions on art and its place in history and in our lives today. Visit artists' studios, art galleries, and museums, and have discussions of painting.

In the first representational drawings, children are in the center of their world and drawings. There are no correct proportions. Objects and people do not appear realistically (as we as adults think of realism) but express what the children know and how they feel. The first drawings use shapes that are more geometric, such as circles for the head, eyes, and mouth, and lines for feet, hands, and legs. Drawings are one type of communication of ideas and feelings, and they express what the child knows.

Drawing does not depend on what the child actually sees but, rather, on the child's active knowledge about the subjects. The drawing includes parts and images that are important and meaningful to children. Parts that are not important are left out. Parts of the self that have special meaning are often exaggerated. There is little or no relationship between the color selected and the objects represented. Grass could be orange or purple. Selection of color becomes more emotional. Children put many objects on a base line along the bottom of the paper. The sky is drawn at the top.

For two- and three-dimensional experiences and materials, please refer to the kindergarten section that follows.

KINDERGARTEN OBJECTIVES

Five-year-olds are adventurous, intuitive, and eager for new discoveries. Often-repeated experiences encourage them to experiment and to "boundary-push" previous awareness. Frequent opportunities encourage discovery, and exploration reveals new possibilities. For example, painting experiences reveal that the mixing of two colors produces a third color and that a brush can dance, hop, or draw a straight line across a paper surface.

Include physical activity as part of kindergartners' art experience, and consider the length of the experience—shorter time spans are most effective. Include opportunities for individual as well as group experiences. Do not interfere with spontaneous self-expression, and do not impose adult standards, such as coloring books. (Chart 2.4 at the end of the chapter summarizes art objectives for kindergarten students.)

Artistic and Perceptual Skills: Art Production

Five-year-olds are free, spontaneous, and direct in their artistic expression, relying more on intuition than on past experiences. Encourage open, free, spontaneous behavior by providing such media and tools as large brushes, vivid colors, and large-size papers that permit children to describe ideas and concepts of space.

Because of the intense perceptual development of the child at this time, many kinds of perceptual experiences should be encouraged. Invent and provide a variety of meaningful, sensory experiences, such as singing walks, tape-recorded stories, smelling experiences, feeling games, and listening walks. Motivations might include such subjects as "Throwing a Ball," "Brushing My Hair," "My House," and "My Favorite Shirt."

Kindergartners do not use correct proportions or draw what adults might think of as correct proportions. Proportions relate to the object's significance, importance, and meaning to the child. These children do not include parts that are not important to them. They do include parts that *are* important to them. How they draw an object does not depend on what they see visually, but more on what they know about the person or object they are drawing.

Line

Kindergartners can identify straight, curved, and diagonal lines, as well as lines that are long-short, thick-thin, light-dark, and fine-rough (see chapter 3).

Shape

Five-year-olds can identify a variety of shapes, such as square, rectangle, circle, oval, triangle, diamond, and irregular, although some of these shapes may be difficult for them to draw (see chapter 4). They can also point out such differences in shapes as large-small and many-few.

At this age, children recognize geometric forms and shapes that combine to become symbols for representing objects and people. Geometric shapes are often used in first attempts to draw a figure: circles for the head, eyes, mouth, feet, and hands; lines for the arms and legs. The children include, and sometime exaggerate, parts that are important and meaningful to them and omit unimportant parts. They have learned to perceive details within the figure and body parts, noticing how the various parts go together (fig. 2.3).

Space

Visually, kindergartners see one object at a time; they do not see objects as they overlap (see chapter 5). They see length and know about distance but cannot yet draw or express three-dimensional space. Their spatial relationships have more emotional meaning relating to the baseline concept of space. All things take place along a baseline, but forms can be haphazardly placed, perhaps upside down or

(a)

Figure 2.3 Drawings by a four-year-old show *(a)* legs growing from the head, as well as interest in learning letters (to suggest a talking figure), and *(b)* a body from which legs grow. Another significant development is a tree on the right and the ground lines under the figure, which place the figure within an environment and on a baseline.

(b)

unrelated to each other. Sometimes, X-ray concepts, where both inside and outside are drawn in the same picture, are expressed.

Five-year-olds do not use or draw what adults consider "correct" proportions. Instead, they assign proportions that relate to the item's significance, importance, and meaning to them. Never evaluate with regard to correct or realistic proportions children's first attempts to draw a figure. How they draw a person or object does not depend on what they *see* as much as on what they *know* or *feel* about the person or object.

Color

Most children of this age, especially children with preschool experience, enjoy many colors and can name them. They can discriminate between colors that are bright-dull, dark-light, and warm-cool. They enjoy experimenting with mixing colors to see how they change, and they learn what to add to achieve a desired effect.

Color selection for particular objects is often not realistic but is based more on the color's emotional appeal (see chapter 6).

Pattern and Texture

Five-year-olds can identify varying marks, dots, and lines, which create designs and patterns. They recognize differences and similarities in texture and pattern. They also have discovered textural qualities, such as hard-soft and rough-smooth (see chapter 6). Kindergarten students are natural-born designers, spontaneous and intuitive.

Two-Dimensional Art Production

Explore with kindergarten students various expressive and manipulative properties—painting, cutting, gluing, tearing, pasting, sewing, weaving, printing, sawing—using such tools as brushes, paints, crayons, felt-tip pens, clay, hammers and nails, wood, scissors, and sandpaper. Discuss the tools and materials used in different artworks.

Develop students' ability to name and describe various art tools and their function. Language is very important to five-year-olds and helps them to analyze art processes, thereby aiding in their concept formation.

Painting is often a manipulative experience for five-year-olds. The exploration of color and color mixing becomes a discovery experience when the colors accidentally run and blend together. Finger painting is a favorite manipulative and tactile experience for children this age.

Five-year-olds need good-quality crayons in a great variety of colors. Large crayons encourage expansive, free movements but sometimes are difficult for small children to hold. Have these children also use regular-size crayons. Suggest that the children use crayons when the objective is for more detailed work than can be achieved with paint. Crayons do not allow for easy mixing of color, nor do they have the flexibility, intensity, or quick coverage of paint, but they are usually handy, direct, and available and provide for immediate expression of ideas. Felt-tip pens have similar characteristics, with the added advantage of intense color. Oil pastels and charcoal are other drawing media to explore.

Three-Dimensional Art Production

Provide five-year-olds with a variety of three-dimensional experiences. Clay and clay substitutes offer direct manipulation of construction media and develop the additive concept of building, as well as the subtractive concept of taking away. Scrap woods (for nailing and hammering), plastic packing materials, papers, telephone wire, and boxes are helpful for construction experiences. Printmaking techniques, such as vegetable printing, aid in learning the concepts of repetition and design. Puppets, paper and cardboard weaving, rubbings, and collages of different textures emphasize tactile experiences. Cameras and camera techniques, such as making sun prints (printing on light-sensitive paper) and slides, also are good three-dimensional experiences.

Art History and Analysis (Criticism and Aesthetics)

Introduce artworks that relate to kindergartners' interests, which include food, work and play, self-image, body parts, other children, home and family activities, make-believe, television heroes, special events (such as the circus), fantasy, and inventing imaginative forms. Looking at and discussing such artworks will help students to grow in their art appreciation. Work with students to identify items or colors, storytelling factors, and shape and color interrelationships in the artworks.

Exhibit and discuss the students' own paintings and artworks, as well as those found in other school displays. Encourage students to present and explain their drawings and paintings to the rest of the class. Ask students to help you in arranging class displays or interest centers.

Bring in art and artifacts from other cultures for class discussions (see chapters 9 and 10).

FIRST- AND SECOND-GRADE OBJECTIVES

In first and second grade (ages six to eight), students are excited about everything. They like bright, colorful, simple, uncomplicated motivations and experiences. They are instinctive designers and creators. They enjoy fantasy, make-believe, and using their imaginations. Presenting one idea, subject, theme, or tool at a time is best. (Chart 2.4 at the end of the chapter summarizes art objectives for first- and second-grade students.)

Artistic and Perceptual Skills: Art Production

With first- and second-graders, include motivations that activate students' self-awareness—what they do, what they look like, how they feel, and how they relate to others within their expanding environment. Students like ideas that have emotional appeal and that are imaginary and inventive, such as "If I were ice cream, what I would see on the way to my stomach" and "How I felt when I fell off my bike." Students approach drawing intuitively; they do not stop to analyze.

Children are more socially aware now and see themselves as part of the social structure. Include activities that involve them with other people and with what is happening around them. Students enjoy sharing ideas and expressing feelings with others.

Use art experiences to help first- and second-graders to explore and discover everything possible. Encourage them to investigate by observing, touching, listening, smelling, and tasting, while using, for example, prisms, microscopes, telescopes, binoculars, and whistles. Emphasize perceptual and intellectual experiences—analyzing, naming, describing, identifying, classifying.

Verbally describe discovered objects and new experiences in detail. This will help students to develop and use an effective vocabulary regarding their self-image and their environment—words about family, school, body parts, and so on.

Proportions remain emotional, not visual, at this age, so do not correct the children for not producing "proper" proportions in their drawings. Instead, have them look at themselves in full-length mirrors and then draw their images on the mirrors with felt-tip pens. Motivate them with experiences that involve the sensory concepts, body parts, family relationships, friends, animals, plants, food, transportation, and other places and events. Use topics that call attention to size relationships. Provide opportunities for students to practice remembering, and conduct recall games with visual materials.

Line

First- and second-graders can describe various lines (thick-thin, straight-curved, wavy-sharp) and can draw lines to describe feelings, music, and poems (see chapter 3).

Shape

Review basic geometric shapes with first- and second-graders. Help them to find the shapes and forms in flowers, plants, animals, insects, figures, and birds' tails, wings, and bills. Encourage them to discover the varieties of shapes in the classroom. Have them match and sort shapes and forms.

Children in first and second grade usually start paintings with simple shapes that are isolated from one another and whose outlines are filled in with paint. They often use symbols to represent objects and people, and they may add or subtract parts that are emotionally significant to them. Consistent exaggeration of one particular body part may have special significance to the child (fig. 2.4). For example, if the eyes are constantly crossed in figure drawings, the child may have an eye problem. Drawings and paintings depict "real" objects that are important "now" to students and that are not abstractions.

Now students usually change from using geometric, symbolic forms to using more specific characterizations that include greater detail. For example, at first, students tend to represent the human figure with geometric shapes—a circle for the important head and with the arms and legs growing from the head. If you help students to discover differences and similarities of the human form, however, faces and figures will then be drawn with greater awareness of detail. For example, if you motivate students to recognize and be aware of the joints of the body—how we can bend at the waist, neck, knees, and elbows—students' pictures will then often reflect more of these details. First- and second-graders are usually able to recognize and distinguish shapes/sizes, near/far, in/out, natural/human-made, oval/irregular, bright/dull, left/right, up/down, over/under, and open/closed (see chapter 4).

Value

In first- and second-grade, students recognize light and dark but are not yet concerned with variations in lights and darks in their drawings and paintings. They also are not aware of three-dimensional shading but see most forms in terms of flat shapes and values (see chapter 4).

Space

First- and second-grade students are ego-centered and see themselves as the center from which all things extend. Space, therefore, is emotional in concept (see chapter 5).

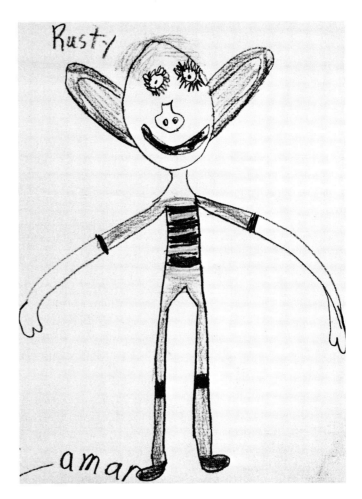

Figure 2.4 A first-grade student exaggerated what to him were his important features—his eyes and ears. He omitted fingers and did not include much body or feet detail. The figure faces front and shows no action.

Students' drawings and paintings show objects exaggerated in size and proportion in relation to their importance. Children may indicate many views of the same object in one drawing because their view of space is conceptual, not visual. Their drawings may reflect an X-ray concept, where both inside and outside are drawn in the same picture. Also, because they do not rely on observing the object they are drawing, they simplify the object in their drawing and show only what is remembered and is essential. Important parts are exaggerated, while unimportant ones may be omitted altogether. Many first- and second-graders handle space by including baselines, foldovers, and overlapping, and they sometimes mix planes and elevations.

In the second grade, students begin to group objects and realistic events, including families, animals, and friends. School appears in the artwork. Students can distinguish right from left and center from corner. The previous single baseline may change to two or more, indicating that some objects are closer. The sky may be shown to come down to meet the ground.

Having students build with clay or wood helps them to develop a two-dimensional/three dimensional concept.

Color

First- and second-graders can identify the primary colors and some secondary colors, and are able to discuss how color relates to feelings and moods (see chapter 6).

First-graders tend to use color more emotionally, but by second grade, most children begin to use color in a more realistic way. For example, they realize that grass is green and therefore use that color to depict grass.

While first- and second-graders are able to discuss differences and similarities in colors, they do not see variations within a color unless they have a meaningful experience that extends their concept.

Pattern and Texture

First- and second-graders can practice pattern by repeating designs with stencils, rubbings, and vegetable prints. Help them to identify patterns in clothing, furniture, wallpaper, architecture, and city planning. Encourage them to practice orderly/disorderly repetition (see chapter 6).

Also, continue exploring tactile surfaces with students. Encourage them to feel walls, floors, and coins, and to produce rubbings. Examine different textures together, and then have students attempt to reproduce the textures in drawings (see chapter 6).

Composition

Experiment with students in combining various lines, shapes, and so on into pleasing relationships. Study symmetrical and asymmetrical balance, contrast, dominance, and similarities and differences with students (see chapter 7).

Two-Dimensional Art Production

First- and second-graders need time for discovery, experimentation, and exploratory manipulation. Repeat experiences with new media often enough that students gain confidence and coordination in manipulating the media. Always provide sufficient time for experimenting and discovering with new tools and materials. Encourage students to verbalize about and dramatize their art experiences. For example, they could invent and act out fantasies, or they could improvise what might happen next in an artwork.

Explore with first- and second-grade students many tools and materials. Draw and paint with felt-tip markers, charcoal, oil pastels, chalk pastels, crayons, watercolor paints, and tempera paints, and experiment with crayon resist.

Provide numerous painting experiences that are purely manipulative so that students can explore paint and what it will do. Have students experiment by running together and blending a variety of paint colors. Demonstrate and have them try spatter painting, sponge painting, and string painting.

Provide both large and small crayons for art experiences, but the smaller crayons are usually better suited for this age group. The smaller crayons also come in a greater variety of colors. While first- and second-graders like primary colors, they are also intrigued by such colors as turquoise, gold, silver, crimson, ocher, and Prussian blue. Crayons usually have their color names printed on their labels, which helps students to build a working vocabulary with colors.

Three-Dimensional Art Production

First- and second-grade students enjoy and are capable of a wide variety of three-dimensional art experiences. For example, have students:

- Make three-dimensional paper objects by bending, curling, folding, cutting, building with slots, and gluing.
- Make masks from paper plates.
- Sculpt and construct with clay by rolling, pinching, pulling, pressing, squeezing, and adding to forms.
- Use boxes of all sizes and materials to construct simple to complex items.
- Build mobile kinetic structures from paper, string, cardboard, reed, wire, and cellophane.
- Construct with "found" items, such as egg cartons, stuffed paper bags, and cloth (for soft sculptures).
- Hammer, glue, and join soft woods and sticks.
- Weave with paper, plastics, and large yarn.
- Tie-dye with paint on cloth and T-shirts.
- Learn knots for tying.
- Design yarn and fabric shapes with glue on cardboard.
- Weave on cardboard looms.
- Make simple stitching with yarn on open-weave cloth.
- Stamp-print with "found" objects, such as kitchen utensils and old toys, by placing the object into paint and then stamping it onto surfaces.
- Create paper bag, sock, and cloth puppets, and then produce plays.

Art History and Analysis (Criticism and Aesthetics)

First- and second-grade students are interested in easily understood artworks about subjects they like, such as animals, the circus, imaginary people, and people engaged in a variety of activities. They like bright colors and artworks with textures.

Encourage students to express their ideas and feelings about what is happening in an artwork and what they see. Students then begin to make decisions about what they like. For example, students may like a painting because it has bright colors, because it reminds them of a place they have seen, or because the painting is about their favorite subject—for example, animals or space (fig. 2.5).

First- and second-graders can begin to describe how an artwork was made: They can classify the media (crayon,

Figure 2.5   This drawing indicates a second-grade student's interest in space and the astronauts landing on the moon.

chalk, pen and ink, felt-tip pen, watercolor paint, oil paint, and so on) used in the artwork; describe the subject; begin to recognize the elements of line, shape, and color; and explain what they like about the artwork and why.

Continue to build students' active art vocabulary. Discuss the names and types of colors, tools, lines, textures, simple designs, and shapes used in an artwork.

Display and discuss students' art, as well as art and artifacts from ancient cultures (see chapters 10 and 11).

THIRD- AND FOURTH-GRADE OBJECTIVES

Third- and fourth-grade students (ages eight to ten) are growing out of the egocentric stage and into the sociocentric stage. They are strongly social and feel a need to belong and to be like their friends. These students have a greater attention span and are enthusiastic, able to work more independently, flexible, interested in each other and in the events around them, helpful and anxious to cooperate, and full of ideas but willing to listen to opposing viewpoints. They like to share in the planning, to practice skills, and to excel in something. Their drawings often depict group situations, with several objects, people, and places. At this age, students need to learn the importance of finishing an assignment. Emphasize each student's individuality and unique contribution to the group. These students need their share of approval and attention. (Chart 2.4 at the end of the chapter summarizes art objectives for third- and fourth-grade students.)

Artistic and Perceptual Skills: Art Production

Third- and fourth-graders are still direct, expressive, and spontaneous, and are pleased with their ability to represent objects more realistically. They are more critically aware of how objects "really" look in their environment and of how they previously drew these objects with visual symbols and schemata. Their drawings may become less expressive and more rigid because of their perception of detail with greater accuracy. Their eye-hand coordination and small muscle development improve.

Discuss with students differences and similarities in forms; in color variations; in landscape forms; in still-life compositions, and in shapes of eyes, noses, mouths, and hands. Encourage the use of details. This will help students to analyze their world visually and will aid them in their drawing.

Third- and fourth-grade students can draw more solid geometric forms, such as cylinders, cubes, and pyramids, with greater accuracy (fig. 2.6). They begin to draw the figure with three-dimensional qualities, using variations in color, forms, and shading. They prefer drawing from models, nature landscapes, and still lifes to aid their vision, but also enjoy painting from their own ideas, stories, and imaginations.

Motivate students by using "we" and "action" words and by suggesting such themes as sports, summer and winter activities, social events, school, where they live and play, and family activities.

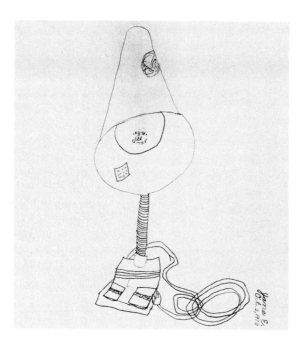

Figure 2.6   A third-grade student's drawing shows rounded forms with lines only.

Encourage students to draw from memory, and have them practice contour drawing (see chapter 3). Suggest including several objects in a drawing to approach a conscious combining of images into an arrangement.

Third- and fourth-graders like to collect objects (such as rocks, tree bark, flowers, and foods) and then name and categorize the collected items to show differences and similarities (such as color variations, shades, intensities, forms, sizes, and functions).

Challenge students with ideas that have many potential solutions. Encourage them to "boundary-push"—to not be satisfied with the simplest or first solution, but to study, investigate, focus, organize, reevaluate, and make changes before settling on a final solution. Emphasize the individuality of the student and the unique contribution of each to the group.

Line

Lines have infinite variety according to the medium and tool used and the hand of the artist. Have third- and fourth-graders look for examples of lines in the classroom that repeat and form patterns. Point out how a line continues, changes form, and recedes in space. Name and describe for students various types of lines and how they can make us feel. With students, experiment with various tools and produce different lines. Have them practice contour lines and draw their own images from mirrors. Suggest that they look at contours of skylines and horizons. Create lines with various materials, such as thread, yarn, and string, and emphasize that lines create shapes, patterns, and textures. Introduce gesture drawing (see chapter 3).

Shape

Third- and fourth-graders know and can describe similarities and differences in various shapes, such as cubes, cones, and spheres. Suggest that they practice finding shapes in people, animals, buildings, and natural forms in the environment. Discuss how organic and human-made shapes are similar and different, and how shape and form can influence feelings and attitudes. Present a simplified explanation of abstract shapes, and work with students to discriminate among realistic shapes and abstract shapes (see chapter 4).

Value

By this age, students begin to see values—changes in lights and darks (see chapter 4). Keep your explanation of this concept simple at this stage. For example, show students a value scale with a range of values from one to ten. Then point out and closely examine values on form, and show students how value changes can make objects appear round or give mass to a form. Demonstrate how moving a light source (such as a lamp) around an object provides opportunities for value changes. Have students practice drawing various values on objects or surfaces. Discuss how value can also create a mood and feeling.

Study of value changes will result in students beginning to add shading on forms (modeled drawing). Experience and practice will lead students to greater development in this area.

Space

A space concept is a significant development for third- and fourth-graders (see chapter 5). They know that more than one object occupies space and that these objects are organized in some way within surrounding spaces. They realize that objects can be viewed from more than one perspective—for example, from the top, bottom, side, front, and back.

While aware of differences between two- and three-dimensional space, third-grade students cannot yet represent the third dimension in perspective. Objects do appear in an order, and third-graders like to design and arrange the objects. They understand nearness, enclosure, and continuity.

Fourth-graders indicate an understanding of space by using single-viewpoint approaches, overlapping, value changes, and distance indicators. They can distinguish differences and similarities and discuss relationships. Plan experiences that involve students moving into and through spaces. Call their attention to various viewpoints, such as a "bird's-eye view" or an "ant's-eye view."

Discuss ways of indicating receding spaces—how objects may appear in foreground, middle ground, and background through overlapping, color changes, size differences, and the use of lights and darks. These concepts are the beginning of perspective (fig. 2.7).

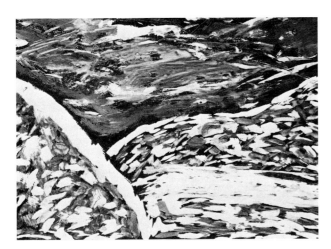

Figure 2.7 A painting by a third-grade student after studying impressionism and impressionistic painters also indicates space by overlapping hills.

Plan and discuss how to arrange furniture and other objects within a room using three-dimensional materials. Discuss arrangements of physical spaces in rooms, buildings, and communities. Have students plan both living and playing spaces.

With students, investigate how artists and architects interpret space. Study art reproductions dealing with cubistic space, surrealistic space, and abstract space.

Color

Third- and fourth-grade students tend to use color more realistically in their artworks (see chapter 6). Question students to look for variations within a color. Have them explore the many subtle relations found in nature's use of color. Suggest that students examine color as it is reflected off of surfaces. Encourage students to make color choices and to discuss how color makes them feel.

Talk about how changes in color can create mood and atmosphere. Help students to experience color contrasts, such as light-dark, bright-dull, rough-smooth, and warm-cool. Discuss how one color affects the colors around it. Invite students to experiment by blending, mixing, and swirling colors. Have them compare transparent color in thin washes with thick, opaque colors. Demonstrate monochromatic painting (painting with all of the shades, tints, values, and intensities of one color hue), and invite students to experiment with this concept.

Pattern

At this age, students can practice pattern by creating designs involving repetition of several shapes (see chapter 6). Discuss with students how pattern can be useful in designing more aesthetic home and school surroundings. Have students examine how nature uses pattern in organic objects, especially in plants and flowers. Then suggest that they experiment with various tools to adapt patterns from natural forms.

Explore patterns and designs in fabrics with students. Study how other cultures use decorative patterns—for example, the patterns that appear in Native American Navaho rugs. Plan a tie-dye activity that emphasizes pattern arranging.

Texture

Children in third and fourth grade have a natural curiosity that invites activities involving looking and touching. Have them discuss the similarities and differences of looking at and touching such materials as a brick wall, clay, fur, and sandpaper. Discover with them how to create textures with various tools. Explore with them by touching, pounding, squeezing, and grasping. Discuss and experiment with students to determine how two- and three-dimensional textures and surfaces differ. Have them attempt to create two-dimensional textural illusions with the use of lines, shapes, and dots (see chapter 6).

Composition

Analyze and discuss with third- and fourth-grade students how composition is used in nature, art objects, buildings, manufactured objects, and students' environments. Then have students practice three-dimensional composition with flexible materials that can be moved, changed, and reorganized. Involve them in composing everything from fabric design, to murals, to model construction, to community planning. Discuss visual movements within a composition, such as directional lines that create centers of interest. Have students create compositions that are based on using harmony, variety, and contrasts of art elements, such as line, shape, value, balance, dominance, and so on. Review the concepts of symmetrical and asymmetrical balance with students and introduce the concept of radial balance (see chapter 7).

Portraits and Figures

By third and fourth grade, students are increasingly interested in the functions and appearances of their bodies. In their drawings, for example, they show more awareness of body parts, such as lips, fingernails, and hairstyles, and of body movements. Their artwork also reflects a concern with figure placement within a group, with changes in clothing styles, and with boy/girl interests.

Have students practice contour drawings of figures (see chapters 3 and 8). Suggest that they:

- Look for details.
- Analyze body organization—how parts go together.
- Analyze peoples' similarities and differences.
- Draw figures in action—moving, playing sports, gesturing.
- Add inventive costumes and uniforms to their figures.
- Show the figure in relation to other objects in the environment.
- Draw the figure as they feel about their own bodies.

- Put figures in group social situations, such as a family or other group at, for example, the circus, state fair, or a political campaign.
- Express emotions—happiness, sorrow, exaggeration, distortion—through the use of the figure. For example, they might want to draw a figure showing sorrow and all the details that make up sorrow.
- Express a theme or idea, using just certain parts of the figure—for example, a large nose or mouth or a grouping of hands.

Fourth-graders begin to draw three-dimensional qualities of the figure. They also begin to shade and show color differences, rounded forms, and realistic proportions.

Landscape

As already mentioned, students in third and fourth grade are developing concepts of depth and space (the distance between objects) and of all objects occupying space. In landscape drawing, students begin to indicate depth by showing a foreground, middle ground, and background (see chapters 5 and 8). Review composition objectives with students, helping them to see size and space differences and to select and focus on certain shapes, lines, colors, textures, and patterns. For example, guide students in finding basic shapes within natural and architectural forms, which they can then combine and compose into an exciting arrangement. Have them do many sketches with a variety of media.

Still Life

Encourage students to practice selecting and arranging a variety of objects, taking into consideration the objects' similarities and differences in shape, balance, depth, texture, form, color, variety, balance, and rhythm (see chapter 8). Then analyze and discuss students' arrangements and composition, focusing on positive and negative shapes, shading, cast shadows, harmonious and disharmonious colors, pleasing and displeasing proportions, two- and three-dimensional qualities of shapes, and how shapes depend on viewpoint.

Two-Dimensional Art Production

Manipulative experiences at this age help to refine small muscle growth, which leads to greater control in handling tools and media. Group activities, such as creating murals, group sculptures, and mobiles; staging puppet shows, light shows, or dramatic plays (with the corresponding stage and costume design); and making videos and films, are also important.

Continue exploring and developing students' skills in drawing and painting with various media, such as felt-tip markers, charcoal, pencils, oil pastels, chalk pastels, watercolor paints, tempera paints, and crayon resist. Students like to draw and paint from their own ideas and stories. Motivate them by saying things like: "Close your eyes and imagine an animal. Is this an imaginary animal? Is it huge or tiny? Is it plump or slim? Does it have dots? Stripes? A pointed head?"

Have students experiment with monoprints, vegetable printing, and rubbings (see chapter 8). Encourage them to use their prints and rubbings to create designs for such items as note cards, posters, wrapping paper, wallpaper, and book jackets.

Three-Dimensional Art Production

Continue to develop third- and fourth-graders' skills in three-dimensional media by engaging them in such activities as sculpting with paper, plaster, clay, and papier-maché; paper cutting and folding; making paper and cloth collages; appliquéing, stitching, batiking, weaving, and tie-dyeing cloth; wood carving and construction; assembling and constructing with "found" objects; jewelry construction; and producing experimental slides, videos, films, filmstrips, and animated films. Specific projects you might want to consider include having students:

- Make masks from cardboard, large paper bags, or papier-maché.
- Use clay and clay substitutes to sculpt small animals, storybook characters, dioramas, murals, pots, and simple jewelry; and to construct with slab and coil methods. Experiment with decorative glazing, textures, and applied designs.
- Construct and sculpt mobiles and sculptures from cardboard, wood, cloth, wire, and other materials.
- Create original designs with stitches and appliqué cloth shapes to make banners, flags, and soft sculptures.
- Weave on fingers or on cardboard, wooden, and free-form looms.
- Experiment with rug hooking and basketry.
- Learn macrame knots, and add beads to creations.
- Practice carving techniques with plaster and clay.
- Fold and cut a variety of papers, such as foils, wrapping papers, wallpapers, colored construction paper, tissues, and doilies, using origami techniques, hole punchers, and pinking shears.
- Use paper pulp for modeling. Build papier-maché over more complex armatures.

Art History and Analysis (Criticism and Aesthetics)

Continue building students' art vocabulary. Have them make a dictionary of art terms that they add to as terms are defined. Keep an art center for displays.

Encourage students to study reproductions and original artworks. Learn all about the artists, their ideas, their place in history, and their purpose in producing art (see chapters 10 and 11). Discuss how the artists may have come up with their subject matter—from other people? From nature? From historic events? From imaginary fantasies? Study art examples that relate to the community, to the school, and to civic structures.

Discuss with students how artists have used art elements and design principles—color, line, texture, pattern, shape, space, value, and so on—in particular artworks and how these elements and principles relate to each other. In other words, how have the art elements been composed? For example, ask students to name and describe the colors the artist used; to point out areas of interest created by lines, shapes, colors, textures, and so on; to analyze space (positive and negative); to look for foreground, middle ground, and background relationships; and to describe the various textures, materials used, processes, and techniques apparent in the artwork. Compare and discuss compositional similarities and differences in artworks.

Discuss emotional response to color. Ask students how they feel about certain combinations of color and about the way a particular artist used color to express an idea.

Encourage students to continue making aesthetic judgments about their own and others' artworks. Ask them to verbalize about how the artwork makes them feel (mysterious? wondrous? excited?), about what they do and do not like about the artwork, and why. Suggest that they analyze and interpret their ideas and meanings (see chapter 11).

FIFTH- AND SIXTH-GRADE OBJECTIVES

Fifth- and sixth-grade students (ages ten to twelve) are maturing in their understanding of art. If they have had adequate artistic and perceptual experiences, if they have had opportunities to engage in creative art production, if they have had numerous chances to study art history as a part of their heritage, if they have been able to develop an aesthetic appreciation for their own and others' artworks, then all of this should culminate in more mature art understandings, preferences, opinions, and capabilities.

Special interests of these students include social awareness, community and world responsibilities, environmental pollution, social structures, how the human body functions, family interrelationships, war, drugs, and disease (fig. 2.8). They like space-time relationships, enjoy research, and can interpret scientific and historical data. They understand past-present, simple-complex, and near-far concepts, and desire to learn more about life and about how art relates to life, nature, science, and history (fig. 2.9).

Students in this age group have begun to take an interest in personal grooming and are sensitive to personal inadequacies. They are loyal to their peers and to the group. They openly discuss likes and dislikes, respect differences of opinion, and enjoy learning about others' points of view. (Chart 2.4 at the end of the chapter summarizes art objectives for fifth- and sixth-grade students.)

Artistic and Perceptual Skills: Art Production

Some fifth- and sixth-graders are now more analytical about their visual world, while others think in more imaginative terms and express their ideas more emotionally.

Figure 2.8 Fifth- and sixth-graders are interested in social issues, and art expression is one way they communicate their concerns.

Their increased motor skills and dexterity with various artistic tools allow them more individuality in their artistic expression and techniques.

Students now have a longer attention span and are interested in pursuing independent directions. They feel a need to express their ideas through artworks. They are interested in planning projects, selecting appropriate materials and tools, following through, and maintaining a quality of workmanship.

Encourage them to expand their personal horizons by exploring new artistic ideas and tools, investigating resources for inspiration and information, establishing their own art interest areas, interpreting and using related ideas with art, being flexible and inventive, valuing originality, and expressing moods and feelings within their own art creations.

Provide opportunities for more in-depth artistic experiences, rather than a smattering of brief, superficial ones. Continue to emphasize observation of detail and memory drawing (see chapter 3). Go on field trips and involve students in a variety of perceptual activities involving scents, sounds, touch, movement, and observations. Demonstrate the interrelation of art forms to music, dance, drama, theater, and writing.

(a)

(b)

Figure 2.9 Drawings by fifth- and sixth-grade students illustrate their interest in drawing realistic depictions of animals and mechanical subjects.

Fifth- and sixth-grade students are already familiar with some artists—with their artworks, their ideas, and their place and function in past and present society. Ask them to compare and contrast artworks with regard to their sensory qualities, their style, and the materials, processes, and techniques used to create them. Fifth- and sixth-graders are also capable of making personal, informed judgments about artworks and the artistic design quality of utilitarian products and community environments. Have them discuss likes, dislikes, and why.

Line

Ask students to observe line qualities in nature and manufactured objects. Then experiment with them in using different tools and materials to invent as many types of lines as possible and to demonstrate how lines can add detail and create movement, perspective, and dimension. Have students practice using a variety of lines in a composition. Suggest that they draw using contour, gesture, outline, memory, calligraphy, and cartooning techniques (see chapter 3) and that they attempt to create shading and depth with lines.

Shape

Review basic shapes with fifth- and sixth-graders, and suggest that they look for new and more complex shapes in nature and the human-made environment. Have students practice: (1) using simple shapes for simplified forms in a composition; (2) using geometric shapes to depict objects in a landscape, a still life, or nature; (3) creating realistic forms; and (4) simplifying realistic shapes into abstraction. Compare and contrast different shapes, and discuss which shapes are harmonious and disharmonious. Discuss and experiment with students in creating shapes using textures, colors, lines, and shadows (see chapter 4).

Value

Encourage students to observe how shadows can be soft or sharp. Discuss artworks with shadows that suggest multiple light sources, and ask students to create paintings or drawings that suggest light coming from one or more directions. Suggest that students study and use shading to show the form of objects, of folds in drapery, and of muscles and bones in the body (see chapter 4).

Demonstrate and have students practice making a value scale with a range of values. Ask students to use only shapes and values in a compositional design.

Space

Observe space in nature with fifth- and sixth-grade students, and discuss the definition of *perspective* (see chapter 5). Show them how to create three-dimensional depth through placement, overlapping, and changes in scale, color, size, and value (light to dark).

Define and discuss with students the terms *horizon line, vanishing point,* and *center of vision.* Show them how to use lines and forms to make a vanishing point, and how it is possible to work with more than one vanishing point in a single drawing. Suggest that they employ different viewpoints in their drawings, such as a "bird's-eye view," a "worm's-eye view," or an overhead view.

Discuss positive-negative shape relationships, and ask students to demonstrate this concept in their artworks. Explain how the concept of space differs in two-dimensional space (flat forms) and three-dimensional space (volume and dimension), and in realistic space versus abstract space.

Color

In fifth and sixth grade, students recognize primary, secondary, and intermediate color hues. Practice awareness of color in the environment, and help students to develop a color consciousness. Define and discuss with them the concepts of *hue, value,* and *intensity* (see chapter 6). Suggest that students observe how different colors are influenced by their adjacency to other colors. Demonstrate how to indicate volume with color and with shading (light to dark).

Encourage students to experiment freely with mixing pigments and painting materials. Suggest that they use black and white (tints and shades) to alter a color for a given purpose or value study and that they use various colors to note changes in shading. Provide opportunities to explore differences in tints and shades.

Provide prisms for students to study the color spectrum. Discuss how colors affect moods, atmosphere, feelings. For example, ask students to identify what colors are "warm" and "cool."

Encourage students to experiment with varied light sources, such as projectors, and with using colored acetates in front of lights, thereby casting colors onto a form, such as a still life or figure.

Pattern

Ask fifth- and sixth-grade students to observe natural patterns in flowers, trees, hills, and mountains, as well as manufactured patterns in fabrics, buildings, and furniture. Suggest that students keep a collection of patterns—patterns that they see and patterns that they create in their imaginations. Encourage them to practice using lines, colors, textures, and shapes to create patterns. Suggest that they try developing patterns and compositions using rhythm, movement, and spacing (see chapter 6).

Texture

Collect and display as many visual and tactile textures as possible. Ask students to practice discriminating between two- and three-dimensional textures.

Then demonstrate and discuss with students how to show texture using various types of lines, media, and washes (see chapter 6). Suggest that they try creating two-dimensional textures that represent three-dimensional surfaces in nature, such as tree bark, leaves, and so on. Encourage them to use various textures in forming a composition or in drawing shadows.

Composition

Explain that composition involves the whole drawing, painting, or art project, that it is the unification of all of the concepts into a whole. Demonstrate how the concepts of the art elements (line, shape, value, space, color, texture, and pattern) as well as the design principles (balance, dominance, rhythm, and contrast) are applied in composition (see chapter 7). Suggest that students continue to practice and apply all of these concepts to their artworks.

Portraits

Artworks of students in fifth and sixth grade demonstrate observation of more detailed features of the human head and a better grasp of realistic proportions. Encourage students to try a variety of portrait possibilities: feeling their own head and then sketching it without looking; then sketching from mirror images of their faces; shading to accentuate highlights, bones, and muscles; and using various types of lines and other materials and tools to create the portrait. Provide and discuss examples of portraits done with contour, gesture, modeled, and memory drawing (see chapters 3 and 8). Suggest that students try taking an imaginative approach to portrait drawing.

Figures

During fifth and sixth grade, students experience great physical and emotional changes in body awareness, and their drawings often reflect male and female differences in characteristics and clothing. They may take two approaches to the human figure: One is realistic with correct proportions and modeling; the other is a more emotional and exaggerated approach. Both are appropriate, depending on students' preferred form of expression (fig. 2.10).

Suggest that students study the proportions and other characteristics of the human figure by closely observing people in daily life and on television. Encourage them to make quick gesture sketches of the human body and its parts, and to also apply contour, modeled, memory, and imaginative drawing techniques to the human figure (see chapters 3 and 8). Ask them to experiment with combining more than one figure in a composition and with using a variety of media in creating a figurative composition.

Landscape and Still Life

Ask fifth- and sixth-grade students to plan a landscape or still-life composition. They should decide what objects, textures, and colors will be harmonious, as well as find and utilize contrast and variety. Then ask students to make several variations on their composition—for example, by selecting objects, textures, or colors that are harmonious or disharmonious. Encourage students to produce landscape and still-life drawings and paintings using various art materials (see chapter 8).

Two-Dimensional Art Production

Students in fifth and sixth grade enjoy more complex exploration of and experimentation with materials and tools and have developed more advanced skills in using these media. Encourage them to invent and discover new, personal ways of applying tools and materials to artworks. Continue to identify and name various art tools, materials, techniques, and processes so that students are able to use this vocabulary to expressively state their individual ideas. Continue to emphasize group activities.

Encourage students to continue to identify and practice with a variety of drawing and painting media: pen and ink, pencil, colored pencils, charcoal, felt-tip pens, crayons, chalk, oil pastels, watercolor paints, and tempera paints.

(a)

(b)

(c)

Figure 2.10 Fifth- and sixth-grade students may take *(a)* a more emotional and exaggerated approach to the human figure or *(b and c)* a more realistic approach.

Suggest that they practice contour, gesture, and modeled drawings (see chapter 3). Engage them in color mixing, from simple to complex. Request that they apply design concepts to their paintings and drawings.

You also might want to consider having students:

- Continue printmaking processes, such as monoprinting, to produce book covers, note cards, and so on (see chapter 8).
- Draw and develop stories in sequence.
- Experiment with creating flip books.
- Draw on mylar paper, using an overhead projector, and then develop color overlays.
- Make sun pictures (printing on light-sensitive paper).
- Bleach 16-millimeter film and draw with permanent felt-tip pens on the film.
- Learn the parts of a camera.
- Photograph and develop their own pictures.
- Create their own slides.
- Produce light shows.
- Experiment with communication media, such as television cameras, video cameras, graphics, and murals.

Three-Dimensional Art Production

Working with three-dimensional materials is manipulative and offers fifth- and sixth-grade students opportunities to experience both visual and tactile thinking.

As mentioned earlier in the chapter, when sculpting or building in three dimensions, students need a working knowledge of design. Most craft processes deal with ways to use tools and to work with materials, rather than with subject or content. Some sculpture and craft processes require students to sketch ideas beforehand. This allows them to make changes and improve the design in the sketches, rather than the actual art product. Such planning is helpful in crafts like batik, weaving, and mask making.

Figure 2.11   Students involved in a group science project created a three-dimensional papier-maché sculpture.

In crafts, there may or may not be a realistic image represented. This is an advantage for students who are more critically aware of their own artwork. They might prefer to work with craft media and processes that allow greater freedom with ideas and are therefore nonthreatening in terms of realism.

With some crafts, the media often dictate what happens in the design. The design can be inherent in the materials used and the form of the object produced, as well as in the design applied to the object. For example, weaving can be spontaneous, as can work with clay and other sculpture materials, tie-dye, collages, and puppets.

Three-dimensional art activities that fifth- and sixth-graders enjoy include:

- Using clay to sculpt larger and more complex forms, such as heads, figures, and animals.
- Building clay pottery with pinch, coil, and slab methods.
- Weaving on cardboard as well as backstrap looms and larger tapestry looms.
- Producing batik cloths for wall hangings, pillows, lamp shades, scarves, and clothing.
- Exploring stitchery projects.
- Practicing tie-dye techniques.
- Studying and constructing architectural models of buildings, neighborhoods, and communities.
- Constructing and sculpting with varieties of materials (fig. 2.11).

Art History and Analysis (Criticism and Aesthetics)

Art analysis will have greater meaning for fifth- and sixth-grade students if it is related to an experience they have had. Take trips to museums and artists' studios, and invite artists to visit the classroom.

Display reproductions and/or original artworks that are appropriate to student understanding and interest. Continue working with students to develop an effective art vocabulary. Students at this level can begin to group artworks as to artists, styles, and techniques and to classify various sculptures as made of wood, metal, stone, and so on.

When discussing artworks with students, encourage them to describe:

- **What is shown in the artwork.** Is it a funny happening? Is a real or imaginary place shown? Does the artwork tell a story? If there are people in the artwork, what emotions are they showing? What are they doing? What are they wearing? How does the artwork relate to your interests and understandings?
- **The tools, materials, techniques, processes, and style that the artist used.** What are the names of the tools that the artist used, and how do the tools work? Is the artwork pen and ink, pencil, pastel, paint, clay, wood, steel, etc.?
- **The artwork's visual structure—its art elements and design principles, such as contrast, unity, and balance.** How do the colors make you feel (sad, quiet, loud, beautiful)? What kind of textures do you see (rough, smooth, soft, hard)? What types of lines are used

(straight, curved, diagonal, crooked, graceful)? How did the artist achieve unity? How did the artist achieve balance? What is dominant in the composition?

- **The interpretation and meaning behind the artwork.** What was the artist's intent? What does the artwork tell you about?
- **Personal likes and dislikes about the artwork.** How do you feel about this artwork? Why?

Explain that interpretations and evaluations of art often depend on an assessment of how well the artist executed formal art elements and design principles, on the idea being presented, and on knowledge about the artist, the times, and the culture. Hold open discussions, and ask students to express and discuss their feelings, decisions, and choices about displayed artworks. Have them analyze and interpret the art elements and design principles exemplified by the artwork. Encourage active, verbal descriptions. Ask students to evaluate their personal response to an artwork and to then explain what they do and do not like and why (see chapter 11). In addition to clarifying their own ideas, students will develop an appreciation for the attitudes and judgments of others.

Discuss artists of yesterday and today. Have students investigate art movements of the past, such as impressionism, surrealism, and expressionism (see chapter 10). Select one or several artists for students to study intensively. Explore the artists' lives, ideas, artworks, styles, the art elements they chose, their preferred colors, why they painted as they did, the meaning behind their work, and so on. If possible, take students on field trips to museums and galleries for further study of the selected artists.

Research art in science, history, literary subjects, music, dance, theater, television, photography, film, architecture, and industrial and commercial design. Suggest that students study art and artifacts of other cultures and countries and of other times (fig. 2.12).

Encourage a variety of group discussions. Discussion topics might include:

- What part has art and artists played in our past?
- What is the meaning of art in our lives today?
- How is art used in communication (books, magazines, computers, videos, television, film), and what meaning does this have for society?
- How do commercially made objects differ from artist-made works?
- What types of art careers are available?
- How is art a part of our environment?

THE GIFTED AND TALENTED PROGRAM IN ART

Many school districts today have a gifted program in which students from all grade levels are selected by means of achievement tests, portfolios, and teachers' recommendations for more individualized instruction to help them realize

Figure 2.12 After studying Navajo art, students planned and designed color sand paintings.

their art potential. The gifted are identified by the way they use art materials imaginatively; show a fervent interest in art; complete projects in innovative, unique ways; or show exceptional craftsmanship.

The average elementary art teacher reaches approximately 750 to 1,000 students each week; the advantages of a gifted program, in which the teacher/student ratio is often one to ten, are understandable. The many art experiences, concepts, and instructional procedures offered in this book are excellent for use with gifted students in general and especially for those who have been identified as gifted in art. Guest artists, art appreciation methods, and field trips to art galleries and museums are also encouraged.

In the Cartwright School District in Phoenix, Arizona, the art teacher in each school recommends twenty outstanding art students, whose portfolios are reviewed. The students are then asked to complete a drawing from one of four sets of instructions, such as:

"Draw an imaginary animal by combining various parts from various animals. Make your imaginary animal as detailed as you can. Use regular or colored pencils."

chart 2.2
Lesson Plan for Teaching Geometric Shapes to Exceptional Students

I. Goals
The goal of this lesson is to have students with disabilities learn different geometric shapes and comprehend how the shapes can be used in the aspect of drawing. Students begin by learning the names of the various shapes, how the shapes are made, and how the shapes can be incorporated with other shapes to produce different objects.

II. Objectives
A. Students will be shown a three-dimensional model of each specific shape, told the shape's name, and given the opportunity to touch and examine the shape.

B. Students will be shown drawings of the different shapes to determine if they can relate the drawings to the corresponding three-dimensional shapes.

C. Students will be shown simple drawings that incorporate the different shapes to see if students are able to pick out the different shapes and also name them.

D. Students will begin by using only one shape at a time to see if they can make a picture using only that shape.

E. Students will continue using only one shape at a time to make different pictures until they become familiar with all the different shapes and comprehend the different ways the shapes can be used.

F. After working with all the different shapes extensively, students will combine the shapes to make a complete picture.

G. After completion of steps A–F, students should know the names of each of the different shapes and also how the shapes can be used in drawing.

III. Evaluation
I found this to be a very exciting lesson for my students. Many of my students had a great deal of trouble with making a picture using only one shape. When they were able to use many shapes, they did much better and were also much more satisfied with their work. I used this discovery to explain to my students the importance that different shapes play in our world and all the different ways shapes can be used.

Many other areas also showed an improvement when the students learned the different shapes. My students are presently learning about traffic safety and street signs, and this was an excellent way to incorporate the idea of the shape and to relate the shape with different signs.

We have worked on learning the different shapes for almost a month, with many of my students still having a great deal of trouble. This particular lesson will continue to be taught for many weeks to come.

In conclusion, I would like to say that I am very pleased with the results and will continue to build on this idea and to incorporate different ideas about teaching it in the years to come.

Source: Andrea Fenton.

"In four frames, draw a story about a person, an animal, plants or insects, cars or planes, an imaginary character, or anything you would like. In the story, show something exciting or dangerous happening, what happens next, and how things finally turn out. Use regular or colored pencils."

The students' drawings are then assessed as to:

1. Theme—quality and subject originality
2. Composition—overall arrangement and placement of subjects
3. Color—blends and application of color
4. Drawing—creative use of line, shape, form, figure correctness, and perspective
5. Imagination—unusual approach to subject and creative design

Students' grades and work examples are also considered. Of the approximately two hundred students who are evaluated, fifty are selected for an after-school art program, once a week for two hours.[2]

ART THERAPY

The goal of **art therapy** is to focus the individual's energies on creating artworks that promote self-actualization. Art therapy specialists use art in children's centers, health clinics, hospitals, counseling centers, and schools to empathize with the individual's conflicts and interpersonal relationships and to establish conditions that foster acceptance and encouragement of self-expression. Such self-actualization of the individual through art includes art as a nonverbal means of communication through various art media. Along with verbal association, such art often has a strong relationship to understanding and working through emotional conflicts and problems.

When working with the exceptional child (a child with mental and/or physical disabilities), the art teacher must focus on practicing one skill at a time and achieving repeated success with this one skill before moving on to another. These students demonstrate various speeds of accomplishment, requiring the teacher to be flexible and to adjust lessons accordingly. Chart 2.2 presents a lesson plan for teaching exceptional students about geometric shapes. Chart 2.3 provides suggestions for art activities for students with special needs.

When art is used as a mirror of the mind, individuals can examine the expression and develop greater self-acceptance, personal self-worth, higher aspirations, and inner harmony. A person who feels balanced on the inside is more likely to be in harmony with the outer world as well. Feelings of self-worth and inner acceptance through success are especially important.

chart 2.3

Art for Students with Special Needs

Behavior Disorders

Characteristics: Poor self-image, low self-confidence, easily distracted with short attention span, involved with self, has feelings of failure, hyperactive.

Art motivations: Motivations should be repeated activities (with limits) and simple tasks, and should provide students with positive reinforcement. Content could include bright-colored, thick paint; finger paints; colored felt-tip pens; manipulative media, such as clay or clay substitutes; papier-mâché; simple construction processes with wood, paper; puppets; costumes; masks; and expressive opportunities for feelings, body awareness.

Learning Disabilities

Characteristics: Difficulties with form and space perception, hand-eye coordination, kinesthetic abilities; hyperactive; easily distracted; has feelings of frustration and failure.

Art motivations: Keep art content simple; repeat activities for success. Develop sequential activities. Stress rhythm, pattern, and motion, such as moving and drawing to music, and body exercises and calisthenics. For hand-eye development, use tactile media, such as collages and weaving; construction; puppets; drawing; painting; and paper sculpture. Include matching colors, shapes, lines, patterns, textures, and so on.

Mental Retardation

Characteristics: Slow to learn with short attention span; poor self-image and body image; problems with visual perception, space; difficulties in social situations; depending on disability, is easily frustrated and distracted.

Art motivations: Instruction should include repeated and slow instruction, concrete experiences, simple ideas, simple skills with gradual, added steps in sequence and order. Stress success. Include emotional expressions of feelings and direct manipulation of materials, such as finger painting, clay, puppets, fabrics (collage and simple weaving), junk printing, papier-mâché, clay substitutes, and thick, bright paint. Paint on mirrors, formica tabletops, large papers. Try simple constructions, such as glued boxes, wood shapes.

Stress body self-awareness activities and action, as well as tactile experiences. Practice self-adornment, such as body painting; use costumes, hats, jewelry, masks.

Visually Impaired

Characteristics: Has difficulty with perceiving the total image and unfamiliar environments. Learns through tactile and auditory activities.

Art motivations: Include activities focused on motion sequencing patterns, rhythm, space, body awareness, self-image, and environment. Also include many tactile experiences, such as clay and clay substitutes, textural collages, feeling boxes, sand casting, weaving, matching and sorting, and shape discrimination activities.

Hearing Impaired

Characteristics: Lack of communication due to hearing loss; language may be limited; poor environmental awareness; is often difficult to motivate; easily withdraws from activities.

Art motivations: Emphasize tactile and visual experiences. Provide very good demonstrations and visual illustrations. Stress nonverbal communication through bodily movement and awareness activities, space and sequencing, patterns, motion and rhythm activities. Other good activities include large drawing (even on chalkboard), painting, clay, collage, weaving, printing, and sculpture.

Physically Handicapped

Characteristics: Students with cerebral palsy may have spastic movements, lack muscle control, and exhibit stiff, involuntary movements. They may have difficulty with speech, eye-hand coordination, and communication, and may need extended art time and assistance.

Art motivations: Motivations depend on handicaps. Special attention should be given to appropriate materials, adequate space, and extra needed art time. If needed, add handles to brushes, pencils, felt-tip pens with tied-on cloth, foam rubber, or plasticine. Tie these to the individual's wrists, if necessary. Include tactile media, such as collage, clay and clay substitutes, thick paint, felt-tip pens.

In the field of mental health, art therapy is used for emotionally disturbed, brain-damaged children and for special education students in public schools. Its value as a means of identifying behavioral problems and inner conflicts has been documented by psychiatrists, psychologists, and art therapists. The emphasis here is not on skills for skills' sake or for any purpose other than as expression (figs. 2.13 and 2.14).

Individuals with physical disabilities have a normal probability of being creative and talented. For example, deaf individuals have the ability to compete in the world of the performing arts, blind performers have demonstrated success in the music world, and individuals with other physical disabilities have often developed unusual and creative talents in the graphic arts. Art tools can be adapted for special needs. For example, fabric or foam can be tied around brush or pencil handles for easier handling.

The Very Special Arts Festival is a noncompetitive forum for exceptional individuals to share their accomplishments through the visual and performing arts. The program integrates the arts into the general education of exceptional individuals throughout the United States. The festival's goals are: (1) to provide opportunities to discover new skills and to increase future potential for employment for the participants, (2) to help recognize the importance of the arts in the lives of exceptional individuals, (3) to provide social and personally satisfying activity, (4) to recognize efforts, (5) to develop communication skills, and (6) to aid in motor skills, social skills, and fine arts skills (such as imagination, flexibility, adaptability, appreciation, and environmental sensitivity). Such skills can heighten confidence levels, develop self-reliance in thinking and self-esteem, and encourage an active interest in all areas of learning, as well as decrease segregation of individuals with disabilities from society and its cultural activities.

Figure 2.13   A twelve-year-old brain-damaged student drew how he and his sister looked when they had the chicken pox.

Figure 2.14   A fifteen-year-old student with disabilities expressed his feelings in painting a design that reminded him of letters.

chart 2.4

Summary of Characteristics/Objectives for Elementary Students

The Kindergarten Student:

May be in the scribbling stage and may name the scribbles.
Is direct, spontaneous, intuitive in drawing and painting.
Is a natural designer.

Line (chapter 3)
Identifies straight, curved, and diagonal lines.
Describes lines as long-short, thick-thin, light-dark, fine-rough.

Shape (chapter 4)
Identifies basic geometric shapes: square, rectangle, circle, oval, triangle, diamond.
Points out differences in shapes: large-small, many-few, etc.

Uses geometric shapes in first attempts to draw the figure.

Value (chapter 4)
Does not indicate values at this time. Is spontaneous and intuitive.

Space (chapter 5)
May not indicate space but places objects randomly.
May develop a baseline concept of space and may also mix planes and elevations.
Sometimes expresses an X-ray concept, where both inside and outside are drawn in the same picture.

Does not use realistic proportions, but proportions that relate to the item's personal and emotional significance.

Color (chapter 6)
Can identify the primary colors.
Can discriminate between colors that are bright-dull, dark-light, warm-cool.
Selects color based on color's emotional appeal, not for realism.

Pattern (chapter 6)
Identifies patterns in the environment.
Can recognize differences and similarities in patterns.

Texture (chapter 6)
Identifies such textural qualities as hard-soft, rough-smooth.

Design (chapter 7)
Is a natural, intuitive, and spontaneous designer and should not be subjected to adult standards regarding artwork.

Artists to Study
Marc Chagall, Paul Klee, Henri Matisse, Walt Disney, children's book illustrators.

chart 2.4
Summary of Characteristics/Objectives for Elementary Students (continued)

The First- and Second-Grade Student:

Is direct, intuitive, and spontaneous.

Line (chapter 3)
Names and uses various lines (thick, thin, straight, curved, wavy, sharp, soft, hard).
Identifies lines in own art and in artists' works.
Practices making lines with variety of tools.
Practices spacing lines on paper.
Draws lines to describe feelings, music, poems.

Shape (chapter 4)
Identifies and describes basic shapes and sizes: circle, square, rectangle, triangle, oval, diamond.
Identifies and describes organic shapes in the environment.
Observes differences in shapes: large-small, in-out, etc.

Value (chapter 4)
May recognize light and dark, but does not yet visualize shading.
Draws and paints values that are primarily flat in tone.

Space (chapter 5)
Practices the baseline, foldover, and overlapping concepts.
Identifies right-left, center-corner.
Mixes planes and elevations.
Sometimes expresses an X-ray concept, where both inside and outside are drawn in the same picture.
Does not necessarily use realistic proportions.
Sees objects in order, one after another.
Often shows tops, sides, fronts together.
Practices building forms with clay or wood to develop the concepts of change of form and two-dimensional/three-dimensional.

Color (chapter 6)
In first grade, often uses color emotionally. By second grade, begins to use more realistic color.

Discusses differences and similarities in colors.
Discusses color as it relates to feelings, moods.
Practices many painting experiences, mixing of colors.
Can identify the primary colors and some secondary colors.

Pattern (chapter 6)
Identifies patterns in the environment (breathing, sounds, plants, flowers, houses, etc.).
Identifies the use of patterns, such as bricks in a wall, designs on cloth, windows in a building.
Repeats shapes in a design in a rhythmic flow.
Looks at and discusses how artists use pattern.
Practices creating patterns with printing techniques (may be orderly or disorderly repetition).

Texture (chapter 6)
Identifies natural textures: tree bark, sand, rocks, etc.
Identifies manufactured textures: glass, cloth, dishes, etc.
Discusses how artists use texture in paintings, sculpture.
Practices making rubbings of various environmental textures.
Practices feeling textures and discusses how they make him or her feel.

Design (chapter 7)
Is a natural, intuitive designer.
Knows what balance is; how one feels balanced.
Identifies symmetrical balance and finds it in nature.
Identifies asymmetrical balance and finds it in environment.
Can participate in simple discussions regarding balance, dominance, point of interest, what makes an object dominant, and contrast and variety in lines, shapes, textures, etc.

Artists to Study
Paul Klee, Joan Miró, Pablo Picasso, Vincent van Gogh, Marc Chagall, Henri Rousseau, Georgia O'Keeffe.

chart 2.4

Summary of Characteristics/Objectives for Elementary Students (continued)

The Third- and Fourth-Grade Student:

Is still direct, expressive, and spontaneous.

Line (chapter 3)
Observes and practices line directions—vertical, horizontal, diagonal, curved, jagged.
Practices making lines with a variety of tools.
Finds examples of lines in nature, manufactured objects, artists' works.
Identifies how lines create movement, patterns, textures, shapes.
Begins contour drawing, gesture drawing.
Analyzes lines in artworks.

Shape (chapter 4)
Identifies basic shapes: circles, cubes, triangles, squares, cones, spheres.
Discusses differences and similarities in shapes, sizes.
Practices finding organic and geometric shapes in buildings, animals, natural forms, etc.
Identifies realistic shapes, abstract shapes.
Identifies how abstract shapes are formed (simplification).
Analyzes how artists use shapes: for overlapping, to show near-far, etc.

Value (chapter 4)
Begins to see values, changes in lights and darks.
Sees how values change and result in shading as one moves around a form.
Understands shading concept—that light causes shadows and shading (modeled drawing).

Space (chapter 5)
Understands that more than one object occupies space and that these objects are organized somehow.
Identifies objects from more than one position: top, bottom, side, front, etc.
Realizes various viewpoints: ant's-eye view, bird's-eye view, etc.
Experiments with placing objects in order through overlapping, color changes, size differences, and value changes.
Practices organizing physical environmental spaces.
Studies how artists use surrealistic, abstract, cubistic spaces.
Studies uses of physical spaces in rooms, buildings, and communities.
Discusses foreground, middle ground, and background concepts and placement (sky-ground relationships).
Is aware of differences between two-dimensional and three-dimensional space. Third-graders do not yet represent third dimension in perspective; fourth-graders show third dimension by using single viewpoint approaches, overlapping, changes in value, and distance indicators.

Color (chapter 6)
Tends to use color more realistically, but colors may still be selected emotionally.
Identifies differences within a color.
Practices mixing primary, secondary colors.
Practices mixing shades and tints of colors.
Paints monochromatic paintings (lights and darks of one color).
Compares transparent colors in thin washes with thick, opaque colors.
Practices making color choices.
Analyzes how color influences moods, feelings.
Analyzes color in nature, in manufactured objects.
Analyzes color contrasts, such as light-dark, bright-dull, warm-cool, rough-smooth.
Analyzes how artists use color in artworks.

Pattern (chapter 6)
Analyzes patterns in nature, such as the repetition of shapes and rhythms.
Practices adapting patterns from nature.
Creates a design using several repeated shapes.
Analyzes decorative patterns in fabrics.
Explores how various cultures use decorative patterns.
Analyzes how artists use patterns in artworks.
Practices patterns in weaving, tie-dye, batik, clay works.

Texture (chapter 6)
Practices looking and touching sensory experiences.
Identifies various textural qualities in materials and surfaces, such as sandpaper, fur, bricks, woods, cloth, etc.
Analyzes how artists use textures in crafts, paintings, and sculptures.
Discusses the differences and similarities between two- and three-dimensional textures and surfaces.
Practices using lines, shapes, and dots to create textural illusions.

Design (chapter 7)
Identifies and uses symmetrical and asymmetrical balance.
Practices radial balance using compasses.
Analyzes how artists use balance and composition in artworks.
Practices variety, emphasis in designs.
Considers center of interest and dominance created by lines, shapes, colors, textures, patterns, balance, etc.
Creates compositions using unity, harmony, as well as contrast with art components.

Artists to Study
Norman Rockwell, Mary Cassatt, Georgia O'Keeffe, Rufino Tamayo, Karel Appel.

chart 2.4

Summary of Characteristics/Objectives for Elementary Students (continued)

The Fifth- and Sixth-Grade Student:

Line (chapter 3)
Identifies various types of lines.
Uses lines in all directions.
Uses lines to create movement and three dimensions.
Practices using converging lines to show perspective.
Practices adding greater detail with line.
Analyzes how artists use line to create form, texture, pattern, space, etc.
Practices and experiments with detail, contour, gesture, memory, and outline drawing; calligraphy; and cartooning.

Shape (chapter 4)
Observes more complex shapes in nature and human-made environment.
Compares and contrasts different shapes: large to small, simple to complex, etc.
Analyzes and practices using basic geometric shapes—cones, cubes, cylinders, triangles, etc.—and organic shapes in compositions.
Observes similarities and differences in usage of shapes in portraits, figures, landscapes, still lifes.
Practices simplifying realistic shapes into abstraction.
Creates shapes with textures, lines, shadows, colors, etc.
Practices positive-negative shape relationships.
Analyzes how artists use shapes in artworks.

Value (chapter 4)
Can create a value scale with a range of values.
Discusses how artists use values to indicate dimension and space.
Observes soft and sharp shadows.
Practices modeled drawing.
Practices using shading and shadows to suggest form, folds in cloth.
Uses shading and shadows to indicate the third dimension in a composition.

Space (chapter 5)
Analyzes and comprehends size, color, scale, placement, value, overlapping relationships to create depth illusions.
Understands and practices initial concepts of perspective.
Understands such terms as *horizon line, vanishing point, center of vision.*
Practices foreground, middle ground, and background relationships.
Analyzes differences in realistic and abstract space.
Analyzes how artists use space in artworks.

Identifies and practices differences in two-dimensional (flat) and three-dimensional (volume) space.

Color (chapter 6)
Expands color knowledge; recognizes primary, secondary, and intermediate color hues.
Understands and practices mixing tints and shades.
Practices color contrasts, intensities, values, and indicates volume with color.
Understands and uses color vocabulary when analyzing how artists use color in artworks.
Discusses how colors affect moods, atmosphere, feelings.
Analyzes personal color preferences and choices.
May continue to express ideas using color, line, etc. in a more emotional than realistic way.

Pattern (chapter 6)
Develops patterns using rhythm, movement, and spacing.
Practices using up to five to seven shapes and developing patterns.
Continues to study how pattern is used by other artists and cultures.
Practices using lines, colors, shapes, textures to create patterns.

Texture (chapter 6)
Discriminates between two- and three-dimensional textures.
Continues to experience visual as well as tactile textures.
Practices creating two-dimensional textures to represent three-dimensional surfaces.
Practices using textures in drawings, paintings, clay works, weavings, sculptures, fiber works, printmaking.
Analyzes how artists use texture in artworks and crafts.

Design (chapter 7)
Continues to identify symmetrical, asymmetrical, and radial balance.
Combines all art elements to create balanced compositions.
Examines artists' works for dominance/emphasis, variety, etc.
Practices design principles in creating artworks.
Practices contrast, variety, and harmony in selection of art elements and design principles.

Artists to Study
Albrecht Dürer, Henri Matisse, Leonardo da Vinci, Michelangelo, Winslow Homer, Ben Shahn, Paul Cézanne, John Marin, Rijn van Rembrandt, Pierre Renoir, Edgar Degas, Edward Hopper, Salvador Dalí, Kaethe Kollwitz, Gustave Courbet, Mary Cassatt, and contemporary artists.

NOTES

1. *The National Visual Arts Standards*, Jeanne Rollins, chairperson (Reston, Va.: National Art Education Association Publications, 1994).

2. Gifted program developed by Pat Jones Hunt, art consultant for Cartwright School District, Phoenix, Arizona.

The Structure of Art

Art Elements, Design Principles, and Art Production

Line

Painting depends above all on a gift of delicious sensuality, which can with a little of the most simple liquid substance, reconstitute or amplify life and leave its imprint on a surface, from which will emerge a human presence, the supreme irradiation of the spirit.

Odile Redon, 1987

The creative artist learns what he needs to know to fulfill his vision and discards the rest; in short, he absorbs only that which is personally meaningful. . . . To speak about texture or line, for example, divorced from all other considerations within a work of art, can be misleading, for texture, line, value, and the rest are tools in the services of vision and not an end in themselves.

Bernard Chaet, 1970

Artworks consist of the subject matter (realistic or abstract), the medium used (such as pencils, paints, clay, and wood), and art concepts. **Art concepts** are the **art elements** (line, shape, value, space, color, pattern, texture) and the **design principles** (balance, dominance, rhythm, contrast). Within an artwork, each art concept is intertwined with and inseparable from the others so that they work together to influence the total vision.

This chapter explores the art element of line in detail. Chart 3.1 offers a definition of line, as well as of the other art elements. Lines are everywhere in our vision.

LINE

As a very young child, you probably expressed yourself in various scribble line drawings. The pure joy of defining a line seems to hold kinetic fascination for all of us, as it has for humanity throughout history.

Some of humankind's earliest expressions of art are found in cave drawings in Spain and France. These direct, sophisticated artworks, which date from about 20,000 years ago, are deeply sensitive, expressive, symbolic, interpretive, and individual.

The Egyptians used symbolic forms to express their religious and social attitudes. Their wall drawings and paintings, dating from about 3500 B.C., were conceived in flat forms, with little indication of depth. Young children similarly demonstrate such space when they put people, houses, and other items along a baseline at the bottom of the paper.

Beginning in the catacombs in Rome, early Christian artists used simplified, repeated shapes drawn with flat lines to represent the human form, much as a child draws during the schematic or symbolic years, from approximately ages six to eight. (A child's **schema** is a personally developed symbol for a person or object that is repeated again and again. The child may use the same schema for the head of a man as he or she uses for the head of a child because this is what the child symbolizes for a head.) The forms of the early Christian artists were symbols of what the artists felt, rather than of how the forms were actually seen. Medieval artists (from approximately the fifth to the thirteenth centuries) concerned themselves with illustrating scriptures, but also worked on glass windows, carvings, mosaics, tapestries, and the building of architectural structures to glorify Christianity.

chart 3.1

Vocabulary of Art Elements

Line The edges of a form. Lines can be drawn in a variety of directions with many kinds of tools. Sometimes, lines are used to express spatial illusions or the artist's feelings.

Shape The contour of a form or mass, whether a real, imaginary, or abstract object. Shapes come in different proportions and sizes, in two and three dimensions. Sometimes, shapes create tension by their proximity; they can also be overlapped.

Value The amount of light or dark seen on an object or in a color. Value can establish mood, flow, direction, and form.

Space The interval of distance between you and the objects in your environment. Where you exist in space determines your point of view. Shapes, colors, sizes, patterns, and line direction all change as you move within space because all objects in space have a position and direction relative to each other. Within an artwork, space is determined by placement on the picture plane (near or far) and is created by color, value, and shape.

Color A visual sensation derived from pigment or light. Color has hue, value and intensity, can be transparent or opaque, and is related to colors around it. Color sometimes has symbolic meaning or expresses moods.

Pattern Formed by intervals of repeated lines, shapes, colors, or textures. Nature is repetitious with pattern. Pattern is also found on human-made objects, such as textiles and pottery, as well as in music, dance, and poetry. Pattern can introduce order and unity, or contrast and variety.

Texture The illusion of an artwork's surface quality. It can be touched (tactile) and seen (visual), may be natural or synthetic. Line and color can simulate texture.

It was not until the Renaissance (beginning with the artist Giotto [1267–1337]) that artists began to draw a visually representative image that showed an awareness of depth, shadows, and perspective. The artist Masaccio (1401–1428) in Florence, Italy, further developed the concepts of perspective, cast shadows, figures modeled in lights and darks, volume, and depth. Students begin to indicate an awareness of space (foreground, middle ground, and background) in third grade and better mastery of volume, depth, shadow, and perspective in about the fifth or sixth grade.

LINE AS EXPRESSION

As your finger moves, you create a line, a record of action, a defined motion that moves in space. Your eye's path of vision is also a line. Your finger and eye need to become one unit of thought so that they can explore lines in space together. When you use a tool to draw a line, you can feel the line through your fingers, hand, arm, and entire body because you are training your eye, mind, and hand to work in unison.

Try thinking of your body movements in terms of directions and lines. Even the paper that you draw on has an outside edge or line, and the drawing you create is defined by this outside edge. Lines define form (fig. 3.1).

CONTOUR DRAWING

Contour drawing involves looking at the object you want to draw and imagining that you are touching it with the drawing tool. In a sense, your eye becomes the drawing tool, and both your eye and the actual drawing tool should move at the same time, very slowly and sensitively. In contour drawing, you do not look at your paper as you draw.

Figure 3.1 Lines can express edges, feelings, direction, and space. What do these lines suggest to you?

Instead, you sit close to the model and look only at the point your eye and pencil are on, trying not to let your eye get ahead of your hand. If you stop at some point to look at your drawing, then you should start at that same point when you begin to draw again (fig. 3.2).

If you draw while looking at the model (not your paper), the proportions and relationships of your drawing probably will not be realistic and may be more exaggerated and unrelated. However, in this type of drawing, as in any other, the more that you practice, the better contour drawer you will become. Proportions and relationships will improve, and your lines will become more sensitive.

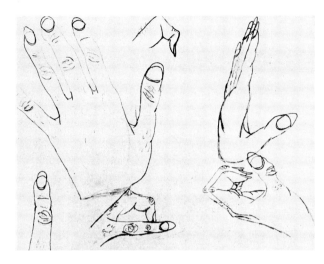

Figure 3.2   Contour drawings like these require the eyes to become, in a sense, the drawing tool.

Tips for improving your contour drawing include:

- Before you begin to draw, study the contours of your model for several seconds. Then close your eyes and try to visualize the contours.
- Touch the surfaces of your models before you contour-draw them.
- When looking at your model, study the line that exists between line changes (from corner to corner, or curve to curve).
- Often, a line does not end on the outline but continues moving inside and then outside. Sometimes, lines meet other lines, they overlap, or the lines may end suddenly. You should have many lines going up and down, as well as in and out.
- While drawing, be aware of your line quality. By applying various pressures to your drawing tool, you can make lines heavy or light. You might want to make important edges and surfaces darker, less important ones lighter. Shadows might be indicated by darker contour lines (fig. 3.3).

Figure 3.3   By applying various pressures to your drawing tool, you can make lines heavy or light. The overlapping, interpenetrating lines in this drawing show greater abstract quality.

Figure 3.4 *All That Is Beautiful* by Ben Shahn. Serigraph. (Courtesy of Gallerie Ann, Houston.)

Figure 3.5 *Au Cirque* by Pablo Picasso. Wash drawing, 9½ inches by 12½ inches. (Courtesy of Lee Ault and Company.)

- Include lines that add to the overall composition. Eliminate lines that do not add interest to the whole.
- Study the drawings of Henri Matisse (see fig. 4.16), Paul Klee, Ben Shahn (fig. 3.4), and Pablo Picasso (fig. 3.5).

though your drawing tool were actually touching the model's contour surface. The distortions and exaggerations that often result tend to add to the abstract quality or uniqueness of the drawing.

QUICK-CONTOUR DRAWING

Quick-contour drawing requires working faster than with regular contour drawing and determining which lines are most essential to the total form. Again, quick-contour drawing involves drawing without looking at your paper. Instead, you should concentrate on the form and draw as

GESTURE (ACTION) DRAWING

Gesture drawing captures a movement, a posture, what a person is doing, or the feeling of a figure or object in a very short time (sometimes less than ten seconds). It involves discovering and feeling the dynamic sensation of the form— the life force of an action, the inner thrust or weight of a

Figure 3.6   Gesture drawing stresses action of the figure and is drawn very quickly.

figure—and responding to that with a line drawing that is descriptive of the action as you, the drawer, see it (fig. 3.6).

Gesture drawing is a learning exercise. The results, which often look like scribbles, are never meant to show details or to be finished drawings. However, they will indicate whether or not the essence of a gesture has been captured.

In gesture drawing, think of the object or figure as a whole unit, and use lines to express the interaction of the whole. For example, in a gesture drawing of a figure, you need to feel the figure's weight. If the figure is resting on an arm, you must remember that the arm is not separate from the torso. Each part of the body influences and forces other body parts to respond to movements and balance.

MEMORY DRAWING

Memory drawing involves drawing from memory, without a model. It requires practice in remembering, and it trains and disciplines your visual recall. You practice remembering by, for example, consciously trying to recall all of the details you saw on your way to school or the color of the walls in the room you were just in. By exercising your memory in this way, you develop a keener awareness of existing relationships and perceptions.

OTHER TYPES OF LINES

The Calligraphic Line

The **calligraphic line** tends to vary from thin to thick in one, quick stroke. A very light brush stroke results in a faint, thin line, while a heavy brush stroke causes a thick, dark line (fig. 3.7). Oriental artists are well known for this

Figure 3.7   The calligraphic line tends to vary from thin to thick in one skillful stroke.

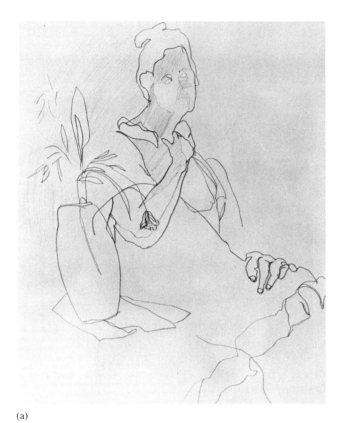

(a)

(b)

Figure 3.8   Line drawing examples, all of the same model in the same pose, illustrate the variety of approaches available to the artist. (*a*) Outline drawing. (*b*) Calligraphic line drawing (wash drawing with brush and ink). (*c*) Building of tones and values with lines, few edges. Broken, unfinished lines permit the eye to move back and forth into space. (*d*) Combination pastel and ink line drawing.

linear drawing technique. A piece of clothing or a figure in action are good subjects for calligraphic drawing. In addition, many people enjoy drawing letters with the calligraphic technique.

The Outline

The **outline** is simply a line that describes the edges of a form. It may be a continuous line that is rather hard and unvarying, or it may be a soft line that describes a rough or smooth texture. Sometimes, discriminating between contour lines and outlines is difficult. Contour lines generally are more sensitive and include more details.

Figure 3.8 shows a variety of line drawings of the same model in the same pose and illustrates the many possible approaches.

Cartooning

Cartooning involves developing one or a series of line drawings to tell a story or joke (for example, comic books, and cartoons and comic strips in newspapers and magazines), to make a statement (for example, political cartoons), or to animate (for example, Walt Disney cartoons) (fig. 3.9).

Most children are introduced to cartoons by watching television. From that time on, much communication with and education of children is processed through cartoon ideas.

The five key words for cartooning are:

1. **Imagination.** Tapping into personal creativity.
2. **Humor.** Bringing funny incidents and stories to life through cartoons.
3. **Exaggeration.** Giving cartoon characters exaggerated body features or apparel to emphasize ideas—for example, Popeye is very muscular, Superman has a special costume, Mickey Mouse has gloves.
4. **Action.** Having cartoon characters show exaggerated movements as well as perform great action feats in a storyline.
5. **Expression.** Having cartoon characters show lots of emotion through facial expressions and action or movement.

(c)

(d)

Figure 3.8 (Continued).

Figure 3.9 Minnie and Mickey Mouse are cartoon characters created by artist/cartoonist Walt Disney.

HOW STUDENTS UNDERSTAND LINE

Kindergarten through Second Grade

Students in kindergarten are usually spontaneous, direct, and intuitive. By the first and second grade, they can understand the concept of lines as edges and outlines that combine to produce forms and shapes. Explain that a line starts at a point and often changes direction. A line can also often change in a variety of other ways that these students can identify and name—for example, light to dark, straight to curved, short to long, thick to thin, vertical to horizontal, hard to soft, sharp to gentle, and wavy to diagonal. Discuss with students how lines can sometimes express feelings and emotions. With students in this age group, focus on studying and drawing individual objects, rather than groups of objects.

Encourage students to find lines in the environment. Examples include: bricks, piano keyboards, necklaces, lines of print, tunnels, strings of car lights, streetlights, pipelines, sewers, rainbows, sunbeams, rubber hoses, chains, irrigation ditches, telephone wires, curbing, barbed wire, cracks, the horizon line, feathers, zippers, hair, stitching, chain-link fences, trellises, the jet stream, age wrinkles, thread, ribbon.

Have students practice making lines with various tools: pencils, brushes, crayons, felt-tip pens. Demonstrate how the tool and the way in which the artist chooses to use the tool can give lines infinite variety. Encourage students to experiment with making various kinds of lines. Urge them to use and fill their whole paper space when drawing or painting.

Third and Fourth Grade

Third- and fourth-graders understand that geometric lines form basic environmental shapes, such as figures, houses, and flowers. In their drawings, they tend to include important lines and shapes and to omit unimportant ones. Encourage students to observe carefully, to feel objects, and to name and describe details in objects. These types of meaningful experiences will result in students including more detail in their drawings.

Continue to have students look for and point out lines in nature, human-made objects, architecture, and the environment.

Explain to students that contour lines are the outer edges—the limits—of objects. Emphasize and have students touch the contour lines of concrete objects.

Have third- and fourth-graders practice line drawing with a variety of tools, such as pencils, felt-tip pens, crayons, and paint, and then discuss the differences and similarities of the lines and tools. Introduce and have students practice contour drawing, gesture drawing, memory drawing, cartooning, and calligraphy.

Display and discuss with students reproductions of linear drawings by recognized artists (see the "Artists to Study" section at the end of the chapter). Encourage students to make judgments about these drawings: Do they like or dislike them, and why? Describe various lines found in paintings, sculptures, and architecture.

Fifth and Sixth Grade

Fifth- and sixth-grade students are able to analyze the environment more accurately and have a better understanding of relationships among objects. They begin to perceive distance in space and achieve a more complex understanding of perspective. They use converging lines to represent depth and space as they demonstrate perspective with a single viewpoint. Their lines become more complex as they begin to represent people and objects with volume and greater three-dimensional accuracy.

As these students acquire a greater understanding of line, they are able to compare and contrast different types of lines. They also learn to use lines to describe surfaces, textures, and patterns; to create movement, perspective, and dimension; and to express moods, emotions, feelings, and atmosphere.

Work with fifth- and sixth-graders to develop their individual drawing techniques. Have them practice line drawing with a variety of tools, such as pencils, felt-tip pens, crayons, and paint, and then discuss the differences and similarities of the lines and tools. Continue to have them practice contour drawing, gesture drawing, memory drawing, and others. Challenge them to draw more complex groupings, such as still lifes or groups of people.

Continue study of linear drawings of respected artists (see the "Artists to Study" section at the end of the chapter). Ask students to describe various lines found in paintings, sculpture, and architecture. Discuss how lines are used in decorative art, alphabets, signs, newspapers, and various cultural artifacts, such as Hopi pottery.

Discuss careers, such as illustrators, cartoonists, draftspersons, and architects, that require skills with lines.

IDEAS AND MOTIVATIONS

Adapt to students' abilities and grade levels.

Lines

1. Using a pencil, pen, crayon, felt-tip pen, charcoal, chalk, brush, or colored pencil, spend some time discovering different kinds of lines and edges and how they move and feel. Let your hand and eye become one unit of thought.
2. Select an object to draw, and then look at that object and try to visualize it in terms of lines, or edges. When you have finished looking, pick up your tool and experiment. Try to remember and re-create the various kinds of lines that you saw (fig. 3.10).
3. If you have been using a pencil, try another tool, such as a pen or a piece of charcoal. What happens when you push down hard with the tool? What happens when you hold it very lightly? What happens when you twist the tool as you draw? Can you discover a new way to hold the tool, such as on the side, or on the point?
4. Try drawing with your other hand and with both hands together.
5. Draw a picture that combines two or more tools together— for example, felt-tip pens with pencils, crayons with watercolors.
6. Compare drawing tools. Does drawing lines with a pencil give you the same feeling as drawing lines with a crayon? Can you get the same details, textures, and colors in crayon lines that you do with pencil or pen lines?
7. Try creating a drawing with only straight, curved, wavy, or zigzag lines. Keep sketch books.

Contour Drawing

1. Do contour drawings of figures; portraits; natural forms, such as weeds, trees, flowers, insects, hands, feet, and eyes; and irregular forms, such as hats, shoes, antiques, and vegetables.
2. Try using only one continuous line to draw your model (fig. 3.11).

(a)

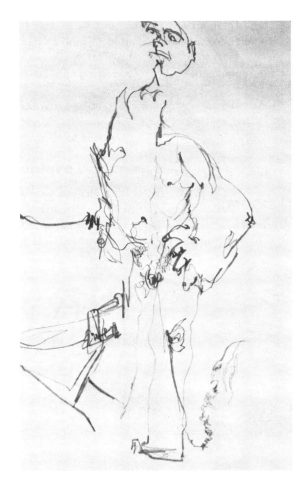

Figure 3.11 Continuous-line contour drawing shows exaggerated proportions and relationships.

(b)

Figure 3.10 Students draw their favorite models—their pets. Cats, dogs, snakes, and other animals, whether real or imaginary, have always been subject matter for artists to interpret personally.

3. Do a contour drawing of a group of objects, such as heads, hands (fig. 3.12), and still lifes of odd combinations (for example, old dolls piled on a table). You might want to emphasize and distort certain parts—for example, drawing one eye on a head while omitting the other might add mystery to your drawing.
4. Do contour drawings of interesting patterned objects, such as large plants (for example, philodendron).
5. Try creating more complex contour drawings of musical instruments and machines (fig. 3.13).
6. Contour-draw a costumed figure. Have the model wear items like large, floppy hats; long, patterned gloves; old-fashioned shoes and boots; and long, lacy dresses. Try to capture the pattern and form of the clothes.
7. After you have done one contour drawing of a model, do another contour drawing of the model, but from a different viewpoint, on the same page.
8. Try contour-drawing various views of the same subject (for example, the corner of a room or a detailed enlargement of an eye), but vary the sizes of the drawings and let them overlap.
9. Try contour-drawing with your other hand.

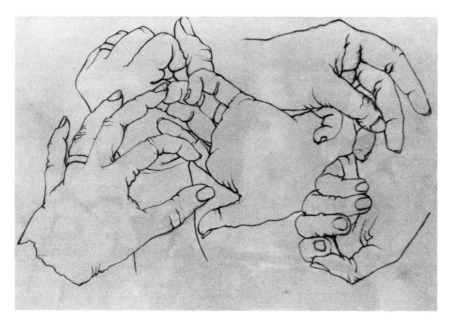

Figure 3.12   Overlapping lines in this contour drawing indicate three dimensions.

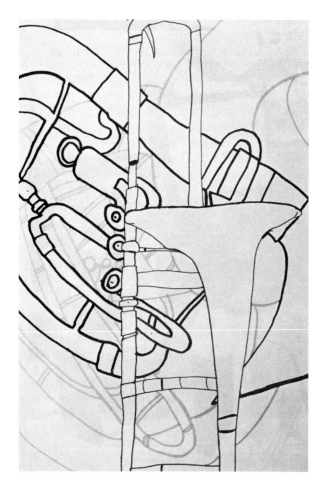

Figure 3.13   In this artwork, contour drawing extends beyond the edges of the paper to create an exciting spatial composition. The different value lines were made by different-colored felt-tipped pens.

10. Contour-draw on black paper with a white pencil.
11. Instead of always beginning your contour drawing at the same point on the paper, start your drawing at the top of the paper and work toward the bottom, or start at the sides and work toward the center, or start in the center and work toward the sides.

Quick-Contour Drawing

1. Select three objects to draw. Do not arrange them into a still life, but place them randomly on a surface. Quick-contour draw each object separately, but consider the placement of each object with regard to composition and how each object will relate to the other two. Permit the lines from each object to intersect and overlap.
2. Ask a model to change poses every thirty seconds. Do a quick-contour drawing of each pose, but place all of the drawings on one page.
3. Try quick contours on a large scale: Work on large mural paper spread out on a wall or the floor.
4. Practice doing quick-contour drawings at parks, baseball games, restaurants, zoos, and schools.

Gesture Drawing

1. Allow yourselves only ten seconds to make gesture drawings of many moving figures in crowds at such places as the supermarket, the school lunch line, or a football game.
2. Try to gesture-draw images on television.
3. Experiment with making gesture drawings of moving animals.

4. Make a gesture drawing of just a head. Feel the changes and movement of the surfaces and forms.

5. Try to gesture-draw with pencil, as well as with crayons or charcoal, using the sides of the tool. Experiment also with brush and ink or paint.

6. Combine gesture drawing with contour drawing: first gesture, and then contour over that; or first contour, and then gesture over that.

7. Experiment with making gesture drawings of inanimate objects, such as glasses, shirts, or drapery, while thinking of them as having action and movement.

8. Begin by making a gesture drawing of a figure, a landscape, a still life. Then continue with more detailed drawings.

Memory Drawing

1. Observe a model for thirty seconds. While the model rests, draw what you remember about the pose.

2. Draw from memory subjects seen in the past: different animals, people on television, people in crowds.

3. Draw from memory still-life objects, such as a favorite toy, an old doll.

4. Observe projected slides or photographs for one minute. Then turn off the projector, and try to draw what you saw.

5. Draw what you did last Saturday. Include your feelings.

6. Try to capture the likeness of a friend who is not now in the room.

7. Select a happy time that you remember, such as a party, circus, or basketball game, and draw everything you remember about it. Do the same with an unhappy time.

Birds

Refer students to photographs or drawings of birds in books or magazines, or arrange to have students observe a live bird, either in the classroom, outside in a park or on a playground, or at a zoo or bird sanctuary. Then ask students to:

1. Look for basic geometric shapes in the bird, and analyze how they are attached. Compare the sizes and proportions of the shapes.

2. Identify various kinds of birds, and note their similarities and differences and any special characteristics (such as waddles) that set them apart from other birds.

3. Observe the texture of the bird's legs and feet. Ask students if lines can be combined to indicate texture (fig. 3.14).

4. Note the proportions of the bird's feet in relation to its body and head, and where the legs extend from the body.

Figure 3.14 A fifth-grader used lines to express patterns, textures, and surfaces. Motivations included photographs, as well as pets and trips to the zoo.

5. Carefully examine the details of the bird's wings, observing their basic shape when extended and when held close to the body.

6. Observe the bird's feathers in detail—their varying lengths and sizes and the underlying bone structure.

7. Note the locations of the bird's eyes and beak, and observe how the beak is attached to the head.

8. Describe the colors and color changes on the bird's body, wings, feet, head, and eyes.

9. Closely observe the different positionings of the bird's body, head, feet, and wings as it flies, lands, walks, eats, and sleeps.

10. Apply their observations to a contour, gesture, memory, or realistic drawing of the bird (figs. 3.15 and 3.16).

Precision Instruments

Gather a variety of precision instruments, such as old clocks, the insides of radios and televisions, musical instruments, microscopes, earphones, typewriters, motors, and so on, for students to look over. Have students study one object very carefully, looking for intricate details. Then suggest that students use such line and detail tools as pencils, felt-tip pens, and ballpoint pens to draw the object (fig. 3.17).

Insects

Ask students to find and bring in a variety of insects, such as butterflies, beetles, and spiders. Then ask students to:

1. Look at the insects' basic body shapes and at how large the shapes are in contrast to the insects' legs and antennas.

2. Study the design and organization of insects, and determine how insects' body parts (head, torso, legs, and so on) are put together.

Figure 3.15   Flying motion is indicated in the above drawings by first- and second-graders. The various sizes of birds in (*a*) and (*b*) suggest families of birds. Several members of the family in (*a*) are crying. The drawing in (*c*) was done with a stencil and suggests motion by overlapping.

Figure 3.16   Upper-level artwork of birds express more realistic interpretations. Note the variety of flowers.

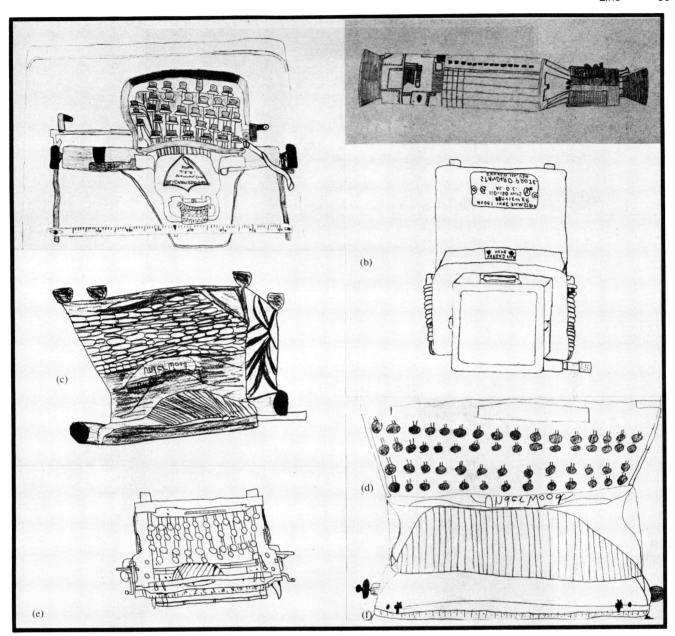

Figure 3.17 Drawings of precision instruments created by students in third through sixth grade. Note that drawing (*c*) shows front and side elevation. Drawing (*d*) shows top view. Drawings (*e*) and (*f*) show greater detail, rounded forms, and indicate lights and darks.

3. Count how many legs different insects have, and observe where the legs extend from the body.
4. Look at the insects through microscopes and magnifying glasses for closer details.
5. Closely observe the different positionings of insects' bodies, heads, legs, and wings as the insects move, fly, eat, rest, and interact with their environment.
6. Compare and contrast the different types of insects observed. Discuss how and where insects live.
7. Use various art tools and apply all of their observations when drawing the insects.
8. Draw a picture of an insect that they invent in their minds (fig. 3.18).

Plants and Flowers

Arrange to have students observe live plants and flowers. (See fig. 8.18b, 8.19a and b, and 9.14c for artwork examples.) Then ask students to:

1. Keep a record of how the plants grow, noting changes in and relationships of the various plant parts.
2. Look at, feel, and do rubbings of the textural surfaces of the plants and flowers.
3. Determine the underlying structure of the flowers and their many parts.
4. Determine whether the leaves grow opposite each other or alternate up the stalk toward the flowers.

Figure 3.18   Imaginary insect drawings by students from various grade levels. Motivations included studying insects under a microscope. Students reveal their individual personalities in their drawings.

5. Hold a leaf up to a light to see the lines in the leaf's internal structure.
6. Determine whether the petals on flowers remain the same size, texture, color, and form, or change from the center out.
7. Feel, smell, taste, and take apart the flowers to intensely "see" them.
8. Use various art tools and apply all of their observations when drawing plants or flowers.
9. Try contour, gesture, and realistic drawings of plants and flowers.

Skeletal Parts

Bring a collection of skulls, skeletons, fish bones, fossils, and even beef bones from the supermarket into the classroom for drawing studies. Point out to students how a skeletal form is the underlying structure of an object. Have students look closely at size relationships of the skeletal parts. Suggest that they examine and touch the different textures. Then ask them to create an interesting drawing with bones and structural objects (fig. 3.19).

Drawing Lines to Music

Have students use felt-tip pens, crayons, or chalk to draw to music. Tell them to first close their eyes and listen for changes in the patterns and movement of the music. Encourage them to move their arms as though conducting the music. Then they should let their drawing tools "dance" across the paper as they "feel" the music, responding to the music action with dynamic strokes, bends, ripples, and glides. Suggest that they try to capture the sound of each instrument with a color.

"Doodle" Drawing

Encourage students to create "doodle" drawings in which they practice drawing many varieties of lines (scratchy, bumpy, flowing, bold, and so on) and then develop the lines and patterns into a design.

ARTISTS TO STUDY

Aubrey Vincent Beardsley

Although he died at an early age, Aubrey Vincent Beardsley (1872–1898) created many highly decorative pen-and-ink book illustrations. Some art historians feel that Beardsley was strongly influenced by the sharp contrasts of black and white used by Oriental artists popular at that time. He delighted in using dotted lines, lacy scroll lines, intricate patterns, and delicate lines against strong blacks. One shape

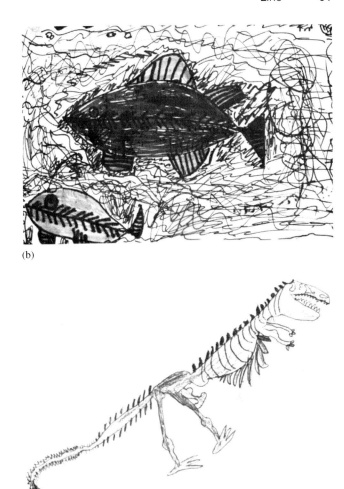

(b)

(a)

(c)

Figure 3.19 Drawings show skeletal parts and structures.

might be a dark form against a light background, contrasted with a light form against a dark background. Beardsley was aware of how surface lines could create forms, and he used these lines to indicate rounded forms. His contrasting of sensitive, delicate lines and simple areas with busy areas added intrigue and expression to his drawings. The period of art during which Beardsley lived is often referred to as Art Nouveau.

Stuart Davis

Stuart Davis (1894–1964) used lines to show patterns, and linear letters often became important in the design. He used other elements, such as color and patterns, but line was central to his concept (fig. 3.20). Davis painted popular American themes, such as jazz, cars, gas stations, airplanes, and signs. He was one of the first artists to make lettering part of the composition.

Albrecht Dürer

Sixteenth-century German artist Albrecht Dürer (1471–1528) mastered many printing techniques, such as

woodcuts and etchings, and used a linear method that appears as pen-and-ink drawings (fig. 3.21).

Joan Miró

The abstract paintings of Joan Miró (1893–1983) include shapes and lines that are happy, moving, humorous, inventive, imaginative, and colorful (see fig. 10.34). Miró's paintings look almost childlike in concept but were executed with a sophisticated understanding of design and theme combinations.

Paul Klee

Paul Klee (1879–1940) was another artist whose work is known for its happy, humorous, and delightful feeling. Klee varied his lines and gave them different qualities, depending on the themes he used.

Figure 3.20 *Composition with Boats.* Stuart Davis, American, 1894–1964. Oil on canvas, c. 1932–34. San Diego Museum of Art (Gift of Mrs. Edith G. Halpert).

Figure 3.21 Albrecht Dürer, German, 1471–1528, *Four Horsemen of the Apocalypse,* woodblock print, 1498, 39.3 × 28.3 cm, Clarence Buckingham Collection, photograph © 1995 The Art Institute of Chicago. All Rights Reserved.

Shape, Value, Shading, and Shadows

I found that I could say things with color and shapes that I had no words for.

Georgia O'Keeffe, artist

My aim is always to get hold of the magic of reality and to transfer this reality into painting . . . to make the invisible visible through reality. . . . It may sound paradoxical, but it is, in fact, reality which forms the mystery of our existence.

Max Beckman, *On My Painting*

As discussed in chapter 3, the art elements consist of line, shape, value, space, color, pattern, and texture, all of which intermingle and affect each other in the final artwork.

Shape (as defined in chart 3.1) is the contour of a form or mass (whether real, imaginary, or abstract). **Value** is the amount of light or dark seen on the object or in a color that can establish mood, flow, direction, and form. **Shading,** volume, and **shadows** result from blending (modeling) shape and value. Look around; everything is a shape.

SHAPE

When a line moves through space, meets itself, and forms an enclosure, it becomes a **shape.** Everything is composed of one or more shapes. For example, study a plank of wood. Both the bottom and top are large rectangles. The long edge is another rectangle, as is the short edge.

Young children often draw an object as they *know* it. For example, they may show the top and bottom of an object

in the same picture, or they may include front and side views of houses and buildings shown together. They may understand that the object has three dimensions, but they represent the object with many sides showing as flat surfaces.

Older students and adults, on the other hand, want to draw an object as they *see* it. They understand that, when lines or edges meet and come together, different shapes are possible. Their viewpoint of an object affects the shape of the object they see and draw. For example, the top of a book may be in reality a rectangle, but when the book is viewed from an angle, the top looks like a trapezoid.

Thus, shapes are not only what you know them to be but also depend on how you view them—where you are in relation to the object.

POSITIVE AND NEGATIVE SHAPES

When composing a picture, you begin with a determined size of paper. The paper is the **format**—the outside edges of the surface. The format influences the design and various shapes that you draw on the paper.

A **positive shape** is the physical object or figure represented in an artwork. Empty space around the form is considered the **negative shape.** Your design consists of the arrangement of positive and negative shapes within the format (fig. 4.1).

To help you understand this concept, use an empty slide holder as a viewfinder. Hold the viewfinder next to one eye, and look through the opening (see fig. 5.3). The viewfinder acts as a border. Select an object, such as a plant, and direct your gaze at the positive shape (the plant). Then concentrate on finding the negative shapes surrounding the plant. Wait

(a)

(b)

Figure 4.1 Positive shapes are the light areas; negative shapes are the dark areas.

until your vision accepts the negative shapes and thinks of them as separate forms. Now imagine that the plant vanishes and that only the negative shapes are left. If you try drawing the negative shapes, you will find that, as you focus on individual spaces, they become forms in themselves, but as they build together, they begin to reveal the form of the plant (or the positive shape).

Practice this "positive shape/negative shape seeing" with all kinds of objects, shapes, and figures to hone your skills in perceiving detail and form. Artists must be constantly aware of both positive and negative shapes as organizing devices for artworks.

VALUE

Value is the amount of light and dark. It is also dependent on the amount of light (tint) or dark (shade) contained in a color. A **value scale** ranges from white to black (fig. 4.2).

To help you understand the art element of value, practice drawing with a range of flat tonal values to represent a surface. Select a subject, then divide the drawing into sections like a map, and assign one flat tonal value to

each form (fig. 4.3). Begin with black, white, and three grays. The grayed flat tones lend more of an abstract quality or decorative effect to your work. Commercial artists often use this approach for poster, fabric, and silk-screen printed designs. Experiment with this concept in drawing faces, landscapes, and still lifes.

Subjects can suggest values to be used. A light, happy, bright subject suggests a light tonal range, while an ominous, evil, fearful, mysterious subject suggests a very dark range of tonal values. Tonal ranges and values can suggest ideas in themselves. For example, a middle-gray-tone picture—that is, one with very close value relationships—might suggest a rainy, gray, foggy day or somewhat unreal attitudes. A strong contrast of darks and lights might suggest a bright day at the beach or skiing down a slope.

SHADING

Shading, or **modeling,** is the representation of three-dimensional, rounded forms through the use of a variety of values from light to dark. Shading and contrast is determined by the amount and source of the light and the

Figure 4.2 A value scale is a series of gray tones that range from white to black. This scale changes about twelve times. The human eye can distinguish many values. An elementary student usually indicates three to four values when producing a drawing.

Figure 4.3   Artwork with flat tonal value by a fourth-grader.

shadows created on the form. Chart 4.1 provides a brief vocabulary of light.

Shading techniques vary, depending on whether the object being drawn is made up of **flat** planes or surfaces, or **rounded forms** (volumes). An object consisting only of flat surfaces, such as a box, has fairly flat tones or shadows and flat, simple values. For example, the brightest surface of the box will be the plane facing or nearest the light. The sides will be grayer or lower in value, and the darkest plane or surface will be the one farthest from the light. Changes in value from one side of the box to the next are sharp—not gradual or blurred.

With rounded forms (such as a ball), the edges of the surface are softer, and the shadows blend from one form to the next. Forms closest to the light will still be the lightest and brightest. However, as the forms recede, the values gradually become darker until the forms farthest from the light source are the darkest (fig. 4.4).

Shading represents nature as ordinarily seen. Artists often add their personal signature to their artworks through shading changes and modifications.

Figure 4.4   A modeled drawing example of rounded shapes shows shading with soft edges between lights and darks. Fifth grade. The forms here appear to be rounded because they recede with dark on some edges and graduate toward lighter tones on others.

chart 4.1

Vocabulary of Light

Transparent Describes materials, such as glass, air, and water, that permit light to pass through them unchanged. Transparent materials do not cast shadows.

Opaque Describes objects and materials, such as people and buildings, that stop light waves. Opaque materials cast shadows.

Translucent Describes materials, such as certain plastics, that you cannot see through but that permit light waves to pass through.

Reflection The return of light waves from a surface. On smooth or shiny surfaces, light is changed from its normal straight line and bounced off (reflected) at an angle (see fig. 4.7). On uneven surfaces, light is reflected in many directions by small surfaces reflecting at various angles.

Refraction Light goes through different materials at different speeds. The bending of light waves from their normal straight path as they pass from one medium (such as air) into another (such as water).

Illumination The amount of light reflected by an object. Illumination depends on the brightness of the light source and on the distance between the light and the receiving object.

Shadow Determined by the size of the light source, the number of light sources, the size of the opaque object, and the size or length of the angle at which the light hits the opaque object.

SHADOWS

Shadows are created when rays from one or more light sources are cut off by an opaque object (fig. 4.5). The object's shadows and tonal values help to reveal the object's three-dimensional form.

The distance of an object from a light source determines a shadow's strength and shape. The brighter the light source, the brighter the object and the darker the shadows. When the light is dull, there is little contrast in value between object and shadow. Moving a light source closer to or farther away from the object also changes the shadow's shape (fig. 4.6).

When you draw a shadow, you are drawing a shape with value. Therefore, as with negative shapes that become forms in themselves, shadows also can be thought of as shapes.

If you were to draw just shadows (without the object), the shadows themselves would reveal the object. Artists practice this kind of light/dark relationship by using just black ink to draw in shadows as independent shapes. Eventually, separate shadow shapes begin to relate to each other, almost like placing parts of a puzzle together, and the total form can be visualized.

Discovering the shapes of shadows will sharpen your vision. After you have practiced seeing shadows as shapes, begin to develop an eye for seeing tonal differences within a shadow.

Artists decide how many shadows to include in a drawing and base their decisions on the design and concept of the entire composition. They may decide to sharpen a shadow or soften it, or perhaps exaggerate it or change its shape.

Figure 4.5   Mount cut, white, paper forms on white paper to study shadow shapes.

In realistic, representational drawings, you will be more concerned with the actual shadows, although sometimes it is better not to try to include all of the shadows that you actually see. Keep the shadows more subdued than the object itself. Placing a dark shadow next to a light object can assign more importance to the object.

Shadows are sometimes made from reflected light (light reflected from glass, mirrors, shiny metal, and so on), but these shadows are best used only when they help to describe the form (fig. 4.7). Reflected shadows can become very complex and are difficult for beginners. Close, opaque objects also cast subtle shadows and reflections on each other and are difficult to draw.

(a)   (b)

Figure 4.6   Without light there is darkness. Shading and shadows are determined by the light source.

HOW STUDENTS UNDERSTAND SHAPE, VALUE, SHADING, AND SHADOW

Kindergarten through Second Grade

Have short, simple, dynamic lessons in kindergarten. In first and second grade, there is interest in naming and identifying basic geometric shapes: circle, square, rectangle, triangle, oval, and diamond (fig. 4.8); in describing similarities and differences in these shapes, such as large-small, light-dark, in-out, and smooth-rough; and in drawing likenesses of these basic shapes. Work with students to identify shapes in their environment. Provide opportunities for exciting, perceptual **looking** and **feeling** experiences with shapes and forms.

Discuss how artists use shapes in artworks. Ask students if shapes in artworks create moods. Help them to identify near and far shapes in artworks.

At this time, students do not comprehend shading or drawing with values.

Objects drawn may not be related, but appear all over the page in random order.

Suggest that students use repeated shapes to create new patterns. Encourage students to invent new shapes and forms. For example, students at this age level enjoy creating imaginative insects, animals, and designs.

Using paint, show students how to produce three values by mixing black with white. Then ask students to find light-toned, middle-toned, and dark-toned objects—both natural and human-made—in their environment.

Keep in mind that students in this age group have a space concept that consists of all forms on a baseline. In addition, these students' representations of shapes, proportions, and sizes are often invented, emotional, and not realistic.

Third and Fourth Grade

Third- and fourth-grade students begin to classify objects and enjoy discovering many shapes in their environment that they can find, list, and categorize. Describe and discuss with them how architects combine various shapes in houses, buildings, and bridges.

Students now begin to see and understand dimension, volume, and shading. Discuss how light affects and changes the forms we see.

(a)

Figure 4.7 Look around! Everything is a shape. (*a*) Photographer Jack Stuler interprets body reflections in metal to create unique and imaginitive shapes. (Photograph courtesy of Jack Stuler.) (*b*) Reflections form shapes.

Figure 4.7 (Continued).

(b)

Figure 4.8 First-graders begin drawing with flat, basic, geometric shapes. Shapes are placed randomly.

Analyze with students how artists have used various shapes in their artworks to indicate space, pattern, texture, contrast, balance, and rhythm. Discuss sizes and proportions, similarities and differences of objects shown in artworks, and work with students on the concept of near-far.

Explain to students the differences between abstract artworks. Demonstrate how to draw objects and how then to abstract the objects into geometric shapes. Note similarities and differences of shapes in objects.

Have students analyze artworks as to light, middle, and dark values, and ask them to describe how values create moods. Discuss how light, middle, and dark values are used in realistic and abstract works. Point out how architects use values in buildings and on surfaces to create textures. Discuss with students how natural light changes during the day and how those changes can affect mood and atmosphere.

Point out how artists indicate volume, shading, and shadows in artworks. Suggest that students produce drawings with cast-shadow shapes. Begin to have students practice creating volume and mass using simple shading techniques.

Keep in mind that, while third- and fourth-graders can see proximity (how close objects are to each other) and understand that an object can be surrounded by something else, they still have difficulty with three-dimensional perspective and correct proportions. In addition, they do not always draw an object from the angle seen. For example, they may draw several sides of an object, such as the front and both sides of a house, or their drawing may indicate that they can look through the walls of a house.

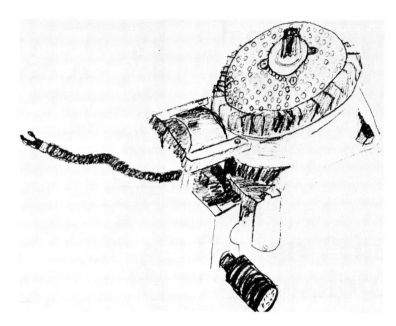

Figure 4.9   A sixth-grader's drawing of a motor indicates three-dimensional form. Students enjoy drawing details of a single object, as well as a grouping of objects.

Figure 4.10   Drawings of shapes extend the design of the photo. Third grade.

Figure 4.11   Above drawing indicates sixth-grader's interest in shapes of hairstyles, hats, shoes, clothing, and the "real" world.

Fifth and Sixth Grade

Fifth- and sixth-grade students can identify the difference between basic two- and three-dimensional shapes, and can draw more complex organic and geometric shapes, such as cylinders, cubes, pyramids, and pentagons, quite accurately (figs. 4.9, 4.10, and 4.11). Initiate a variety of discussions about shapes with students. For example, discuss:

- How viewpoint changes a visual shape and shading
- How shapes can create movement in space
- How placement of shapes creates visual tension and illustrates the concept of near-far
- Harmonious and disharmonious shapes. Look for relationships.

- Ability to draw grouping of objects.
- How shapes are used in signs, logos, flags, books, furniture, and architecture
- How shapes are influenced by textures, colors, and patterns
- The concepts of positive/negative shape

Ask students to identify light, medium, and dark values in the environment. Then discuss kinds of light and how it affects vision. Show students how light can change shapes and forms.

Demonstrate and have students draw a value scale of contrasting values (see fig. 4.2). Provide a number of black-and-white photographs, and ask students to find, analyze, and differentiate the values.

Figure 4.12   Observe shapes, values, and shadows as they occur in nature and changing light.

Suggest that students practice creating values with various media and with massed lines. Encourage them to create drawings with close (similar) values and with contrasting values, to experiment with changing the value of drawn shapes, and to practice developing five values in a drawing.

Provide various media, such as pencils, pen and ink, charcoal, and crayon, for students to practice shading forms. Study shadows in nature (fig. 4.12), in changing light, and in various artworks.

Display selected art reproductions, and ask students to identify various shapes, values, and shading techniques. Discuss how shapes can affect balance, rhythm, dominance, contrast, color, pattern, and texture.

IDEAS AND MOTIVATIONS

Adapt to students' abilities and grade levels.

Shape

1. Find one basic shape that is repeated over and over in a painting.
2. Find and draw basic shapes in figures of animals and people, and in the environment.
3. Name and describe some basic shapes used in architecture (see color plate 5).
4. Try building shapes in sand, in clay, with sticks, and with blocks of wood to get a "feel" for mass and form.
5. Use paper shapes to build sculptures, architectural forms, animals, and so on. Cut out silhouettes.

Value

1. Experiment with making a variety of gray tones with pencils (sides and point) and with charcoal.
2. Experiment with using other tools—crayons, ink, chalks, paints—to make tones and values.
3. Using one color of chalk, experiment to see how many values you can achieve.
4. Make a value scale (see fig. 4.2). Divide a 10-inch by 1-inch rectangle into ten boxes. In the first box, put white; in the last box, put black. In the eight boxes in between, create a series of graduated gray tones.
5. Build a value scale with just lines. Place one layer of lines on top of another to achieve darker values.
6. Experiment with the interesting texture created when a middle-gray tone is produced with pencil or charcoal and then an eraser is used to take away areas to create light tones.

7. Use the wax from a white candle to draw in the whites of a picture. The whites will not show, so you will have to remember where you have put them. Then, paint in wash tones, including darks. The tones can be wet as you work, or let one gray dry before adding the next gray tone. The waxed areas will appear as white in the final drawing. This is similar to the **crayon-resist** technique, in which colored crayons are used and then dark paint is placed over the crayons.

8. On a sheet of acetate paper, draw organic shapes or one or more geometric shapes, and then repeat them, letting the lines intercept and overlap. Fill in the areas of overlap with colors, plus black and white. The filled-in areas become forms. Place your acetate on top of that of someone else's and rotate the two sheets. The resulting design is an optical illusion.

Shading

1. Select a simple form, such as a cylinder, block, ball, apple, or egg, to draw. Study the lights and shadows on and surrounding the form. Then draw the form, using a range of four tones from light to dark. Pencils of different weights (and using various hand pressures) will permit different tones, as will various other tools, such as crayons, charcoal, and chalk.

2. Use shading to draw a feather and then a door. How do the drawings differ in value?

3. Draw pieces of fruit. Study one shape and its value at a time, and draw each shape in detail. Note the changes and directions of the forms. For example, an apple will have a different form from a grape, but both apples and grapes have reflective surfaces.

4. Discuss various careers and what shape, value, and shading mean in architecture, commercial art, television, advertising, interior design, photography, etc.

5. Select a simple object to draw. Do not draw any outlines—just blend in the grays and darks to create form, volume, and shading.

6. Drape a piece of cloth or clothing over a chair, or tack it onto a wall and then drape it. Using a range of four or five tones, draw the changes in drapery very carefully, concentrating on the lights and darks. Where the cloth goes under or behind is often where the greatest darks are. The parts of the cloth that come forward are often the lightest forms. Consider the background as part of the total composition so that you create tones behind the cloth as well. Think of the cloth as a form that is being modeled (pushed in and pulled out) in clay.

7. Crumple up a paper bag, and then draw all the tones you can see. Do another drawing after you have flattened the paper bag out again.

Figure 4.13   A sixth-grader used dots to create modeled form and shadows.

8. Try to draw the various lights and darks of a mineral specimen. Amethyst crystals are particularly beautiful and are visually exciting.

9. Experiment by thinking in reverse. Try shading techniques with white chalk or crayons on dark paper. Or where forms appear darkest visually, draw them lightest, and where they appear lightest visually, draw them darkest.

10. Experiment with building up lines or using dots or crosshatching to create tones (fig. 4.13).

11. Make a contour drawing of one of your hands, looking for the cross-contour and surface qualities (see chapter 3). Then build up the forms of the fingers with shading, tones, and values.

12. After you have practiced some shading techniques, try doing portraits. Keep in mind the changes of the forms as they move in and out, behind and under, as though you were a sculptor creating in clay.

13. Try using your nondominant hand to make a drawing with values only.

Shadows

1. Try drawing with different tools to create different feelings with shadows. Experiment with charcoal, pen and ink, watercolor paints, chalk, oil paints, pencil.

2. Make a drawing using only cast shadows (fig. 4.14).

Figure 4.14   A teacher, along with her shadow, greets her class. Drawing by a second-grade student.

3. Draw a picture with interesting lines and shadows. Keep in mind that interest is created by variety—in dark and light, in strength and delicacy, in different types of lines, in soft and hard edges, in large and small shapes, in busy and quiet areas, and so on.

4. Study how shadows change the colors of an object. For example, an orange or grapefruit may be basically yellow or orange, but the shadows cast on them from a light or other objects may alter their natural color.

5. Look at a Rembrandt painting. Decide which is most important in the painting—outside edges, shading, shadows that describe forms, or cast shadows.

6. Using a contour drawing or outline drawing that you have already completed, (a) draw in the shadows where you remember them to be. Or, using your imagination, (b) draw in a separation of areas and add random tones to make the drawing unrealistic and more abstract. Or, (c) experiment with adding only stark whites and blacks, and eliminating the middle tones.

7. Experiment and have fun drawing a bottle and its reflections. This will challenge you because of absorbed as well as reflected light.

ARTISTS TO STUDY

Milton Avery

The paintings of Milton Avery (1885–1965) can best be described as lyrical poems. Each painting contains within itself a fluid statement of simplicity, creating a mood and feeling with primarily clear, simple shapes and related colors filled with light patterns. His work emphasizes the importance of the shapes and forms used flatly and related to the design of the format (fig. 4.15). Familiar forms at once recall a landscape, a bird, a figure, with control and expression.

Henri Matisse

Henri Matisse (1869–1954), like Milton Avery, used flat tones of color, but in each painting, he also employed many more decorative elements (fig. 4.16). Both artists were interested in objects within the environment. Matisse concentrated to a great extent on the forms surrounding the figure, rather than on the forms within the figures. His paints are rich and heavy with decoration; his colors and shapes are clear.

Figure 4.15   *Bicycle Rider*, Milton Avery. Courtesy of Milton Avery Trust. Oil on canvas, 38 inches by 55 inches.

Figure 4.16   Henri Matisse, *Reclining Woman.* Collection of Phoenix Art Museum, Gift of Carl Bimson. Lithograph, 28.1 centimeters by 44.5 centimeters.

Figure 4.17   Henry Moore, British, 1898–1986, *Reclining Figure*, bronze, 1945, 1.: 19.1 cm, Gift of Mr. and Mrs. Joel Starrels, photograph © 1995. The Art Institute of Chicago. All Rights Reserved.

Henry Moore

During World War II, Henry Moore (1898–1986) was in England, where he made good use of the dark paper that blacked out house windows at night and helped to prevent detection during bombing raids. Moore drew sketches of future sculptures by using white lines on the black paper to indicate the moving forms as they turned from one shape to another. These linear drawings later took solid, rounded forms in sculpture (fig. 4.17).

chapter

5

Space

The dimensions of space determine the world in which we move and live; and space, in turn, is established by the objects or forms that occupy it.

Graham Collier, *Form, Space, Vision*

W hen we draw and paint, we create the visual illusion of space within artworks on a flat surface. We also actively deal with space in our environment. We move through space, both in interiors and exteriors. Existing enclosed spaces are in our homes, schools, communities, neighborhoods, and cities. When we build, construct, or move three-dimensionally, we design spaces within an environment.

SPACE: A VISUAL ILLUSION

Space is the interval of distance between you and the objects in your environment. Where you exist in space determines your point of view. Shapes, colors, sizes, patterns, and line direction all change as you move within space because all objects in space have a position and direction relative to each other. When you change your position—your viewpoint—you change the illusion of an object. Movement alters what you see. Just moving your head from side to side or taking a step to the left changes your existing space relationship and therefore alters the illusion (fig. 5.1).

How you know, see, and feel about space is always changing. You *know* that a person at the end of the room is the same size as one close to you. You *know* that the room is the same width at the other side. You *know* that the sky does not touch the ground at the horizon. Yet, what you *see* and *feel* may disagree with what you *know* about space.

Thus, visual imagery and concrete reality are not the same. What you create in your art is an illusion determined by what you know, see, and feel about your subject. And what you know, see, and feel about your subject is enhanced by greater observation of details. The following list suggests motivational questions to inspire greater observation of detail:

Before drawing:

1. Where is the object located?
2. What is the space around it like?
3. How many parts does it have?
4. Is it larger or smaller than another object?
5. How much space does the object occupy?
6. What is the object made of?
7. How is it similar to another object?
8. How is it different from another object?

After drawing:

1. How did you create such an illusion?
2. What drawing technique did you use?
3. What surface textural quality is there?
4. What is the light source for the object?
5. How did you indicate the value—the light, middle, and dark tones?
6. How did the time of day change your perception of the object?
7. What shapes, textures, patterns, and colors changed as you got farther away from the object? Closer to the object?
8. What is your view of the object (top, bottom, side, etc.)?

Figure 5.1 Space is an illusion—an interval of distance.

REPRESENTING SPACE IN TWO DIMENSIONS

Artists create illusions of space in all art forms. In other words, instead of seeing the concrete object that the artist has drawn, viewers see the art product, the artist's illusion of the idea. When attempting to represent three-dimensional space in two dimensions, artists can work to create a realistic visual illusion of space, or they may choose to have their creation reflect their imaginative illusion of space.

Realistic Representations of Space/Perspective

Throughout history, artists have devised various systems for representing realistic space. During the Renaissance, great emphasis was placed on a system called **perspective.** The word *perspective* comes from the Latin word meaning "to look into, view, perceive." It is the art of representing solid objects on a flat or curved surface so as to give them the same appearance as in nature when viewed from a given point.

Figure 5.2 shows an etching by Albrecht Dürer of how Renaissance artists drew objects on clear "window" surfaces or "picture planes" to achieve realistic perspective. A simpler way of finding illusions of depth is to use a

viewfinder (such as a slide holder), which is a device for showing the area of a subject to be included in a picture. While helping you to eliminate extraneous, nonessential elements from a picture, viewfinders also allow you to select and "see" realistic perspective (fig. 5.3).

Hold a viewfinder in front of one eye while closing the other eye. The outside edges of the viewfinder create a window with boundaries in the same way that the edges of a piece of paper are your drawing boundary. Select a view within the window, and study the angles and line directions that you see. Draw these angles and line directions on your paper in the same way that you see them within the window (fig. 5.4).

Another technique for "seeing" perspective is to use a pencil as an angle-finding device. Hold the pencil either vertically or horizontally in front of one eye and about an arm's length away. Visually estimate the angle of an object, and compare the angle to the vertical or horizontal pencil. Move the pencil to the angle and then back again. Now you can estimate and draw the angle in your drawing in relation to the edges of your paper.

The same process is used in comparing size (length) measurements. Hold the pencil about an arm's length from one eye, and visually measure the lines of an object. For example, position the pencil eraser at one point on the object, and move your thumb to the point on the pencil where the object ends. Now change the positioning of the pencil to measure another edge of the object, and compare the second length to the first. Be sure to keep your arm fairly stiff so that the measurements are consistent. Use these observed size proportions when drawing the object on your paper.

Visual relationships, whether they are angles of lines or size proportions, are out in front of you. What you are doing is seeing clearly what is before your eyes. You are drawing what you find in ratio to an outside imaginary border (determined by horizontal and vertical edges). The proportions and comparisons you find exist only in relation to how you see them.

The camera duplicates the reality that we see in the same manner that our eyes do. Today, many artists use cameras to capture images of subject matter. The camera image helps artists to select gray values and to see more readily the line angles and directions that create the illusion of space. It can also emphasize the modeling of rounded forms.

The study and concept of perspective and receding vanishing points is most appropriate for upper-level students.

Chart 5.1 lists a number of space concepts and techniques that are helpful in creating a realistic representation of space in art.

Imaginative Illusions of Space

Some artists prefer that their artworks portray imaginative illusions of space, rather than realistic spatial interpretations.

Figure 5.2   This drawing by Albrecht Dürer explains perspective. Albrecht Dürer, German, 1471–1528. *Book of Proportions,* woodcut, page 508, 13 × 178 cm, Clarence Buckingham Collection, photograph © 1995 The Art Institute of Chicago. All Rights Reserved.

Figure 5.3   A slide mount makes an excellent viewfinder. Viewfinders aid in sorting out information, as well as in establishing the horizon line and the vanishing point.

Space 79

(a)

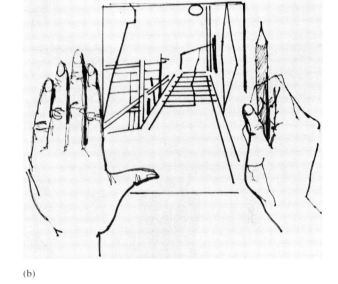

(b)

Figure 5.4 (*a*) Receding lines converge at vanishing points. These points are on horizon lines, which are actually eye-level lines. Your position in space and movement cause your perspective views to change constantly. Many artists today disregard perspective space and interpret depth in more imaginative ways. (*b*) A pencil or hands can be used to establish vertical or horizontal lines. Look for angles where lines meet. Practice using photographs you find in magazines. (*c*) In one-point perspective, all lines recede to one vanishing point on the horizon line. (*d*) Illustrates two-point perspective where receding lines converge at **two** vanishing points on the horizon line. A slide mount makes an excellent viewfinder.

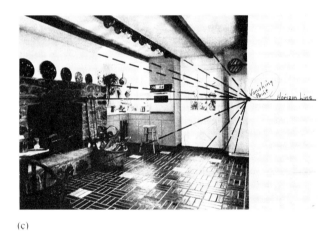

(c)

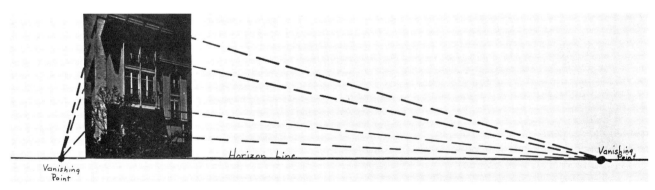

(d)

chart 5.1

Vocabulary of Space

Eye or station point The concept that where you are determines your viewpoint.

Converging lines Receding lines that appear to converge at distant points to show perspective. For examples, look at the receding lines in a long table, up a skyscraper, along a railroad track, or up a stairway (fig. 5.4).

Horizon line/eye-level line A perspective term that refers to an imaginary line ahead of you that is level with your horizontal line of sight and on which is located the vanishing point. All edges and lines of the object pictured converge to what is called the vanishing point (see the next definition). Those above eye level recede down to the eye-level line, and those below eye level converge up to the eye-level line.

Vanishing point A perspective term that refers to the point on the horizon or eye-level line where receding parallel lines appear to converge.

Picture plane The flat, two-dimensional drawing surface on which you create three-dimensional space.

Overlapping Partially covering one form with another form. The whole form that is in front of the overlapped (partially covered) form seems closer. Overlapping forms create distance.

Foreground, Middle ground, Background (See Spatial levels.)

Detail variation Placing the clearest detail in the foreground of a picture, while having other details become less distinct with distance.

Color variation Having the brightest colors appear in the foreground of a picture, while having other colors become less distinct with distance.

Size variation Having the larger forms appear in the foreground of a picture, while having smaller forms recede with distance.

Placement Placing forms lower in the picture so that they appear to come forward and placing forms higher up in the picture to cause them to appear to recede.

Spatial levels Establishing various levels, such as **foreground, middle ground,** and **background,** to create distance and to indicate which objects are nearest, in between, and furthest away.

Shading and shadow variation As discussed in more detail in chapter 4, the technique of using shading and shadows to show the three-dimensional characteristics of an object.

Foreshortening A drawing technique showing an object projecting sharply toward or receding from the viewer. Foreshortening creates a visual impact.

In many contemporary artworks, the space illusion is flat and related more to design principles, such as balance, unity, contrast, dominance, rhythm, and movement across the surface, and what the artist selects as line, color, shape, value, texture, and pattern (fig. 5.5). The placement and distance between forms, sometimes called **tension,** plays a major role in such space designs.

For example, Joan Miró's *Personage with a Star* (see fig. 10.34) shows invented shapes that appear to be flat. The shapes sometimes overlap and appear transparent so that they create new forms. No shadows, ground lines, horizontal lines, or perspective hints indicate where these forms are in space. Multiple, overlapping, penetrating forms create an abstract space illusion.

Artworks that illustrate **imaginary spaces** include Salvador Dalí's *Spectre de Soir* (see fig. 10.10), the photograph by Jack Stuler (see fig. 4.7a), Stuart Davis's *Composition with Boats* (see fig. 3.20), Marc Chagall's *White Crucifixion* (see fig. 10.37), and Ben Shahn's *Television Antennae* (see fig. 10.17). In these imaginary spaces, paintings appear to float, sometimes in the sky, or objects are turned upside down. In *White Crucifixion,* for example, the bodies float, the boat and houses appear together, the candles are as large as some figures, there is no horizon line, body parts have unreal proportions, and the invented lighting does not cast realistic shadows.

In Milton Avery's *Bicycle Rider* (see fig. 4.15), Ben Shahn's *Television Antennae* (see fig. 10.17), Rufino Tamayo's *Woman with a Bird Cage* (see fig. A.2 in appen-

dix A), and George Braque's *Fruits and Guitar* (see fig. 10.26), the shapes are flat. The lines do not appear to recede into space, but do create an illusion of space by placing an object in front. Objects also appear in the middle ground and background.

Considerations for creating imaginative space follow.

- Multiple views of a particular object
- Disregard of perspective
- Flat forms—forms that only possess length and breadth, not thickness, depth, or volume
- Interpenetration of forms—forms appear transparent, thereby allowing shapes to overlap and the shapes behind to show through the front shapes
- Disregard for reflected light, values, and color (artist's choice)
- Imaginative forms—invented, unknown shapes related to each other in unconnected floating space
- Positive shapes—forms, masses, or areas that artists create and manipulate
- Negative shapes—unoccupied spaces existing around positive shapes
- Exaggeration or distortion of forms or space

REPRESENTING SPACE IN THREE DIMENSIONS

Up until this point, chapter discussion has focused on how artists create the illusion of space with two-dimensional

Figure 5.5   Flat, transparent shapes that lack dimension and perspective are considered more abstract and imaginative.

shapes that have only height and width. However, some artists deal with shapes that have height, width, and also depth—objects that are three-dimensional and solid, and that occupy and enclose space. Sculpture and architecture are common three-dimensional areas of art.

Sculpture

A sculpture can exist **in the round**—that is, it is freestanding, and you can look all around it—or it can be **in relief,** having forms that project from a background. It may have irregular contours, resulting in an **organic shape,** or it may have straight or curved lines or both, resulting in a **geometric shape.** A **mobile** is sculpture that moves in space.

To create sculptures, artists generally use one of two processes. With the **subtractive method,** sculptors start with a large piece of material, such as clay, wood, or stone, and carve away the form. With the **additive method,** sculptors add parts to each other to build the form. Sculptors also sometimes combine a mixture of three-dimensional media to form what is known as an **assemblage.** Often, tapestries, or fabrics, are combined with wood, metal, wire, branches, reeds, or any other materials that will enhance the artist's concept.

Architecture

Architecture as a form of art reflects the history, culture, and aesthetic concerns of societies throughout the ages (fig. 5.6).

The Sumerians lived in Mesopotamia, the land between the Tigris and Euphrates rivers, between 3500 and 2500 B.C. Because they believed that mountaintops were the dwelling places for gods, they built their temples to resemble mountaintops. The temple as the center of both spiritual and physical existence was reflected by city layouts that featured the temple of the local god at its center (on a plat-

Figure 5.6   The history, culture, and aesthetic concerns of societies throughout history are reflected in their architectural structures.

form). The architecture, which was made of wood and mud-brick, is gone now except for the foundations and some richly endowed tombs built below ground. Many of the bronze, stone, and diorite sculptures are associated with deities found in the tombs.

The Egyptians used 2.5 million blocks of limestone to build the fifty-story Great Pyramid around 2500 B.C. as the burial tomb for the Pharaoh Cheops. Since all ancient Egyptians believed that, after they died, their soul, called Ka, would live forever in the Land of the Dead, they put all the items they thought the soul might need for the next life in the tomb. Other important tombs include Queen Hatshepsut's Temple at Deir-El-Bahari (1800 B.C.) and King Tutankhamen's tomb in the Valley of the Kings (1300 B.C.).

Egyptian temples were built of rows of stone columns that held beams of stone. To bring light into the temples, the Egyptians placed the columns close together, with the shorter side columns next to tall center columns, thereby creating clerestory windows. Builders in the Middle Ages used this same concept in their great cathedrals, and it is still used today.

Greek temples, such as the Parthenon, were constructed of marble or stone. The temples had columns all around the outside so that people could enter the building from any outside space. The temples were where the ancient Greeks worshipped their gods and goddesses, and the steps and areas outside the temples were the settings for orators, athletic games, and processions. Phideas designed the Parthenon and sculpted the figures on the pediment around 438 B.C.

The Greeks developed the various columns, such as the Doric (the capital, or top, is plain and simple), the Ionic (the capital has a scroll on each end and the column has flutes), and the Corinthian (the capital is decorated with flowerlike petals, and the column also has vertical flutes). They adorned their temples with ornate sculptures of gods and goddesses.

The Romans were great engineers who developed the concept of the stone arch and also designed aqueducts to carry water from the mountains to the cities. Many Roman aqueducts are still in existence today in Italy and parts of Israel and Jordan. The oval-shaped Colosseum, in Rome, held 45,000 people and was built by Emperor Vespasian in A.D. 80 to present games and circuses to the people of Rome. The Pantheon, built by Roman Emperor Hadrian in A.D. 118, is round with a front porch. Its stone walls support a huge concrete dome 142 feet in diameter. The Roman baths, built in A.D. 200, had groin vaults (four arches that buttress, or push together, at the center).

The Hagia Sophia in Istanbul, Turkey (once known as the city of Constantinople), was built in A.D. 532–537. This former church, now a museum, has many arches and domes. It is an example of what is called Byzantine architecture because Constantinople was built on the ruins of the city of Byzantium.

Churches of the Middle Ages, such as the Gothic church in Rheims, France (A.D. 1225–1299), or Notre Dame in Paris, are noted for their pointed arches; thin, spiring columns; multicolored glass windows; and flying buttresses.

In the mid-nineteenth century, new technologies and the Industrial Revolution encouraged mass production of buildings and houses. Improved sawmill machinery and mass-produced nails helped to achieve a new method of construction called the wooden balloon frame, or as it is known today, wood-frame construction.

Today, architectural forms are determined not only by structural needs, but by technical advances (fig. 5.7). New

Figure 5.7   The Tempe Municipal Building, Tempe, Arizona, is an example of modern architecture. (Photograph by Scott Pfister.)

Figure 5.8 Navajo Native Americans use available materials—mud and logs—to make structures called hogans.

materials provide unique architectural possibilities, such as the steel skeleton of a skyscraper permitting an exterior facade of glass.

Regardless of advances, the architects of today are still faced with the same basic challenges as their predecessors: enclosing functional space, providing light, and using available materials (fig. 5.8).

HOW STUDENTS UNDERSTAND SPACE
Kindergarten through Second Grade

Very young children draw what they know about; they do not draw objects realistically. For instance, a drawing of a face may simply be a circle with eyes, nose, and mouth. At this point, a child's drawing is whatever the child says it is. Young children's drawings often tell a story—describing a person, an object, or what is happening. Drawings are visual symbols for communicating ideas.

By the time children enter school, their drawings are more complex story-telling devices, describe events, and often reveal aspects of the child's emotions. For example, in a drawing of a family portrait, the sizes of the figures, the exaggerations of people or parts of figures, and many other details may reflect inner emotions and reveal the child's feelings about self and the world. Such drawings represent symbols of people and objects and are not realistic visual representations. The symbols are primarily flat, without roundness or depth.

Around age six, children realize that they are within the world and place themselves in relationship to other people and places in their art. Their drawings show representations of houses, trees, schools, the sun, flowers, and animals. They search for a sense of space—for an understanding of near and far. They are still the center of their world and emotionally express this spatial relationship. Proportions may be exaggerated as to how important

the subject is. Sizes and placement are expressed according to how developed the children's concepts of the subject are, the schema, and what types of experiences the children have had with the subject. At this time, presenting enriching information related to the subject will deepen children's understanding and be reflected in drawings with increased detail. (See p. 86 for a list of suggestions for motivating students' observation of detail.)

Students in this age group draw space as they feel and know about it, rather than how it looks. They can perceive length and realize something about distance, but do not represent these spatially. They also do not perceive overlapping of objects to represent depth or three dimensions.

A significant development at around six to seven years of age is students' development of a **baseline concept** in their drawings: They show spatial relationships between the objects they are drawing by placing the objects on a line that represents the ground. The sky is usually indicated by a line running along the top of the page. The open space in between is "air." The objects are colored in with flat, bright, primary colors. Space is flat, two-dimensional, and without rounded forms. By second grade, the previous single baseline may change to two or more, indicating that some objects are closer (fig. 5.9).

Once the baseline concept is established, students also may begin to represent space using other concepts, such as the **foldover concept,** which involves the baseline running horizontally across the middle of the paper, with students showing objects both above and below the baseline (fig. 5.10). However, they still may confuse planes and elevations, showing top, side, and front views all mixed together. They may also sometimes express an **X-ray concept,** where both inside and outside are drawn in the same picture (fig. 5.11). **Space-time** drawings show various sequences in a single space, like "walking from my house to school."

Third and Fourth Grade

Beginning around age nine, students are intrigued by how things work and what things are made of. The more you tell them, the more they want to know. They want to draw objects more realistically (as well as imaginatively). When their drawing skills increase, suggest ways to present the illusion of three-dimensional "real" space on a two-dimensional surface. Have them practice drawing more complex geometric shapes, such as cylinders, cubes, and pyramids, with greater accuracy.

Third- and fourth-graders know that more than one object occupies space and that these objects are organized in some way, such as in an order of succession, within surrounding space. Because they are very interested in detail and in classifying and grouping objects, many objects and people begin to appear in their drawings. They tend to represent objects from a frontal view because they do not understand perspective, and they ignore correct proportions. Discuss how to place objects in order through overlapping,

Figure 5.9   A double baseline drawn by a second-grader.

Figure 5.10   Here, a child used the foldover concept: The baseline runs horizontally across the middle of the paper, with objects drawn above and below the baseline.

color changes, size differences, and value changes. Give them opportunities to understand the concepts of foreground, middle ground, background, and how objects placed in the space nearest the bottom of the page will appear closer to the viewer (figs. 5.12 and 5.13). Discuss how the sky is shown coming down to the horizon, and how the sky and other objects in the drawing overlap, indicating deptn. Students also enjoy imaginative space, such as including multiple views of an object and using interpenetrating and flat forms (see figs. 4.3 and 4.5).

Fifth and Sixth Grade

Fifth- and sixth-grade students want to expand their spatial concepts. While first-graders tend to see objects from a single point of view, fifth- and sixth-graders begin to see changes in objects' depth and dimension. Look at art reproductions, and teach them various art techniques for making objects look round and for blending and shading to suggest form and space. Practice creating three-dimensional depth through placement, overlapping, and changes in scale,

Figure 5.11 An X-ray drawing shows both exterior and interior spaces.

Figure 5.12 Beginning one-point perspective. Drawing also shows foreground, middle ground, and background.

Figure 5.13   A scratchboard drawing by a Navajo student shows foreground, middle ground, and background. Ganado Elementary School, Ganado, Arizona.

color, size, and value. Discuss and demonstrate the use of some of the initial concepts of perspective, such as horizon line, vanishing point, and center of vision (figs. 5.14 and 5.15).

IDEAS AND MOTIVATIONS

Adapt to students' abilities and grade levels.

Space

1. Use an empty slide mount as a viewfinder, and practice selecting views for line angles, line directions, overlapping, and spatial levels.
2. Analyze how artists represent space both realistically and imaginatively.
3. Analyze space in magazine photographs.
4. Use a pencil or your hands as a guide to establish the vertical and horizontal lines (or edges) of a scene you want to draw. Within the scene, find all the vertical lines, all the horizontal lines, and all the directional lines. Now, "eyeball" the angles where the lines meet and where the lines form shapes. Practice drawing a negative shape next to a negative shape until you build the entire drawing. This kind of perception increases your ability to visualize line directions and angles as well as to see a shape as a form.
5. Draw what you would see if:
   - you could climb into a television.
   - you were a piece of candy just swallowed.
   - you were a bird (bird's-eye view).
   - you were inside a typewriter.
   - you were an ant (ant's-eye view).
   - you were the Mickey Mouse balloon in Macy's Thanksgiving Day parade.
6. Draw a still life with foreground, middle ground, and background.

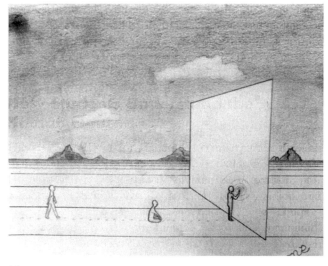

(a)

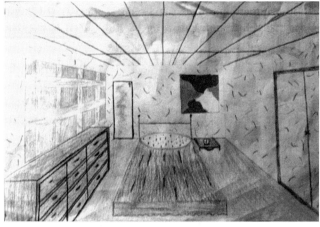

(b)

Figure 5.14   Fifth- and sixth-graders demonstrate beginning one-point perspective drawing, in which all lines recede to one point.

Figure 5.15   A student artwork demonstrating two-point perspective.

7. Draw a drinking glass from many viewpoints.
8. Draw cakes, pies, and other foods and objects on a table.
9. Draw a view looking down the street.
10. Draw what you see when you look up at a tall building.
11. Draw what you see when you look down a staircase from the top of the stairs.
12. Initiate group participation drawings with such ideas as "Building a Spook House," "Our Rocket Ship to Saturn," "Organizing a Fashion Show or Car Show," and "The Circus."
13. Draw unusual combinations of objects in a composition. Draw imaginative still lifes.
14. Draw a map of your town from a bird's-eye view.
15. Design an art center in your classroom.
16. Make a drawing of the interior space of a familiar room (fig. 5.16).
17. Redesign your house, school, or community.
18. Build three-dimensional dioramas.
19. Design a model of a new city, a future city.
20. Study and discuss how spaces have changed throughout history.

Sculpture

1. Create animals with clay (fig. 5.17).
2. Design and build sculptures out of wood.
3. Use paper for sculpting three-dimensional forms (fig. 5.18). Build a house of the 21st century.

(a)

(b)

Figure 5.16   Both of these examples are views of interior space: (*a*) is an imaginative study, while (*b*) is a more realistic approach. Fifth grade.

Figure 5.17   Favorite animals can be subjects for realistic and imaginary clay sculptures.

Figure 5.18   Three-dimensional forms sculpted from paper.

Figure 5.19   Construction techniques and history are combined with the study of architecture.

Figure 5.20   Medieval castles built from clay.

4. Build bridges out of straws, wood, and toothpicks (fig. 5.19).
5. Carve forms out of sand.
6. Build houses, castles, and architectural forms out of clay or cardboard and paper (fig. 5.20).
7. Carve faces, masks, and figures from clay. Build papier-maché masks.
8. Use various materials (such as cardboard boxes, telephone wire, and so on) to create assemblage sculptures.
9. Construct large sculptures from Styrofoam.
10. Create "soft" sculptures, such as dolls.

Architecture

1. Define, find, and draw examples of the following architectural terms:

arch	fence
dome	aqueduct
Doric column	proportion
beam	Corinthian column
chamber	capital
wood-frame construction	flying buttress
clapboard	bracket
pilaster	shaft
plaque	cupola
siding	transom
balcony	pedestal
pointed arch	barrel vault
column	post
Ionic column	clerestory window
temple	skeleton
post and lintel	eaves
geodesic dome	capital
base	fountain
cornice	shingle
gable	gingerbread
window sash	

2. Broaden your view of architecture as a three-dimensional art form that occupies and encloses space by asking yourself and discussing such questions as:

    - What is architecture?
    - What is the purpose and function of a building?
    - What is a city?
    - How do buildings fit into a community?
    - How is my city planned?
    - How did growth and expansion occur in my community?
    - What makes a city unique?
    - What makes cities different?
    - How do time period, style, materials, climate, land levels, type of terrain, and various cultures affect types of architecture? For example, why are some homes in the southwestern United States built of adobe? Where else in the world would one find adobe structures? Why did the Egyptians use stones as their building materials?

3. Compare the architectural designs of the ancient Greek Phidias to those of the modern American architect Frank Lloyd Wright.

4. Study how a building's interior, colors, and furnishings relate to its exterior design.

5. Study architectural examples from the Near East, Europe, and the Far East, paying particular attention to the climate, needs, and available materials used for buildings in various locations.

6. Examine architectural examples over the centuries, and describe how various cultures have chosen to adorn building exteriors. For example, the Greeks placed sculptures of figures on the exteriors, while the Egyptians added picture writing.

7. Discuss and analyze photographs and blueprints of buildings as to forms the buildings contain, such as squares, cubes, cones, cylinders, pyramids, spheres, and slabs.

8. Select a building, such as a school, library, theater, or shopping center, and analyze and draw how the building's space is divided, as in a floor plan.

9. Select several buildings in the immediate area, and analyze them in terms of design, distinctive features, style, age, and materials used (fig. 5.21).

10. Design, as an architect would, buildings to be used for (*a*) the heart of a city, (*b*) a new home, and (*c*) a twenty-first century school.

11. Develop three-dimensional models of buildings. For example, construct models of a group of neighborhood buildings or of ancient structures, like the Acropolis in Greece or an Egyptian pyramid (fig. 5.22).

12. Collage parts of photographic examples together to construct a dream house. Design your own dream house.

ARTISTS TO STUDY

Different artists have developed distinct and diverse ways of showing space. Compare and contrast how particular artists used space in the following artworks:

Night Shadows (fig. 5.23) and *Nighthawks* by Edward Hopper (see fig. 10.16)

On the Terrace by Pierre Auguste Renoir (see fig. 10.7)

Young Girl at an Open Half-Door by Rembrandt van Rijn (see fig. 10.3)

The Basket of Apples by Paul Cézanne (see fig. 10.8)

Book of Proportions by Albrecht Dürer (see fig. 5.2)

The Bath by Mary Cassatt (see fig. 10.9)

Spectre de Soir by Salvador Dalí (see fig. 10.10)

Woman in a Rose Hat by Edgar Degas (see fig. 11.14)

The Tolling Bell by Andrew Wyeth (see fig. 10.14)

Figure 5.21 For an architectural study, students created large paper designs of a local historical building and then drew in individual architectural features.

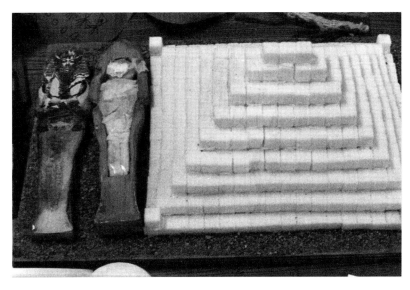

Figure 5.22   When studying ancient Egyptian architecture, sugar cubes are used to build a pyramid.

Figure 5.23   *Night Shadows* by Edward Hopper. Hopper emphasized the emotional quality of mystery by employing scratchy black lines; strong black-and-white contrasts; diagonal lines; a single, lone figure in the night; a long shadow; and a deep bird's-eye-view perspective. 6¾ inches by 8 inches. (Reproduced by courtesy of Gallerie Ann, Houston, Texas.)

Color, Pattern, and Texture

It should not be hard for you to stop sometimes and look in the stains of walls, or ashes of fire, or clouds, or mud, or like places, in which . . . you may find really marvelous ideas.

Leonardo da Vinci

As music is the poetry of sound, so is painting the poetry of sight, and the subject matter has nothing to do with the harmony of sound or color.

James McNeill Whistler

Color and light are the essence of man's spirit and so is my painting palette. . . . Color heals and gives joy.

Susan Cervantes

By the combination of lines and colors, under the pretext of some motif taken from nature I create symphonies and harmonies which represent nothing absolutely real in the ordinary sense of the word but are intended to give rise to thoughts as music does.

Paul Gauguin

For all of us, color is more complex than the perception of a light stimulus. It is a very personal form of expression that is interdependent with the other visual elements in an artwork.

COLOR

Color is unique, like a melody. Separate musical notes are beautiful in themselves. When placed in special relationships to each other, the notes can produce melodies that arouse a variety of feelings—from exhilaration, inspiration, and joy, to sadness and a profusion of others.

It is the same with color. Individual colors are beautiful, and when the shapes, amounts, placements, and relationships of colors are varied, so too are the feelings the colors create in us.

Color Preference

We have always been intrigued by the phenomena of the perception and psychology of color. Colors influence us emotionally; some believe that color preference is a result of learning, while others think it is purely an emotional response determined innately.

What we do know is that colors can have a variety of meanings for each individual; our learned past experiences, our total emotional perception and response, and the symbolic meaning it may have for us. For students, color can be a personal form of artistic expression, and color preferences may be due to a child's personality. Most students enjoy using lots of colors, and its sensual appeal is captivating for all of us.

When students were asked, What is your favorite color?, some responses were: "Blue, because it is alive like myself—it can be sad, glad, dreamy and because it has so many shades." "Blue, because my eyes are blue and it is like the sky and sea." "Green, it makes me think of candy." "Hot pink." "Psychedelic green." Pink makes me feel good, purple because it's pretty and also makes me sleepy." "Red . . . it's a hot fast, happy color." "Black makes me feel sad, cold, slow, dead, strong." "Gray, because I had a cat that was hit by a truck and I loved her very much." "Color has feeling and some kind of mood, temperature and motion." "Color makes life bright, happy and funny." "Color makes pictures alive." "Orange—I do not know why." "I like blue and red because they jump and flash to your eyes."

Rose Alschuler and LaBerta Hartwick conducted a study with one hundred and fifty preschool children in eight separate nursery groups. Each child's artwork was recorded for one year, along with the child's social and developmental date. Case studies and statistical analysis did indicate that color gave insight into the child's emotional life. Their findings indicate that red is the most emotionally toned of the colors studied. During the preschool years when color is somewhat of an impulsive choice, red is the preferred color. As the child gains more emotional control and develops into the age of reasoning, the interest in red decreases, and the interest in cooler colors increases. Red is associated with feelings of affection and love, as well as feelings of aggression and hate.

Blue is more often associated with drives toward control; green is associated with those functioning with more control and showing little emotional reactions. Orange tends to be used with tempered emotions such as friendliness and sympathy and by students who turn more to fantasy and imaginative realism. Black is associated with intense anxieties and fears. Other findings indicate that color placement also gives clues to personality.

Start students in the first grade with a large box of sixty-four color crayons. So much fun to try, why limit to eight primary colors? Plan on time for experimenting. After they have freely explored the many possibilities of mixing at random, ask them to mix a very definite color. Refer to the color chart for inspiration or obtain color swatches from paint stores. Hold up a swatch and see if they can match it. Write on the board how the colors were achieved. You will find that individual discovery of a mixed color will be more meaningful to the child, rather than having you explain how to mix the color. Mixing colors with crayons, paints, chalks, or pastels will determine the intensity of the color you achieve.

THE VISUAL PERCEPTION OF COLOR

In 1665, Sir Isaac Newton found that, when he passed a narrow beam of sunlight ("white light") through a triangular prism, the white light broke down into a multicolored **spectrum** of red, orange, yellow, green, blue, indigo, and violet. He also found that by passing the spectrum back through another triangular prism, he could again produce white light. Thus, Newton showed that pure sunlight is composed of many different colors all mixed together into the white light that we normally see.

These colors can become "unmixed," however, when white light attempts to pass through an object. At that point, some of the white light is absorbed, while some is reflected. The light that is reflected is what we perceive as color. Thus, when we perceive an object as blue, it means that the object reflects blue light waves while absorbing all other colors.

In addition, color also depends on the light in which the object is seen. For example, in sunlight, a daffodil looks yellow because the flower reflects yellow light waves and absorbs all other colors. Under a blue light, however, a daffodil looks black, since there are no yellow light waves to be reflected.

Thus, **color** is the perception of a light stimulus by your mind and eye. The color that you see depends on the light in which the object is seen and the color that is reflected. White (that you see) indicates the presence of all colors, while black (that you see) indicates the absence of all colors. Keep in mind that, like a melody of notes, we see color in relation to the colors that exist around it.

Chart 6.1 provides a brief vocabulary of color.

HOW STUDENTS UNDERSTAND COLOR
Kindergarten through Second Grade

Students in kindergarten through second grade tend to use color spontaneously, directly, and intuitively—not deliberately. That is, their color selection tends to be based on a color's emotional appeal. By second grade, however, some students may begin to use color more realistically.

Kindergarten, first-, and second-grade students can usually name and identify the primary and secondary colors. Explore many creative and uninterrupted painting and color mixing experiences. Large brushes encourage broad arm movements. Crayons and felt-tip pens encourage smaller details.

Students in this age group can identify and discriminate between colors that are light-dark, bright-dull, and warm-cool. Initiate discussions with them about (1) color as it relates to feelings and moods, (2) differences and similarities in colors, and (3) the use of color in artworks. Suggest activities that involve them in sorting and matching colors, such as different blues.

Provide a variety of simple, short, colorful, bright art experiences with one object, tool, or medium at a time. Explore and experiment with students in color mixing, both on and off the paper. Help them to investigate relationships of color—for example, how the color of their hair looks next to the color of their eyes, next to their skin, next to their

chart 6.1

Vocabulary of Color

Refer to color plate 1, The Color Wheel, as you read the following descriptions.

Hue The classification or name of a color. Artists often use the word *hue* to indicate color. Technically, the hue of an object is the wavelength of light reflected from it. When the reflected wavelength of light changes, the color changes.

Value Describes the amount of light (tint) or dark (shade) contained in the color on a scale ranging from black to white. Adding white to a color lightens the value. Adding black to a color darkens the value.

Intensity The strength or weakness (brightness or dullness) of a color. Sometimes called the saturation chroma, or purity of a color. A hue that is not mixed with any other color is at its maximum intensity. Mixing a color with another color lowers the hue's intensity. Bright red, for example, has greater intensity than brown or dark blue.

Warm colors Red, orange, yellow—and derivatives.

Cool colors Green, blue, violet—and derivatives.

Monochromatic Describes all of the shades, tints, values, and intensities of one color (hue).

Opaque With regard to color, describes thick, nontransparent color, such as that provided by tempera paints and oil paints.

Wash With regard to color, describes a thin, transparent, watered-down use of paint or ink.

Related colors Personal selection of colors that "go well" together.

Achromatic A color scheme using white, gray, and black.

Chroma The brilliance or intensity of a color.

Spectrum The continuum of color formed when a beam of white light is dispersed, as by passage through a prism, into red, orange, yellow, green, blue, indigo, and violet.

Primary colors Red, yellow, and blue—the colors that cannot be made by mixing other hues and from which all secondary colors are created.

Secondary colors The colors that contain about equal amounts of two primary colors: Yellow and blue make green, blue and red make violet, and red and yellow make orange.

Tertiary colors Colors that are a result of mixing unequal amounts of two primary colors (for example, a green that is produced by mixing more yellow than blue) or of mixing primary and secondary colors (for example, the red-violet produced by mixing red and violet).

Complementary colors Colors that, when used side by side, such as red next to green, offer the visual illusion of maximum contrast. On a color wheel, complementary colors are opposite one another: Red is opposite green, blue is opposite orange, and yellow is opposite violet. When opposites are mixed, complementary colors are "grayed" or neutralized. Artists often "gray" colors this way, rather than adding black or white to a hue.

Analogous colors Colors that are side by side on the color wheel and that are similar in hue, such as red, red-orange, and orange.

Tint A color that is lightened and whose intensity is reduced by adding white. For example, pink is a tint of red.

Shade A color that is darkened by adding black. For example, maroon is a shade of red.

Tone A color to which both black and white have been added.

Pigment The coloring matter that is mixed with oil, water, wax, and other substances to make paints, crayons, chalks, etc.

Color purity The degree of maximum strength (or saturation) of any given color.

Color relativity The quality of color that is dependent on the color's relationship to other colors.

Color balance The color arrangement in a design that indicates harmony or disharmony.

Color blend The effect achieved when two similar colors are placed side by side.

Color contrast The effect achieved when two distinctly different colors are placed side by side.

Color effect The effect achieved when a color impression is conveyed to the viewer through the use of color.

Color advance and recede The effect achieved when color is sensed as being in front of or in back of another color. Warm colors advance; cool colors recede.

---

shirt. Students will use at least four colors in their drawings, and more when given the opportunity. First-graders should have a large box of sixty-four crayons, instead of just the eight primary colors. They can blend and mix the sixty-four to get different colors. An added bonus is that the crayons usually have the color name printed on them. This adds to students' art vocabulary.

Third and Fourth Grade

Third- and fourth-grade students begin to think of color in a more realistic way—that is, the grass is green, the sky is blue. Their concept of color, however, is simplified in that all sky is blue, not a variety of blues, and all daffodils are yellow, not a subtle variety of yellows. They do not necessarily see variation in color unless they have a meaningful experience with color variations.

Color schemata and preferences, which are often based on visual or emotional experiences, can change due to significant learning experiences. Have students experiment with color, and work with them on seeing variations within a color. For example, you might want to demonstrate how mixing different values of colors produces different results. For example, mixing different values of blues and yellows results in varying values of green. Work with students to learn the names of different colors—for example, the names of different blues, yellows, and greens. Have them experiment with mixing primary, secondary, and tertiary colors, and with making shades and tints of colors. Discuss how one color affects the colors around it. Continue discussions regarding how colors can make us feel and why.

Fifth and Sixth Grade

Fifth- and sixth-grade students are beginning to develop a color consciousness. They can choose certain colors and analyze why they like them. They may select personal colors to indicate moods, atmosphere, and feelings. Define and discuss with them the concepts of *hue, value,* and *intensity.* Continue to explore how different artists have used and interpreted color. Discuss color preferences.

Students may use color emotionally or depict color realistically. Suggest that they use various colors to note changes in shading and that they explore using black and white to produce a tint or shade. For example, you might want to hold up a swatch of color (easily obtained from a paint store) and ask students to mix paints and try to match that color as closely as possible. If they can, have them recount exactly what they used to make particular colors. Use these written "formulas" to make a color chart. Individual discovery of a color is always more meaningful to students than having you simply explain how to mix it.

Such experimentation also helps students to learn to differentiate colors. That is, all reds are not the same; there are blue-reds, orange-reds, green-reds, and so on. This will lead students to learn the names of various colors, such as crimson red, Chinese red, cadmium red light, cadmium red medium, and so on.

Fifth- and sixth-graders are beginning to understand how color is one aspect of an artwork's overall design and composition. Show them examples of artworks in which color is used to create contrast, balance, harmony-disharmony, movement, dominance, space, repetition, and rhythm. Demonstrate how warm colors and cool colors can be used to indicate depth, modeling, roundness, and form. Discuss how light on a surface changes color, such as in a landscape. Explore how perspective changes color and light.

Students in this age range are beginning to understand the importance of color relationships in the environment. Have them describe color in nature (flowers, gardens, trees, animals), as well as in manufactured objects. Suggest that they study the use of color in various kinds of interior spaces (the library, theater, school, home); in clothing, cosmetics, and food; on television and photographs.

PATTERN

Pattern is created by *repetition* in a particular *rhythm* (fig. 6.1). A regular pattern—one that is based on repetition of units at regularly spaced intervals—provides order and unity. An irregular pattern is more random.

In art, when a shape is repeated, the resulting pattern often becomes decorative and is used to embellish a surface. However, patterns are also created by repeating qualities other than shape, such as color, line, positive and negative space, light and dark, and so on (fig. 6.2). We are especially aware of patterns when the image is flat, rather than rounded.

In nature, we see patterns everywhere: ripples in water, the petals of flowers, clusters of leaves, a row of trees (fig. 6.3). Patterns are also found in numerous human-made items: bricks in a wall, wheels on a bike, shingles on a roof, holes in a pegboard, windows in a building, designs in a rug or on clothing.

Patterns have been used since ancient times in the expression of the arts. Musical rhythms and beats are repeated. Melodies of tone often repeat themselves and form a pattern. In poetry, sounds may be repeated, with the number of sounds forming a pattern. Dance forms are organized in patterns.

Patterns have also been common in architecture throughout history. The Greeks, inspired by stands of trees, repeated the columns of the Parthenon. The ancient Colosseum in Rome has repeated rounded openings. Today, many buildings have patterns that reflect geometric shapes, such as cylinders, spheres, cones, and cubes.

TEXTURE

Texture is an object's surface quality. It can be touched (*tactile*) and seen (*visual*). It may be natural, such as tree bark or sand (fig. 6.4), or synthetic, such as glass or cloth.

In painting and drawing, texture is the representation of the surface quality of the object being drawn. If the surface of the object is smooth like skin, then a soft, blended texture is needed. A surface that is rough like sandpaper requires a scratchy, uneven texture. Texture can be simulated using various kinds of lines, colors, and media.

HOW STUDENTS UNDERSTAND PATTERN AND TEXTURE
Kindergarten through Second Grade

Students in kindergarten through second grade can identify patterns and textures in the environment and recognize differences and similarities in natural and manufactured patterns and textures. They also have discovered textural qualities, such as hard-soft and rough-smooth.

Students' understanding of pattern and texture increases with visual and tactile experiences. Have them explore a variety of surfaces with both their hands and their eyes. Demonstrate and have them experiment with making rubbings of various environmental surfaces. Show them how to create patterns using various printing techniques.

(a)

(b)

(c)

(d)

Figure 6.1   Patterns express repetition and rhythm and may also be decorative.

Figure 6.2 Japanese paper folding (origami) utilizes repetition of shapes and forms.

Figure 6.3 Patterns and textures are everywhere in nature.

Figure 6.4 Sand has a rough textural quality. Try using it in a collage.

Have students experiment with a variety of media to achieve different patterns and interesting textures. Discuss with them both natural and human-made textures and patterns.

Third and Fourth Grade

Looking and touching activities come naturally to third- and fourth-graders because of their innate curiosity. Have them look at and touch textures and patterns in such items as plants, trees, furniture, clothing, weavings, ceramics, jewelry, and sculpture.

Begin discussions of the various ways artists have used pattern and texture in artworks. Discuss with students the relationship of pattern and texture to line, shape, value, space, color, contrast, dominance, balance, and rhythm. Display artworks and artifacts from a variety of cultures to show alternative uses of pattern and texture.

Continue to work with students to help them discover various tools and media for producing different patterns and textures (fig. 6.5).

Fifth and Sixth Grade

Fifth- and sixth-grade students need continued visual and tactile stimulation in seeing patterns and textures. Have them observe natural patterns and textures in flowers, trees, hills, and mountains, as well as manufactured patterns and textures in fabrics, buildings, and furniture.

Students are ready to use a variety of lines, colors, shapes, and media to create patterns and textures. Suggest that they experiment with developing patterns that use fast rhythms, slow rhythms, and repeating shapes as they move across the paper surface (fig. 6.6). Encourage them to practice creating both two-dimensional (visual) and three-dimensional (tactile) textures in drawings, paintings, clay works, weavings, and sculptures.

Provide opportunities for students to analyze how pattern and texture are used in architecture in the placement of columns, windows, doors, and other parts, and on building facades. Continue discussions with them about how artists have used patterns and textures in artworks and about how we use them in our homes and environments. Display and discuss such items as African masks, Indian batik cloth, Navajo rugs, and Hopi pottery to show how different cultures use pattern and texture (fig. 6.7).

IDEAS AND MOTIVATIONS

Adapt the following as to students' grade-level capabilities.

Color

1. Paint is a medium that allows colors to mix either on the palette or on the paper after the paint is applied. Explore the many possibilities of mixing paint colors at random. Discover new colors.

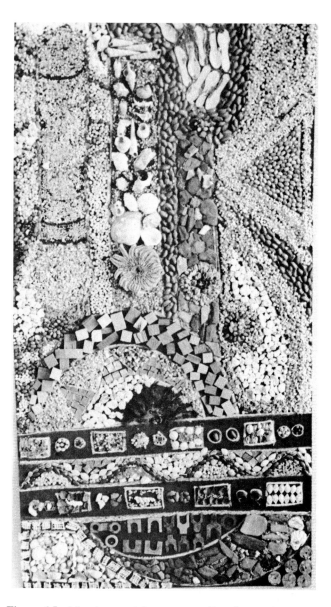

Figure 6.5 Mosaic materials are one medium for creating pattern and texture.

2. Experiment with mixing colors of chalk to see how chalk mixtures differ from paint mixtures. For example, when blue chalk is mixed with yellow chalk, the resulting green is very different from the green produced when blue and yellow paint are mixed.
3. Blow bubbles, and then look at them through a concave lens.
4. Look through a prism, through a convex lens, and through a magnifying glass.
5. Look at paintings through sheets of colored acetate or film.
6. Observe how the colors of a tree and the sky subtly change over the course of a day.
7. Find the colors in an oily puddle, a rainbow, in the mist around street lights.

Figure 6.6   Patterns with fast rhythms, slow rhythms, and repetition move across a paper surface.

8. Identify the colors that, to you, express different feelings—happy, sad, love, hate, etc.

9. Stare at something red for one minute. Then look away and close your eyes. You will see red's complementary color—green.

10. Examine the colors in a painting while inside, under artificial light, and while outside, in natural light.

11. Look at the leaves on a tree. Are they all the same color green?

12. Examine others' drawings and paintings and then experiment with your own to determine what colors appear to come forward and what colors appear to recede.

13. Examine others' drawings and paintings and then experiment with your own to identify colors that you feel go together or clash.

Figure 6.7 Navajo rugs are famous for their individual pattern designs. (Hubbell's Trading Post, Ganado, Arizona.)

14. Listen to a variety of musical selections to see if you can identify moods and effects that relate to a color. Experiment with painting to music.
15. Think of a story. Which color would express the idea in the story?
16. Create a painting using just:

 • Primary colors
 • Secondary colors
 • Complementary colors
 • Tints
 • Shades
 • Opaque colors
 • Wash colors, warm colors, cool colors
 • Related colors, unrelated colors
 • Colors that are close in value
 • Colors with contrasting values
 • High-intensity colors
 • Monochromatic color

17. Wear something black on a hot day, and then wear something white on a hot day. In which color were you more comfortable? Can you explain why?
18. Examine color in movies and on television. Why does a desert scene look hot? Why does snow look cold?
19. Look at the sky and the clouds. Is the sky always a clear blue? Is it ever red? Purple? Green?
20. Some paintings tend to make us feel calm, while others excite us. What colors create a feeling of calmness? What colors create a feeling of excitement?
21. Visit factories, department stores, hospitals, grocery stores, restaurants, and so on in your community. What colors are used in these buildings? Can you suggest a reason for using particular colors in particular buildings?

22. Look at objects under a white light bulb, a red light bulb, and a blue light bulb. How do the colors of the objects change?
23. Make a spectrum with a prism or a glass of water.
24. The average person can see about nine steps in the progression from white to black. Experiment with a variety of media, and attempt to draw or paint the nine steps from white to black. Then compare and contrast the progressions made with the different media.
25. Mix two colors together, varying the amounts of each color added, to see how the resulting colors compare.
26. Try putting dabs of color on paper to form shapes. From a distance, your eyes should fuse the colors so that the shapes appear. This is called **pointillism** (fig. 2.7).
27. Look at the colors of something, such as a mountain, from far away. Then get close to the object, and see how its colors change.
28. Experiment with mixing colors. What happens when you mix blue with all other colors? What happens when you mix yellow with all other colors? Can you mix gray? Brown? Other neutral colors?
29. Find and use in a design four colors that are ugly together. Then do the same with four colors that are pleasing together.
30. Create a "strong" painting—one that uses "strong" colors. Create a "weak" painting.
31. Discuss the symbolic use of color for certain holidays, such as red for Valentine's Day and orange and black for Halloween.
32. Create an artwork in which color is the dominant element and the center of interest.
33. Discuss how color is used in various environments. Look in magazines for color combinations in clothing, interiors, and nature. Then design collages from magazine samples.
34. Discuss color relationships (how colors affect each other) in rooms at home, in school, in the cafeteria, in a movie theater. How could they be improved?
35. Design a new color scheme for your wardrobe.
36. Study how artists through the centuries have used color in different or similar ways (such as Vincent van Gogh).
37. Use color chips (available from paint stores) to experiment with combinations.

Pattern and Texture

1. Design a pattern for a rug, textiles, pottery. Refer to Native American patterns in rugs and pottery.
2. Design a pattern for a quilt, for wrapping papers, book covers.
3. Design a motif, and practice repeating it in a drawing, painting, in printmaking, in architectural forms.
4. Look through a kaleidoscope. Then draw what you see.
5. Draw patterns from leaves on various bushes.
6. Make a pattern collage (see fig. 6.8).
7. Cut a sponge into a design. Apply (print) the sponge design with paint, using organized intervals and disorganized intervals (patterns).

8. Experiment with crayons, charcoal, pencils, pen and ink, and dry and wet washes to see the textures they make.

9. Draw the surface of an old wall and also make rubbings of it.

10. Select a small area of an interesting surface, like the skin of a gourd, and examine it closely. Then draw an enlargement of the surface on paper. See what textures you can create in an interesting abstract design. Try using extra-strong lighting or strong contrasts of darks and lights to change the texture.

11. Look for textured surfaces as you walk around school, and make rubbings of them, using a crayon or soft pencil.

12. Use a crayon to make drawings on a piece of sandpaper.

13. Do a texture collage. Collect unusual scraps of papers, woods, and cloth, and combine these textures into a design.

14. Make a collage of photographic textures (fig. 6.9).

15. Experiment with painting on a variety of textures, such as velvet, grass, wood bark, and lace.

16. Go on a looking and touching trip to discover many types of textures. How do wood grains look? How do feathers look and feel? How does velvet look and feel? Does a tree branch feel the same as it looks? Does paint have a texture? Can you draw the textures you have found? Look at artworks.

17. Select a theme—such as textures found in the desert, on a walk through a forest, on tree bark—and create a design emphasizing the feelings of the theme.

18. Using a variety of media—chalks, charcoal, pencils, pens—draw a still life that emphasizes objects' textural differences. For example, fruits and vegetables have a variety of textures and shapes, yet are closely related in subject.

19. Draw an egg, showing its textured form. This is difficult because of an egg's simplicity of form and texture.

20. Draw a still life or subject using one all-over texture. Only change the tonal range to describe the form.

21. Cut open an apple or orange, and draw its internal texture and pattern.

ARTISTS TO STUDY

For color, study the works of Rembrandt, Marc Chagall, Georgia O'Keeffe, and many others. For pattern and texture, study the works of Larry Poons, Ben Shahn, Norman Rockwell, Kathe Kollwitz, Paul Gauguin, Henri Rousseau, and many contemporary artists.

For example, in *All That Is Beautiful* (see fig. 3.4), Ben Shahn used various patterns for windows in the buildings.

Figure 6.8 Collages of various patterns make interesting designs and visual displays.

Figure 6.9 Imaginative texture and pattern collage.

He also varied the sizes, shapes, and intensities of the patterns to create interest and variety. In Radio Tubes (see fig. 10.11) by Stuart Davis, patterns are the major focus of his painting.

chapter

7

Design Principles/ Composing the Picture

Design has many connotations. It is the organization of materials and processes in the most productive, economic way, in a harmonious balance of all elements necessary for a certain function. . . . [The artist] must know that design is indivisible, that the internal and external characteristics of a dish, a chair, a table, a machine, a painting, a sculpture, are not to be separated. There is a design in organization of emotional experiences, in family life, in city planning, in working together as civilized human beings . . . there is no hierarchy of the arts, painting, photography, music, poetry, sculpture, architecture . . . they are equally valid departures toward the fusion of function and content in "design."

L. Moholy-Nagy and Sibyl Moholy-Nagy, *Vision in Motion*

Art is a reflection of your special self. To create art, you focus on visual perception. Through your eyes—your optical receivers—the brain transforms energy to your computerlike nerves and sends skill forces to your hands. The resulting artworks are distinctive, nonverbal expressions of your unique self that tell others how you see and feel about the world and also tell *you* about *you.* How you put everything together to express yourself in your art is called the artwork's design or composition.

DESIGN/COMPOSITION

According to noted philosopher and educator John Dewey, design is an essential seeking for order, reason, and structure out of chaos.[1] Design exists everywhere—in all of

nature, the arts, architecture, music, dance, theater, writings, and in all of life's activities, from preparing foods to arranging furniture.

In art, **design** or **composition** is the structure, arrangement, and organization of the art elements—line, shape, value, space, color, pattern, and texture—into a unified structure (fig. 7.1). It begins with the first pencil mark or brush stroke on a surface and continues until the final detail is completed.

Artists—both young and old—attempt to organize the art elements into visual relationships. This designing or composing is one of the *creative* processes in a work of art and is what gives all designs an individual mark, reflecting the personalities, feelings, emotions, messages, perceptions, and experiences of the artist (fig. 7.2).

The act of organizing the art elements into a design or composition can be conscious or unconscious, deliberate or spontaneous. Young students are natural, intuitive designers. The strokes and marks that they make on a sheet of paper are spontaneous, instinctive expressions. These "unconscious" designs usually have a high sense of organic unity. Mature artists' designs, on the other hand, often consist of complex, conscious, visual relationships among art elements. Both approaches to design—whether conscious and deliberate, or unconscious and spontaneous—are valid and should be nurtured and incorporated into your personal, unique design style. Remember: You are the artist and so have the privilege to change the design as you like.

While there are no formulas for producing "good" designs, the search for organizing the art elements begins by analyzing, sorting out, and trying to create some order in what you *see.* Look for similarities and differences, for

Figure 7.1 Composition is determined by the structure, arrangement, and organization of all the art elements.

Figure 7.2 Geometric designs are a significant aspect of Hopi pottery.

order and variety. You rarely see forms in isolation; you see them in relation to each other. For example, the impact of a color depends on the impact of other colors in relation to it and surrounding it and on how the colors are used together. Relationships change, depending on, for example, the tension (balance) between spaces, which form is the center of interest (dominance), the movement and direction of forms (rhythm), and the interaction among opposites (contrast).

As you begin an artwork, ask yourself the conceptual questions that follow. These kinds of questions are also helpful for clarifying your thinking regarding how to interpret art objects, how to respond to your environment, how to establish your own visual value system, and how to assess and form judgments in art preferences.

1. Which objects will you include in the artwork? Which will you exclude?
2. Will the design be intuitive and spontaneous, or conscious and deliberate?
3. What idea do you want to express?
4. Will your point of view be realistic or imaginative?
5. Will the art elements and their arrangement focus on your idea?
6. How will the materials and tools selected expand the idea?
7. How will the rhythms of the colors, lines, and shapes suggest a beat or visual music?
8. How will the textures, patterns, spaces, and values add to the orchestration of the art piece?
9. What will be dominant? What type of balance, contrast, and rhythm is there?
10. What sizes will the objects be—will some be larger than others?
11. Will the forms have volume, or will they be flat and two-dimensional?
12. Will there be shading from a light source?
13. Will the forms be realistic, or exaggerated and distorted?

14. Will the forms overlap and/or interpenetrate?
15. How much space will there be between objects?
16. How will you provide movement into and across the picture?
17. Will colors be realistic or emotional?
18. Will there be light against dark or dark against light?
19. What will be the positive and negative shapes?
20. What will be the artwork's outside shape—square, rectangle, round, irregular?

How do you know when you have designed or composed something to its best advantage? Much of the decision is based on your knowledge, previous experience, exposure to the problem, study of other artists' solutions, and, very often, feelings and pure intuition. A design is successful when you feel that it is complete in itself and that you can respond to it with interest and excitement. Since you are the artist, you can change it as you will (fig. 7.3).

However, certain design principles—balance, dominance, rhythm, and contrast—underlie many design decisions. These design principles are the focus of this chapter. All artworks can be discussed and analyzed for design.

BALANCE

Balance is the design principle of visual equilibrium (**harmony** or **disharmony**) achieved in an artwork. It is determined by weight, directional forces, and opposing tensions. You have an awareness of balance with regard to your physical body: When you are balanced within a space, you feel comfortable; when you fall or are off balance, you feel uncomfortable.

In art, balance is an illusion affected by everything happening in the artwork (see fig. 7.4). For example, the design within a picture is in balance when no one part of the picture overpowers any other part, when the visual illusion created is one of equilibrium and stability. In contrast, the design or composition of an artwork can also create a visual illusion of instability, of a visual pulling or inequality, an imbalance that can be psychologically upsetting to the viewer.

To achieve balance in your artwork, you must organize the lines, shapes, values, spaces, colors, patterns, and textures until they feel "right" to you. Among the hundreds of possible balance "solutions," you will have to choose the one that most clearly conveys your message.

Chart 7.1 presents a brief vocabulary of balance.

DOMINANCE

Dominance is the design principle of giving a focal point greater emphasis or stress and making it the center of interest (fig. 7.5). Dominance is achieved with such techniques as:

- Placement in or near the center
- Using a brighter color surrounded by more muted colors
- Balancing a large object with smaller objects, or vice versa
- Placing the darkest form in the center of lighter forms, or vice versa
- Using differences in forms, colors, textures, shapes
- Changing the sequence in a pattern to create a focal point

chart 7.1
Vocabulary of Balance

Symmetrical balance The balance achieved when there is equal distribution of forces on both sides of a picture (see fig. 7.4).

Asymmetrical balance The balance achieved when there is unequal distribution of forces on either side of a picture—for example, when a large object on one side of the drawing creates an overpowering feeling, a heavy weight.

Radial balance The balance achieved when all of the art elements radiate from a central point. In nature, radial balance is exemplified in the petals of a daisy or the cross section of a grapefruit.

Weight The perceived "heaviness" of an object or art element. Weight often depends on location, size, shape, color, and relationships to other art elements. For example, a weight (or large form) in the center of a composition does not disturb balance. However, a large object placed in the upper part of a design appears heavier than one located lower. A large object on the right feels heavier than one placed on the left. An object placed at the bottom of a picture feels more stable and appears to have weight because of gravitational pull. An object placed alone appears heavier than an object surrounded by other forms. A geometric shape appears heavier than an irregular shape. A dark-colored object appears heavier than a light-colored one. A large, heavy weight on one side of a picture can be balanced by three smaller weights on the other side.

Figure 7.3 Visual structuring can range from simple to complex. Deciding when a design is complete is often an intuitive judgment.

Figure 7.4   Usually, masks are symmetrically balanced on both sides of a central axis.

Figure 7.5   In this artwork, the central circle is the dominant shape and the point of emphasis.

CONTRAST

When the art elements in an artwork are similar or complementary—for example, when objects are similar in line, value, shape, color, texture, pattern, or space—the overall effect is one of **harmony** and **unity.** However, when the art elements are opposites of or contradict each other, the interaction of the art elements results in a sense of **variety** and **contrast** that adds interest and focal points (fig. 7.7). For example, contrast can be created by such dissimilarities as light and dark values, thick and thin lines, hard and soft edges, and smooth and rough textures.

IDEAS AND MOTIVATIONS

Adapt to students' abilities and grade levels.

Balance

1. Discuss "feeling" balanced as being an intuitive response.
2. Display photographs of and discuss examples of balance in nature, as well as architectural balance.
3. Examine a variety of inside building spaces, such as a dorm room, a hotel lobby, a church, and so on, and comment on the balance of the interior design.
4. Select several decorative, abstract, and realistic artworks, and compare and contrast the visual balance achieved in each.
5. Discuss symmetrical design as it applies to architecture. Do you think that it is desirable in architecture to create a balanced, symmetrical structure? Why or why not?
6. Find and discuss artworks that exhibit symmetrical and asymmetrical design.
7. Create a drawing that applies radial design to achieve a feeling of balance.

RHYTHM

In art, **rhythm** is suggested by **repetition** of a line, shape, value, color, or other art element to provide a regulated, uninterrupted flow that suggests a moving force and direction. Rhythm or movement created in this way can be regular or irregular, pleasing or unsettling, just as in music. For example, equally spaced objects create a sense of order and **unity,** while irregularly spaced objects suggest **variety** and little order.

Rhythm or movement can be conveyed in a number of ways (fig. 7.6). For example, a sequence of images often suggests motion and rhythm, while multiple, overlapping imagery suggests movement through space. Repetition of an object with some changes, such as diminishing size or value, also can indicate movement. A curved line suggests a different movement than a straight line. Movement can be across the picture, or it can be implied by the path of a line traveling from deep space toward the picture plane, or from foreground to middle ground to background.

Figure 7.6 Curved lines indicate movement and rhythm.

Figure 7.7 The above artwork demonstrates harmony, unity, variety, and contrast.

8. Experiment with how weight affects balance in a drawing or painting. Try different locations, sizes, colors, shapes, and so on to determine when a weight appears visually to be "heavier."
9. Discuss ways that balance can create a mood or feeling.
10. Use cut paper shapes of various colors and "balance" in a design.
11. Select an artwork that you feel is balanced. Analyze and draw a diagram to show how the artist achieved this.
12. Create a decorative design that is pleasing to your sensibilities.
13. Create a design that you feel is not balanced.

Dominance

1. Make a number of drawings that differ in how a center of interest is created. Try showing dominance with (*a*) size, (*b*) placement, (*c*) contrast, (*d*) balance, and (*e*) rhythm.

2. Experiment with making drawings that illustrate how to create dominance using (*a*) line, (*b*) shape, (*c*) value, (*d*) space, (*e*) color, (*f*) pattern, and (*g*) texture.
3. Find and discuss examples of dominance in decorative artworks, in abstract artworks, and in artworks with subject matter.
4. Select and display a variety of artworks. Discuss how the artists used dominance to create centers of interest, focal points, and emphasis.
5. Find examples of artworks that use dominance to express moods and feelings. What moods and feelings does dominance express?
6. Find examples of architecture with established centers of interest. How was this dominance achieved?
7. Practice achieving the illusion of dominance using a variety of media.
8. Discuss the psychological use of dominance in art. For example, in Edward Hopper's *Night Shadows* (see fig. 5.23), the strong diagonal shadow is placed near the center, and angles create emphasis. The man, being central and isolated, becomes dominant in the design.

Rhythm

1. Draw a design that shows rhythm and movement with sequential images.
2. Draw a design that varies the sequence of images. How does this affect the design's rhythm and movement?
3. Draw a design with equally spaced objects and another with unequally spaced objects. How do the rhythms in each design differ?
4. Experiment with creating rhythm through repetition of lines, values, shapes, spaces, colors, patterns, and textures.
5. Experiment with creating movement (*a*) across a picture, (*b*) from deep space forward, and (*c*) from forms in middle ground and foreground to background.
6. Discuss the relationship between rhythm and pattern.
7. Create a sense of rhythm in (*a*) a decorative design, (*b*) an abstract design, and (*c*) a drawing with subject matter.
8. Find examples of rhythm in (*a*) nature, (*b*) architecture, and (*c*) manufactured products.
9. Discuss the rhythm and pattern found in cultural objects, such as Navajo rugs.
10. Select three art reproductions in this book, and look for how the artists communicated rhythm and movement through similarity, repetition, unity, and variation.

Contrast

1. Find different ways of creating contrast with each of the art elements—for example, thick and thin lines, bright and dull colors, dark and light values.
2. Experiment in simple drawings with providing contrast in (*a*) lines, (*b*) shapes, (*c*) values, (*d*) spaces, (*e*) colors, (*f*) patterns, and (*g*) textures.
3. Find examples of and discuss contrast and variety in nature. Can you also find examples of harmony and unity in nature?
4. Create a sense of contrast in (*a*) a decorative design, (*b*) an abstract design, and (*c*) a drawing with subject matter.
5. Create a sense of harmony and unity in (*a*) a decorative design, (*b*) an abstract design, and (*c*) a drawing with subject matter.
6. Analyze a variety of artworks in this book to identify how the artists achieved a sense of harmony and unity.
7. Analyze a variety of artworks in this book to identify how the artists achieved a sense of contrast and variety.

NOTES

1. John Dewey, *Art as Experience* (New York: Putman, 1958).

8

Art Production: Ideas and Techniques

Expression, to my way of thinking, does not consist of the passion mirrored upon a human face or betrayed by a violent gesture. The whole arrangement of my picture is expressive. The place occupied by the figure or objects, the empty spaces around them, the proportions, everything plays a part.

Henri Matisse

We all have inherited abilities. Your desire to learn about art is the only limit. When you create art, you may discover things you have never seen or known before.

Only rarely are people born with an artistic gift like that of Michelangelo. More often, their skill is acquired with practice and study. Just like playing an instrument or being involved in a sport, becoming an artist takes enthusiasm, time, and practice. Like the pianist who must practice the basic scales, you must start with a basic understanding of the tools of design. Do not expect to create a masterpiece the first time you draw. The more you practice, the more you learn and the more you increase your skills.

This chapter provides ideas and some basics on drawing and painting portraits, figures, still lifes, and landscapes/cityscapes. (See Other Artists to Study, in Appendix A, pp. 261–265.) The chapter also suggests a variety of techniques and ideas for exploring painting and drawing, printmaking, puppets, clay, weaving, and art and technology. While a knowledge of basic techniques is helpful, the creation of artworks also requires inspiration, a capacity to "see" artistically, and a thoughtful approach.

GETTING STARTED

Creating art means (1) knowing what you want to express and why, (2) thinking about how you "see" and understand your subject, and (3) deciding on what approach you want to take to your art.

Why Create Art?

Individuals create art for a variety of reasons:

- To express images of people, places, landscapes, oceans, animals, and so on
- To express their feelings
- To illustrate events, history, religion, literature
- To invent ways of expressing ideas
- To express dreams and fantasy
- To compose with the art elements (color, line, space, and so on)
- To produce designed objects for functional use
- To record observations, drawing from life experiences
- To capture visual memories of images
- To innovate, to express ideas that have no predetermined expectations (open-ended)
- To interact with materials (discovery)
- To reflect on life experiences
- To be independent thinkers, to set goals and engage in problem solving for themselves

Ideas and inspirations for artworks are gathered from a variety of sources, including memories about other times, places, peoples, events, and objects; photographs; the works of other artists and cultures; found objects, such as rocks, flowers, branches; various materials, such as fabrics and tools; and diverse themes, such as different cultures, religions, nature, animals and birds, literature, and myths and legends.

Learning to "See"

In addition to feeling compelled and inspired to create art, individuals who want to create art must learn how to "see." "Seeing," in the artistic sense, involves calling on the imaginative and inventive forces stored in your mind and opening your visual potential so that the two can work together to permit a "higher" visual processing. Then it is up to your eye-hand-brain coordination to improve your drawing skill so that the processed information can be expressed in a nonverbal way. Many artists say that creating art places them in a special awareness state, in a freeing mood that helps transport them to another plateau—something like listening to music or "letting your mind go."

Children and adults see differently, and they also draw differently. A second-grader can instinctively draw charming, delightful pictures that are excellent for that age level, but the same drawing from an adult might be judged very differently. Certain standards exist at certain levels of understanding. There is no one "best" way to see and draw, however, since each person explores what he or she feels is most interesting and exciting.

For example, the artist Joan Miró spent his whole life cultivating the freedom of a child in his art expression. He did not mirror nature in a traditional way or consider proper proportions or perspective. Instead, he mixed realism and fantasy. He saw with his eyes the same things we all see, but then he took from what he saw and knew and "played" with it, improvising in a unique way, until all the forms resolved themselves in a personal statement. Miró's paintings are gay, often humorous, full of vitality and symbolism, and very much alive. They reflect his temperament, inspiration, and unrestricted imagination, as well as his skills, years of study of and involvement with art, and personal statement of ideas, thoughts, and feelings (see fig. 10.34).

Rembrandt and Pablo Picasso also "saw" in their own unique ways. Rembrandt, a Dutch painter of the seventeenth century, was concerned with the way light reflected on objects, the atmosphere created by different lights, the shadows cast by light, and composition. Picasso, a contemporary artist, was more concerned with abstracting the art elements and with experimenting with lines, variations, textural qualities, forms, imaginative shapes, and unusual composition. No one can say which of the two was the "better" artist because different artists "see" differently, take different approaches to art, and are motivated in different ways.

Approaches to Art

Once you have decided what you want to depict in your artwork and have given some thought to how you "see" your subject, you can usually take one of three approaches to the actual creation of art:

1. **The imaginative (or abstract) approach.** This approach involves using invented forms and ideas developed from the imagination. Sometimes, real objects, models, or photos stimulate imaginative ideas (fig. 8.1). Figure 8.2 shows the work of artist Kenneth Kerslake, who explained his imaginative approach to this particular artwork as follows:

   I had been interested in establishing a process of working that would allow interchange of my thought patterns and greatly expand the possibilities of seeing precisely the same image in new and ever-changing relationships. It has always been fascinating to me how incidental events in one's life can become major concerns. Perhaps as much as a year before beginning the suite [of etchings], I received in the mail a brochure from Time-Life Corporation, advertising a book and illustrated with a series of anatomical drawings from an eleventh-century manuscript. I liked it and pinned it on my studio wall. About the same time, I purchased a sabre saw. Both things had little to do with my immediate interests at the time; but over the course of the year, a distillation of the figure from the manuscript reproduction became the model for the suite, involving the anatomy of the contemporary human condition, and the sabre saw became the primary means of realizing the idea. The central innovation was cutting the plate apart—once I had decided to do that, anything became possible. When all the plates were complete, or near completion, I assembled them on the press bed. At this point, the whole image was brought together for the first time.[1]

2. **The visual approach.** This approach involves seeing and representing the object as accurately as possible. A direct light source and shading are often used to represent the object realistically in space (figs. 8.3, 8.5).

3. **The emotional approach.** This approach involves interpreting subjects with exaggeration and distortion to emphasize an idea or express a feeling (fig. 8.4).

ART PRODUCTION

Elementary students can be inspired to "see" the world in unique ways and to take different approaches to their art, as discussed in the previous section. Art offers opportunities for students to explore, enjoy, invent, discover, expand, and become deeply involved. It awakens each student's potential and abilities, suggests new possibilities, and provides creative experiences. Students' artworks are unique expressions that reflect individual, natural talents and are a personal statement of what is seen, known, and felt.

As such, art is critical to students' education, and elementary teachers are instrumental in initiating art experiences that motivate, spark excitement, stretch imaginations, and cause students to hunger for more. How, as a teacher, do you provide this artistic motivation?

Positive art experiences must begin early. Young elementary students, in kindergarten through second grade, are adventurers. A splash of color on a surface, whether it be the wall, the floor, or a sheet of paper, is enormously

(a)

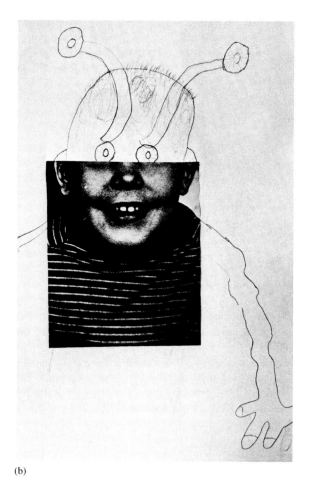

(b)

Figure 8.1   Imaginative approaches involve using a variety of materials, ideas, and inventive themes.

exciting. The students are intuitive, free, and spontaneous, and they reflect little on past experiences. As a teacher, you need to encourage this freedom and to provide time for just "awareness." Suggest new and challenging ideas, and provide a choice of tools and materials that offer many art opportunities: large crayons; large brushes; large papers; vivid, bright colors; paints that respond opaquely as well as transparently.

As students progress into third and fourth grade, they begin to use personalized symbols to represent forms and objects. They are more sensitive to and aware of existing objects and relationships and their existence within the environment. They want to communicate ideas. As a teacher, you can provide frequent art opportunities to inspire discovery, exploration, and enthusiasm, and to reveal new possibilities.

By fifth or sixth grade, students are more reflective and draw the existing world as they see it in a more realistic representation. They are consciously aware of design and of the art elements that structure design (line, shape, value, space, color, pattern, and texture). This awareness provides working tools to express strong feelings and new ideas. As a teacher, you can provide art experiences that encourage these older students to experiment, build, and boundary-push. Once-in-a-while art experiences are not often enough to promote real artistic development.

PORTRAITS

A **portrait** is a drawing or painting of a human model. When artists paint portraits, they attempt to capture the spirit and character of the person, as well as the person's likeness (fig. 8.5). When you draw a face, you reveal not only the person you are drawing but your own spirit as well—the artistic vision in each of us.

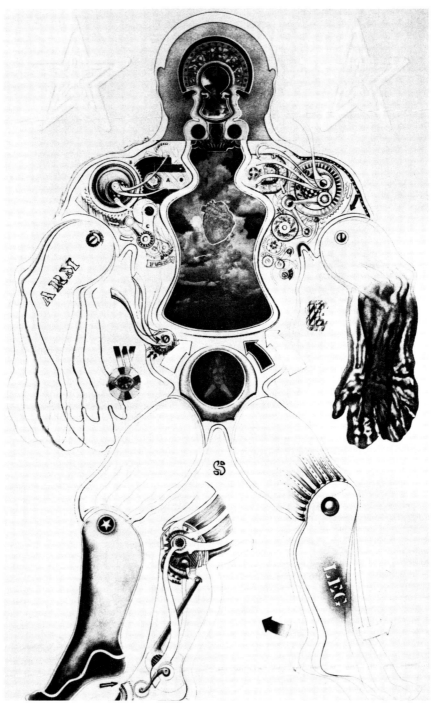

Figure 8.2   From the series *The Anatomies of the Star-Spangled Man* by Kenneth Kerslake, University of Florida.

How Students Understand Portraits

Drawing a portrait is a growing process. In most very young children's development, the circular movements of a pencil on paper symbolize the head of a person, usually "Mommy" or "Daddy." Later, the child draws arms and legs that grow out directly from the head. Thus, the head appears to be the central focus from the very beginning.

Young students emphasize the inner emotional attitudes of the subject, rather than the person's exterior visual qualities. They draw the way they feel about themselves, how they see and what they know about other people, and how they see life. Not until the third, fourth, fifth, and sixth grades do students become aware of differences in features and changes due to light, atmosphere, and emotional expressions, such as love, fear, and sorrow.

(a)

(b)

Figure 8.3   A more **visual** approach is used in the above drawings using models and photographs as motivation.

In working with students in drawing portraits, you might want to have students feel the three-dimensional forms of their own faces. They already have some idea of the basic structure of their bones and the shape of their features, but this passive knowledge about themselves must be brought into active consciousness. After students have thought about, felt, and explored their own features, they are ready to try drawing a face.

Another possible approach with all students is to sculpt a face in clay. In experimenting with this three-dimensional form, students are able to feel the changes in the curves and angles, the movements in and out, and the shape variations for the nose, mouth, and eyes.

A third approach to drawing portraits is to have students draw self-portraits on mirrors with felt-tip pens. Have them stand at arm's length from a mirror. Then, they can

start by drawing the basic oval shape of the face, measuring to find the distances between features, and adding personal details.

For fifth- and sixth-grade students, portrait study should include numerous experiences in drawing the basic portrait proportions, as outlined in chart 8.1. After awhile, these guidelines become second nature to students.

Select and do at least several of the portrait activities presented in the "Ideas and Motivations" section at the end of this chapter. These will be helpful to you and also can be adapted for use with elementary-age students.

Lessons in Basic Portrait Proportions

Begin the portrait proportions lesson by having students draw a blank oval and marking the various lines mentioned in chart 8.1 lightly on the paper (fig. 8.6). Before proceed-

(a)

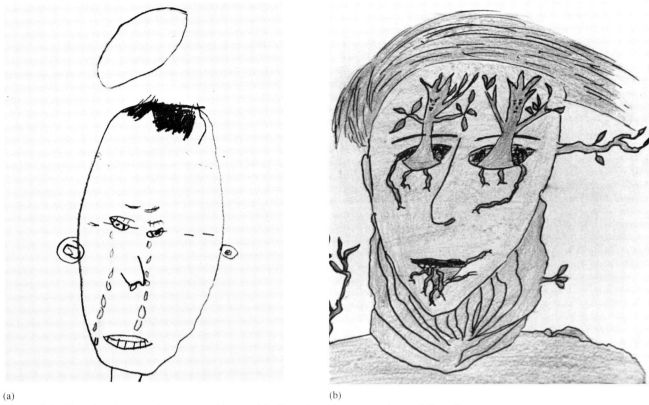

(b)

Figure 8.4   Emotional approaches express ideas and feelings through exaggeration and distortion.

(a)   (b)

Figure 8.5   Self-portraits often reflect the visual image as well as the different personalities of the artists. In both portraits shown here, the light source is different, creating different shadows. Notice the artists' brushstrokes. (*a*) *Self-Portrait,* Gustave Courbet, c. 1866. Oil on board, 17 inches × 13⅞ inches. The Fine Arts Museums of San Francisco, Memorial Gift from Dr. T. Edward and Tullah Hanley, Bradford, Pennsylvania. (*b*) Vincent Van Gogh, Dutch, 1853–1890, *Self-Portrait,* oil on artist's board mounted on cradled panel, 1886/87, 41 × 32.5 cm, Joseph Winterbothom Collection, photograph © 1995 The Art Institute of Chicago. All Rights Reserved.

chart   8.1

Portrait Proportions

First, study and draw the basic structure, from both the front and the side, of a skeleton of a head.

Then draw a basic oval shape. This oval shape may require slight variations toward a heart, square, round, or long shape, depending on the individual being drawn. Finally, draw a light vertical line down the center of the oval. Now you are ready to consider the placement of facial structures.

1. The eyes are halfway between the top of the head and the chin line. (Beginners tend to place the eyes closer to the top of the head.)
2. The nose is halfway between the eye and the chin line.
3. The center line for the mouth is a little less than halfway between the nose and the chin.
4. The space between the eyes is about the same as the width of another eye.
5. The width of the mouth is about the distance from pupil to pupil when the eyes are looking straight ahead.
6. The eyebrows are about one-third the distance from the top of the head to the chin line.
7. The space between the eyebrows is basically triangular.
8. The forehead is a rectangle.
9. The ears run approximately from the eyebrows to the bottom of the nose.
10. The eyes fit into holes in the skull—the eye sockets. They are round, like balls, and are controlled by four muscles—one at the top, one at the bottom, and two side muscles.
11. The eyelids surround and rest on the eye. The eyelids are important because they determine the eye's shape. Some are heavy (in older people), while others are hardly seen at all. Eyelid shape varies greatly and needs close observation.
12. The upper eyelid is longer and follows somewhat the shape of the forehead and the cheekbone. It moves during blinking.
13. The bottom eyelid appears to have a shelf form close to the eye.
14. The eyes are placed deeper in than the eyebrows or cheekbones.
15. There are definite planes (surfaces) of the forehead, nose, cheeks, and chin that move in and out, back and forth.
16. When the head is viewed from various angles, the planes change.
17. The nose is primarily a triangle that juts out from the face.
18. There is a plane under the nose. The nostrils have definite shapes.
19. The lips can be thought of as two different shapes.
20. Basically, the head is a cube shape, having four sides and top and bottom.
21. The head sits on the spine, which intercepts approximately at the ear. The spine is the axis, and the head pivots on the axis. Beginners tend to make the neck too narrow.
22. The cheekbones are round on the sides, following the skull.
23. Hair grows away from the skull.
24. Hair also has a basic shape and adds to the person's individual character. When drawing hair, examine its form—from its general shape to smaller details. Do not draw each hair, but indicate the form with lights and darks.
25. To draw a profile, use the same basic proportions. Study the negative shape (the shape surrounding the profile) before beginning. Compare the size of the head to the neck. Study differences in nose contours.

ing, request that students close their eyes and "feel" the way their faces move and change. Tell them to pretend that an ant on top of their head is going to crawl over their head and face. They should think about how the ant moves and crawls in and out over the forms. Then they should move their finger, as if it were the ant, along the cheekbones, over the eyes, and down and under the chin. Next, they should investigate with their finger from one side of their face to the other side. Encourage students to explore their head and face as if they were discoverers roaming over a new land. Suggest that they then discuss, examine, and feel each other's eyes, noses, and various contour edges and shapes.

Then stop and demonstrate how to draw the basic individual features as separate elements, such as the eye (fig. 8.7). Have students study the shape of the nose (fig. 8.8) and cheekbones. The nose is the most perplexing form to draw because it has no defined edges and must be drawn primarily with shading. Encourage students to discuss and feel the form of the nose, to see how the nose begins at the eyebrow and has individual bumps and turns. Suggest that they feel how each cheekbone moves from the front plane around to the side, which will give students a better feeling for its rounded form.

Discuss with students how everyone's noses, eyes, cheekbones, mouths, and chins all have individual forms (fig. 8.9). No two are exactly alike. Explain that it is in looking at the differences in each face that they are likely to find the characteristics that create the "look" of the individual.

Students are usually excited to learn the basic portrait foundations provided in chart 8.1. They often go home and practice drawing people in their families or work from family photographs (fig. 8.10). For fun, when students have completed drawings of themselves and family members, display the drawings and have students try to pick out which of the drawings depict class members (fig. 8.11).

Figure 8.6 The drawings above illustrate portrait proportions, as found in chart 8.1.

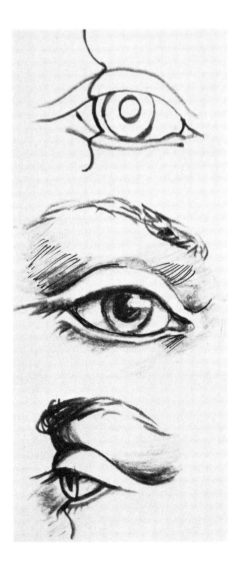

Figure 8.7 Eyelids determine the shape of the eye and vary greatly from person to person. The upper eyelid is longer and follows somewhat the shape of the forehead and cheekbone. The bottom eyelid appears to form a shelf close to the eye.

Figure 8.8   The nose is a challenging form to draw because it has no defined edges and must be drawn primarily with shading. It is a triangle that juts out from the face. The head is a cube shape having six sides—four sides and a top and bottom.

Figure 8.9   Think of lips as having two different shapes.

Figure 8.10   Drawing portraits and figures from photographs increases observation of detail.

Figure 8.11 Various portraits drawn by students at different grade levels. Some are feeling portraits; others are drawn from mirror images. Note the individuality of each.

THE HUMAN FIGURE

Drawing the human figure requires a basic understanding of figure structure and proportion, as well as the perception of the figure as a complete organization of rhythmic parts into a whole. Equally important to figurative art, however, is a comprehension of how the figure exists, moves, and relates to its environment within a given space. Just as one color in a painting never exists by itself, but only in relationship to the colors surrounding it, so the figure never exists by itself, but only in relationship to the forces generating from within and about the figure (fig. 8.12).

Children somehow instinctively capture these relationships in their drawings of human figures. The mood, emotional tone, and movement always seem to be present, along with the details and proportions that comprise the complete statement of the form.

Students who tend to shy away from drawing figures and portraits probably lack drawing experience and knowledge. However, once they have learned simple figure proportions and have been offered many opportunities to learn to draw the head, the figure, and the figure in action, most students are motivated by their achievement and feelings of confidence. Emphasis on practice, questioning, learning, and "let's try it" attitudes contributes to feelings of positive self-awareness and successful creation of figurative art.

How Students Understand the Human Figure

The figure concept for students in kindergarten through sixth grade develops from very young children's symbolic use of shapes to sixth-graders' greater use of realistic proportions and their awareness of detail, shading, action, and atmosphere. It also expands from a narrow, "ego" comprehension of the figure in the family, school, and community to a more broad-based concept of the figure concerned with real life in a world force of communities and cultures.

Very young students, in kindergarten through approximately second grade, use basic forms to represent the body (fig. 8.13). A circle is a head (the most important part of the body), and from the head grow the arms and legs. If you

(a)

(b)

Figure 8.12   The human figure exists, moves, and relates to its environment within a given space. (*a*) The white pastel on black paper surrounds the figure. (*b*) Here, the negative shapes around the figure reveal the figure.

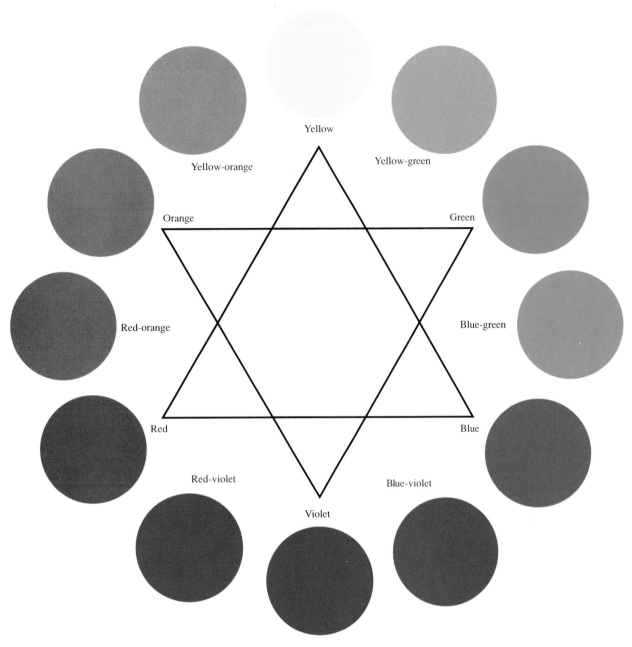

Plate 1   Color wheel. Can you find the primary colors? Secondary colors? Complementary colors?

Plate 2   Upper grade students painted a mural of life in the desert. (Continued on plate 3.)

Plate 3   (Plate 2 continued)

Plate 4 Clay animal sculptures are painted with tempra and acrylic paints by first-, second-, and third-grade students.

Plate 5 Following a lesson on architectural details and spatial relationships, students created this eight-foot replica of The Peterson House. Project directed by Peter Nearing and Patrick Miller, Tempe Elementary Schools.

Plate 6 Details to look for in portraits include hair texture and shape, face shape and special features, glasses, clothing patterns and textures.

Plate 7 Social interests include clothing and hair styles in upper grades.

Plate 8   After studying cubism, a fifth-grader painted this still life. Characteristics include defined outlines, black shapes, flat colors, and some overlapping shapes.

Plate 9   Student painting in the style of Miro, which includes primary colors and symbols such as stars, circles, curved lines, and rectangles.

Plate 10   A cowboy and horse on the roof, cacti, and a figure inside the window appear in this student's landscape of desert life.

Plate 11 Tissue-paper collage forms the background for this Native American figure dressed in traditional costume, which reveals social customs and traditions.

Plate 12 Nam June Paik, *Electro-Symbio Phonics,* 1992, American West Arena, Phoenix, AZ. Photo courtesy of Chris Gomien.

Plate 13 "Heroes" such as Dr. Martin Luther King, Jr., provide art motivations and expression as in this watercolor portrait by a sixth grader.

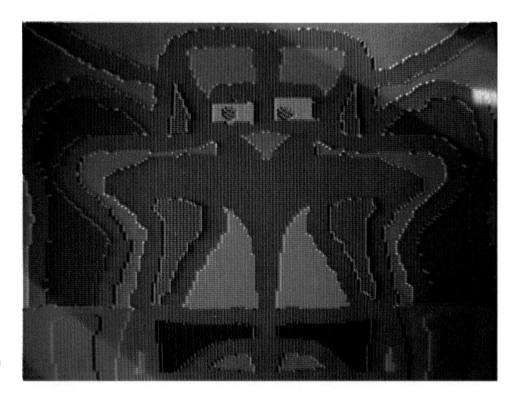

Plate 14 Imaginative computer drawing created by a student in the classroom of Barbara Hartman.

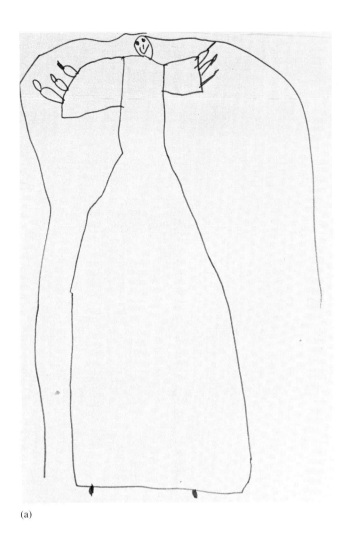

(a)

(c)

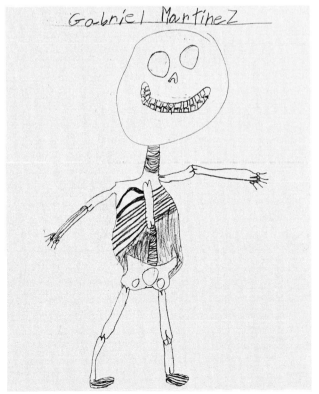

(b)

(d)

Figure 8.13   Students in kindergarten through second grade use basic shapes to represent the human figure.

motivate with strong, significant art experiences that focus on different parts of the body, students will develop awareness of their own bodies, and their concepts of the figure will be enriched. The concepts will include much more detail and will reflect a better understanding of the parts and how they move together and of the forms as they change and move. Students will repeat symbols that are personally meaningful and will develop strong schemas.

In third and fourth grade, students tend to find that geometric lines are unsuitable for their expression, and they move toward a more realistic approach. They do not see folds and ripples yet. Their representations are more characterizations, not visualizations, and figures are stiff, due to the continuing egocentric view of students in this age group (fig. 8.14). These students like to characterize hairstyles, girl-boy clothing, and costumes.

Fifth- and sixth-grade students have developed an awareness of and interest in real-life situations, and also enjoy imaginative and inventive themes. They feel a new

(b)

(a)

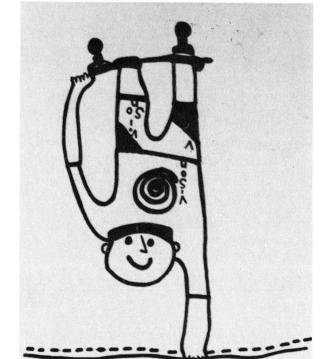

(c)

Figure 8.14 As third- and fourth-graders begin to perceive details and differences, their figures indicate "men" and "women" and show more realistic imagery. While the legs remain stiff, the drawings reveal very personal statements. Circus ideas.

and serious concern with their changing bodies and are forming self-images (fig. 8.15). As a teacher, you need to motivate these students' awareness of the figure in both a realistic sense and also an emotional sense.

Visually expressive students are most interested in realistic attempts to create the human figure. They are concerned with changing appearances due to changing light, space, and atmosphere. They need art experiences focused on correct figure proportions, exterior qualities of the figure, shading of the figure, bending and moving of body parts, where the joints are, and how clothes fold and wrinkle around the joints.

Nonvisually expressive students, on the other hand, want art experiences that concentrate more on the figure's emotional attitudes—its gestures, feelings, and expressions (how the figure feels inside)—rather than its exterior qualities. They also want to focus on the parts of the figure they feel are more important, exaggerating some parts and omitting others.

With all elementary students, practice drawing the figure often, since practice brings improvement and development. Students can be motivated by experiences that include figures—for example, see figure 8.16.

Select and do at least several of the figure activities presented in the "Ideas and Motivations" section at the end of this chapter. These will be helpful to you and also can be adapted for use with elementary-age students.

Figure Proportions and Structure

The search for perfect proportions of the human figure has intrigued many artists. During the first century B.C., Vitruvius established a measurement for the body: A person lying on the floor with arms and legs spread out is perfectly held within a square. Vitruvius also proportioned the head as one-eighth the overall length of the body, with the face being divided into three equal parts—the forehead, nose, and the space between the nose and chin.

(a)

Figure 8.15 Fifth- and sixth-grade students are forming self-images and need motivations that increase both their realistic and emotional awareness of the human figure. In (b), (c) and (d), the students posed as the models.

(b)

(c)

Figure 8.15   Continued

(d)

(a)

(b)

Figure 8.16   People, situations, and experiences that motivate students may include figures.

The following explanation of general human figure proportions often works well with elementary students:

One way to conceptualize the human figure is as consisting of three large body masses: the head, the chest, and the pelvis. Attached to these three masses are the arms, legs, neck, spine, and abdominal muscles. All of these move by *bending, turning,* and *twisting.* A general rule is that the top of the leg where it meets the hip is the halfway

mark in the figure. A center line (using the spine as the center) establishes the action of the figure and holds all figure masses together (fig. 8.17).

The center of gravity (the distribution of body weight) is an imaginary vertical line through the figure that acts as a balancing scale, creating counteracting forces on both sides. This center of gravity line runs through the pit of the neck down to the supporting weights (feet) and can only be established when the figure is stationary. When the figure is in motion, such as running, determining the center of gravity is difficult.

The best way to begin a figure drawing is to study the pose carefully. Look for the center of gravity line, at how weight is distributed, at the positioning of the three figure masses, and for the bends, twists, and turns of the figure. Then begin the drawing by placing a short line at both the top and bottom of the paper to indicate the figure's top and bottom dimensions.

Perfectly proportioned figures are rare—most of us vary from the "ideal" proportions in one way or another. Keep this in mind as you draw. Look for the "imperfect" proportions in your subject. They show how one person is different from another. Remember also that the appearance of your figure will depend on your viewpoint (your position in relation to the model). In addition, the model's action and movement may alter figure proportions.

In the book *The Natural Way to Draw,* Kimon Nicolaides recommends an advanced approach to drawing the human figure that you and your older students might find helpful:

The torso is divided into two equal parts, shoulders to waist and waist to thigh, and we use a half-section of the torso as the unit of measure. From the shoulders to the waist, then, we count as *one.* From the waist to the thigh is also *one.* From the collarbone to the top of the head is approximately *one or somewhat less.* From the highest point of the leg to the

Figure 8.17   In figure drawing, look for the action lines, the twists, the bends, the supporting weight of the figure, and the large masses (the head, chest, and pelvis). Proportions aid in describing a figure, but most real figures will vary from them in one way or another.

middle of the knee is *one and one-half.* From the middle of the knee through the foot, if it is placed flat on the floor, is also *one and one-half.* The highest point of the leg on the outside is less than half of the way up into the lower part of the torso.

The width of the shoulders equals *one,* and the neck occupies a third of the distance across the top of the shoulders. The arms fit into the torso at the shoulders, just as sleeves are set into a coat. From the shoulder to the elbow is *one,* and from the elbow to the wrist is *one.* The head is longer in the front than it is at the back, so it sits on the neck at an angle, and the neck seems to be set down farther in the front than it is in the back.

The upper part of the torso is supported by the basket of the ribs and the lower section by the pelvic bone, and the spine holds these two sections together in the back. In the front, they are held together by the large perpendicular muscle of the abdomen. From the side, the two sections of the torso have the same proportions as from the front, but because the spine has a slight curve, they appear to be joined together in

the back and somewhat separated in the front. When the body bends, either forward or back, the torso seems to fall in or expand, rather like an accordion.

From the back, the proportions are naturally the same because the silhouette is exactly the same. (The front view and the back view of any object must be the same in silhouette.) The back of the figure, however, looks different from the front. It is a good deal flatter, and a difference in muscular construction makes the torso seem longer and the legs shorter. In the front, the muscles of the chest do not overlap the arms as the muscles of the back do. But the bone construction, front, side, and back, is necessarily one thing, and it is the bone construction which causes the proportions.[2]

STILL LIFE

A **still life** is a drawing or painting of a grouping of inanimate objects. Before the actual drawing or painting, however, the objects to be shown must be selected and arranged.

Select a variety of interesting objects. You might want the objects to comprise a particular grouping—for example, objects that are commonplace, unusual, manufactured, or organic forms from nature. You might want to express a theme or idea. Chart 8.2 lists a variety of potential objects for a still life. Figures 8.18 and 8.19 show examples of various still-life motivations.

Consider all of the following questions as you design a sensitive, aesthetic, and interesting arrangement of your selected objects:

- Do you plan to include all of your selected objects in the grouping, or just one or a few?
- What shape is the paper you intend to paint or draw on—rectangle, square, circle, triangle? How will this affect your arrangement?
- What contrasts (if any) do you want to emphasize: simple against detailed, tall against short, round against rectangular?
- From what point do you want to view the arrangement as you draw or paint it—for example, head-on front view, side view, behind view, bird's-eye view, ant's-eye view?
- Are all the objects on the same level (for example, a table), or are there a variety of levels, as well as foreground, middle ground, and background?
- Do the shapes overlap or connect in some way? Study the edges or contours of the forms and how they relate.
- Are there dark forms as well as lighter-valued forms? How are they placed?
- Is there a theme or idea to the still-life?
- Will shadows add to the design/composition of your painting or drawing?
- Does your arrangement show contrasting lines? Contrasting colors? Contrasting textures and patterns? Variety? Interest? Balance?
- Have you created a rhythm in your arrangement?

(a)

(c)

(b)

(d)

Figure 8.18   Various themes, such as (*a*) shoes, (*b*) flowers, (*c*) art tools, and (*d*) table settings, can be motivations for still lifes.

(a)

(b)

Figure 8.19 Art materials can help express different feelings, moods, and detail. (a) Pastel; (b) felt pens and crayon.

chart 8.2
Ideas for Still-Life

antiques	small sculptures	mirrors
old bones	tools	dolls
old sewing machines	round items (jars,	musical
old shoes and clothing	glasses,cans, etc.)	instruments
gears, motors, cars	toys	lace
shells	skeletons	old machinery
sticks and twigs	interesting plants	weeds
old furniture	old clocks	seeds
flowers (real and	grasses	bottles
synthetic)	rocks	fans
vases	lamps	driftwood
different cloths (patterned,	stuffed animals	pottery, dishes
velvet, satin, etc.)	fruit, vegetables	screens
insides of radios	televisions	sports items
pocketbooks, contents	lanterns	wristwatches
typewriters	bicycles	eyeglasses
chairs	cereal boxes	shoes
hats, clothing	gloves	candy wrappers
paintbrushes	pop and food cans	kitchen utensils

LANDSCAPES/CITYSCAPES

A **landscape** is a painting or drawing of natural scenery, while a **cityscape** is a painting or drawing of a city scene. The most important considerations in either of these are what you decide to include and what you decide to leave out. Your decision could be based on ideas, as well as on contrasts of color, texture, and forms, and on spatial interest. You may want to create a mood and visual excitement by distorting, rearranging, and simplifying (fig. 8.20). Consider all of the following as you plan your landscape/cityscape vision:

- Compositional balance
- Center of interest—the object(s) that dominate
- Feelings and moods of harmony and contrast
- Rhythm and movement
- Important lines
- Proportions of shapes
- How to indicate space (background, middle ground, foreground)
- Areas of simplicity and areas of detail
- Outside shape (rectangle, square, circle) of the paper you will be drawing or painting on
- Contrasting shapes, values, patterns, and textures
- Positive and negative shapes
- Color relationships (experiment on scratch paper)
- Variety of forms—simple/detailed, horizontal/vertical, tall/short, and so on

(a)

(b)

Figure 8.20 Landscape examples: (*a* and *b*) Drawings by students in kindergarten through second grade indicate spatial depth. (*c*) This third-grade example of a landscape illustrates the use of overlapping to show depth. (*d–f*) Fifth- and sixth-grade landscape drawings show greater detail, overlapping of shapes as well as aerial views.

(c)

(e)

(d)

(f)

Figure 8.20   Continued. (a) is crayon; (b) crayon-resist; (c) cut paper; (d) felt-tip pens; (e) crayon-resist; and (f) pencil and pen.

- Placement of the horizon line—will you show more sky or more ground?
- How your proposed scene looks through a viewfinder

When you are ready to begin drawing or painting, sketch in basic line directions and basic forms (circles, rectangles, squares, triangles) first. You might want to begin with the object nearest to the bottom of the paper and build from there, or you might select and draw a shape in the middle and build out from there.

DRAWING TECHNIQUES

The following is a summary of various drawing concepts and techniques to teach and/or review with students and to increase drawing skills. Keep a sketchbook of your drawings, and encourage your students to do likewise.

1. Deciding what will be included and what will be omitted in a drawing is essential to the overall composition.
2. The basic structure and shapes of what is going to be drawn—whether leaves, trees, people, still-life objects, muscles, skeletons, or flowers—should be studied.
3. Thinking of the contour edges of the shape (as if the object were black and silhouetted against a bright light) is helpful.
4. Lines that move over the forms and across the surface show roundness without shading (fig 8.39). Cross-hatching indicates form and three dimensions.
5. Objects lighter in value appear to be in the distance, while objects darker in value appear closer. Similarity in value gives an overall feeling of oneness.
6. Objects appear to be in front of items they overlap.
7. Heavy lines coming forward and lighter lines receding create a sense of depth.
8. Grouped lines and marks indicate patterns and textures.
9. Different drawing tools (crayon, pen, pencil, and so on) create different lines, feelings, and textures.
10. For variety, some lines can be created with dots.
11. Graphite, charcoal, the sides of a pencil, and lithograph crayons create soft tones.
12. Curved lines give a different feeling from straight, horizontal, or diagonal lines.
13. Quiet, simple areas of a drawing convey a different feeling and contrast with busy, active areas.
14. Colors create depth: Bright, intense colors come forward; dark, muted colors recede.
15. Similar colors, values, shapes, and lines give feelings of harmony and unity, while opposing ones give feelings of opposition and discordance.
16. The spacing or interval between objects conveys a sense of movement.
17. Exaggerated proportions and strong distortions, such as a large hand to a small head, indicate space, create strong feelings, and transmit emotions.
18. Objects with greatest detail appear closest. Objects are less distinct with distance.
19. In drawings of drapery and folds, the relationship of the curves and planes must be considered: Light values come forward, and dark tones recede.
20. Variety and contrast—in dark and light, strength and delicacy, types of lines, soft and hard edges, complex and simple areas, large and small shapes, and so on—create interest.

PAINTING TECHNIQUES

In kindergarten and in first and second grade, most painting is direct, spontaneous, and expressive of ideas. What follows is a summary of various painting concepts and techniques to teach and/or review with students in third through sixth grade as they undertake painting projects.

1. Watercolor is a transparent medium. Many artists prefer to work quickly, boldly, confidently, and directly to keep the painting alive and spontaneous.
2. The general idea or design of the artwork can be sketched in with pencil or light-colored paint and brush.
3. A large, flat brush is useful for painting in large areas of color. Background colors, like skies, should be painted in first.
4. Smaller, round brushes are good for adding lines.
5. Adding colors from the background into the foreground, and vice versa, helps to pull a painting together.
6. Details and textures should be added last.
7. Different brushes, such as oil brushes, varnish brushes, scrub brushes, and toothbrushes, produce different textures.
8. The edge of a large, flat brush can give a fine line, which, when turned in one stroke, becomes a wide line. Some artists prefer only large brushes.
9. A pointed brush gives a graceful thick-to-thin line when the pressure applied on the point of the brush is varied. Oriental painting is based on this technique.
10. Dipping the brush in paint, removing the excess, and then flaring the brush (so that it looks like a messed-up hairdo) allows the creation of many fine lines with one stroke.
11. A broad, flat brush can be separated into three parts, each of which is loaded with a different-colored paint. This creates three different-colored lines with one stroke. An alternative is to load one side of the brush with one color and the other side with a different color.
12. A broad brush loaded with paint and a little water dragged over a rough paper gives an effect called dry brush. Dry brush is used to indicate foliage and to produce a stippled effect.
13. Brush-cleaning water should be changed regularly so that it is fresh and clean, not muddy.
14. Brushes must be thoroughly cleaned before changing paint colors.
15. Colors can be mixed either on the palette or on the paper or canvas.
16. Sponges, clean damp brushes, cotton swabs, or cloth can be used to remove paint while it is still damp, if changes need to be made. These tools can also be used to add color.
17. Ordinary household bleach will remove unwanted areas of color. It works best with colored inks.
18. Crayon, wax, or rubber cement "resist" water and paints applied over them. This technique is called **crayon-resist.**
19. Blending involves laying in the top stroke with a dark color and then adding more water with each stroke down the page.
20. Clear, unmixed colors give the strongest contrast. More pigment and less water produce the deepest, most intense color.

21. In watercolor, overlays of paint create interesting color combinations and more intense color. The underlayer of paint must be dry before the overlay is applied. This is called **glazing.**
22. Strong contrasts of light and dark values give paintings vitality and crispness.
23. Space can be indicated with washes, if color is graduated from intense to light. Strong colors come forward; muted colors recede.
24. Textures can represent forms. For example, dry sponge or paper towel painting can make textures that indicate leaves on a tree.
25. Each cake of paint should be brushed clean. Paints squeezed from tubes will harden and can be saved and mixed with water for use another time.
26. Paintings can be matted, framed, or mounted.

PRINTMAKING

Printmaking involves printing from various surfaces. For example, the ancient Chinese carved seals from stone and then inked the stone carvings, applied them to paper or fabric, and used the printed seals as identification symbols. In the fifteenth century, the invention of the first printing press by Johannes Gutenberg changed the course of printing history. Today, books, magazines, and prints are taken for granted because they are so readily available.

Elementary students are capable of exploring a number of interesting print processes, including:

1. **Rubbings** are the images made by placing paper over a raised, incised, or textured surface and then rubbing over the paper with crayons, pencils, chalk, or other colored substances. Interesting surfaces to experiment with include coins, leaves, lace, walls, and concrete floors.
2. **Stamped prints** are the images made by incising designs into various materials, such as potatoes, plasticene, clay, sponges, and cardboard, dipping the incised material into paint or ink, and then pressing (stamping) onto paper or fabric. Stamped designs can also be made with jar lids, sticks, "found" objects, doilies, shells, linoleum blocks, Styrofoam, and forks and spoons (fig. 8.21). A simple stamping pad can be made from Styrofoam trays, pie tins, or plastic boxes by placing a sponge or toweling paper into the container and adding water (if needed) and tempera paint. One pad can be shared by several students.
3. **Stencil prints** are the images created by cutting out a design or shape from a piece of cardboard or other material, thereby leaving an open shape, and then placing the stencil over a piece of paper, and filling in the design with chalks or paints (fig. 8.22). Oak tagboard works well for this.
4. **Monoprints** ("one print") are the images created by using brushes, brayer rollers, or even cotton swabs to

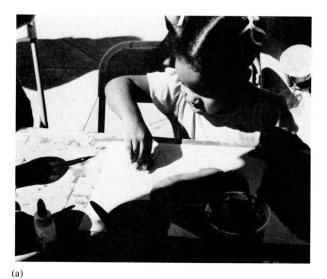

(a)

(b)

(c)

Figure 8.21   Stamped prints can be made from a variety of items, including vegetables and sponges. In (*b*), students combined their linoleum block prints as a group project to make a calendar. In (*c*), incised styrofoam is inked and printed. Note reverse word "skull."

Figure 8.22 Stencil and chalk prints can create interesting visual illusions.

Figure 8.23 Monoprinting involves applying paint to plastic or glass. The completed print design is then transferred to the paper.

apply paint (tempera for classroom use) to a nonporous surface, such as metal, plastic, or glass, and then drawing designs or images into the paint. A sheet of paper is then placed on top of the finished design, and the back of the paper is rubbed gently with the hand or the back of a spoon to transfer the paint to the paper (fig. 8.23).

PUPPETS

Puppets invite elementary students to create, perform, imagine, and express ideas. They also provide a means of tying in with other areas of elementary study in that students can, for example, use puppets to act out historical events or to portray characters from books or paintings. Because puppets usually require group activity, they encourage social interaction among students.

Puppet construction can range from the simple sock or paper-bag puppet to the more complex marionette. Papier-mâché heads are excellent for hand, stick, or marionette puppets (fig. 8.24). Chart 8.3 provides directions for making papier-mâché puppets.

CLAY

Clay is a manipulative material that can be molded to form aesthetic and utilitarian objects (figs. 8.26 and 8.27). The basic methods of construction include:

1. **Hand or pinch method.** The thumb is inserted into a ball of clay. The clay ball is then rotated while the thumb pushes out and "pinches" a pot shape. Elbows, knees, or such objects as stones or balls also can be used to press into the center.
2. **Slab construction.** A slab of clay is rolled out like pie dough. Then shapes are cut from the clay and joined

Figure 8.24 Construction of hand puppets included making papier-mâché heads.

together to form other shapes. Clay boxes or cups are often made in this way (fig. 8.28). Outside clay surfaces can then be inscribed with designs or "found" objects.
3. **Draping.** Clay slabs can also be draped over forms, such as bowls, rocks, dishes, flower holders, and so on, to achieve that particular shape (fig. 8.29).
4. **Coil method.** Rolls of clay (like snake forms) are used to build such items as large or small containers, model buildings, and animals. The coils can be any size and are rolled on a flat surface. The coils are joined by wetting and scoring the surfaces where the sides and ends meet and blending them together (fig. 8.30).

Clay must be fired in a kiln to dry it completely and to make it hard. Then glazing techniques can be brushed, dipped, or poured over the clay.

If a kiln is not available, a clay substitute for modeling is salt ceramic. Two recipes for salt ceramic are provided in chart 8.4.

chart 8.3

How to Make Papier-Maché Puppets

1. **Materials:** Newspaper strips (about ½-inch wide), white paper towels torn into ½-inch strips, wheat paste, shallow bowl, paint, felt-tip pens, large and small paint brushes, newspaper, masking tape, fabric for making the body, sandpaper, and various miscellaneous materials, such as yarn, lace, braid, feathers, cloth, or old jewelry.

2. **Procedure:** Decide on the size of puppet head that you want, and then crunch or roll the newspaper into a ball that size and secure the ball with masking tape. Push one or two of your fingers into the newspaper ball to make a hole. Mix the wheat paste and water in a shallow bowl. Pull the newspaper strips through the paste, and then wipe off excess paste with your fingers. Carefully wrap the strips around the newspaper ball, keeping your fingers tucked inside the hole. Do this three times with newspaper strips and one time with white paper-towel strips. Allow the papier-maché puppet head to dry thoroughly in the air for several days.

   After the papier-maché is dry, sandpaper any surfaces that you want to have a smooth texture. Cover the papier-maché with a single coat of white paint. After the paint has dried thoroughly, add features to the puppet head with a brush or felt-tip pens (fig. 8.25). Fabric for the puppet's body can be gathered and glued to the inside of the hole in the puppet head. Additional materials, such as yarn, construction paper, lace, buttons, and gift wrap, can be glued on for features or decorative elements.

Figure 8.25 Fashioned from a crunched newspaper ball, "instant" papier-maché was applied to the basic shape and painted to create this puppet head.

Figure 8.26 Pancake shapes were formed with clay, then various tools and materials were used to apply textures. The shapes became neck ornaments.

Figure 8.27 A creative dinosaur is formed from clay, using a variety of construction techniques.

Figure 8.28 Slab shapes are built into clay containers.

Figure 8.29 Clay slabs can be draped over forms to achieve a particular shape—in this case, a plate.

Figure 8.30 Coils can be used to create a variety of clay items, including interesting sculptures.

WEAVING AND TEXTILES

Weavings (interlacings of various materials to form a fabric, texture, or design) can be created from various yarns, grasses, twigs, feathers, straws, and other found materials. Simple looms can be made out of Styrofoam trays, as well as old picture frames. (See figs. 2.2 and 9.8, and p. 167.)

Other possible textile activities for the classroom include:

- **Tie-dye,** the process whereby knots are tied in cloth, such as a T-shirt, and then the cloth is dipped into liquid cloth dyes.
- **Stenciling,** the process whereby an impervious material, such as a sheet of paper or cardboard, that is perforated with lettering or a design is placed on cloth. Paint or dye is then applied over the stencil, and the lettering or design is transferred to the cloth.
- **Batik,** the process whereby designs are applied to cloth with candle wax or crayons and then paint is brushed over the designs.

chart   8.4

How to Make Salt Ceramic

Salt ceramic can be made with either of the two recipes that follow. Salt ceramic dries to a rock hardness without being baked.

1. Mix equal amounts of salt and flour. Add water and food coloring until you get the proper consistency for modeling.
2. Mix 1 cup salt with ½ cup cornstarch in the top of a double boiler. Then pour in ¾ cup water and a small amount of food coloring. Place this mixture over the bottom part of the double boiler and warm it slowly, over low heat. Stir continuously until the mixture has a thick, smooth consistency (about four minutes). Place on a sheet of waxed paper and cool. Knead to make it soft and pliable.

ART AND COMPUTERS

As new technology is developed, students and artists find ways to apply these methods in their artwork. Exciting areas of technology are opening unexplored artistic frontiers, providing opportunities to create in different and visually stimulating ways.

This discussion of technology looks at two aspects: using the computer to produce artworks and using the computer to learn about art.

Producing Art with the Computer

Computers can be fascinating tools for creative problem solving in art. Students practice active learning, learn programs, are self-directed, work independently, question information, sustain greater periods of concentration, and reflect on their own thinking as they develop and analyze independent solutions and create expressive visual effects and imagery. Often, the final learning outcomes are challenging and unpredictable (fig. 8.31).

Software programs that are useful for creating art on the computer include: Fine Artist, Painter, Kid Pix, Flying Colors, Draw to Learn/Dinosaur Edition, Coreldraw, Adobe Illustrator, Super Paint, Sketcher, and 3D Swivel Pro. Most of these programs involve using an array of paint tools and visual effects to invent, magnify, shrink, rotate, brighten, fill, and even animate images (fig. 8.32).

For example, the software program Fine Artist contains seventy-six patterns and colors and seventy-two paintbrush styles with brushes of different sizes and shapes. The program also includes lessons on basic art techniques, such as three-dimensional perspective and drawing on a grid. Special tools allow you to enlarge, magnify, stretch, flip, rotate, and move images. You can also add sounds and animation and create posters, comic strips, stickers, and multimedia picture shows, to name several possible projects.

Other fascinating software programs allow you to take a photograph and change it into a drawing, which can then be modified in an infinite number of ways. Or a photograph or image can be scanned into the computer. The image can then be transferred into a paint program and modified at will.

Computer images can also be printed and then used with other media. They can be drawn upon, painted, photocopied, or collaged. After such changes, they can be scanned back into the computer for even more modifications. The creative potential and inventive process of computers excite the imagination, as the teaching example that follows exemplifies.

Figure 8.31   Computers become tools for creating art imagery as students experiment with new technology. Photo by James Cowlin © 1995.

(a)   (b)

Figure 8.32   Young student artworks were created with a computer.

In addition to this teaching example, motivations that will give you ideas for how to relate computers and art in the classroom are presented in the "Ideas and Motivations" section at the end of the chapter. Adapt the activities to your students' grade-level capabilities. Chart 8.5 provides a vocabulary of computer terms.

Teaching Example: Modern Matisse

Lesson Plan

>   **Objective:** To create a lesson plan that incorporates art history and art elements and that uses the computer as the medium.
>   **Materials:** Computer and monitor, input device (mouse or stylus), graphics software, visual materials for art history background on Henri Matisse, computer printer
>   **Class time:** Four one-hour classes
>   **Student prerequisite skills:** Basic computer skills incorporated into lesson plan

Motivation: When I was first introduced to the computer at an in-service for art teachers last year, the possibilities for incorporating computer graphics into my grades 1–6 art curriculum excited me. How could I use this modern technology, with its built-in student motivation, to help teach art? By the end of last year, I had convinced our principal of the benefits of buying graphics hardware and software programs with our computer budget. Each school in our district is equipped with a computer lab consisting of twenty Apple IIe computers and a printer. With our budget, we purchased five mice, five koala pads, and two graphics software programs. A computer demonstration for the students, teachers, assistant principal, and principal confirmed my belief in the computer as a highly motivating art medium.

Since computer room time was limited, I could only fit a short introduction to computer graphics at all grade levels into the school year. After-school computer graphics labs served as the hands-on time for those students who could attend. The labs were filled, and names crowded waiting lists every day. The excitement and curiosity of computer graphics did not wane.

I wanted to start this new school year with a more concentrated computer graphics program with fifth- and sixth-grade level students. Our major limitation is having only ten input devices and an average of thirty students per class with only one hour for art each week. I wanted a project that would reinforce traditionally learned art elements, such as line, shape, color, pattern, and space, and that would also incorporate art history and computer graphics. Thus, the lesson I call "Modern Matisse" was developed.

Procedure: Henri Matisse (1869–1954) is considered one of the major forces in the development of modern art. He is famous for his simplification of form, sense of space, and use of brilliant color and bold patterns in his compositions. I presented an introduction to Matisse to my fifth- and sixth-grade classes, concentrating on his use of interior spaces including a figure, a table, and a vase of flowers, such as in his work *The Purple Robe.*

The students' first assignment was to create a composition incorporating a figure, a table, and a vase of flowers with contour lines. We used student models to get our figure drawing started.

Next, we entered the computer room for a demonstration of the unique advantages the computer has to offer this lesson. Instructions are given to the computer by touching a stylus to a graphics tablet or by moving a mouse and using commands in a menu at the edges of the monitor screen. The commands create effects, such as repetition of pattern; change of stroke width; variation of colors, shapes, and lines; editing; and zooming in on one portion to create detail. Wouldn't Henri Matisse have loved to create colors and patterns at the click of a button, rearranging and changing compositions until the "right" look was achieved?

During the first demonstration for students, a Matisse-like composition was sketched on a computer, using the

chart 8.5

Vocabulary of Computers

Baud A unit that measures the speed of electronic data transmission through a modem. The higher the number, the faster the modem operates. Often used interchangeably with bits per second, or bps, although the two terms mean different things technically.

BBS A computer bulletin board system. Thousands exist around the world. They can be operated by anyone with the right equipment and software. Most are text-only and offer discussion areas, games, and software that can be downloaded. Some offer access to the Internet. Some charge membership fees.

Commercial online service A giant BBS that charges users monthly fees for access to vast libraries of software, games, clubs, discussion groups, and information, including newspapers and magazines. Most offer colorful graphics and the ability to navigate by clicking with a mouse. The three largest services are America Online, CompuServe, and Prodigy.

Communications software Programs that enable computers to "talk" via modems and telephone lines. Most computers running Windows already have a simple communications program, called Terminal. Others include ProComm and Crosstalk.

Cyberspace A generic term used to describe the intangible "place" computer users visit when they go online.

Download The process of using a modem and telephone line to copy computer files from a remote computer—such as a BBS or a commercial online service—to your computer, where they can be saved and used. Software, graphics, text, video, and even audio files can be downloaded. Opposite of *upload*.

E-mail Electronic mail sent from one computer user to another. E-mail can be sent over networks, such as within an office building, or through modems and telephone lines to users on BBSs, commercial online services, or the Internet.

FAQ Frequently asked questions. New users tend to ask the same questions, so many spots in cyberspace offer FAQ files that can be read at leisure. Reading FAQs can avoid online blunders.

Fax modem Computer device that operates both as a modem and a fax machine, enabling users to link with remote computers via telephone lines, and to send and receive faxes.

Information superhighway Term used to describe electronic networks that link people around the world. To purists, that means the Internet. Others include cable television and telephone networks. Same as *information highway*, the *infobahn*, and the *I-way*.

Internet The worldwide computer network that links millions of computer users at schools, businesses, government institutions, military installations, and homes.

Modem A device that enables remote computers to be linked via telephone lines. Some are installed inside computers. Others are external, connected to computers with cables.

Online Electronically linked, as in, "I'm online with America Online." Similar to *cyberspace*.

World Wide Web A part of the Internet that supports graphics and allows users to navigate by clicking with a mouse. It features hypertext, or words, phrases, or images usually outlined in blue that, when clicked on, send users to related files or other computer systems anywhere in the world. Also referred to as WWW or the Web.

---

black outlines prominent in Matisse's style. Students' excitement grew as the composition was filled with color and pattern using the FLOOD/FILL command. To create a wallpaper pattern for the background of the composition, we created one floral element, "captured" it, "copied" it, and then "pasted" that element over and over to the walls of the composition. The same technique, using the CAPTURE, COPY, and PASTE commands, was used to fill a vase with a perfect rose. We used the ZOOM command on the figure's face to add a touch of color to her eyes and to even up her nose and chin. Because we could change one pixel at a time, students saw the program's touch-up and refinement capabilities. After this vast amount of technical information had been presented, each eager student had a ten-minute hands-on session with a computer to explore the possibilities.

During the next sessions, students began drawing their Matisse composition on the computer screen and mastering their control of the elusive cursor with a mouse or koala pad. Frustration was common because control results only

from practice, and our short hands-on time of ten to fifteen minutes per student did not allow much practice. The ideal situation would be one computer and one input device per student. After-school computer labs, however, helped to alleviate some of the time problems.

Measuring Achievement and Conclusion: The results of this lesson were very satisfying for both teacher and students. The students learned about composition, figure drawing, Henri Matisse, color, pattern, and the use of the computer as an art tool in one four-week lesson (fig. 8.33). This lesson could be the sketchpad for a painting project, the first in a series of art history lessons, an introduction to computer graphics, or the stepping-stone to more complex and challenging art assignments. We have only begun to "click" on how the computer can be used in the art curriculum. If only Henri Matisse could see us now! (See chart 8.6 for a sample computer art quiz and chart 8.7 for a sample computer art vocabulary quiz.)

Submitted by Barbara Hartman, art teacher

(a)

(b)

Figure 8.33   Computer-generated artwork for the "Modern Matisse" lesson by fifth- and sixth-grade students. Teacher: Barbara Hartman.

Learning about Art with the Computer

Would you like to visit the Louvre Museum in Paris? How about the National Gallery of Art in Washington, D.C.? Would you be interested in sampling art, music, or literature from around the world? All of this is possible with the use of **commercial online services,** such as America Online, the Internet's World Wide Web, CompuServe, Prodigy, Microsoft, and AT&T. You can zoom along the information superhighway with just a click of your mouse. Online services allow you to be a modern-day explorer, limited only by your imagination. (See chart 8.5 for a vocabulary of terms familiar to users of computer online services.)

The Internet Connection offers a World Wide Web browser that will take the user to the corner of Internet that supports graphics and permits the use of hypertext. **Hypertext** is the words, phrases, or images that, when clicked on, electronically link the user to related files or even other computers around the world. Once you are connected to the

Web, the world is at your fingertips. Among many others, there are Web sites for the Louvre Museum, for schools and universities, and for government agencies.

New **interactive multimedia programs** usually are developed to involve a computer, CD-ROM, and laser videodisc player. These programs can consist of any or all integrations of a variety of media, such as text, graphics, animation, still photos, video, music, and voice. These programs also permit users to interact with the text, graphics, audio, and video information that is offered. For example, some programs have options for reducing, enlarging, and navigating around and to a graphic image and for pausing, fast forwarding, rewinding, stopping, and freezing a video frame. Some allow interaction with texts in a variety of languages and have on-screen dictionaries with word pronunciation recordings, as well as audio recordings that can be slowed or accelerated. Many of these programs are effective because they are multisensory and have great appeal due to the digital quality, voice, music, sound effects, photos, dynamic graphics, animation, and video.

A list of some interactive multimedia programs follows. The museum offerings are more indexing than instructional and are valuable resources for both teachers and students.

- American Art from the National Gallery. Laser videodisc with Voyager's laserguide. The Voyager Company.
- Ancient Lands. Interactive CD-ROM. Microsoft.
- Annabel's Dream of Ancient Egypt. Interactive CD-ROM. Texas Caviar.
- The Art Institute of Chicago: With Open Eyes. Interactive CD-ROM, with over two hundred works from the permanent collection. Art Institute of Chicago.
- Columbus: Encounter, Discovery, and Beyond. Interactive videodisc. IBM (EduQuest).

chart 8.6
Computer Art Quiz

Student name _____

1. Describe your project.
2. What artist(s) or style of art did you look at for ideas?
3. How did you design your project? Describe the art elements and principles used.
4. What did you like, and dislike, about using the computer as the art medium for this project?
5. What tools and menu options did you use?
6. What problems did you have with your project, and how did you solve them?
7. How did you accomplish your goals?

chart 8.7
Computer Art Vocabulary Quiz: Example

1. The famous artist we studied for our computer graphics unit was

    a. Vincent van Gogh.
    b. Henri Matisse.
    c. Pablo Picasso.

2. One of the famous paintings we examined to study this artist's style was titled

    a. The Starry Night.
    b. The Three Musicians.
    c. The Purple Robe.

3. The three compositional elements that needed to be included in your picture were _____ , _____ , and _____ .

   Use some of the following vocabulary words to fill in the blanks for items 4–15:

Menu	Figure	Input device	Goodies	Edit
SAVE	Cursor	Dazzle Draw	Pattern	File
Tools	DELETE	Scroll bar	Monitor	LOAD

4. The center of interest in your composition was the _____ .

5. Repeating lines, shapes, colors or designs creates a _____ .

6. The LOAD, SAVE, and DELETE commands are under _____ .

7. The CLEAR PICTURE command is under _____ .

8. The CUT and PASTE commands are under _____ .

9. The PAINTBRUSH, SPRAY PAINT, and ZOOM options are under _____ .

10. The screen we viewed our graphics images on is called a _____ .

11. The program we used for computer graphics is called _____ .

12. To draw on the computer with this program, you need an _____ , such as a mouse or koala pad.

13. _____ is the command used to take information from a data disk and put it on the computer monitor.

14. _____ is the command used to take information from the computer monitor and put it on a data disk.

15. _____ is the command that will erase your file.

16. The disk drive light should be on when you load or unload a disk. **T or F**

17. Handle a disk carefully by holding it by the label edge. **T or F**

- The Further Adventures of Annabel the Cat. Interactive CD-ROM. Texas Caviar.
- The Louvre Art Museum. Vols. 1, 2, and 3. Videodisc. The Voyager Company.
- Ludwig van Beethoven's Symphony No. 9. Interactive computer and CD-ROM program. The Voyager Company.
- The National Galley of Art. Laser videodisc with Voyager's laserguide. The Voyager Company.
- The National Gallery of London. Interactive CD-ROM. Microsoft, Inc.
- The North American Indians: 500 Nations. CD-ROM. Microsoft, Inc.
- The Ultimate Frank Lloyd Wright. CD-ROM. Microsoft, Inc.
- Van Gogh Revisited. Laser videodisc with Voyager's laserguide. The Voyager Company.

Figure 8.34 Perception is increased when using a camera.

PHOTOGRAPHY

Cameras are powerful tools of creative expression. They capture the magic of our world—from microscopic organisms to heavenly bodies at the far reaches of the universe (fig. 8.34).

Even more than that, however, cameras allow us to express a unique point of view. When you put your eye to the camera viewfinder, you immediately isolate for an instant in space and time a particular view that you alone can see. The resulting photograph shows your view—your composition, your contrasts of lights and darks, your combinations of certain colors, forms, and action—a view that can be studied and perceived again and again.

When you draw or paint on a surface, you are doing the same thing: You are isolating some forms and saying that these are the most interesting and most expressive of the way you feel about something. There are infinite ways of saying the same thing—whether with words, paint, movement, music, unlimited combinations of forms, or

chart 8.8
Vocabulary of Photography

Aperture The opening in the camera lens that permits light to enter.

Point of view The position of the viewer in relationship to the scene.

Foreground The area of a photograph that is nearest the viewer.

Middle ground The area of a photograph that is between the foreground and the background.

Background The area of a photograph that is farthest from the viewer.

Low-angle shot A shot taken with the camera held at a low angle.

High-angle shot A shot taken with the camera held at a high angle.

Contrast Variation between light and dark objects in a photograph. Determined by the amount, source, and direction of the light source.

Shadows Created when rays from one or more light sources are cut off by an interposed opaque object. Shadows may be sharp or diffused (scattered), depending on the light source and distance.

Value The variation of grays or tones in the photograph.

F-stop The aperture size indicated on the camera by an F-number. The larger the opening, the smaller the number. In many cameras, the F-stop is fixed and not adjustable.

Lens A glass or transparent plastic material that is made with two opposing surfaces. The surfaces change the direction of light, focusing it at a place on the film. Lenses are classified on the basis of how they bend light rays.

Exposure The length of time light is applied to light-sensitive materials (for example, film).

Emulsion The shiny, light-sensitive coating on photographic film or paper. The coating is a gelatin substance that contains silver halide crystals.

Shutter The camera device for opening and closing the aperture of a lens in order to expose the film.

Viewfinder A small, rectangular window that shows the area of a subject to be included in a picture. While helping to eliminate extraneous, nonessential elements from a picture, viewfinders also allow the viewer to select and "see" realistic perspective.

Focus To adjust a lens so that the image it projects has maximum sharpness.

Stop bath A mildly acidic solution used to check photographic development of a negative or print.

Fixer A solution that fixes, or makes permanent, on film or paper the image brought out in development.

film. You say it in the way you feel is the most expressive for you, and your way will be unique because you are seeing through your eyes and your mind.

Cameras range in complexity from the very sophisticated to the very simple and to even "disposable" varieties. Every classroom should have at least one camera available for student use. Chart 8.8 provides a vocabulary of photography terms.

VIDEO AND FILM

Video and film cameras produce some of the newer art forms of our visual world today—a moving picture whose excitement is heightened by action and a constantly changing scene. Video and film cameras can instantly gather information, capture interactions, document events, and spontaneously incorporate movement and sound into a creatively told story.

Because video and film cameras do not record static scenes, but scenes in which the challenge of action has been added, the final film can be a curious collection of intentional, planned happenings, mixed in with unforeseen "accidents" that may add to or detract from the film's intended message. For example, images may become out of focus or have inadequate light exposure; or the zoom feature may increase feelings of depth and/or provide ultra-closeups (see chart 8.9 for a vocabulary of video and film terms). At any rate, the final video camera film can accentuate and recreate definite feelings and emotions with details that the mind alone is not fast enough to capture.

In many schools, students have access to video cameras. Some schools provide video studio experiences for their gifted students (fig. 8.35). Students at other schools write and produce daily newscasts that are broadcast over closed circuit television to the student body. Many school districts conduct video workshops for teachers and students to illustrate how to use video equipment, the equipment's capabilities, and the many and varied uses for video cameras within the classroom.

Sometimes, teachers videotape art demonstrations or the talks of visiting artists so that students who were not present at the time can still benefit from the talk or demonstration. Other teachers have students select a topic or theme, do background research, write skits or stories, and prepare storyboards and graphics. Then they videotape the students' presentation.

Various cameras can also be used to document elementary school displays and events, such as concerts, dance performances, and social gatherings; to record information on various cultures and on students' ethnic backgrounds; to document field trips to galleries, museums, and other classrooms; to preserve on tape a slice of community life; to capture students creating art in the classroom; and to document historical events (fig. 8.36). These videos can then be shared and reviewed in the classroom, or they can be sent

Figure 8.35 In a gifted program, students produce their own video.

chart 8.9
Vocabulary of Video and Film

Dolly To move the camera toward or away from the object being filmed, using a wheeled platform.

Pan To move the camera left or right.

Tilt To move the camera up toward the ceiling or down toward the floor.

CU Close-up shot.

MCU Medium close-up shot.

LS Long shot (full view of the background).

WS Wide shot.

Zoom To change the focus of the lens without moving the camera (the effect of moving toward or away from the object being filmed).

Dissolve To fade into one picture from another or to fade out of one picture to another.

Fade To lessen the sound or brightness of the picture (such as "fade to black").

Freeze-frame A static picture produced from a videotape recording.

Soft focus To produce an image having unsharp outlines.

Backlight To illuminate the object being filmed from behind.

Figure 8.36   Video or film cameras document events at a teacher workshop.

home with students to be used for written reviews and self-critiques. They also can be presented at community locations, such as libraries, to illustrate, for example, the quality of the school's art program or to recruit new students. Videotapes such as these are also often welcome and worthwhile at parent-teacher meetings and at meetings with school administrators.

Students' visual perceptions are enhanced as they use light, space, movement, time, and the art elements (line, shape, value, shading, pattern, and so on) in their compositions. Critical analysis of professional techniques and tapes, as well as of other students' tapes, is especially helpful in this regard.

PROJECTORS

In the regular classroom, overhead projectors and slide projectors usually are used to magnify information, images, or photographs on transparencies onto a vertical screen or wall. In the art classroom, however, use of both of these technologies can provide students with an amazing spectrum of creative possibilities and viewpoints.

For example, students can create their own slides from a variety of materials and then experiment with projecting one or more of these slides onto screens or some other type of surface to create unique images (figs. 8.37 and 8.38). Artists often use slide projectors to project images onto paper or canvas. In this way, they can copy images and lettering. Or overhead projectors can be used to create dynamic light shows that offer a spectrum of visual distortions, exaggerations, and illusions. Motivations in the "Ideas and Motivations" section provide all the details.

IDEAS AND MOTIVATIONS

Adapt the following ideas as to students' grade-level capabilities.

Portraits

The ideas that follow will help you to become more skilled at drawing portraits and also can be used with elementary students.

1. Study and draw the shapes and proportions of the skull and skeleton.
2. Feel the forms in your face, neck, and shoulders. Let your finger move from forehead to chin, then from side to side (cheekbone to cheekbone).
3. Use a pencil to compare the measurements and proportions of various facial features.
4. Ask three individuals to stand next to each other, and compare the shapes of their heads, eyes, noses, mouths, and hairstyles.
5. Build clay models of heads.
6. Draw self-portraits on mirrors with felt-tip markers, and compare proportions of your head.
7. Make contour drawings of faces and features (see chapter 3 for an explanation of contour drawing).
8. Practice cross-contour drawings of faces and features (see the example in figure 8.39).
9. Make gesture drawings of faces and features (see chapter 3 for an explanation of gesture drawing).
10. Make positive/negative-shape drawings of faces.
11. Pretend that there is a fly crawling across your face. Draw what the insect sees and finds.
12. Place a spotlight on the face—first from the side, then from the front, from the back, from above, and finally, from below. Study how the different positions of the light change the way the forms appear on the face.
13. Draw a face with just shadows (no lines).
14. Experiment with drawing faces using different tools and media (for example, pencils, pens, charcoal, brushes and ink).
15. Study a variety of artwork reproductions, and analyze how other artists have drawn faces.

(a)

(b)

Figure 8.37 Using slides of themselves, students project their own images onto T-shirts to create self-portraits.

16. Draw individual features and fragments of faces.
17. Combine an assortment of different eyes, noses, mouths, and so on in new faces.
18. Abstract a face.
19. Make a face collage with magazine photos.
20. Make "feeling" portraits that show how you look when you are angry, happy, sad, and so on.

21. Pretend that you are a character in history, such as George Washington. Draw a portrait of what you think you would look like.
22. How do you think Pablo Picasso would draw you? Draw a portrait.
23. Pretend that you are an insect, a bird, or an animal. Draw a portrait of what you think you would look like (fig. 8.40).
24. What do you think you would look like if you came from the planet Saturn? Draw a portrait.
25. Draw a portrait of what you think you would look like if sitting under a red light. Do the same for sitting under a blue light. How do you think you would feel in each of these situations?
26. Draw self-portraits that show you:
    - Brushing your hair
    - Cleaning your teeth
    - Eating your favorite candy
    - Turning your head inside out
    - Your brain
    - Wearing your favorite hat or jewelry
    - The secret you
27. In a self-portrait, use the two or three colors that best express the way you think or feel.
28. Experiment with using unusual materials, such as string, sandpaper, beads, and so on, to make portraits.
29. What can you do with just your eyes—stare, blink, squint, wink, frown, cross? With just your nose? With just your mouth?
30. Experiment with drawing different facial expressions. What expressions do you make with your eyes, nose, mouth, and ears when you are sad, happy, and angry? When you are eating, sleeping, laughing, crying, yawning, shouting, whistling, and sneezing? How do moods change your appearance? What do you look like when you have a cold?
31. Make portraits that reflect a feeling or mood (fig. 8.41). For example:
    - Put color washes in the background, leaving the space for the face white. Then draw only the eyes in the portrait.

Figure 8.38   During a workshop, teachers experiment with projectors for visual effects to create light shows.

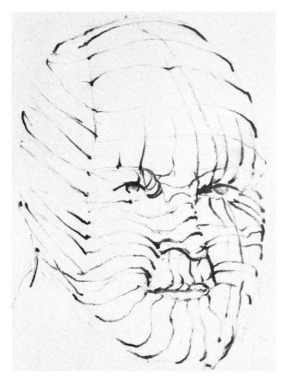

Figure 8.39   Cross-contour drawings help you to "feel the form."

Figure 8.40   Student drawings of self-portraits as an insect, bird, or animal can be self-revealing.

(a)

- Draw a profile face, emphasizing the hair's importance by putting various brush strokes and forms into the hair, while only suggesting with broad color the forms for the features.
- Split the paper in half, putting one color on one side, another color on the other. Then draw into the painting with a delicate line for the features.
- Make the portrait one color (monochromatic), which usually invokes a strong mood.

32. Draw three contour or gesture poses of the head from three views, and superimpose the poses, letting the forms intersect and overlap.
33. Make photocopies of a portrait photograph, and then draw into the photocopies with various interpretations (fig. 8.42).
34. Try drawing portraits of famous heroes (see plate 13).

The Human Figure

1. Posing the model is important for informal and exciting compositions. Study and discuss various figure styles, techniques, and poses as painted by

(b)

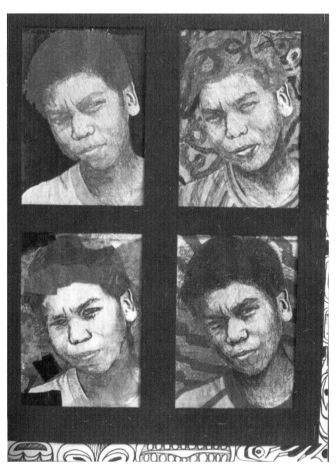

Figure 8.41   Both (*a*) and (*b*) are self-portraits of the same individual (Geneva Farthing, art teacher) but reflect dramatically different feelings.

Figure 8.42   Portrait photographs are photocopied and then embellished with art tools to show different interpretations.

Leonardo da Vinci, Rembrandt, Edgar Degas, Henry Matisse, Vincent van Gogh, Pablo Picasso, Ben Shahn, Maurice Lasansky, Roy Lichtenstein, and Mel Ramos.

2. Study and draw the skeleton of the human body, paying particular attention to the structure of the hand and foot and to where the figure bends, turns, and twists. Do several gesture drawings of these areas.

3. Lie on white butcher paper, and have someone draw a silhouette around your body. Then within the silhouette, draw in significant forms and details (fig. 8.43).

4. Use flat, angular shapes to do an abstract drawing of the head and figure.

5. Draw the roundness of facial forms using shading. Then try drawing hands this way.

6. Draw the face and figure with cross-contour surface lines only (see fig. 8.39 for an example).

7. Draw parts of figures, using models (fig. 8.44).

8. Draw the head and figure of the person you would be if you could be anyone in the world.

9. Experiment with head placement in head and figure drawings. The head sometimes appears more balanced when placed near the top, rather than in the middle, of the paper. Try placing only half of the head on the paper, with the other half off the side.

10. Draw a figure while paying particular attention to clothing details, such as collars, cuffs, and clothing curves around the body. Carefully observe and draw seams, wrinkles, and folds.

11. Practice many contour drawings (see chapter 3) of both the head and the figure. Look for significant details and unusual identifying forms. Exaggeration and distortion are part of the excitement of contour drawing.

12. Experiment with drawing friends and family members, focusing on their differences and similarities.

13. Study and draw the frameworks and proportions of different individuals.

14. Change your view of a figure—look at the model from behind, above, below—and try to draw this viewpoint.

15. Have the model hold an instrument, favorite object, or sports equipment, while dressed in costumes or uniforms. Pose the model in some interesting action. Add backgrounds and props to the composition.

16. Practice several quick gesture drawings (see chapter 3) of a figure to add to your understanding of the figure's placement in space. Show actions like playing baseball, doing gymnastics, playing golf, running, and so on.

17. Draw quick sketches of figures you see on television or in public places, such as the library or cafeteria.

18. Draw figures in environments. When does the figure dominate? When does the environment dominate?

19. Draw figures in composite groups—for example, a marching band in a parade, the characters in a play, people at the market.

Figure 8.43   Life-size figures (drawn around students as they lay on the floor) were decorated and painted by third-graders. The figures were then stuffed with newspapers and suspended from the ceiling to add whimsy and fantasy as they move in the air.

Figure 8.44   Ask students to model and draw parts of the figure. A sixth-grade student made this charcoal-and-pencil drawing.

20. Make a figure drawing that shows how you feel about your body.

21. Show emotions—happiness, sorrow, fear—through the drawing of the figure. Incorporate exaggeration and distortion.

22. Include only important parts in your figure drawing, and omit unimportant parts.

23. Draw yourself as a comic-strip character in a comic-strip situation.

24. Draw how you would look and feel if you were a puppet.

25. Engage in some body awareness exercises: How small (or big) are you compared to the rest of your family? How does your size compare to that of a cat? Assume the shape of a ball; how does your body feel? Squeeze your hands and fingers together—do you feel the joints? Reach for a tall branch; how do you feel when you are stretching your spine and are on your tiptoes? Can you balance on one leg with the other leg straight out in back? Do a somersault; how does your spine curve?

26. What do a person's clothes tell you about that person? Do clothes tell others who you are and what you feel like?

27. Study the portraits and figures created by artists and reproduced in this book. For example, in this chapter, examine the self-portraits of Gustave Courbet and Vincent van Gogh in figure 8.5, *Young Girl at an Open Half-Door* by Rembrandt van Rijn (see fig. 10.3), *Lady with Beads* by Kees Van Dongen (fig. 8.45), *Indian Spinning* by Diego Rivera (fig. A.4 in appendix A), *Woman with Bird Cage* by Rufino Tamayo (fig. A.2 in appendix A), *The Bath* by Mary Cassatt (fig. 10.9), *On the Terrace* by Renoir (fig. 10.7), *At the Milliner's* by Edouard Manet (fig. 10.4), and the drawing by Norman Rockwell (fig. A.1 in appendix A). Analyze the various methods the artists used. What are the figures doing? What are they feeling? Are they realistic or more abstract?

Still Life

1. Do several gesture drawings (see chapter 3) of "found" objects around the room, such as the "squat" of a chair, the "droop" of a coat. Select and enlarge the drawing you feel is most successful.

2. Create a still-life composition from "found" objects. Draw the objects larger than life-size, and compose the arrangement as the objects are drawn. Some forms will go off the edge of the paper.

3. Select five objects in the room. Arrange them on a cloth and then draw only the basic geometric forms.

4. Draw closeups and details of fragments or sections of objects.

5. Make numerous contour drawings (see chapter 3) of still-life objects, including objects that have been randomly arranged.

6. Explore a theme, such as musical instruments, with contour drawing (see chapter 3), gesture drawing (see chapter 3), and modeled drawing (see chapter 4).

7. Attach one or several cut-up photographs to your drawing paper, and extend the ideas of the photographs by drawing.

8. Draw a selected object as it would look in three ways: (*a*) with X-ray vision (where both inside and outside are drawn in the same picture), (*b*) if it were exploding, and (*c*) if five views (top, bottom, sides, foreshortened, and exaggerated) of the object were superimposed.

9. Select three related or unrelated objects, and draw a still-life that suggests an emotion, such as fear, love, or hate.

10. Paint a still life using flat colors.

11. Explore how other artists have drawn still lifes. Then see how many ways you can draw them.

12. Analyze a variety of artworks to see how other artists arrange, interpret, and invent still lifes. For example, examine *Vas de Fleurs* by Odilon Redon (fig. 8.46) and *The Basket of Apples* by Paul Cézanne (see fig. 10.8).

Landscapes/Cityscapes

1. Draw imaginative views of earth and other planets from outer space.

2. Draw a landscape or cityscape as it would look in three ways: (*a*) with X-ray vision (where both inside and outside are drawn in the same picture), (*b*) if it were exploding, and (*c*) if three views of the landscape/cityscape were superimposed.

3. Draw a landscape of irregular free-form shapes, such as clouds.

4. Draw landscapes of imaginary forests, trips to an antique shop or junk store, invented stories or fantasies, flowers.

5. Create a composition based on an imaginary dream.

6. Create a composition that combines five unrelated objects or places.

7. Try drawing animals. Visit a taxidermist or nature museum to do sketches. If possible, bring in your own pets to draw.

8. Create a composition based on a poetic theme, such as poems about "If I Could Visit Anywhere in the World" or "If I Were a Christmas Tree in a Forest."

9. Create landscape/cityscape compositions that convey moods (a foggy morning, a sunrise).

10. Create landscape/cityscape compositions that convey "noise" and "silence."

11. With a group, make sketching tours of the school and community. Then, as a group, enlarge the sketches to mural size.

12. Draw the view of looking down an alley. Exaggerate foreshortenings.

13. Draw blowups of architectural details seen in churches, government buildings, and old houses.

14. Practice drawing factories, bridges, rivers, harbors, zoos, amusement parks, tennis courts, football games, unusual houses, skyscrapers, and other city buildings.

15. Study and draw nature forms under a microscope. Then enlarge your drawing to mural size.

16. Find, compare, and draw similar shapes in magnified leaf cells. Do the same with textures of a hillside.

Figure 8.45   Kees Van Dongen, *Lady with Beads.* 1923. Collection of Phoenix Art Museum, Gift of Mr. and Mrs. Donald D. Harrington.

17. Select one particular landscape view, and draw or paint it during different seasons and at different times of the day.

18. Draw and paint other "scapes," such as "flowerscapes," "moonscapes," "motorscapes," and "found-object scapes." You may want to place single drawings onto mural-size paper.

19. Study how other artists through the centuries have painted landscapes and cityscapes. For example, see *Purple Mountains, Vence* by Marsden Hartley (see fig. A.7 in appendix A), *Brooklyn Bridge* by John Marin (see fig. 10.19), and *Picnic of Changes* by Roland Peterson (fig. 8.47).

Figure 8.46 Odilon Redon, *Vas de Fleurs* (Vase of Flowers). Collection of Phoenix Art Museum, Bequest of Mrs. Oliver B. James.

Drawing

1. Use only geometric forms in a drawing. Use only free forms (indefinite shapes or invented forms) in a drawing. Combine geometric shapes and free forms in a single drawing.
2. Select an emotion—such as, love, hate, fear, anxiety, exhilaration, anger, loneliness, hope, joy—and express it in a drawing in abstract forms. Use color intuitively to describe the emotion.
3. Select two emotions, such as anger and joy, and try to make a drawing that expresses them in a psychological relationship, as in "anger giving way to joy."
4. Using free forms, geometric forms, and naturalistic forms, draw a blowup of the inside view of a flower until it fills the whole page. Show all the inside parts, such as the pistil and stamen. Explore the flower from the inside out. Add some imaginative forms to the basic flower.
5. Design a new flag, a new stamp, a label for a new product (see fig. 8.48).
6. Make pop-art blowup drawings of a single object, such as a shoe, an apple, or a coffeepot.
7. Draw optical illusions, such as a red circle on a green background next to a green circle on a red background.
8. Draw on various sizes and shapes of paper—long, skinny, round, triangular, and so on.

Figure 8.47 *Picnic of Changes* by Roland Petersen, University of California, Davis.

9. Draw a picture of what you would most like to do—for example, play sports or fly the space shuttle (fig. 8.49).

10. Make an "add-to" drawing mural. Tack up a 10-foot piece of mural-size paper. Ask students to add new ideas to it—how they feel and important happenings—whenever they wish.

11. Explore group mural drawing projects with such topics as "Life under the Sea," "The Workings of a Factory," "How Motors Work," "The Modern Abstract Artist," "Impressionist Artists," "Artists from Early America," "Women Artists," "Black Artists," "Costumes from

around the World," and many story-line themes (*Kidnapped, Through the Looking Glass, The Wizard of Oz,* and other favorites from literature).

12. Design a pattern for cloth.
13. Select a favorite artist, and draw using the same style (see fig. 8.50).
14. Create dress designs.
15. Draw designs for cars or furniture of the future.
16. Create drawings that illustrate other times and places.
17. Draw yourself as you would like to be in another life.
18. Draw and illustrate a story you have written.
19. Draw fantasy topics. Examples include: "The World of the Fingerprint," "My Secret Dream," "Mystery Island," "Through the Crystal Ball," "Inside a Dot," "The Bottom of the Sea," "When I Was an Elephant in Africa," "The Sorceress," "The Night I Caught Harry, the Giant," "Being a Tornado," "When I Was a Raindrop," "January 1, 1999," "My Trip on a Flying Saucer" (fig. 8.51).
20. Draw buildings and other important places in your town.
21. Use movie titles and television shows (for example, *The Lion King, Snow White, Aladdin*) as motivations for drawings.

(a)

Figure 8.48   A new, imaginative label for a can of beef ravioli created by a fifth-grader.

(b)

Figure 8.49   Aspirations—whether (*a*) playing sports or (*b*) flying the space shuttle—can be stimulating motivations.

Figure 8.51 Fantasy topics are excellent motivations for art.

Figure 8.50 After studying Joan Miró, students incorporated Miró's style and symbols into their own art work.

22. Study various artists' drawings through the centuries. Describe and analyze drawing techniques and materials.

Painting

1. Try the following exercise:
    a. Soak your paper under cold water. Then wet the table on which you plan to paint so that the paper will stay flat on it.
    b. Use 2- or 3-inch flat brushes, and brush on the paint in large areas. If the areas are still wet, the colors will run.
    c. Paint thin washes as well as thick pigment layers. Build up layers of paint, called **glazing.**
    d. Sponge over the painted areas, wet or dry. What happens?
    e. Soak up and wipe away some of the pigment with a sponge. Paint another area with the same sponge.
    f. Drip, blow, or run paint onto the wet paper. Watch how the paint moves.
    g. Pick up the paper and move the paint and washes around, causing them to flow in various directions and to create patterns and designs. Then use squeeze bottles or 4-inch pie tins to add paint to the paper. Some artists *pour* paint on surfaces.

    h. Use sticks or tongue depressors to scratch into the painted washes.
    i. Drop some ink into the wet wash and watch how the ink reacts differently from the paint. Experiment with dropping oil, starch, and glue into the wash.
    j. Try drawing into the wet paper and washes with pen and ink—black as well as colors. Different sizes of pen points create different lines. Watch how the ink spreads and creates colors and textures.
    k. Keep some areas of your painting wet; let other areas dry. Keep some white spaces open. The whites move throughout the design and keep the painting fresh and clean looking.
    l. Use heavy pigment to get intense color because, as your painting dries, some of the color will lose its intensity.
    m. Keep the washes fresh and clean. After your paper has dried, go into the painting again with transparent washes. This will build up and create depth and will also change the color.
    n. If you do not like an area, wipe out some color with a wet cloth, tissue, or brush.
    o. If you do not like the painting at all, try washing it out under the faucet and start again. You can do this with good watercolor paper but not with thin paper or drawing paper.
2. Try painting on different types of paper (such as butcher paper in various colors, newsprint, manila, sandpaper, and drawing paper), and investigate their resistance to the media.
3. Paint with unusual tools, such as combs, sides of cardboards, tongue depressors, squeeze bottles, facial tissues, toweling, aluminum foil, medicine droppers, brayer rollers, or small dowels or sticks.

4. Place ice on your paper, and add paints around the ice. Try adding table salt to wet paint for a different texture.

5. Paint glue on the paper. While the glue is still wet, add sand, soil, pencil shavings, table salt, or coffee grounds for different textures.

6. Hold the brush in different ways—like a pencil or like a spoon gripped like a shovel. Try twirling the brush.

7. Draw a single rhythmic line. Then repeat this line over and over, varying the pressure you apply.

8. Let water "drip" over the paper in spontaneous flows. Add color at the top of the drip, and observe what happens as the color flows.

9. Soak your paper, and then crinkle, wad, or crush the paper to create lines. Let the paper sit about five minutes. Then carefully add some color washes. Water will collect at the wrinkles, creating a "batik" look. Add more colors. Draw with pen lines over all.

10. Try covering your painting surface with wheat paste or glue as a base. Let the base dry before you paint.

11. "Doodle" with a paint brush to see what colors, feelings, and ideas emerge from your inner self.

12. Experiment with painting over a pencil, charcoal, or grease pencil drawing. Moisten the edges of color with a spray atomizer.

13. Try rubbing sandpaper across your paper surface to create textural effects, either before or after painting.

14. Experiment with the textures created by rubbing steel wool across the surface of a dry painting.

15. Try "puddling" colors onto an absorbent paper. Rather than have the colors run and blend, let each color dry before adding the next color.

16. Experiment with dripping, blowing (through straws), and blotting of paint, as well as with painting with string, sticks, bottle caps, and so on to add interesting textures.

17. Experiment with string painting, spatter painting (using old toothbrushes and combs), stencil painting (incorporating both the positive and negative cut stencil into the design), and spray painting.

18. Try painting with colors made from soaking old coffee grounds or tea. Experiment with other potential color sources.

19. Paint a head as if you were modeling it from clay. Think of the head as a series of forms, rather than as an outline. Use color to help pull out the forms from within the structure. Incorporate the background into the painting.

20. Write down a place, a favorite person, and the name of an object. Create a painting about these three ideas.

21. Make a "wish" painting. Tack up a piece of 10-foot mural-size paper. Have all of the students draw themselves on the paper as they wish they were ("I wish I were . . . an eagle, Big Bird, an astronaut, . . . etc."). Next to each student's drawing, add a balloon that describes the student's feeling about his or her wish.

22. Create paintings about "What It Feels Like to Be a . . . ," "I Had a Dream about . . . ," and "If I Were . . . (sand on the desert, a bird, a fish, an animal, a rainbow, an ice cube, etc.)" (fig. 8.52), and about moods, such as joyful, angry, and stormy (fig. 8.53).

23. Create "mistake" paintings. See what mistakes you can make on purpose. Then let them become "happy accidents" as you see what you can do with them. Try painting with your opposite hand (left hand if you are right-handed, and vice versa).

24. Practice painting rounded forms, such as a vase. First, brush in a light tone all over. While the paint is still wet, add a darker shade on the side of the form. The colors will blend together, with the dark shade blending toward the center.

25. Paint abstract designs after selecting a 2-inch-by-2-inch section of a photo and enlarging the forms. A rectangular viewer helps in selecting interesting sections (fig. 8.54).

26. Make a dot painting by placing small areas of color next to each other, as in pointillism (see chapter 6).

27. Paint a mural of the community and its significant architectural structures. Then paint a mural of how you think the community will look in the future.

28. Study how artists have painted over the centuries. Analyze the many artworks in this book.

Computers

All of the following motivations require a computer and draw or paint software. Be able to demonstrate a working knowledge of your software program through your use of tools and pull-down menu options. All of these motivations can also be adapted for use with elementary students.

1. Create a repeating tile pattern, using tools and the COPY, CUT, and PASTE commands. Invert, flip, and exchange colors in some of the tiles to add interest to your design. Look at cutouts by Henri Matisse for ideas.

2. Draw an image. Then redraw to show the image from three different viewpoints. Consider flipping one of the images. Combine these viewpoints into one composition. Explore the works of the cubist artists Georges Braque and Pablo Picasso.

3. Make a design in black and white. Select at least one area to convert into negative space. Add color, and convert one area to color opposites, or complementary colors. Add patterns. Study the op art movement and the works of Victor Vasarely and Frank Stella.

4. Make a painting that includes a woman, a table, and a vase of flowers. Use bright colors and vibrant patterns of your own design. Examine paintings by Henri Matisse, especially *The Purple Robe.*

5. Create a design of overlapping shapes. Add words or text to the images. Consider the artworks of Stuart Davis, Robert Rauschenberg, and Kurt Schwitters.

6. Create a painting using pointillism, or small dots of color. Use complementary colors next to each other for

(a)

Figure 8.53   What type of mood or story does this painting convey?

(b)

Figure 8.52   Imaginative paintings are the result of students motivated to imagine what it would be like to be a fish or other animal.

Figure 8.54   Fourth- and fifth-graders painted abstract designs after selecting a 2-inch-by-2-inch section of a photograph and enlarging the forms.

color interaction. Examine the works of the impressionists and neo-impressionists (Georges Seurat, in particular) for ideas.

7. Create other graphic images, incorporating idea and words to enhance messages.

Photography

1. Make a cutout rectangle (viewfinder) from a firm piece of paper (oak tag). Use it to "frame" different scenes and ideas and to find exciting contrasts and interesting perspectives. Look for the most interesting way to express a subject, subjective contrasts of lights and darks, perspective (for example, unusual angles), shadows and feelings, depth, forms, textures, lines, size relationships, patterns, colors, and so on.

2. Compare and contrast photographs by well-known photographers. Discuss how the elements of content, expression, composition, space, light, shapes, textures, patterns, design, and so on contribute to the photographs.

3. Take lots of photographs. Critique your photographs and those done by classmates and other students with regard to the same elements mentioned in number 2.

4. Discuss how the camera has documented significant world events.

5. Select themes for photographs.

6. Montage photos together in designs.

7. Discuss how the camera and photography have changed in the last fifty years.

8. Discuss the many types of cameras and features available today.

9. Discuss how the camera is an important part of society today (in books, magazines, television).

10. Study photographic artists, such as Edward Weston.

11. Pinhole cameras (about 3 inches by 6 inches) can be made in the classroom with few materials: small boxes; flat, black paint; heavy aluminum foil (2 inches by 2 inches); a fine needle (like a #10 sewing needle) or awl; and black and white film (Kodak Tri-X or Verichrome Pan) (fig. 8.55).

    Rotate the metal foil with the needle punched through it. Attach it to the front of the box, and cover with light cardboard, which acts as a shutter. In a dark closet, load the film into the opposite side of the inside of the box facing the foil. Tape any joints of the box with tape.

    Approximate exposure times are: 1 to 2 seconds in sunlight and 4 to 8 seconds in cloudy light for the Tri-X film; and 2 to 4 seconds in sunlight and 8 to 16 seconds in cloudy light for the Verichrome film.

    Encourage students to be spontaneous with the photographs to capture impressions. Consider lights and darks, shadows, positive and negative space, and composition.

    Film can be developed in a darkened room or leakproof bag. With the image and negative, print on photographic or blue print paper.

Figure 8.55   In this pinhole camera, a small hole in the piece of brass permits light to enter. Film is loaded into the camera in a darkened room.

12. Photograms are prints made without a camera, using light-sensitive papers, such as blueprint paper (figs. 8.56 and 8.57). Collect objects with interesting shapes and silhouettes, such as lace, doilies, jewelry, buttons, flowers, leaves, ferns, crumpled plastic wrap, figures and animals cut from paper, and other cut shapes with interesting textures and patterns.

    Arrange shapes on a firm piece of clear plastic, and consider design and repetition, unity, variety, positive/negative, and overlapping arrangements and composition.

    To print, place a sheet of printing paper (the same size as your piece of plastic) underneath the plastic with arranged objects on it, and quickly go out into the sunlight for exposure for approximately 15 seconds or until the paper turns white. Rinse the paper in clear water, and then rinse again in a solution of half bleach/half water, and then once more in clear water. Use caution when using bleach.

13. After taking a photograph with a Polaroid camera, and while the image is processing, use a blunt pencil to draw designs on the surface. As the photo develops, the drawn lines will take on different colors due to the chemicals. Afterward, decorate with felt pens, fabric paint, glitter, and sequins.

Video and Film

1. Video and film cameras can be used creatively to encourage young students to become movie-makers. All students can be involved—as directors, writers, camera operators, actors, stage directors, set designers, makeup artists, costume designers, and so on. While this may be an ambitious undertaking, it could be a very rewarding experience for students, since it would involve all of the arts.

2. Use video and film to document many types of events, such as school displays, arts demonstrations, cultural and ethnic activities, discussions, and field trips to

(a)

(b)

(c)

Figure 8.56   (*a*) Fourth graders created photograms using light-sensitive paper to reveal the exposed image. (*b*) Photogram drawn with a cotton swab on light-sensitive paper. (*c*) Developing photograms.

galleries, museums, and other classrooms. Musical events, dance performances, social events, student presentations, and student progress in their artworks can also be documented using film and video.

3. Have student groups review videos and films.

4. Tape presentations so that students who missed them can view them later.

5. Have students view videos and films at home and then write reviews and self-critiques.

6. Present films or videos at various community locations, such as libraries, to illustrate the quality of the art program, as well as to recruit students.

7. Share art curriculum videos with parents, teachers, and administrators to inform others of student achievement and the art curriculum.

8. Use film or video to record an artist's step-by-step procedure.

9. Use film or video to study longitudinally such phenomena as clouds in the sky, birds, the life of a flower, how a cat moves, and other items in the environment.

10. Select a theme and develop a short story. Then videotape it.

11. Use video to record a dialogue and class discussion about a painting or artist's works.

12. Use film or video to keep track of a class project as it develops, such as a papier-maché project.

13. Use film or video to preserve a record of class projects.

Filmmaking

The motivations that follow involve both animated and experimental filmmaking. Motivations 1–4 require the use of a camera with a single-frame exposure, a tripod, photo lights, and film or tape. Motivation 5 requires a 16-millimeter projector and old 16-millimeter film (possibly donated by a photo store).

1. Make a short animated film, using figures and ideas that you draw yourself. Figures will need to be disjointed, and several body parts will need to be drawn in a variety of different positions to allow for the illusion of movement.

Figure 8.57   Photogram, gum bichromate on paper. 1995 © Desert Flora by Linda Ingraham.

2. Make a short animated film using cutouts from magazines. Use collages of photos to change, move, and to express ideas.
3. Make a short animated film using paintings or drawings of movie heroes for which you have created a variety of different features: new eyes, mouths, noses, beards, mustaches, teeth, glasses, and so on.
4. Make a short animated film using figures made out of soft clay. Add or subtract clay as necessary to create a collage of fun images and movement.
5. Strip some old 16-millimeter film. Applying liquid bleach directly to the film dissolves the emulsion.

Leaving some images and sound on the film adds interest and variety. Place long strips of film on tables for students to work in groups.

Then draw images on the stripped film with colored inks and pens, felt-tip pens, ballpoint pens, brushes and ink, pens with fluorescent ink, and so on. Applying clear Cryst-L-Craze paint (or similar paint from hobby shops) over the drawn areas will make the images on the screen look like snowflake crystals. The paint is transparent as it goes on, but crystallizes on drying. Later, film strips can be spliced together.

Sixteen-millimeter leader (a blank section at the beginning or end of a reel of film or tape) can also be used for this lesson. The emulsion can be scratched away or holes punched, leaving designs. Color is then added to the lines and textures.

Projectors and Slides

You will be impressed with the excitement and interest in painting generated by the inventive images you can create with experimental slides. Discuss design and compositional elements.

1. Obtain inexpensive slide mounts (available at stores selling photographic supplies). Cut pieces of clear acetate to fit the slide mounts. Then experiment:

    - Glue some of the acetate pieces into place on the slide mounts. Then draw directly on the acetate with felt-tip pens or pen and ink. Apply ink and marker designs rather heavily; the heavier the ink, the stronger the color.
    - Glue forms and scraps, such as feathers, hairs, dust, gelatin, petroleum jelly, tissue papers, salt and sugar crystals, vegetable dyes, old negatives, colored acetate shapes, lace, and netting, between two of the acetate pieces, and then attach this acetate "sandwich" to a slide mount. Spread glue thinly, since it will become opaque if applied heavily.
    - Optional: Paint the outside of the acetate with crystallized paint.

2. Use a slide projector to project your invented slides one at a time onto a wall or screen. Then consider projecting two at a time, and experiment with overlapping images. When projected from a distance, the images are much larger. Experiment with the effects of having one or more individuals in light clothing stand and move in front of the images. Try projecting the images onto objects or onto mirror balls. Experiment until you have discovered the image that you want to paint.

3. When you are ready to paint, project the image closer to the screen so that the image is smaller and colors are more intense. You might even place your paper in front of the image to see what relationships you wish to include and perhaps exaggerate in the painting. Consider the design and the composition created by the art elements in the image. What moods or emotions are indicated?

4. Try painting the projected image. Your painting can be realistic or abstract. Try to capture the free, experimental, loose, abstract forms that appear in the slide.

Multimedia Shows

1. Place a roll of acetate painted with brightly colored inks in abstract designs and patterns on one overhead projector. Place a variety of colored acetates—cutout patterns, filigree designs, pinhole designs, or grids, for example—on top of this roll. Manipulate these manually to the tempo of music.

2. Pour a mixture of colored alcohol and mineral oil into each of two graduated crystal dishes—approximately 10 and 12 inches in diameter. Then stack the dishes inside one another on an overhead projector. Move them gently. The mixture of colored alcohol and mineral oil in each of the dishes will project changing, amoeba-like images on the screen. Hold colored acetate sheets in front of the overhead scope to change the color effects.

3. Place a glass dish of automotive oil on an overhead projector. This will black out the projection. Then use your finger or another device to wipe through the oil. This will create images of light traveling across the screen.

4. Fill plastic bags with colored water, and place them on an overhead projector. Experiment with adding different materials to the water and noting the effects these have on the projected image. For example, try adding vegetable oil to the water. Use eyedroppers to add coloring to the oil. Try adding rubber cement and liquid soap and blowing with straws. The bubbles appear as huge white circles swirling on the screen. Add a fizzy for bubbles.

5. Glue broken pieces of mirrors to a piece of felt suspended by rubber bands in a wooden frame to reflect a fractured image on an overhead projector. Move the mirrors, and the image will split in many directions and scatter rhythmically across the projection screen.

6. Tape three 12-inch-long mirrors into a triangular tube. Place this device in front of the overhead scope while the acetate roll from activity 1 is turned. A radial kaleidoscopic pattern will appear on the projection screen.

7. Glue mirror pieces onto a papier-maché ball formed over a balloon. Hang this mirror ball in the center of the ceiling, and suspend colored mini-spotlights near it. As the mirror ball turns, the projected lights move.

8. Use several slide projectors to provide multiple projections that can be blended and faded by using hands in front of the lenses. Friction wheels of colored acetate, rotated by motors, allow ease of color changes. Slides of current events, faces, local scenes, students, and imaginative designs are appropriate.

9. Try combining a number of the techniques outlined in activities 1–8 into one light show. This will require that you practice handling the technical equipment and be familiar with all the procedures. Experiment with optical distortions, exaggerations, and illusions. You might also want to add a student-produced film to the lineup. Program the techniques together, following a crescendo approach. Begin with low-key, subtle changes of color and images. Build to an intensity of rhythm, light, and color. Choreograph the presentation to appropriate music. Consider adding individuals to the overall effect. Students enjoy standing in front of the images, and by moving, they add still another dimension. Add a student-produced video. Coordinate music, dance, and so on for maximum effects and participation.

NOTES

1. Kenneth Kerslake, artist, University of Florida, speaking about his series *The Anatomies of the Star-Spangled Man.*
2. Kimon Nicolaides, *The Natural Way to Draw* (Boston: Houghton Mifflin; London: Andre Deutsch Limited, 1941), 106–7.

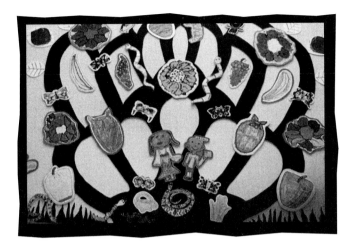

Multicultural and Interdisciplinary Art

The air is precious to the red man, for all things share the same breath—the beast, the tree, the man—they all share the same breath. You must remember that the air shares its spirit with all the life it supports.

The white man must treat the beast of this land as his brothers. I am a savage and do not understand any other way. I have seen a thousand rotting buffaloes on the prairie, left by the white man who shot them from a passing train. I do not understand how the smoking iron horse can be more important than the buffalo that we kill only to stay alive.

What is man without the beasts? If all the beasts were gone, man would die from great loneliness of spirit. For whatever happens to the beasts soon happens to man.

We know that the white man does not understand our ways. The earth is not his brother, but his enemy, and when he has conquered it, he moves on. His appetite will devour the earth and leave only a desert. You must teach your children that the ground beneath their feet is the ashes of our grandfathers. So that they will respect the land. Teach your children what we have taught our children, that the earth is our mother. Whatever befalls the earth, befalls the sons of the earth. If man spits upon the ground, they spit upon themselves. This we know, the earth does not belong to man; man belongs to the earth.

Chief Seattle, chief of the Dwamish tribe of the
Pacific Northwest, 1850

C hief Seattle's words are a testament to the need for basic understanding among all cultures. Technology permits us to travel to and attempt to communicate with all cultures, even those in distant corners

of the earth. We are becoming a global society in which multicultural learning and understanding have increasing importance.

Art can be a vehicle for promoting multicultural learning, for making us aware of other peoples, their needs, and their traditions, both past and present. Artworks and artifacts from different cultures and different times provide insight into geographic, ceremonial, religious, political, philosophical, and technological differences among cultures.

In addition to art being a source of multicultural study and understanding, it can also be a means of teaching skills in other disciplines. The integration of art with other areas of study is valuable in that art learning involves creative thinking—probing the senses, through experiencing, to shape mental imagery. This type of thinking is also critical to learning skills in other disciplines. Learning is a natural development of all of the experiences and activities of human life and occurs when we are able to see and form meaningful relationships among concepts.

Research has clearly shown that the integrated arts have value in general education. For example, drawing skills aid in reading skills. Reading music helps in reading and in computing math. In many experimental curriculums, where the arts have been used as disciplines in themselves and also as vehicles to teach other disciplines, reading and math skills have improved dramatically.[1]

While multicultural and interdisciplinary art learning has real value, art should also be taught for its own merits, separate and distinct from other subjects. According to the National Art Education Association:

The [National Visual Arts] Standards address competence in the arts disciplines first of all. But that competence provides a firm foundation for connecting arts-related concepts and facts across the art forms and from them to the sciences and humanities. For example, the intellectual methods of the arts are precisely those used to transform scientific disciplines and discoveries into everyday technology. . . . The educational success of our children depends on creating a society that is both literate and imaginative, both competent and creative. That goal depends, in turn, on providing children with tools not only for understanding that world but for contributing to it and making their own way. Without the arts to help shape students' perceptions and imaginations, our children stand every chance of growing into adulthood as culturally disabled. We must not allow that to happen.[2]

This chapter explores both aspects of art learning: multicultural and interdisciplinary. A variety of teaching examples help to demonstrate how art is central to the entire general education curriculum.

MULTICULTURAL ART

Multicultural art learning involves studying and learning from the arts created by different peoples at different times and places for various reasons. For example, artifacts such

as masks vary in appearance and purpose because of the beliefs, interests, and needs of the various cultures that used masks at social functions, festivals, celebrations, funerals, initiations, and other spiritual activities. Comparing masks of different cultures and times can provide insight into a variety of differences among cultures (fig. 9.1).

Paintings, sculptures, costumes, adornment, vessels, funerary objects, tools, boxes, musical instruments, furniture, architectural structures, and utilitarian objects are several of the other themes found cross-culturally. These arts are distinct in form, construction, design, symbolism, meaning, and importance.

Multicultural learning has never been more important. Advanced technology and mobility are "shrinking" the globe and allowing us to communicate and interact with all of the earth's countries, cultures, and peoples. For that communication and interaction to be effective requires an understanding of the world's cultural diversity.

Art offers unique opportunities for students to recognize and respect every culture's integrity and validity (fig. 9.2). The teaching examples that follow show how some teachers have used art as a vehicle for motivating multicultural learning. In addition, the chapter also briefly examines

(a)

(b)

Figure 9.1   Throughout history, masks have reflected cultural beliefs, rituals, and emotions. They are pathways into various cultures. (*a*) This African mask represents the life and customs of its creator. (*b*) This mask was created by a fifth-grader.

(a)

(b)

(c)

(d)

Figure 9.2   Clothing, costumes, and environments help us to know and understand various cultures.

(e)

(f)

(g)

(h)

Figure 9.2   continued

how multicultural art learning can be promoted through study of myths and legends and examination of textiles. Ideas and motivations that will give you some ideas for how to relate multicultural education and art in the classroom are presented at the end of the chapter. Adapt the activities to your students' grade-level capabilities.

TEACHING EXAMPLES
Third Grade: Clay Vessels, Stagecoaches, and Plants

We researched the cultural aspects, the climatic conditions, and the plant and animal life of our state (Arizona), and then discussed our results together. The lesson was planned so that the students would realize what an exceptional state they live in and would broaden their view of Arizona. We compiled a list of our researched facts and information. Each child received a copy of the list as a guide for later classes. Then we went to the library and in books about Arizona found more information to contribute to our list. We collected photographs of Arizona and displayed them. We discussed *Arizona Highways* magazine and what the students found of interest in it. We watched films, filmstrips, and slides about Arizona. We took field trips to the zoo, pioneer village, botanical gardens, Pueblo Grande Museum to see Native American ruins, and the Heard Museum to see early artifacts.

The students' special project was the final unit and was to model something from clay, as our Arizona heritage involves Native Americans and pioneers using clay. We first sketched our ideas. Most students chose to make vessels, stagecoaches, and cactus plants.

Submitted by Lois Field, third-grade teacher

Fifth Grade: Hopi Tribe and Kachina Dolls

As part of our study of the state of Arizona, we studied the different Native American tribes, with emphasis on the Hopi tribe and their kachina dolls. We learned the legend of the kachina dolls and how the dolls are thought of today. We read about the Hopi tribe, viewed films, filmstrips, and slides, and looked at photographs from magazines. Then the students created their own kachina dolls. The students had no model to look at but worked from what they remembered (fig. 9.3).

Submitted by Pat Pollard, fifth-grade teacher

Sixth Grade: Country Shadowboxes

To enrich our curriculum, I had students make shadowboxes to typify a scene in a country in the Eastern Hemi-

Figure 9.3   After studying the Hopi culture, students created their own Hopi kachina dolls.

sphere. We discussed backgrounds and environments of such places as a German farm, African huts in rural Uganda, a sidewalk cafe in Paris, a Polish farmstead, windmills in Holland, and an African rain forest. For English, the students researched their topic and wrote a paragraph about materials to include in the shadowbox. In their shadowboxes, they used available materials in creative ways, such as toothpicks for fences, soda straws for candles, and fruits and vegetables for clay and ceramic tile. Then the students made clothespin dolls wearing native costumes. We displayed the shadowboxes, and now students from other sixth grades want to make them, too.

Submitted by Virginia Breed, sixth-grade teacher

African Mural

The classroom teacher worked with the art teacher and divided the activities for a unit on Africa. With the classroom teacher, the students looked at and discussed pictures about African life, villages, cities, animals, weather, clothing, and so on; played African games; read African stories; created movements to African music; made a mural of African animals; wrote stories about Africa; and made dashikis (brightly colored, loose-fitting, pullover garments).

With the art teacher, the students looked at and discussed African artwork; listened and danced to African music tapes; discussed the dance movements; discussed the use of lines, shapes, colors, and patterns on dashikis; went on an animal walk to look for African animals; and read the African folktale *Why Mosquitoes Buzz in People's Ears* and discussed the book's illustrations. The result was a painted mural on Africa.

Submitted by Yvonne Stitt, Angela Taylor, and Ann Velasquez, in conjunction with the University of North Carolina, Dr. Esther Page Hill, coordinator

MYTHS AND MULTICULTURAL ART

Myths are traditional stories within a culture that attempt to explain the mysterious and unexplainable in nature or that relate to and explain practices, beliefs, and religious rites. For example, ancient humans developed myths to explain such phenomena as the rising and setting of the sun, the waning of the moon, lightning, rain, the changing of seasons, and the growth and aging of people, plants, and animals.

In ancient times, there were no written languages or books, so myths were passed on by word of mouth over the generations. This method of passing myths involved many people over many centuries, which sometimes resulted in the myths being altered to reflect current knowledge or happenings. Consequently, myths are a fusion of the thoughts, feelings, and actions of groups of people over time and have helped to create cultures.

Myths and legends are fertile fields for the imagination and have inspired art and artists since recorded history. Study of these artworks and artifacts is beneficial in that students not only learn about the artistic aspects of the pieces but also discover their cultural value. Some examples of artworks that reflect cultural myths are prehistoric cave art, Mexican clay works, and Egyptian shawabtis figures. (See also the discussions of Australian "Dreamings" and cave paintings in chapter 10.) All of the myths and legends discussed in the sections that follow can be used as motivations for drawing, painting, and creating in the classroom (fig. 9.4).

Prehistoric Cave Art

America's first artists left paintings (pictographs) and carvings (petroglyphs) on rock surfaces as early as ten thousand years ago. These prehistoric images have been found in forty-one of the fifty states, as well as in Canada and Mexico. Some of the earliest examples in North America were found in the Great Basin (what is now Utah and Nevada). These early artworks of animal and human forms are interesting in themselves as examples of early art techniques and media, but they are also valuable as prehistoric visual records of the observations and beliefs of early cultures (fig. 9.5).

Mexican Clay Works

Ancient Mexicans had many myths about the sun. They called themselves "Children of the Sun." They offered the sun a share of their food and drink. They greeted the rising sun with prayers and songs of thanksgiving and praise. Even today, many people in parts of central Mexico throw a kiss to the sun just before entering a church (fig. 9.6).

Some ancient Mexicans believed that the sun was actually the fifth sun that existed. According to the legend, the first sun was washed away in a great flood, the second fell out of the sky, the third caught fire and burnt itself to a crisp,

(a)

(b)

Figure 9.4 Myths, legends, and poems inspire imagery. Can you imagine what the titles of these drawings might be? (*b*) Kachina Behnke, 7 years old. Heidilberg, West Germany.

while the fourth sun was blown away in a violent windstorm. Then, according to the legend, darkness prevailed for twenty-five years, until the present sun was created.

In Metepec, Mexico, a small town not far from Mexico City, the folk artists have been celebrating the warmth and power of the sun for generations and create fascinating sun faces or masks from clay. These smiling faces are a symbol of good fortune at having a warm friend in the sky. Metepec artisans also make the Mexican "Tree of Life" (fig. 9.12), a symbol depicting the universal connection between humanity and nature, from clay. The clay trees often serve as candelabras and have colorful animals, birds, and figures resting among their "branches."

Figure 9.5   After students studied prehistoric cave art, they used some of the symbols in their own clay designs.

The art of working with clay has played an important part of Mexican life from the earliest times and remains an important craft today. The style of clay work is as varied as the many Mexican villages, and clay pieces are so distinctive that the villages where they originated can easily be identified.

Egyptian Shawabtis Figures

In Egypt, the dead were buried with a canopic chest that contained the items the individual would need when life returned, such as jewelry, clothing, furniture, and foods. Also buried were mummy-shaped figures called shawabtis, who took care of the work in the afterlife. Encircling the shawabtis was the following prayer in hieroglyphics:

> O Shawabtis, if the Osirs [name of deceased] is called upon to do any of the work which a man does in necropolis, namely to cultivate the fields, to water the banks, to transport sand from the east to the west, "Here I am," you shall say.

Study of the artistic aspects of the shawabtis figures and the other items found in canopic chests is instructive from an artistic point of view but also reveals a significant Egyptian cultural belief—that is, the existence of an afterlife (fig. 9.7).

Japanese Creation Myth

The following Japanese myth about creation can be used as a motivation for painting and drawing in the classroom:

> In the beginning, as the ancient records of Shinto describe, there was disorder. The world was like an ocean of bubbling oil. Something like a reed grew up through the ocean. It proved to be a god who was called the Eternal Ruling—Lord or God. Many gods and goddesses appeared after this. Finally, a couple appeared who were destined to create many things and many important gods. He was called Izanagi, and she was called Izanami. These two gods were sent to make things on earth. They landed upon an island, were married, and then created such things as the sea, the waterfalls, the wind, the woods, the mountains, and the fields. When the goddess Izanami gave birth to the god of fire, she died of a fever. Hers was the first human death. With her death began the opposite things of life, such as death, darkness, and war.

Figure 9.6   Art has always been an integral part of the Mexican culture.

African Creation Myth

The following African myth about creation can be used as a motivation for painting and drawing in the classroom:

> In the beginning, everything was water. Olodumare was the supreme god. Olodumare sent Obatala down from heaven to create the dry land. Obatala came down a chain, and he carried a snail shell filled with earth, some pieces of iron, and a rooster. When he arrived, he placed the iron on the water, spread the earth over it, and placed the rooster on top. The rooster immediately started to scratch, which spread the land far and wide. When the land had been created, the other gods came down from heaven to live on the land with Obatala. Obatala made man out of earth. He shaped arms, legs, and heads. After shaping men and women, he gave them to Olodumare to blow in the breath of life. Obatala is still the one who gives shape to new babies before they are born.

Ancient Chinese Art Beliefs

The following Chinese story about Fan K'uan can be used as a motivation for painting and drawing in the classroom:

> During the Sung dynasty, about A.D. 1000, Chinese artists painted what was important to them. One great painter was Fan K'uan, a Taoist painter who believed that the way to

(a)

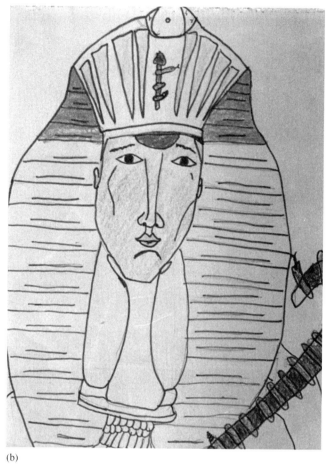

(b)

Figure 9.7   Study of the ancient Egyptian culture motivated these paintings.

happiness was being close to nature. So he lived alone in the mountains, where he found peace and happiness. In his paintings, he made the things that were important to him, such as the mountains, trees, rocks, and waterfalls, large, while he painted the things of humankind, such as temples and packhorses, small.

TEXTILES AND MULTICULTURAL ART: WEAVING, LOOMS, TIE-DYING, AND DRESS DESIGN

When humans first began to cover their bodies for protection from the elements, they had to make their clothing from available materials. In cold countries, such as Alaska, they used the skins of fur-bearing animals. In warm countries, they pounded the bark of certain trees into a kind of cloth, wove grass into garments, or scraped the skins of animals to make a soft leather.

Gradually, clothing became more ornamental (buckles, tassels, and embroidered cloth) and beautiful (hairstyles, ornaments, jewelry), and different cultures developed traditional clothing styles—for example, the Hopi ceremonial dress, the Mexican serape, and the Japanese kimono.

As the craft of weaving became known, textiles became an important part of traditional dress. Different cul-

tures used a variety of materials and wove distinctive designs, patterns, and textures into their fabrics (fig. 9.8). Currently, Native American Hopi men and Navajo women are known for their accomplished weaving skills. In Mexico, the serape weavers are always men. Weaving of cotton cloth began with the Pueblos around A.D. 750. Weaving with wool began about A.D. 1600, after the Spanish introduced sheep into Mexico and the Southwest. Tie-dying of fabrics, a hand method of producing patterns in textiles by tying portions of the fabric so that they will not absorb the dye, was used in almost all parts of the world at some time, particularly Africa.

Study of the craft of weaving, of the variety of looms and materials used, and the unique textiles that were created in the past as well as today offers an illuminating look at how each culture has expressed its artistic design through dress. Contemporary society has great interest in fashion, with fashion magazines highlighting specific designers and changing styles. Elementary students enjoy designing clothes and costumes.

INTERDISCIPLINARY ART

Interdisciplinary art learning can be helpful in a variety of learning areas, such as language, science, math, and social

Figure 9.8   Notice the feathers and clay figure woven into this textile example.

studies. The teaching examples that follow show how some teachers chose to be creative in integrating art instruction with other disciplines. In addition, the chapter also briefly explores how poem painting, English-as-a-second-language instruction, and mural painting can be worthwhile interdisciplinary learning experiences.

LANGUAGE AND ART: TEACHING EXAMPLES

In addition to the teaching examples that follow, activities that will give you some ideas for how to relate language and art in the classroom are presented at the end of the chapter. Adapt the activities as per students' grade-level capabilities.

First Grade: Favorite Stories

The children selected their favorite story and made puppets and scenery to go along with the stories from *A Trip through Wonderland,* from the Open Court Language series.

Submitted by Susan Hoen, first-grade teacher

Fourth Grade: Puppets, Plays, and Scenery

We started by watching a film on the making of different kinds of puppets. Then we talked with the librarian, and she explained how to write a script for a play and how a character communicates his or her ideas and emotions to an audience. The students wrote plays and made puppets. The puppets could be make-believe or realistic. We made scenery, backgrounds, and props, including tables, chairs, a part of a house, and trees. The students practiced their plays in the library, using a desk as a stage. Some titles were: "Steve Hurts His Leg," "Tigger and His Bouncing," "The Skill Trip," and "The Surprise Birthday Party." Then the plays were presented to the first and second grades.

We learned what goes into the making of a puppet show. The children learned to work with various materials. Most of all, they learned to work together in a group situation and how to work with group ideas. Even when they disagreed, they came to a workable solution after a discussion.

Submitted by Barbara Wentz, fourth-grade teacher

First Grade: Painting to Music and Poems

The class was divided into groups. Some groups listened to poems; other groups listened to music with and without words. One poem was "Poem" by Langston Hughes, about a friend going away. The students were asked what they thought of when they listened to the poem. Some thought of friends who had moved away. Others thought of times their mothers or fathers were away from them. We then read the poem again and painted a picture about it. After reading the poem "The Little Turtle," we talked about who the turtle caught and what it might feel like to be a turtle.

The groups that listened to music heard "Clowns," "Five Little Kites," and "Dance of the Little Bells" by Rebikoff. The children were not told the titles. We talked about what they thought of as they listened to the music. We sang to the music. Then we painted as we listened to the music.

Submitted by Lorrie Miller, first-grade teacher

Fifth Grade: Quotations and Visual Mind Pictures

We printed about thirty famous quotations and distributed them to the twenty-seven fifth-graders during language. We had discussed idioms, and the quotations gave us an excellent chance to "think" and analyze these quotes and sayings over a wide range of subject matter. After a class discussion of what each quote could mean, I asked the students to visually picture how each quote could look to them. We called them "visual or mind pictures."

We studied vowels and the long and short vowel sounds. Then the students picked a vowel and drew a picture of one. We wrote a creative story about the vowel. We made vowels from twisted tissue paper, bread dough, macaroni, and colored sand.

Submitted by Terri Jones, fifth-grade teacher

First Grade: Papier-Mâché Hats and Stories

We read the story *Caps for Sale* by Esphyr Slobodkina. Then we papier-machéd hats, using papier-maché mixture, wallpaper, white and colored papers, paint, trims, rickrack, feathers, artificial flowers, and so on. We used our mural of "Our Community Helpers" that we had made after field trips. Some made firefighter hats, police hats, imaginary hats, and hats from true life. Then we shared our art products and talked about the students' ideas and reasons for selections. We made up stories about who they were when wearing the hats, how they felt, what things they would do. We wrote stories and play-acted experiences.

Submitted by Marianne Di Matteo, first-grade teacher

Language and Art: Poem Painting

Writing a poem is much like creating a word painting. Both poems and paintings have textures, rhythms, colors, forms, ideas, free imagination, and discoveries, and both are emotionally inspiring. As in art, the important ideas are the sounds, thoughts, impressions, imaginations, happy experiences, or sorrowful remembrances. Emphasize to students that rhymes, jingles, spontaneity, expression, and personal statements should be the focus.

Children like to write poetry when it is an innermost expression of themselves. After several experiences with writing poems, they are usually bursting with ideas for more poems. Combining visual images with thought images is exciting and challenging for all levels of growth development. Here are several poems written by a fifth-grade student:

CHAIRS
Square, round
They mostly stand
They're good when you want to sit down
But when you don't want to, they're just O.K.

CLOTHES
Clothes are bright and dark,
Shiny and broad,
With all kinds of designs on them.
I think clothes are just wonderful,
Especially for me!

SPRING
Bright, beautiful
Blooming flowers
everywhere
I like old Spring
Happiness.

RED
Red is nice
Red is like a rash
Red is glistening blood
Red is a sunset
Red is a madman
Red is a juicy apple
Red is a ripe plum
Red can be a tear
Red could be an autumn leaf
Red could be lipstick
Or red can be a ribbon
But mostly Red and
Red for always.

GWEN'S GUM
Gwen's gum is
your chum. It's
Chewy, it's bubbly.
You get a freckle in
every chew. It has
that red-headed
flavor. It's tasty,
It's sweet. A real
neat treat that
can't be beat.
Gwen's gum—get some, chum!

Ask your students to read their poems to the class, and ask listening students to jot down phrases that suggest images, excite their awareness, express ideas, cause them to react emotionally, and capture their imagination. Then suggest that they select a phrase and make it an inspiration for a painting.

Chart 9.1 presents possible ideas for poems and paintings.

Language and Art: When English Is a Second Language

Many elementary school classrooms contain students of various nationalities, to whom English is a second language. Activities based on the arts are an integral part of an English-as-a-second-language (ESL) program, both as an instructional tool and as a means of sharing cultures.

For example, when language barriers make words an insufficient means of communication, art is a universal language. If, as a teacher, you are having difficulty explaining a concept, draw a picture. If a student is unable to explain something to you, ask him or her to draw a picture. Regardless of a student's nationality, art can always communicate the message.

chart   9.1
Ideas for Poem and Art Inspirations

"Hello to . . ."
"I wish . . ."
"A color is . . ."
"Spring to me is . . ."
"It's fun to . . ."
"Work is . . ."
"Inside me is . . ."
"My secret feeling is . . ."
"If I were a monster, then I would feel . . ."
"If the ocean could fly, then . . ."
"If clouds had legs, then . . ."
"If spiders were giants, then . . ."
"When I am the president of the United States, then . . ."
"If I could do anything in the world, I would . . ."
"In this magic box is . . ."
"When I turn into a . . ."
"My favorite color is . . ."
"My favorite place is . . ."
"I dreamt that I could . . ."
"My favorite food is . . ."

Take advantage of the varied backgrounds and customs of the cultures represented in your classroom. Encourage students to draw pictures of their native homes, local customs, and holidays. These pictures will lead to many conversational activities and will teach both you and your students about many countries.

Learning a second language usually requires practice in four areas: listening, writing, reading, and speaking. Chart 9.2 presents an outline of artistic listening, writing, reading, and speaking activities for students who are learning English as a second language. These activities were developed for use with a small group but also could be adapted as whole-class or individual exercises. Students of a second language often agree that conversing in the new tongue is the most difficult aspect. Many of the listening, reading, and writing activities in chart 9.2 could be adapted into speaking activities to give students more practice in this area.

SCIENCE AND ART: TEACHING EXAMPLES
First Grade: Prehistoric Animals—Stories, Paintings, Clay

For two days, we read about prehistoric animals—dinosaurs in particular—and looked at pictures of them. We discussed size, eating habits, and various physical features. We watched filmstrips and a cartoon viewmaster story, and made a stand-up diorama. We drew or painted pictures and wrote stories about them. Then we modeled dinosaurs out of clay.

Submitted by Lorrie Miller, first grade teacher

Second Grade: Animal Characteristics—Puppets and Plays

We discussed the various animal stories the three reading groups had read, each group telling the other children. We noticed similarities and differences among animals, including scientific items like the foods they ate, their means of protection, and their abilities to move and to reproduce. We divided animals into vertebrates and invertebrates. (One student brought in a cow vertebra to show.) We also divided animals into categories, such as mammals, birds, reptiles, amphibians, and fish, and talked about what makes each kind unique. The students were surprised to discover that an elephant and a mouse are in the same category. We particularly discussed animal characteristics, such as types of skin covering and the number and positioning of the limbs, that the students could include in puppets. We talked about the animals' distinctive features and how the students could show three dimensions.

I then showed the two animal puppets I had made and suggested that the students try making a different animal puppet. The children did come up with their own ideas and were more aware of the animals' anatomical characteristics. After exhibiting the puppets in class, the children presented improvisational plays based on the stories they read. Many of the children couldn't wait and were acting out their puppets as soon as the puppets were finished.

Submitted by Judy Wallace, second-grade teacher

Animal Homes, Bird Mobiles, and Illustrations

First, we discussed science concepts relating to animals and living things. We talked about the various kinds of animals, animal characteristics, and animal homes. We viewed animal films and filmstrips, listened to and illustrated animal stories and poems, read animal stories, and used study prints to study animal characteristics and habits. The students brought in and observed small animals in class—a land crab, a hamster, kittens, puppies, a rooster, a hen, fish, tadpoles, and a lamb. We constructed animal homes from wood scraps, drew animals with marking pens, painted animals with tempera and watercolor, and cut and pasted bird mobiles. We wrote and illustrated animal "tales," molded salt-dough animals, made science research folders, planned and made a zoo trip, dramatized a play about a lost kitten, and culminated the activities with a motivation to the poem "Brown Bear, Brown Bear, What Do You See?" by Bill Martin. The children interjected different animals, chanted to the poem, and then drew the animal they "saw" on a quilt block. The students drew with crayon directly on 9-by-11-inch fabric blocks.

Submitted by Claudia Spackman

chart   9.2

Outline of Art Activities for an ESL Program

I. Listening
A. Illustrate a story. (Grades K–12)
Tell a small group of students a story at their level of language development. Have students illustrate the story. Example: "Once there was a black bear cub who liked honey very much. Every day, he'd walk into the woods, looking for a tree that was filled with honey. . . ."
B. Draw cartoons. (Grades 2–12)
Tell students a humorous story or poem. Have them draw a cartoon with appropriate captions.
C. Depict moods. (Grades 4–12)
Introduce mood words, such as *angry* or *frustrated*. Use gestures and/or pictures for clarification. Then read students a story that includes descriptions of several strong emotional states. Tell students to draw a line or picture to denote the feelings of a particular character. The result should depict the changes in the character's moods throughout the story.

II. Writing
A. Make an illustrated glossary. (Grades 3–12)
Have students compile a glossary of new words as they learn them. They should write the new word and then use an illustration to show the word's meaning. Words not easily illustrated may be described in the student's first language. Whenever possible, however, illustrations should be used instead of translations, since pictures speed the transfer from thinking in the native language to thinking in English. Students should keep their glossary booklet close by so that they can readily add new terms to it.
B. Make a dictionary. (Grades 1–12)
Draw pictures of basic vocabulary words in alphabetical order, and make a copy for each student. Have students write the corresponding word for each illustration and then store the sheets in a folder or notebook.
C. Write a cartoon. (Grades 3–12)
Either draw your own cartoon or cut the captions from a cartoon in the newspaper. Have students write a story that corresponds with the cartoon.

D. Describe pictures. (Grades 4–12)
Give students a picture you have drawn or cut from a magazine, or have each student draw a picture and then exchange with another student. Ask students to list the objects they see in their picture. Encourage them to write sentences or paragraphs about the picture.

III. Reading
A. Language experience. (Grades 1–3)
Language experience is an excellent vehicle for incorporating reading in English and art. Have students dictate a story, which you write on large paper on a bulletin board. Then have students make copies of the story and add illustrations.
B. Reading experience. (Grades 3–12)
Read plays, newspapers, comic books, and art journals.

IV. Speaking
A. Discuss art prints. (Grades K–12)
Have students look at, discuss, and express their reactions to different works of art. Discussion of the artist's background and other works encourages additional practice in art words and also cultivates an appreciation of art.
B. Make puppets. (Grades K–12)
Have students make puppets from socks, papier-maché, or even a clothespin. Students can then use these characters to tell a story that they make up or that you read. Many newcomers to the United States do not know the traditional stories and nursery rhymes that American children learn. Even high school students are interested in hearing these.
C. Study the various art periods. (Grades 3–12)
For older students, an art unit concerning the various periods or techniques provides a cornucopia of vocabulary and speaking opportunities.
D. Take field trips. (Grades K–12)
Field trips to local museums provide even more meaningful speaking experiences than classroom activities.

Source: Andrew Bartlett, coordinator of the English-as-a-Second-Language program in Scottsdale, Arizona.

MATHEMATICS AND ART: TEACHING EXAMPLES

Third Grade: Art, Music, and Math

As a third-grade teacher, I find that the complement of art and music incorporated into the instructional day makes a world of difference to the student's attitude and consequent desire and ability to learn. Once you have gotten their attention, the sky's the limit!

This is best exemplified in my classroom by an instructional program that I have developed called "The Times Champs Multiplication Program." This program uses arts and crafts, cartoons, music, and graduated, timed tests to assist children in memorizing the multiplication facts.

With each set of facts, I use an arts and crafts activity to apply and bring home the concept of groups, and how many in a group, in a hands-on, experiential way. For example, fours are introduced by creating four salt-dough creatures and twenty-four tiny characters. As each set of factors is acted out, as in $4 \times 6 = 24$, each of the four large creatures is shown to have six, tiny friends in its group. Thus, four groups of six equals twenty-four. The concept of four groups of six is demonstrated by characters that the students have developed through the process of creativity and fun.

The factors of seven are experienced with a craft idea called "Real Eggheads!" Seven egghead characters are created, using blown-out eggs, yarn, construction paper, glitter, and so on, to create each personality. The factors of eleven are demonstrated by creating characters called "Rockys." Ordinary rocks from the yard come to life to create unique characters. Small pebbles can be used to make the nose and ears, and other rocks can even become the rest of the body. Yarn and construction paper help to complete each character and make them ready for mathematical service.

Art and music are loved by everyone, and when you can apply these universal treats to learning important skills, such as mathematics, not only will children associate fun with learning math, but their whole attitude about learning will change.

Submitted by Bill Linderman, third-grade teacher

Kindergarten: Shapes, Pictures, and Stories

In kindergarten, our curriculum includes learning to identify geometric shapes. My goals were to heighten students' awareness in the use of geometric shapes in the environment, and to recognize differences and similarities in texture, size, and pattern of fabrics. We looked at books, such as *Round and Round and Square* by Fredun Shapur, *Shapes* by Jan Pienkowski, and *Shapes* by Miriam Schoien. We looked at shapes around us—in doors, tables, books, windows. The students cut shapes out of paper and fabric and adhered them to paper to make objects or pictures. Then they drew with felt-tip pens to add details. Each child then dictated a story to me about his or her picture.

Submitted by Lois Allen, kindergarten teacher

SOCIAL STUDIES AND ART: TEACHING EXAMPLES
Second Grade: Transportation

For a transportation unit, we discussed ways we travel and the types of travel. We compared the speeds of different types of travel, such as walking; riding animals, bicycles, and motorcycles; and traveling by wagon, car, truck, train, plane, rocket, boat, and ship. We discussed the uses of the different types, how they depended on each other, and in what way they served us. We took a bus trip to the airport and later made pictures about what we liked best about our trip. We wrote a letter to our guides and sent our pictures to them. We painted and cut out buses, cars, people, planes,

trains, and airplanes, and put them on a table with houses to make a town. In the background, we painted a mural showing the various types of travel in our town.

Submitted by Earlene Glaser, second-grade teacher

Fifth Grade: People at Work and Play—Collages

The students discussed what vocation they would like to pursue in later life and why. They came to the conclusion that many vocations overlap with what is considered recreational activities. We made two lists on the chalkboard and titled them "Americans at Work" and "Americans at Play." Our art project was to use magazine pictures in a collage exemplifying the many activities we had discussed. We discussed the art elements and art principles involved. The groups were given an outline map of the United States. The collages were great! They enforced the learning of shapes, organization, depth perception, and being creative.

Submitted by Pat Pollard, fifth-grade teacher

First Grade: Cowboys, Rodeos, and Paintings

Over a two-week period, we discussed cowboys and rodeos, looked at photographs of and saw films about cowboys and rodeos, and read "Cowboy Sam." Students played with a cardboard, cutout, stand-up rodeo during their free time. A rodeo clown came to school to do rope tricks. The children then drew pictures of the rodeo and clown.

Submitted by Lorrie Miller, first-grade teacher

Second Grade: Community—Paintings

We began by studying our community and its helpers. This led us into many interesting discussions about our environment and what *we* can do to preserve and conserve energy and ecology. The resources we used included films, filmstrips, books, pictures, and charts. We wrote creative stories and limericks about pollution and our environment. In conjunction, we made watercolor paintings, drawings, and collages.

Submitted by Mary Anne Pape, second-grade teacher

Third Grade: Awareness of Environment—Designing a Flag

Our goal was to increase students' awareness of the environment and the community. We discussed Arizona's birthday and the symbols related to Arizona, including the flag. Some students were unaware that each state has a flag. We discussed the history and symbolism in the color and design in the American flag and the Arizona flag. We looked at other flag pictures, at historical flags, and at flags from other countries. Then the students were told to create their own flag and to consider something special about themselves or their family they would want to put on a flag. They also could redesign the Arizona flag or design a flag for the state in which they were born.

Submitted by Kathryne Diamond, third-grade teacher

INTEGRATION OF THE ARTS: TEACHING EXAMPLES

While the visual arts of painting, drawing, sculpturing, and so on differ from the performing arts of music, theater, and dance, the visual arts and the performing arts are also interrelated. The most common element of all of the arts is the process of creating. Each artist, in his or her own medium, attempts to solve a problem using the tools of that medium. While the end product—whether a dance, a painting, a sculpture, or a dramatic production—is different, the creative process is the same. A second element that is common to both the visual and performing arts is the use of space, movement, images, and form. The artist must work with these elements on canvas just as the theater director must work with them on stage. The interrelationships of the arts allow for easy crossover among them in the curriculum.

Music, Costumes, and Masks

While listening to various records (from classical to electronic sounds), the students were asked to express the music or the feeling it gave them in a painting. The students realized the variety of moods that music can create, remembered the pieces better, and were motivated to further appreciation and listening on their own.

In rhythm exercises, we listened to 4/4 time being a different picture from, say, 3/4 time. Students were given two bars and eight dots of assorted sizes and colors and asked to express the rhythms played. Sections on the paper were quartered and suggested the various patterns. A number of students selected a large, dark circle for the strong downbeat. Yellow and orange tended to "jump out," and these colors were often used to represent staccato. Students also were invited to "lead the band" to feel the rhythm.

Part of the musical experience is designing costumes for musical productions. Students also enjoy making masks of the various characters portrayed in musical reviews.

Students can learn to read music with colors. They also enjoy drawing musical instruments. Other forms that relate to music and art are rhythms by the regular repetition or growth progression; that is, the form grows in size by progressive repetition of its own shape.

Submitted by Jeanne Shimizu, art teacher

Music, Pantomime, and Clay

The first-graders recognize the music from "Carnival of the Animals" and respond to the animal characters through pantomime. We visited the Phoenix Zoo for further motivation. Sometimes, we sit on the floor of the classroom in a circle and pretend that we are at the zoo or circus. The music plays, and the children pantomime the animals, such as lions, roosters, mules, kangaroos, elephants, turtles, birds, fish, and swans. We also constructed animal figures in clay.

Submitted by Bonnie Williams, art teacher

MURALS: AN INTERDISCIPLINARY ART FORM

Murals are paintings—or frescoes—that are either painted directly on a wall surface or that are fastened to a wall. The earliest of cultures did not have the convenience of paper or canvas, so they painted on rocks and cave surfaces. Prehistoric, Greek, Egyptian, and Renaissance artists painted murals that told about daily life or that had magical or religious meanings. Twentieth-century mural painters, such as Diego Rivera, Marc Chagall, and American Thomas Hart Benton, painted images dealing with more contemporary issues, such as politics, fantasy, and life in America. Paint, clay, ceramic tile, and various other media are often used in making murals.

Today, murals are gaining in popularity in schools for several reasons. Murals beautify walls (such as in a school cafeteria or library) and last as long as desired (fig. 9.9). More important, however, they also are ideal vehicles for integrating various aspects of the curriculum. For example, the organizing and space planning required for murals enhances math and visualization skills. Group planning and execution of murals enhances social cooperation skills (fig. 9.10). The theme of the mural might focus on a science, social studies, or multicultural area. For example, themes might be "Growing Foods," "Animals," "Wildlife," "Birds," "Plant Life," "Water Life," "The American West," "The Fourth of July," "Art of the Native Americans," "African Masks," "Space Travel," "The History of Japanese Kites," "Hopi Basketry," "Quilt Making," "Women in Government," "The Food Chain," and many others (fig. 9.11).

As a teacher, your role in mural painting is one of organizing, providing resources, assisting with images, and supplying materials. Students younger than eight or nine enjoy painting images on a long piece of paper (such as butcher paper) that is either on the floor or at their eye level (fig. 9.12) on the wall. By third or fourth grade, students can engage in cooperative planning of a mural. Appoint three students as chief organizers to plan some sketches, establish sections, and decide on foreground, middle ground, and background. Then students can select areas of the mural to work on—either in groups or individually.

Figure 9.9   A large painted mural in an Arizona school library illustrates the multicultural influences and agriculture in Arizona. Thew School, Tempe Elementary District.

IDEAS AND MOTIVATIONS

Adapt the following ideas as per students' grade-level capabilities.

Relating Multicultural Education and Art

1. Study and discuss prehistoric cave art and artifacts from books and slides. Then use twigs and black tempera paint to draw simple pictures of animals and figures on torn brown paper (or paper painted brown). Cut out the figures and animals and assemble as if on rock and cave walls. Write stories about the meanings and feelings connected with the artworks.
2. Study a particular culture, and then design clothes and costumes of that culture.
3. Research and obtain photographs of how dress in America has changed since 1900. Then draw from the photographs.
4. Design and draw a new wardrobe for yourself.
5. Study Navajo rugs and then experiment with simple weaving projects.
6. Study textiles from other cultures, such as India. Then tie-dye a T-shirt.
7. Study the Egyptian and Mexican myths mentioned in the chapter, and then illustrate these in your own way.
8. Study the Japanese and African creation legends mentioned in the chapter, and then illustrate them in your own way.
9. Study the Chinese artists from a thousand years ago, and then try painting "happiness is being close to nature."
10. Design clay vessels, animals, birds, candelabras, and figures after discussing how art is important in the Mexican culture.
11. As Chinese artists did centuries ago, paint what is important to you as large and what is insignificant to you as small.

Figure 9.10   Students work cooperatively as a group to create a painted stenciled wall mural. Paradise Valley School District. Teacher: Heather Davenport.

12. Study various weaving looms used in different cultures, such as the backstrap loom popular in Central America and the U.S. Southwest.
13. Study pictographs and petroglyphs. Discover if there are examples in your geographic area. Use the basic designs as inspirations for creating your own.
14. Discuss the Mexican "Tree of Life"—the connection between humanity and nature. Design your own "Tree of Life" (fig. 9.12).
15. Design your own sun masks from papier-maché.
16. Study the many significant buildings in history, such as the Great Pyramid or medieval castles. Then create your own.
17. Select a theme, such as "Containers throughout History," "Wearing Apparel," or "Homes throughout History," and create drawings related to the themes. Or create costumes or build clay containers.

Relating Language and Art

1. Write and illustrate poems and stories. Try to write spontaneous interpretations of feelings and ideas. Do not be concerned about rhyming or spelling.

(a)

(b)

Figure 9.11   Mural themes may have a science, social studies, or multicultural focus. (*a*) Each student painted their animal on the mural. (*b*) A large cut paper mural is based on the theme "Life in the Sea."

2. Make paintings, drawings, and murals that reflect books that you have read or other learning topics (fig. 9.13). Include "language balloons," like those used by comic-strip characters. To encourage free flow of ideas, do not be concerned about spelling errors.

3. Make a "magic box" containing "magic" suggestions for exciting, mysterious topics to write and draw about.

4. Conduct games that practice different types of language usage, such as using gestures, action words, or facial expressions instead of words to suggest a mood or feeling. Practice drawing these gestures, actions, and expressions.

5. Create a puppet. Puppets offer opportunities for interpretations and expressions of ideas, thoughts, and feelings. Puppet characters can be make-believe or representative. Often, hidden feelings come forward through puppetry. Students with stuttering difficulties may forget their problem when hidden behind the safety of another character, such as a puppet.

6. Design letters, words, signs, and book jackets.

7. Draw, rather than write, a book report.

8. Make a play from a favorite book or painting.

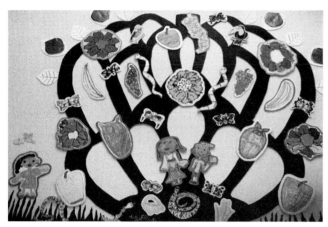

Figure 9.12 Young elementary students added individual artworks to this Mexican "Tree of Life" mural, a symbol depicting the universal connection between humanity and nature.

Figure 9.13 Books, movies, songs, and thoughts can be motivations for artistic expression.

9. Keep a personal journal in which you record and illustrate your daily activities, experiences, and feelings.
10. Send letters and pictures of appreciation to the author of a book you have read.
11. Dramatize a book in dance, costumes, music, and art.
12. Engage in creative dramatics—that is, improvise situations dealing with real life, family, or school; do parodies of commercials, nursery rhymes, books, favorite television shows, and historical events; or create commercials or sales talks for fantasy inventions.
13. Read plays, newspapers, comic books, art magazines, and art journals, and stay current on important issues.
14. Read the works of favorite authors, such as Lewis Carroll and A. A. Milne.
15. Research areas that are of particular personal interest to you by reading and drawing.
16. Make word books—notebooks filled with your favorite words about a particular topic and drawings or paintings that illustrate the words. For example, make art word books (with words used in art) or "just for fun" word books.
17. Study certain cultures, such as the Northwest Indians, and their folklore. Then create models of the totem poles or masks.

Relating Science and Art

1. Study and draw the anatomy, structure, and workings of natural forms, such as the human figure, flowers, animals, and trees (fig. 9.14).
2. Group, select, classify, name, draw, and describe rocks, leaves, plants, and insects.
3. Study and draw the workings of manufactured objects, such as clocks, motors, radios, batteries, transformers, projectors, tape recorders, earphones, and cameras.
4. Plant seeds. Then study, draw, measure, and record seedlings' growth.

5. Make sculptures, using the principles of balance, gravity, and kinesthetics.
6. Look through microscopes, telescopes, magnifying glasses, cameras, prisms, and kaleidoscopes. Try drawing what you see.
7. Illustrate ecology words, such as *noise, waste, litter, pollution, recycling, energy, foods,* and *smoke.* Draw ecology posters.
8. Design "touch pictures" and "feeling boxes" (pictures and boxes made from various textures and materials).
9. Investigate similarities and differences in foods and tastes. Collect menus and design them.
10. Draw diagrams that show how foods are grown, harvested, and cooked.
11. Design and build bird feeders, bridges, and buildings.
12. Study and draw how the sun, wind, and water generate power.
13. Study how scientists use various chemicals to clean and restore paintings and sculptures (such as the Sistine Chapel).

Relating Mathematics and Art

1. Draw pictures that illustrate mathematical problems and solutions that involve weight, balance, measurement, and geometry.
2. Introduce games that offer visual and spatial planning, such as chess and checkers. Relate spatial planning to drawings.
3. Divide spaces and areas on a sheet of paper to create optical designs, such as artists use in "op art" (see chapter 10).
4. Use mathematical tools, such as rulers and compasses, to create drawings and designs.
5. Design and illustrate simple catalogs. Then practice making purchases from the catalogs while conforming to a budget—say, forty dollars.

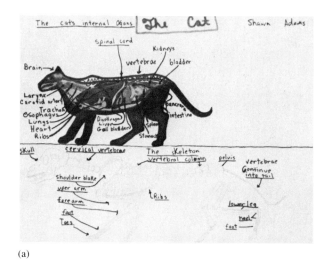

(a)

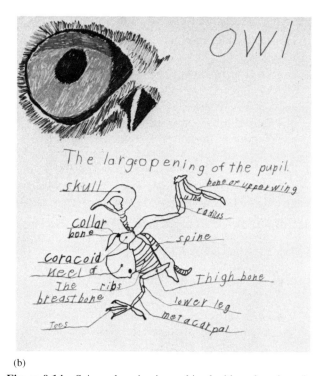

(b)

(c)

Figure 9.14   Science learning is combined with art learning when students draw the anatomy and structure of various plants and animals.

6. Engage in art activities that require measurement and planning, such as weaving (fig. 9.15), macrame, and architectural and other models.

Relating Social Studies and Art

1. History becomes alive through art. Visually interpret—that is, draw or paint—such events as "The Development of the West," "Visiting the Middle East," "The Civil War," "The History of Clowns," and "Transportation."
2. Draw and paint murals or illustrations about the environment, such as "Plant Life," "A Walk in the Desert," and "Hiking in the Mountains."

3. Study the history of a country (or a state like Alaska) through artists' paintings.
4. Draw and compare similar artifacts of various cultures—for example, tools, masks, jewelry, architecture, clothing, textiles, adornment, and furniture.
5. Draw maps of a city as seen through the eyes of an architect and a city planner.
6. Examine the development of architecture within a culture by studying past artworks.

Integrating the Arts

1. Improvise dramatic plays using face masks that you created.

Figure 9.15   Weaving designs requires students to practice their math skills.

Figure 9.16   Words, ideas, and a design are incorporated into this album cover.

2. Design and paint stage props to use with plays.
3. Paint to music.
4. Design album covers (fig. 9.16).
5. Create costumes and then dramatize a story from literature.
6. Design costumes for a dance performance.
7. Improvise feelings and dramatize them. Then express them in drawings or paintings.
8. Create puppets based on characters in a story. Then design scenery and dramatize the story as a puppet show.

9. Select a painting, such as Picasso's *Three Musicians*. Pretend that the characters become alive and perform the music.
10. Select a painting and reinterpret it into a collage.
11. Dramatize a painting—that is, pretend that you are the characters in the painting.
12. Study European cathedrals, such as Notre Dame and Chartres, and relate these to classical music. Then create a painting to the music.
13. Study Navajo sand paintings, and research the meanings and stories of the paintings.
14. Study cultures in history, such as the Incan culture, and their costumes and headdresses. Then have students create their own costumes and dances.

NOTES

1. P. Gregg, "Art and Reading: Is There a Relationship?" *Reading World,* May 1978, 345–51.
2. *The National Visual Arts Standards.* Jeanne Rollins, chairperson. Reston, Va.: National Art Education Association Publications, 1994.

part

3

Art Appreciation

Looking at and Responding to Art—History, Analysis, Aesthetics

chapter

10

Art History

After viewing the cave paintings at Lascaux, France, Pablo Picasso was reported to have said, "We have invented nothing."

The image grows in the sense that man sees what he wants to see. As each tool has its own unique way of living on the picture surface, so each individual has his own way of binding optical signs into shapes and images that he would like to see.

Gyorgy Kepes, *Language of Vision*

Art is an exciting adventure. All artworks are unique expressions of visual thought, defined by art elements and design principles. Each artwork reflects the artist's idea about a subject and is a concept that has been experienced, composed—sometimes spontaneously and intuitively, sometimes carefully and precisely—and then created as a work of art.

As art appreciators, we have the privilege of viewing the artist's creation and perhaps understanding the artist's world that exists only in that particular space. In that respect, artists are heroes and teachers, offering us a glimpse of their reality, their truth, and an appreciation for what art can be.

This chapter highlights artworks and artists from throughout history that together provide a worldwide sampling of a variety of media, styles, techniques, and ideas. As you read through this chapter, use the time line in figure 10.1 as a reference.

ANCIENT ART: YESTERDAY'S ARTISTS

In ancient cultures spread out over various geographic locations, art had many purposes and was used in rituals, magic, worship, and social and political propaganda. Remnants of the art remain, but little is known of the ancient artists and their living and working conditions. Different societies tended to regard artists differently. Usually, throughout history, artists have worked for a society, a wage, or a commission. Only in the last century have artists worked independently, without an agreement or remuneration.

Australian Aborigine "Dreamings"

Rock engravings and other art fragments found in Australia and dating back 32,000 years (twice the age of the Lascaux cave paintings found in France) are evidence of the oldest known continuous art tradition: what Australian aborigines call "Dreamings."

The art of "Dreamings" describes the creation of the world by spirit ancestors who took a variety of mythical forms. At times, they were animals, insects, vegetation, birds, giants, stars, and even movements and concepts like coughing or itchiness. They molded the world into deserts, mountains, forests, stars, and cultures.

Each aborigine inherits the rights to the stories, imagery, and paintings of a particular "Dreaming." In the paintings, the aborigine artists portray the spirit ancestors as significant mythical forms, and everything in the painting must be meaningful. Each artist experiences different aspects of his or her own personal "Dreaming" and can add revelations or forgotten fragments. In this way, the traditional design has changed through the millenniums (see fig. 10.2).

Ancient art forms were painted on bark, on the body, on objects, and in the sand, and were used for reenactment of the "Dreaming" mysteries. More recently, men and women aborigine artists use acrylic paints on canvas spread

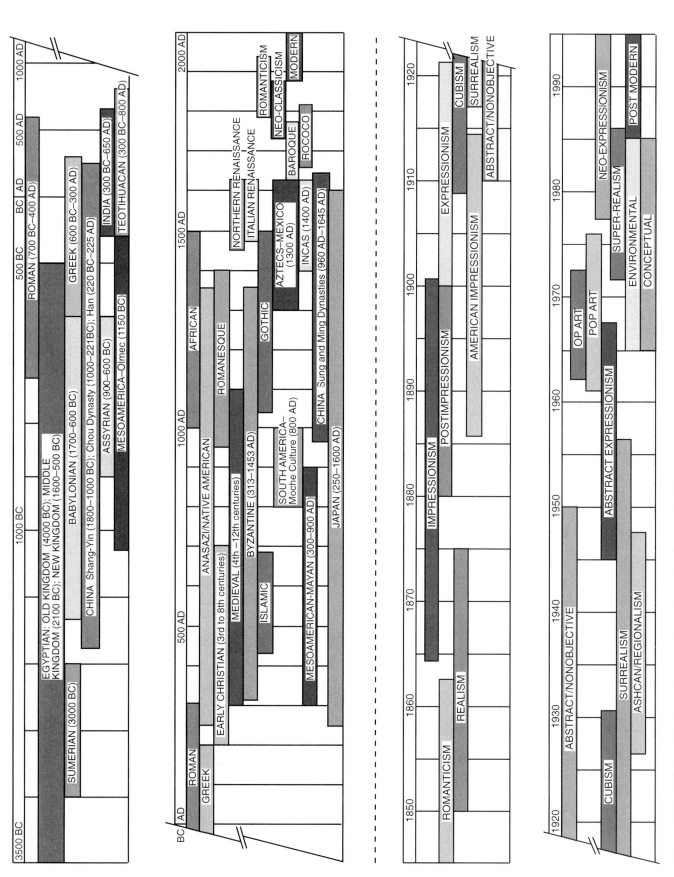

Figure 10.1 This time line shows the approximate dates of various art developments.

Figure 10.2 *Dreamtime V* by aborigine artist Heath Possum. (Courtesy of Gordon R. Marks, San Francisco.)

out in the sand. In the aboriginal community of Yuendumu, about eight hundred out of a thousand inhabitants are artists.[1]

Cave Paintings and Artifacts

The earliest cave paintings were majestic drawings of animals that were incised into rock, marked in soft clay, or drawn with the fingers on decomposing areas of cave walls. Thousands of paintings and artifacts, made between 11,000 and 35,000 years ago, have been discovered at hundreds of different sites.

A beautifully carved ivory head, made about 25,000 years ago, is called the Venus of Brassempouy, after the site where it was discovered in France. A musical flute of the same age was carved from bone. Weapons, such as spears, items of personal adornment, and carved and modeled animals have been found at many sites. Carved and modeled female sculptures, sometimes called Venus figures (fertility symbols), date back to 25,000 years ago and portray women at various stages of womanhood. The sculptures, found in Russia, Austria, and Italy, usually do not have facial features, but some are adorned with jewelry, belts, and elaborate coiffures. A carved male sculpture, estimated to be 32,000 years old, was found in a cave in Germany.

The most famous and elegant cave paintings were found in Lascaux, France, in 1940. The cave's chamber and passages contain over six hundred large and small paintings, fifteen hundred engravings, and artifacts used by the artists, all dated at about 20,000 years ago. The meanings of the paintings are not known, but the paintings may have been related to hunting-magic rituals. The mystery animals are bulls, deer, bison, cows, horses, and combinations of all. Dots under some of the images may be hunting tallies.[2]

Ancient artists used stone tools to shape rock, burins (flint tools with beveled points) to incise outlines, earth-provided colors, animal marrow for binding pigments, and animal bristles as brushes. From the beginning, they imprinted their own hands on cave walls in decorative patterns. In some instances, color was sprayed through a hollow bone, a reed, or directly from the mouth around a hand placed against a wall. When the hand was removed, a silhouette outline remained.

Egypt

In ancient Egypt, art was devoted mainly to funerary purposes and the afterlife. Artists worked in hereditary employment, decorating tombs and working an eight-hour day. Their pay was usually food and clothing.

Artists were thought of as artisans—that is, craftspeople—who worked alongside goldsmiths, potters, and woodworkers. Some achieved more success than others, however, having servants of their own, participating in religious ceremonies at the temples, and reaching high positions in administrative or priestly rank.

Sculptors were more respected than painters, since they had more responsibilities, including knowing painters' techniques. They carved mainly from granite or basalt, both hard stones.

Workshops regulated artistic styles and also prescribed recipes for exact colors. Only six basic colors were used—black, white, red, blue, yellow, and green—and these were mixed to make other shades and tints. Small pots held fluid paints, and animal skin bags held powdered pigment. Colors were mixed on slate palettes. Hollow reeds held mixed colors, and brushes were made from reeds pounded flat on the end till they were fibers.

Greece

During the golden age of Greek art in the fifth century B.C., Phidias was the best-known sculptor and the superintendent of artistic work for the Parthenon. He created the "Zeus" at Olympia and the "Athena" that stood before the Parthenon on the Acropolis. These sculptures were 35 and 40 feet high, respectively, and were made from wood, which was covered with ivory, gold, and bronze.

Most Greek statues were painted. Encaustic wax painting (with hot beeswax) preserved the colors of statues placed outside.

The first independent paintings in Greece were made on wooden panels. The artists used primarily four colors: white, yellows, reds, and black. The Greeks held painting competitions, much like they did for sports.

Pottery vessels were used and needed by every Greek household. On many of the vessels were painted scenes and designs revealing the Greek way of life. Assembly-line techniques made possible the production of large numbers of vessels, and those who painted them were considered secondary artists.

Rome

In ancient Rome, artists were granted exemption from some taxes and the free use of state-owned workshops. Fresco mural paintings on walls of public buildings and private villas were part of everyday life. Statues were everywhere. For example, one theater had some three thousand statues, and the Trojan column in the Roman Forum was decorated with twenty-five hundred low-relief figure sculptures. Roman sculptors copied Greek sculptors in their addition of tree trunks and pedestals to sculptures. Nevertheless, in ancient Rome, architecture was considered the only valid art form.

India and Southeast Asia

In India, communities that date back more than 5,000 years have been discovered near Mohenjo-Dar, on the Indus River in what is now Pakistan. These finds reveal cities with houses, streets, shops, wells, and drainage systems. The residents used carved stone seals to stamp documents written on clay tablets. Pottery and small sculptures have also been found.

Southeast Asian countries, including Thailand, Burma, Sumatra, and Java, were greatly influenced by the Indian culture, including Buddhism. Bas-relief sculptures, carvings, and temples reflect the Buddhist religious belief of rebirth.

China

Some of the earliest known Chinese artifacts are bronze objects used for food or wine in sacrificial rites. These objects date from the Shang dynasty that ruled from 1800 to 1200 B.C. Around 600 B.C., Chinese philosophers began to teach the philosophy of Taoism, which says that the secret of wisdom and happiness is leading a simple, modest, patient life and following the conditions of the laws of nature. Artists of that period liked to combine painting and poetry and painted scenic landscapes as well as fantasy ones. Many artists painted hanging scrolls with ink and watercolor on paper. The pottery, bronze sculptures, gardens, calligraphy, and porcelains of this period are also well known.

Japan

In Japan, ancestor worship evolved into the religion of Shintoism, which teaches reverence for race and for ruling families, who are believed to be descendants of gods. The Japanese Shinto shrine is an early architectural form. Around A.D. 500, Buddhism was brought to Japan by a Korean king. Most Japanese Buddhist temples were post-and-lintel structures with open-frame construction. Japanese artists also were known for their painted scrolls, lacquered wood carvings, and painted screens.

Around A.D. 800, the woodcut was introduced from the Chinese. During the late 1800s, Japanese woodcuts became popular in the West for their aesthetic qualities and greatly influenced European artists, who were inspired by the woodcuts' patterns and compositions.

Islamic Countries

About A.D. 600, the Arabian prophet Muhammad initiated the Islamic religion. Followers, who were called Muslims, believed in Allah as the sole deity and in Muhammad as Allah's prophet. Islam spread from what is now the country of Iran west to Spain and east to India.

Muhammad was against idolatry and forbid any images in the religious mosques. Only abstract decorations, such as arabesques (complex patterns of intertwined lines and shapes) and geometric designs, were allowed to adorn the insides of Islamic buildings.

Islam was a major force in crafts, architecture, government, science, literature, mathematics, and medicine for hundreds of years. Arabesques were often found in Islamic silver works, textiles, rugs, ceramics, and glass creations. Book illustration was permitted, and scholars translated and copied Greek texts. After the Crusades of the eleventh, twelfth, and thirteenth centuries, when Christian military forces tried to win the Holy Land from the Muslims, some Islamic distinctions, such as the pointed arch and stained glass, were taken back to Europe and incorporated into cathedrals.

Today, highly prized Islamic carpets may have from thirty-two to three hundred knots to an inch.

Africa

Africa, a continent separated into deserts, highlands, savannas, rivers, and forests, is also a land of many different peoples, each with their own language and their own style of art. In Africa, art has always been a part of life in that it is featured in social, spiritual, natural, and supernatural beliefs. The art may be created to bring about fertility, to appease and honor spirits, to indicate authority, to ward off enemies, and to celebrate life. However, in modern-day Africa, artworks tend to be tied less to rituals and more to artistic expression.

Ceremonial masks are found in cultures throughout much of Africa and symbolize taking on the identity and power of another person, animal, or both. The wearer may also paint the body and wear costumes to perform.

The Dogon people of Mali in Africa are known for their imaginative carved wooden bowls, jars, masks, and doors. They also carve abstract wooden figures of animals, humans, or a combination of both that are of excellent craftsmanship and that inspired early twentieth-century artists.

In the Ife culture (Nigeria around A.D. 1100–1300), the artists created bronze sculptures using the lost-wax casting method. Because of the fine artistic qualities and craftsmanship of these sculptures, Ife artists are believed to have been influenced by the Egyptians.

South America and Mesoamerica

The earliest civilization found in South America was a group who lived in the central Andes Mountains around 700 B.C. and designed irrigation canals. The Moche culture existed around A.D. 800 and was known for its metallurgy, sun-dried brick pyramids, and handmade ceramics.

By A.D. 1400, the Incas had built an empire of hanging bridges, roads, and framed terraces for irrigation and farming that reached from northern Ecuador to Chile. Llamas and alpacas had been domesticated to provide wool and to be food carriers. Known for their architecture and stone carvings, the Incas built religious temples of stone and decorated them with symbols (carvings) of their gods, most important of which was the sun god. The Incan city of Machu Picchu rested high on a mountaintop and consisted of over two hundred buildings, which at the time was considered a large community.

Mesoamerica was the area from modern Mexico to the northern countries of Central America (including the Gulf of Mexico and Yucatán peninsula). The oldest Mesoamerican culture was found near Olmec and dates back to around 1150 B.C. Olmec art often carried a jaguar face motif and included large sculptures, small jade carvings, and pottery.

In the central highlands of Mesoamerica, north of Mexico City, the Teotihuacan culture dates from about 300 B.C. to A.D. 800. Teotihuacan cities had many ornate temples and palaces, and the center of the city was developed around a broad avenue. Teotihuacanos respected nature, and their gods were of nature, such as Tlaloc, god of rain. They made carvings of their gods and also were known to make human sacrifices as offerings to the gods.

The Mayans, who lived in the lowlands of Guatemala and Honduras from about A.D. 300 to 900, and then moved to the Yucatán peninsula, were advanced in both architecture and mathematics. They designed the corbeled arch so that they had openings for rooms and hallways in their pyramid temples. They also developed a fairly accurate calendar that included mythical and magical stories. Writing and astronomy were two additional accomplishments of the Mayans. Their bas-relief sculptures were of human, animal, and plant forms.

By A.D. 1300, the Aztecs were in power in Mesoamerica and had established a center at the site of modern-day Mexico City. The Aztecs were very warlike and over time expanded their empire to include all of Mexico. They had ornate costumes for their rituals.

North America

Not much is known about Native Americans before A.D. 1500 except for one culture—the Anasazi. The Anasazi lived on the plateaus of New Mexico, northern Arizona, and southwestern Colorado in cliff dwellings made of stone, timbers, and adobe. Each cliff dwelling was like a modern condominium, often containing over two hundred rooms, with twenty-plus underground religious chambers called kivas, and housing many clans. The Anasazi made pottery, weavings, and masonry-walled structures as early as the first century A.D.

The Zuni and Hopi were the Anasazi heirs, as were the Pueblo people, a farming culture. Around A.D. 1600, the Navajo, originally a hunting culture, adopted many of the Pueblo customs. Today, Navajo rugs are highly prized around the world.

The Tlingit, Haida, and Kwakiutl, for example, lived from Alaska to California along the Pacific Coast. They depended on food from the ocean but also farmed and hunted. Their homes were gable-roofed structures of cedar planks. Wood was also used to make totem poles and seaworthy canoes.

Native Americans who lived in the open middle section of the country—the Plains—from the Mississippi to the Rockies included the Crow, Sioux, Comanche, Cheyenne, and Arapahoe. They were noted for their buffalo hunting, tents (tepees), and leather shirts, dresses, and leggings decorated with beads, feathers, thongs, bones, claws, horns, and fur. Face painting was also popular. Artist George Catlin made paintings of forty-eight tribes of warriors and chiefs, which today tell us about the peoples of the Plains. The Iroquois lived on the East Coast.

ART IN THE MIDDLE AGES

During the Middle Ages, from about the fourth to twelfth centuries, monasteries were the art centers in Western Europe. The function of the library workshops in the monasteries was to copy the Bible and other religious works. Each book was printed by hand, one at a time, with monks and nuns as scribes and illuminators. These craftspeople worked endlessly, inscribing intricate designs and scrollwork on the vellum pages (made from calfskin).[3] Gold leaf was used in the ornate initial lettering and painting. Black, brown, or red ink was added with a pen for outlining. A pen was also used for hatchwork and details. Brushwork filled in the drawing with flat colors, and then shadows and modeling in darker shades were added.

The art of the early Middle Ages shows flat handling of paint and decorative style. Divine figures from religious beliefs were usually depicted in symbolic imagery. Mosaics were often used by the Mesopotamians, Greeks, and Romans, with centers at Byzantium and Ravenna.

Medieval art studios produced mosaics and fresco wall murals. Studio artists worked at the site, such as a church. Mosaics were made by covering a wall with a layer of fresh cement and then embedding small pieces of colored marble or enamel into the cement. *Buon fresco* painting meant applying water-based pigments on newly laid wet lime plaster, which formed a durable binding film of crystalline carbonite. *Buon fresco* murals had to be done correctly the first time, since retouching was not possible. *Fresco seccos* meant tempera wall painting where an adhesive-like egg white or gum was mixed with pigments and then applied to a dry plaster surface.

Associations of tradesmen, called **guilds,** were formed during the Middle Ages to protect the individual and to maintain standards of performance and quality. There were three classes in the guild: (1) the master, who bought the materials and sold the finished work; (2) the journeymen, skilled craftsmen who worked by the day and were paid by the master; and (3) the apprentices, or beginners, who did the menial tasks while learning their skills and received room and board in exchange. Apprentices were trained according to a written contract under a master. They learned lifetime skills and adhered to standards set by the guild.

Each guild was run like a small industry, with the master as the director and representative and the journeymen as supervisors of the apprentices. Fees were based on the hours needed to complete a work.

Fine art was highly commercial to the artists, who painted the same pictures several times. Artists worked to the dictates of a patron, who paid the commission. A contract between patron and artist set the theme and price. The artist did complete drawings on toned paper with ink, chalk, watercolor, or tempera. The finished drawing was then "squared" up so that the assistant could repeat the contents of each square on a large panel or canvas.

The old masters derived their pigments from the earth, from minerals, and from semiprecious stones (such as carbon, coal, tar, oxides, and sulfides). Lapis lazuli, found in the mountains of Afghanistan, was needed for painting blue robes and cloth. Painting media, such as water, honey, egg, or oil, were added to the pigments.

Many studios made woodcut or engraving copies of paintings to advertise the skills of the artist. Workshops used stamped signs or monograms that were approved by the master as trademarks.

The Church was an important patron of the arts in the later Middle Ages and during the Renaissance, and the best of art was often found in the churches. In the seventeenth century, royalty became the grand patron of the arts. Rulers often appointed artists to paint extravagant projects to enhance their reputations.

ART DURING THE RENAISSANCE

The Renaissance (or "rebirth") in Italy (from about A.D. 1300 to 1600) is often considered the greatest period in the world history of art. Two of the greatest achievements of this period were the discovery of **perspective** (the illusion of space on a two-dimensional surface) and **chiaroscuro** (the illusion of form through the use of light and dark). Both of these art factors contributed to the development of realism. Florence and Venice, Italy, were the centers for this great art movement.

The early Renaissance artists were Giotto, Donatello, Masaccio, Fra Angelico, Botticelli, Fra Filippo Lippi, Mantegna, and Andrea del Castagno. The sixteenth century brought the "Age of Genius," as there were so many great artists gifted with creative powers. The High Renaissance

artists included Leonardo da Vinci, Michelangelo, Giorgione, Titian, Raphael, Tintoretto, Correggio, Veronese, Uccello, and Piero della Francesca.

POST-RENAISSANCE ART

Baroque art began in Rome between A.D. 1600 and 1700 and then extended to Flanders, France, and Spain. Baroque artists used light and multicurved forms and arrangement to create a romantic mysticism in their compositions. Outstanding artists of this period were Peter Paul Rubens, El Greco, Velazquez, Frans Hals, Caravaggio, Rembrandt (fig. 10.3), Steen, Vermeer, and Poussin.

Rococo art, which was prevalent from A.D. 1700 to 1789, was very decorative, ornamental, and free. Rococo art flourished in France, Italy, Holland, and England and was best exemplified in the works of Watteau, Fragonard, Van Dyck, Holbein, Reynolds, Gainsborough, and Hogarth.

Neoclassicism is the term used to describe the art movement that followed the French Revolution (A.D. 1789 to 1815). Paintings were based on classical themes and heroic ideals. The figure was painted without feelings and with the emphasis on style, which was sophisticated, intellectual, cold, technical, and very realistic. Form was more important than light and color. Neoclassic artists were technical draftsmen and included Jacques-Louis David and Jean-Auguste-Dominique Ingres.

Romanticism (1820–1850) was a reverberation against neoclassicism, traditional classicism, and imitative styles. Paintings stressed the emotion and personality of the individual, dramatic action, and adventure. They told thrilling stories about life and experiences. The paint quality was full of energy and movement, with open, flowing brushwork. Artists of this period included Goya, Gericault, Delacroix, Turner, and Constable.

Realism (1850–1870) was a reaction to the machine age. Artists began to paint the lives of workers and peasants in a serious way. They depicted what they saw in everyday life, not in the imagination. They believed in a new scientific and industrial age that reflected contemporary issues and images. Artists of this period were Gustave Courbet, Edouard Manet (fig. 10.4), Daumier, and Thomas Eakins.

In the late eighteenth century, art schools were founded in various art centers. These schools taught conventional drawing, anatomy, perspective, and copying of the work of masters. The Royal Academy of Art was founded in A.D. 1768 by George III. The Pennsylvania Academy of Fine Arts was founded in 1805 in America.

During the late eighteenth and early nineteenth centuries, art schools often received financial support from the many new industries. This resulted in changes in the programs of art schools. Art became not only a means of self-expression but also a consumer product.

Art became an integral part of everyday life in the Industrial Age. The Bauhaus, founded in Weimar, Germany, in 1919 by Walter Gropius, emphasized the unification of

Figure 10.3   Rembrandt Harmensz, van Rijn (or follower), Dutch, 1609–1669, *Young Girl at an Open Door,* oil on canvas, 1645, 102 × 85.1 cm, Mr. and Mrs. Martin A. Ryerson Collection, photograph © 1995 The Art Institute of Chicago. All Rights Reserved. The young girl seems to be waiting in anticipation. The strong contrasts of light and dark, along with the firm edges of the forms and the simple background with the faint light opening from the left, all add to the mysterious expression on the girl's half-lit face.

Figure 10.4   *At the Milliner's* (Chez La Modiste), Edouard Manet, 1881. The Fine Arts Museums of San Francisco, Mildred Anna Williams Collection.

art and industry. Teachers at the school included such artists as Paul Klee, Käthe Kollwitz, and Wassily Kandinsky. Art schools today offer curriculums in both fine art and commercial art.

CONTEMPORARY ART

The art movements discussed in this section represent the contemporary movements of the nineteenth and twentieth centuries. Beginning with impressionism, the contemporary art movements express a transition from the traditional to a new technical approach to painting. Artworks not only represent the subject matter but go beyond to consider atmosphere and the appearance of light on a surface. The descriptions that follow are simplified and can act as catalysts for further study.

Impressionism

Impressionism (impression of light) was an art movement begun in the 1870s and 1880s by Parisian artists whose purpose was to paint air, sunshine, light, and the reflection of light off of surfaces in their work. These painters sometimes used intense contrast between light and dark, bold shadows, and short strokes of bright, bold color next to each other to make their brush strokes alive with movement. They painted mostly out of doors, and their chief concerns were light and atmosphere. They simplified forms, sometimes losing the outside edges and silhouettes. Claude Monet reportedly said that he was not interested in painting objects but in the atmosphere surrounding them—impossible to do by remaining indoors (fig. 10.5).

Close inspection of an impressionistic painting shows that the color is placed directly on the canvas, with one stroke being placed next to another with a slight space in between. From a distance, the viewer's eye blends the pure colors into combinations, and the colors' brilliance is preserved. When the painting is viewed closely, however, the form is almost lost.

Impressionistic painters included Edgar Degas (fig. 10.6), Pierre Auguste Renoir (fig. 10.7), Claude Monet, Camille Pissarro, Paul Cézanne (fig. 10.8), and Pierre Bonard.

In America, the first impressionist exhibition was in 1874. The group of artists called themselves an "anonymous cooperative society of painters, sculptors, engravers, etc." The press and public considered their creations too sketchy for finished work. Today, however, these works are highly prized. American impressionists included Childe Hassam, Mary Cassatt (fig. 10.9), William Merritt Chase, Maurice Pendergast, John Singer Sargent, John Twachtman, Lillian Wescott Hale, and James McNeill Whistler.

Post-Impressionism

Post-impressionism was a late nineteenth-century avant-garde movement by artists whose paintings resemble those of the impressionists in the use of bright colors. Rather than emphasizing the effects of light, however, post-impressionists expressed and exaggerated their personal feelings about the image.

Post-impressionistic painters included Paul Gauguin and Vincent van Gogh (see fig. 8.5*b*).

Figure 10.5   Claude Monet, *Les arceaux fleuris,* Giverny 1913. Oil on canvas, 32 inches × 36 inches. Collection of Phoenix Art Museum, Gift of Mr. and Mrs. Donald D. Harrington.

Figure 10.6 *Portrait of a Man,* Edgar Degas. Oil on canvas, 16 inches × 13 inches. ca. 1964. The Fine Arts Museums of San Francisco, Gift from Dr. T. Edward and Tullah Hanley, Bradford, Pennsylvania.

Figure 10.7 Pierre Auguste Renoir, French, 1841–1919, *Two Sisters* (On the Terrace), oil on canvas, 1881, 100.3 × 81 cm, Mr. and Mrs. Lewis Larned Coburn Memorial Collection, photograph © 1995 The Art Institute of Chicago. All Rights Reserved. The theme here is delicate, light, and airy. Even the edges of the forms are soft. Renoir was concerned with the airy quality, and the soft brush strokes reflect this feeling.

Figure 10.8 Paul Cézanne, French, 1839–1906, *The Basket of Apples,* oil on canvas, c. 1895, 65.5 × 81.3 cm, Helen Birch Bartlett Memorial Collection, photograph © 1995 The Art Institute of Chicago. All Rights Reserved.

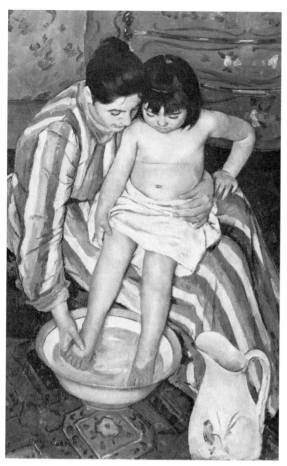

Figure 10.9   Mary Cassatt, American, 1844–1926, *The Bath*, oil on canvas, 1891/92, 39½ × 26 in., Robert A. Waller Fund, photograph © 1995 The Art Institute of Chicago. All Rights Reserved.

Neo-Impressionism or Pointillism

Neo-impressionism, or **pointillism,** was a late nineteenth-century French method of painting in which small dabs of complementary colors, such as red and green, orange and blue, and yellow and purple, were applied side by side. The expectation was that, at a distance, the eye would fuse the colors so that they appeared to blend smoothly. Neo-impressionists expected this technique to provide more vivid coloring than that achieved by mixing the colors on the palette. Neo-impressionistic painters included Georges Seurat and Paul Signac.

Expressionism

Expressionism was a late nineteenth-century art movement, especially popular among German artists, that emphasized portraying what artists felt, rather than what they viewed. Thus, expressionistic paintings reflect powerful emotional feelings concerned with the emotional essence. The paintings have subjects, but the subjects are often distorted in form, color, or space. Light and color are powerfully contrasted, and there is dynamic movement. Expres-

sionism is a highly personal interpretation of life. The distortion of the subject helps to capture and clarify the meaning or idea.

Expressionistic painters included Georges Rouault, Ernst Ludwig Kirchner, Emil Nolde, Wassily Kandinsky, George Grosz, Max Beckmann, Chaim Soutine, and Edvard Munch.

Cubism

Cubism is an art movement in which the semiabstract image is often represented by fragmented, semitransparent shapes. Cubists use regular forms—sometimes architectural, sometimes geometric (without modeled shading)—that become transparent and merge with the background. Many views of the same object may be seen and combined in the same picture. Tops of objects may be tilted to make the objects more interesting and the angles more lively.

In cubism, depth of space is replaced by a flat, two-dimensional surface with no background or foreground as such. Instead, the viewer sees combinations and interrelating of parts. Interpenetration of forms is used for the best composition. To indicate motion and vibration, cubists repeat the same object, overlapping and interpenetrating itself, many times. Major cubists included Pablo Picasso, Georges Braque, Paul Cézanne, and Fernand Leger.

Surrealism

Surrealism is the art movement begun in the 1920s in which artists use supernatural combinations, psychological effects, and new associations to invent a new reality through new relationships with ordinarily unrelated themes. (See Salvador Dalí's *Spectre de Soir,* fig. 10.10.) The subconscious mind dominates the actions.

Subjects can be from any time, any place, and images vary from realistic, to dreamlike or exotic, to semiabstract, to childlike. Surrealists use realistic objects, but the objects are combined in an unrealistic way to convey unusual effects, perhaps to make the viewer wonder. Symbols suggest many things. Deep perspective indicates the movement of time.

Surrealists included Salvador Dalí, Yves Tanguy, Georgia De Chirico, Joan Miró, Mauritz C. Escher, Odilon Redon, and Rene Magritte.

American Ashcan and Regional Art

Beginning in the early 1900s, a group of artists joined together, calling themselves "the Eight." They painted city street life and experiences in American cities. Backyards, saloons, alleys, fights, and slums were often depicted in their paintings. They were rejected by the public and soon nicknamed the **"Ashcan School."** Their independent approach became well known and culminated in an exhibition in New York in 1913. Ashcan artists included Robert Henri (originator), John Sloan, Arthur Davies, William Glakens, Ernest Lawson, George Bellows, and George Luks.

Figure 10.10 *Spectre de Soir* (Spector of the Evening), Salvador Dalí, Spanish, 1904–1989. Oil on canvas, 1930. San Diego Museum of Art (Gift of Mr. and Mrs. Irving T. Snyder). This painting has qualities of mystery, unusual space, interesting shadows, and strong lights and darks. The forms appear to float and to be timeless, since we do not see any surface on which they are resting. The painting is an example of surrealism.

Some artists, called **regionalists,** painted everyday rural life during the Depression in the Midwest. These artists included Thomas Hart Benton, Grant Wood, Charles Burchfield, and Philip Evergood.

Abstract Art

The **abstract** art style describes nonrepresentational or nonnaturalistic forms of expression. The forms may be more or less abstract, varying from simplified, geometric, or identifiable subjects to those that are completely unrecognizable. (See Stuart Davis's *Radio Tubes,* fig. 10.11.)

Abstract artists included Pablo Picasso, Piet Mondrian, Georges Braque, Henri Matisse, Mark Rothko, Stuart Davis, and John Marin.

Nonobjective Art

The **nonobjective** art style describes artworks that have no recognizable object or subject, no reference to natural appearances. Compositional relationships, such as color, shape, and texture, are most important.

Wassily Kandinsky was the founder of nonobjective art. He used simple shapes and believed that painting was composed of three elements: line, color, and shape. Lines assume attitudes and are rhythmical. Colors have emotions of their own, with low-key colors being somber, quiet, and moody, while bright colors are happy. Nonobjective painters might select one shape, such as a circle, and vary the design.

In addition to Kandinsky, nonobjective painters included Joan Miró and Piet Mondrian.

Abstract Expressionism

Abstract expressionism is an American art form that appeared in the late 1940s and 1950s and that is characterized by large, broad, often multicolored strokes of paint and very expressive abstract forms that appear to have been painted quickly and spontaneously. Abstract expressionist painters included Willem de Kooning, Mark Rothko, Robert Motherwell, Helen Frankenthaler, Hans Hofmann, and Jackson Pollock.

Figure 10.11   *Radio Tubes,* Stuart Davis. Govache on paper, 22 inches × 14 inches. Oliver B. James Collection of American Art, Arizona State University Art Museum, Tempe, AZ.

Pop Art

Pop art is a comment on the contemporary, natural environment and on commercial aspects of our culture. Pop artists often use such themes as cakes, pies, and soup cans. Frequently, these objects form patterns and are repeated. Pop artists include Wayne Thiebaud, Andy Warhol, Roy Lichtenstein, Claes Oldenburg, and Robert Rauschenberg.

Op Art

Op art is concerned with the optical illusions achieved with small, patterned shapes and moving visual effects. Op artists include Bridget Riley and Richard Anuszkiewicz.

Minimal Art

Minimal art, a term coined by art critic Barbara Rose, describes a shift in the 1950s toward a new sensibility in art

> whose blank, neutral, mechanical impersonality contrasts so violently with the romantic, biographical abstract-expressionist style which preceded it that spectators are chilled by its apparent lack of feeling or content.[4]

This new kind of art intentionally leaves out the traditional requirements of uniqueness, complexity, and expressive content, and takes visual simplicity to an extreme. For example, minimal artist Robert Rauschenberg gave an exhibition in 1952 that consisted of all white followed by all black canvases.

In addition to Rauschenberg, minimal artists include Josef Albers, Morris Louis, Al Held, Tony Smith, Robert Morris, and Donald Judd.

Computer Graphics

Computer graphics is a popular product of computer-produced art that dates from the mid-1950s. Practiced all over the world, it has centered in large research sections of industrial companies or universities. Aesthetic use of the computer is a result of investigation into its practical uses for industrial designers, engineers, television technicians, and artists and for complicated techniques of computer programming. Students also find the computer fun for drawing (fig. 10.12).

Conceptual Art

Conceptual artists believe that the *concepts* or *ideas* behind an artwork are the real art, not the physical objects (such as paintings) that artists produce. An art style that began in the 1960s, conceptual art focuses on the *process* by which the artwork comes into being and involves the spectator by actual participation. Ideas are often documented with photographs as they develop.

Conceptual artists include Ann Mendieta, Alice Aycock, and Mary Miss.

ART OF TODAY

It is too early to classify the art of today or to delineate it into major new directions because we are still too close to the art concepts to determine which particular movement or group of artists to focus on. However, several trends are apparent.

First, the great variety of materials and techniques being used, often within a single format, results in a huge spectrum of visual imagery, rather than a focus in only one direction. Due to technological advances in, for example, polymers and stronger adhesives, the variety and combinations of art materials being used to express ideas is incredible. For example, earthwork artists change the landscape to conform with the artist's intent. Anselm Keefer, a German artist, adheres molten lead and straw to large canvases to express Germany's emotional landscape.

Second, art of today often is a social commentary, reflecting on social changes, injustices, environmental concerns, and the need for change. In *The Dinner Party*, artist Judy Chicago clarifies women's needs for recognition

Figure 10.12 Stimulating visual images are created by using paint-and-draw software on a computer. Kevin Scully, first grade, Spitalny Elementary School, Phoenix, Arizona. Art teacher Jackie Bondie.

throughout history. Graffiti artist Keith Haring calls attention to social attitudes, many of them dealing with television as a medium and its influence on society (see fig. 10.13). Most recently, political statements are themes for such artists as Leon Golub and Jenny Holzer. Photography and video art also play major roles in art today.

Perhaps the major influence on art of today, however, is the international universality of the artist. For instance, Italian artist Francesco Clemente has studios in New York, Rome, and Madrid. Art exhibitions from around the world travel to major museums across America, and even local galleries feature contemporary foreign artists. Today, artists are not American, Italian, French, or German as much as they are international, and their works are as likely to be found in the Pompideau in Paris as in the Modern Museum in New York City.

Major artists include Enzo Cucchi, Nam June Paik, Susan Rothenburg, Julian Schnabel, Mark di Suvero, Eric Fischl, Mimmo Paladino, and George Baselitz.

SELECTED PROFILES OF MODERN ARTISTS: THE ARTIST AS ROLE MODEL

The artist is the hero and role model. The sections that follow offer brief profiles of some well-known modern artists. Only a few of the many modern artists are profiled here.

There are many others whose lives and works you might want to explore. See Appendix A for lists of selected modern artists, portrait and figure artists, still-life artists, landscape artists, and abstract artists, all in alphabetical order, and for a list of recognized artists grouped by their country of birth. These should make it easier for you to select artists to study in particular areas.

Andrew Wyeth

Andrew Wyeth (1917–) paints familiar favorites—farmhouses, reflections in a pond, empty rooms, kitchens, shiny buckets coated with the grease of cream—with clean, well-scrubbed flair.

His studio is an austere and drab one-room school that epitomizes the simplicity of Maine and New England. Wyeth enjoys sitting in his studio and watching the sun creep along the floor boards and up the wall. In a portrait of the school, he painted every detail—from the color of the curtains to the rag stuck in the upper right-hand window.

To Wyeth, drawing is like fencing. He darts in and puts down a sharp notation and then jabs at it. Then he moves back, recovers, and jabs again. The excitement in his hand—even the shaking—gives life to the line and makes Wyeth impossible to copy. (See Andrew Wyeth's *The Tolling Bell*, fig. 10.14.)

Figure 10.13   Keith Haring, untitled. Collection of Phoenix Art Museum, Museum Purchase and Gift of an Anonymous Donor.

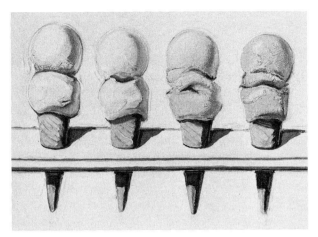

Figure 10.15 Wayne Thiebaud, *Four Ice Cream Cones.* Oil on canvas, 14 inches × 18 inches. Collection of Phoenix Art Museum, Museum Purchase with Funds Provided by COMPAS.

Figure 10.14 *The Tolling Bell,* Andrew Wyeth. Watercolor, 29 inches × 21 inches. Oliver B. James Collection of American Art, Arizona State University Art Museum, Tempe, AZ. Note the wet-wash sky. The darker values were brushed in next, and the fine lines of tree and steeple were painted last.

Wayne Thiebaud

Wayne Thiebaud (1920–) attempts to have his paintings create their own light. Also, the drama of his images is heightened by isolation and insulation, and by emphasizing certain elements in a variety of situations. Thiebaud's subject matter, whether a pie, cake, figure, or landscape, does have iconographic force and interest, but to him, these are less important than the structure of learning to paint as a problem, extending the painting's limits, and playing around with a notion, such as isolation. (See Wayne Thiebaud's *Four Ice Cream Cones,* fig. 10.15.)

For example, in figure painting, Thiebaud's isolated figures become a formal problem of changing the volume from spatial attitudes that are very round to those that are very flat and of infinite space. The viewer wonders what is happening. The figure is posed, not saying, doing, or feeling anything. Most of us go through life with some kind of mask—perhaps a vacant smile, an introversive stare, a frown, a placid attitude—that we put on when we are just sitting with nothing to do or resting. The facial muscles relax, and the face appears to be expressionless. Thiebaud attempts to capture this expression.

Edward Hopper

Edward Hopper (1882–1967) started drawing when he was very young, signing and dating his small sketches by the time he was ten. Hopper was intrigued with the light, the solitude, the feeling of space that he found within the American landscape. Whether it was a lighthouse on a hillside, a Pennsylvania coal town, a room in Brooklyn, a stairway, a bridge, or Jo (his wife) in Wyoming, he focused on capturing the presence of light; the powerful contrast of light and shadows; and the silence, starkness, loneliness, mystery, space, and solitude of the individual within an environment. (See Edward Hopper's *Night Shadows,* fig. 5.23, and *Nighthawks,* fig. 10.16.)

Ben Shahn

Ben Shahn (1898–1969) was born in Lithuania. When he was five, his father was sentenced to Siberia for revolutionary activities. During this time, young Ben would spend all day lettering words from the Bible, memorizing Psalms, and reading Bible stories, study that later revealed itself in the rich biblical imagery of the mature artist. Ben's father escaped Siberia and brought his family to America when Ben was eight. At age thirteen, Ben was apprenticed to a lithographer in New York City.

During his career as an artist, Shahn worked for government agencies and did murals for various federal buildings. He enjoyed a variety of media, such as drawing, painting, mosaics, lithographs, prints, serigraphy (which he often hand colored), frescoes, murals, and graphics. His ideas grew from tragedies, literature, religion, politics, and everyday life. His style was his own: linear, flat areas of color; distorted proportions; patterns; textures; and shallow space. (See Ben Shahn's *Television Antennae,* fig. 10.17, and *All That Is Beautiful,* fig. 3.4.)

Figure 10.16 Edward Hopper, American, 1882–1967, *Nighthawks,* oil on canvas, 84.2 × 152.4 cm, Friends of American Art Collection, photograph © 1995 The Art Institute of Chicago. All Rights Reserved.

Figure 10.17 *Television Antennae,* Ben Shahn. Tempera paint, 10.25 inches × 15.5 inches. Reproduced by courtesy of Gallerie Ann, Houston. The quality of the paint suggests thin wash techniques as well as heavy overpainted areas.

Louise Nevelson

Louise Nevelson (1900–1988) was born in Kiev, Russia, but was brought to America in 1905. She was famous for her sculptured walls—wall-like reliefs made of boxes and abstract shapes placed together with chair legs and other found objects—that she painted a uniform color, usually black. Her construction began as assemblages, and her later sculptures used more permanent materials, such as Lucite, aluminum, glass, and steel. (See Louise Nevelson's sculpture in fig. 10.18.)

John Marin

John Marin (1870–1953) was interested in capturing atmospheric effects, and his paintings might be considered fragmentary, spacious, airy. Tension and balance created a restless expression in his work. Marin believed that he could not create a great work unless he was somehow moved by the objects he painted and then tried to express this perception in his art. (See John Marin's *Brooklyn Bridge*, fig. 10.19).

Figure 10.18 *Windows on the West*, sculpture by Louise Nevelson. Cor-ten steel 14 feet × 14 feet 7½ inches × 24 inches. Photo courtesy of City of Scottsdale, Arizona.

Figure 10.19 *Brooklyn Bridge*, John Marin, American, 1870–1953. Watercolor and pencil on paper, 1910. San Diego Museum of Art (Bequest of Earle W. Grant).

Earl Linderman

Earl Linderman (1931–) takes the raw stuff of life and invents a panorama of electric personalities that exist in media. He chooses to create a new reality in his work, rather than to replicate a given subject or form. The imaginative world of his art is a dynamic adventure derived from selective and aesthetic experiences.

He is a traditionalist in the sense of pictorial composition, and so, the space must work for him. He seeks to thrust forms back and forth to achieve an infinity of depth on a flat surface. At times, the forms ride on top of the plane, or they can drop back. Each part must relate to the whole. The classical ideas of balance, rhythm, and harmony are all present but are interpreted in a contemporary context.

His use of color heightens and expresses form in both an emotional and intellectual sense. He strives to find new modes for the manner in which a color, a line, a shadow can imply or suggest the form or the idea. For

Linderman, art comes together as a visual novel or illustrated fiction, in which no words are necessary. The artworks are timeless and universal. (See Earl Linderman's *Cafe Berlin*, fig. 10.20.)

Joan Hall

Joan Hall considers herself an experimentalist in both image and technique. Color, surface, movement and scale are important aspects of her constructions.

Handmade paper has made an enormous change in Hall's work, allowing her to create free-form shapes, rather than cutting them out of a square sheet of paper. She continually prints and paints with pulp until she achieves the complexity of surface desired.

Hall's constructions are affected by her strong interest in abstraction and in the layering of fragmented images and marks. Her images are drawn from many different ideas, influences, symbols, and impressions centered around her interest in the ocean environment and sailing.

Figure 10.20 *Cafe Berlin* by Earl Linderman. Oil on canvas, 72 inches × 60 inches.

Frida Kahlo

Frida Kahlo (1907–1954), injured in an accident at age eighteen, was subject to ill health most of her life. She explained how she began to paint:

> For many years, my father had kept a box of oil paints and some paint brushes in an old jar and a palette in the corner of his photographic studio. . . . I had my eyes on that box of paints. I couldn't explain why. Being confined to bed for so long, I finally took the opportunity to ask my father for it . . . my mother asked a carpenter to make me an easel, if that's what you can call the special apparatus which could be fixed to my bed, because the plaster cast didn't allow me to sit up. And so I started my first picture, the portrait of a friend.[5]

Kahlo often painted herself because she frequently found herself alone and because she felt that she was the subject she knew best. (See Frida Kahlo's *Self-Portrait with Monkey,* fig. 10.21.)

Alice Neel

Alice Neel (1900–1984) believed that drawing was the great discipline of art. She noted the requirement for drawing a good portrait:

Figure 10.21 *Self-Portrait with Monkey* by Frida Kahlo, 1938. Oil on canvas, 16 inches × 12 inches. (Courtesy of Albright-Knox Art Gallery, Buffalo, New York. Bequest of A. Conger Goodyear, 1966.)

I was incapable of seeing a head as just a head. When I drew a head, it had expression, it had eyes, it had everything. . . . You can't paint any good portrait unless you have a good memory because there are tiny changes all the time, and if you follow those changes, you have nothing. I work fast, and I concentrate so hard that in two or two-and-a-half hours, I've done all I can do.[6]

Neel also felt that painting gave her happiness because it allowed her to be in her own world and to do as she liked in it. (See Alice Neel's *Wellesley Girls,* fig. 10.22.)

Lois Mailou-Jones

Lois Mailou-Jones (1905–) has had a successful career as a painter, teacher (Howard University for forty-seven years), book illustrator, and textile designer. Her oils and watercolors depict African-inspired works, French subjects, and Haitian scenes. Of her work, Mailou-Jones said:

Mine is a quiet exploration—a quest for new meanings in color, texture, and design. . . . Even though I sometimes portray scenes of poor and struggling people, it is a great joy to paint.[7]

Sam Gilliam

Sam Gilliam (1933–) is internationally known for his color field paintings. He has taught in public schools, universities, and workshops. According to Gilliam, "Whether I am teaching or making art, the process is fundamentally the same: I am creating."[8]

Bill Traylor

Bill Traylor (1854–1947) started making art when he was eighty-five years old. Using pencils, a straight edge, and a lap-sized wing board, he drew on any material available, whether paper or shirt-cardboard. He drew simplified

Figure 10.22 *Wellesley Girls* by Alice Neel, 1967. Oil on canvas, 50 inches × 42 inches. © The Estate of Alice Neel. Courtesy of Robert Miller Gallery, New York.

animals, figures, and architectural structures, which he then colored with crayons. Traylor drew prolifically from 1939 to 1942, saying, "It jes' come to me."[9]

Isabel Bishop

Isabel Bishop (1905–1988) worked out of a studio on Union Square in New York City, where she derived subject matter from the people she observed, including workers, passersby, shopgirls, waitresses, straphangers, bums, and shoppers. According to Bishop:

> We never see only what we see; we always see something else with it and through it. If we look at a human face, we see lines and shades, but with it and through it, we see a unique, incomparable personality whose expressions are visible in his face, whose characteristics and destiny have left traces which we understand and in which we can even read something of his future. With and through colors and forms

and movements, we see friendliness and coldness, hostility and devotion, anger and love, sadness and joy. We see infinitely more than we see when we look into a human face.[10]

Barbara Nessim

The primary concern of Barbara Nessim (1939–) is subject matter as content. In her work, she strives to reflect the interaction between women and men, and between humans and the world around them. Her work deals with the psyche and how it integrates in differing lifestyles.

For example, in Nessim's *Thoughts of the Moon* (fig. 10.23), a small, feminine figure is basking in the light of the moon on a large masculine figure's shoulder. She is radiating heat in the darkness, and the male is aware of her presence, but in this particular instance, he is unappreciative of her and is looking elsewhere. The stripes that cover

Figure 10.23 *Thoughts of the Moon* by Barbara Nessim, 1989. Computer drawing with pastel, 44 inches × 34 inches.

the male figure represent his emotional or mental prison—that which is provoking him to search beyond the immediate relationship between the two figures.

Nessim often uses the computer as her medium but stresses that the medium—be it computer, paint on surface, or a combination—is not the main issue. Rather, it is the choice of well-integrated components that helps to illuminate the end result—the work of art.

Esmeralda Delaney

Esmeralda Delaney's (1951–) work is about mystery, love, humor, anxiety, and satire. It is about the human condition; all of humanity's perfections, imperfections, and absurd situations come out in her work. To her, creating art is a necessity. It is a love affair in which she is always involved.

Twenty-three years of studying and collecting in the arts have contributed to Delaney's intuitive abilities as a sculptor. Primitive art, folk art, "Day of the Dead" Mexican

art, and religious art have strongly influenced her work, and she believes that these art forms are some of the most beautiful and universal ever created.

Delaney works primarily in clay and enjoys doing figurative work. Her pieces are large. She works with a stoneware clay body, which she mixes herself. After a piece is thoroughly dried, Delaney uses Duncan underglazes on the eyes and whatever other areas of the piece she chooses to emphasize. Most of her pieces then go through three firings. After a piece is removed from the kiln after the third firing, the nonglazed surfaces are gessoed, and the oil paints are thinned down before they are laid on for a transparent veil of color on the surface. (See Esmeralda Delaney's *Stuck on Forty,* fig. 10.24.)

Georgia O'Keeffe

Georgia O'Keeffe (1887–1986) was one of the important American pioneers of modern art. She began her career as

Figure 10.24 *Stuck on Forty* by Esmeralda Delaney, 1993. Ceramic, 30 inches by 21 inches × 12 inches. Humor and imagination in this artwork make the viewer smile.

an art instructor, teaching at several universities. In her thirties, she gave up teaching after several art exhibits of her paintings in New York. Her paintings of enlargements of flowers and plant forms, her New Mexico landscapes, and her works of clouds and skies are widely known. (See Georgia O'Keeffe's *Pink Abstraction*, fig. 10.25.)

Georges Braque

Georges Braque (1882–1963) was a French painter who, along with Pablo Picasso, originated the cubist style. Braque thought of cubism as the materialization of a new space and saw fragmentation of objects as a way to establish space and movement in space. In his paintings, he

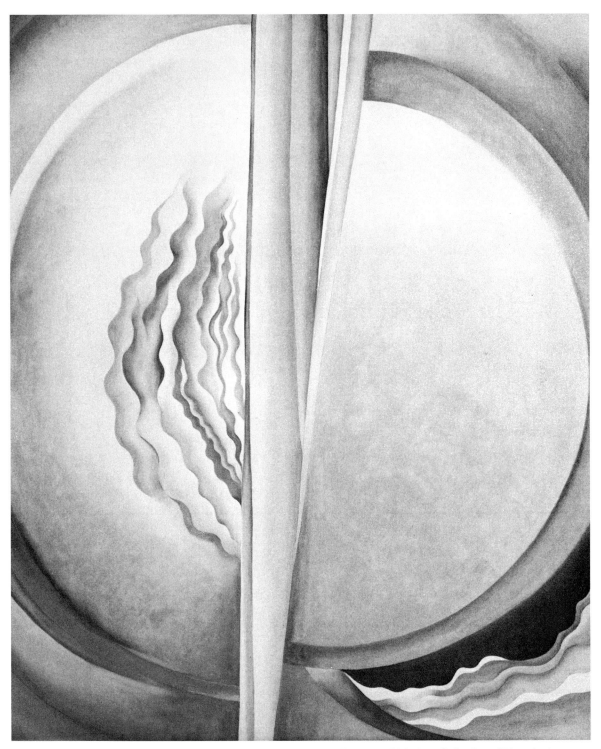

Figure 10.25   Georgia O'Keeffe, *Pink Abstraction.* Oil on canvas, 36 inches × 30 inches. Collection of Phoenix Art Museum, Gift of Friends of Art.

Figure 10.26   Georges Braque, French, 1882–1963, *Fruits and Guitar,* oil on canvas, 1938, 81.3 × 101.1 cm. Gift of Mrs. Albert D. Lasker in memory of her husband Albert D. Lasker, photograph © 1995 The Art Institute of Chicago. All Rights Reserved. © 1996 Artists Rights Society (ARS), New York/ADAGP, Paris.

flattened the planes while continuing the decorative patterning. Around 1912, Braque was the first to introduce the concept of the collage—combining fragments of the real with the illusory image. He also introduced commercial lettering into his paintings. His subjects were still lifes (fruit, guitars), Greek themes, and a series of birds and moons. (See Georges Braque's *Fruits and Guitar,* fig. 10.26.)

Willem de Kooning

Willem de Kooning (1904–1988) was born in Holland but came to the United States in 1926. His portraits and figure studies of the 1930s are considered a more traditional style of his work. At this time, he also did murals, including one for the New York World's Fair in 1939.

After his first exhibit in 1948, de Kooning became the unofficial leader of the artists' group called the abstract expressionists, who emphasized the spontaneity of action painting. He was concerned with abstract spatial problems, the creation of ambiguous and chaotic space, and the merging of the figure into the environment. His originality made de Kooning one of the most influential painters in the abstract expressionist movement.

De Kooning was well known for his figurative theme of the abstract female figure. The figures are distorted and fragmented, often exaggerated, and always painted with an expressive energy of brush strokes. (See Willem de Kooning's *Working Man,* fig. 10.27.)

Figure 10.27   *Working Man* by Willem de Kooning. Pencil on paper. (Courtesy of Allan Stone Galleries, Inc., New York.)

Käthe Kollwitz

German-born artist and sculptor Käthe Kollwitz
(1867–1945) lived in Berlin. Her work expressed her feelings of sympathy for the poor and oppressed and her strong
social convictions. The great tragic themes of life, such as
mother and child, death, and social protest, were her inspiration. She is thought of as belonging to the German expressionist movement. (See Käthe Kollwitz's *Woman with
Folded Hands,* fig. 10.28.)

Helen Frankenthaler

American painter Helen Frankenthaler (1928–) is
thought of as an abstract expressionist. She is known for
her unique staining of unsized canvas by pouring pigment on the canvas rather than brushing it on. She is
considered an innovator in color-field painting (where
large areas of flat color are applied). Her paints are primarily acrylics, and her colors are strong, retaining the
staining technique. (See Helen Frankenthaler's *Lush
Spring,* fig. 10.29.)

Maria Luisa Ruiz/Malintzin

Maria Luisa Ruiz/Malintzin (1953–) was raised in New
Mexico by her grandmother, a curandera (medicine
woman), who knew the village folklore, legends, and traditions. She learned how to make masks and costumes for the
Matachine ritual (a victory celebration dance), which was
brought to the New World by the Spaniards over 450 years
ago and, combined with Aztec rituals, is danced in both
Hispanic villages and Indian pueblos.

The themes for Ruiz/Malintzin's artwork come from
personal childhood memories, when ceremonies were abundant. She tries to link those memories with current rituals to
create contemporary works of art. She uses handmade paper
by breaking down the paper into pulp and then casting onto
molds. Other materials, such as plants, animal hairs, fibers,
silk, rayon, and cotton linters, are mixed in with the paper
pulp. (See Maria L. Ruiz/Malintzin's *Chicomecoatl, Goddess of Corn* and *Shawoman II,* fig. 10.30a and b.)

Figure 10.28 *Woman with Folded Hands* by Käthe Kollwitz,
1989. Etching. 28.6 × 22.8 cm. (Author's collection.)

Figure 10.29   Helen Frankenthaler, *Lush Spring.* Oil on canvas, 94.5
inches × 119.5 inches. Collection of Phoenix Art Museum, Museum
Purchase with Funds Provided by the National Endowment for the Arts.

(a)

(b)

Figure 10.30   (*a*) *Chicomecoatl, Goddess of Corn* by Maria L. Ruiz/Malintzin. Cast paper sculpture, 22 inches × 16½ × 3½ inches.
(*b*) *Shawoman II* by Maria L. Ruiz/Malintzin. Cast paper, 30 inches × 4 inches.

Ruth Weisberg

Internationally exhibited and acclaimed artist Ruth Weisberg also serves as Dean of Fine Arts at the University of Southern California. In 1995, she was awarded a Fullbright Fellowship in Rome to further her art studies and works. She also received a fellowship from the National Endowment for the Humanities. "My work as an artist focuses on figurative narrative and issues of time, memory, and history."[11] Weisburg recently completed an 18´ × 14´ wall piece that attempts to reclaim the voices of biblical women, Rachael and Leah. Several of her large scale installations have addressed women in history. (See Ruth Weisberg's *Everything That Falls Has Wings,* fig. 10.31.)

Suzanne Klotz

Suzanne Klotz has traveled the world as both an artist and teacher, giving and receiving inspiration for her artworks. She views art as a vehicle for the expression of individuality and universal understanding:

> To achieve unity, harmony, and peace, we must consider all citizens of the world as our brothers and sisters and all people as the fingers of one hand. . . . Art is a vehicle for the unity, harmony, and understanding of self, the society in which we live, and the diverse cultures of the world. A garden is beautiful and stimulating because of the different flowers found within it.[12]

(See Suzanne Klotz's *Catching the Golden Moment,* fig. 10.32.)

Artemisia Gentileschi

Artemisia Gentileschi (1593–ca. 1652) developed her own dramatic, forceful style of painting that established her as one of the foremost artists of her generation. Her father was the successful painter Orazio Gentileschi. Her compositions were dynamic and dramatic. Her knowledge of female anatomy displayed her talent. The chiaroscuro (light and shade) in her paintings added secrecy and mystery to the scenes.

Judith Leyster

Judith Leyster (1609–1660) was a versatile artist who painted a variety of subjects—from still lifes to portraits to genre paintings. She created interesting compositions and painted them from a woman's point of view. She was an independent artist with a personal style, although her work has been compared to Frans Hals. Whereas Hals's work had greater painterly brushstroke techniques, Leyster's style was more precise and linear, and the moods of her subjects were more somber.

Figure 10.31 *Everything That Falls Has Wings* by Ruth Weisberg, 1990. Drawing, 39.25 inches × 58 inches.

Figure 10.32 *Catching the Golden Moment* by Suzanne Klotz, 1992. Acrylic, 54 inches × 66 inches. (Photo courtesy of Ron Lundy.)

TEACHING ABOUT ARTISTS: EXAMPLES

Once students become acquainted with the works and artistic characteristics of various artists, they often are able to draw or paint their own interpretations of a particular artist's style (see fig. 10.33). See appendix A for lists of artists to study, organized by country of origin and genre.

Example 1: Fourth-Graders Study Joan Miró

The objectives of the project were for fourth-graders to learn about Joan Miró and surrealism and to create drawings in the manner of Miró. (See Joan Miró's *Personages with Stars,* fig. 10.34.)

Lesson 1

The objective of this lesson was to acquaint students with Joan Miró and his style of painting and surrealism. We began by discussing music and its many variations—rock, country, folk, classical—and the various composers with their individual styles. We carried this idea into discussion of art and the many types of art that students have observed on visits to galleries and museums: landscape, still life, psychedelic, light paintings, and so on. Mention was made of various artists with unique styles.

(a)

(b)

(c)

Figure 10.33 After studying the artworks of a particular artist, students interpreted the artist's style in their own drawings and paintings. (*a*) Interpretation after studying Degas. (*b*) Interpretation of Pieter Brueghel. (*c*) Interpretation of Picasso.

Figure 10.34   Joan Miró, Spanish, 1893–1983, *Personages with Stars,* oil on canvas, 1933, 196.3 × 247.9 cm. Gift of Mr. and Mrs. Maurice E. Culberg, photograph © The Art Institute of Chicago. All Rights Reserved. © 1996 Artists Rights Society (ARS), New York/ADAGP, Paris.

I then presented a simplified explanation of surrealism and mentioned that a variety of artists have practiced this type of art, including the artist Joan Miró. I showed photographs of Miró on the opaque projector and gave a brief resume of his life. I showed a few of his earlier works and then some of his later works to illustrate how he changed his style. The students reacted with interesting comments. Special emphasis was given to his 1940–1955 period.

References used were:

Gasser, Manuel. *Joan Miró.* New York: Barnes and Noble, 1965.

Matthews, J. H. *Introduction to Surrealism.* University Park, Penn.: Pennsylvania State University Press, 1965.

Walton, Paul H. *Dalí/Miró: Masters of Surrealism.* New York: Tudor Publishing, 1967.

Lesson 2

I asked some of the students to look again at their favorite Miró works and engaged them in a more detailed discussion of the style, ideas, and repeated symbols—colors, shapes, lines—Miró used. I asked students to close their eyes and do two things: (1) invent a symbol of their own to be their trademark, and (2) think of some feeling, place, or idea they would like to represent in a drawing. They then folded a large piece of newsprint and jotted the idea and secret symbol inside. The students then tried making two illustrations in the style of Miró, using one of his characteristic symbols, along with their own symbol in each illustration (fig. 10.35).

Lesson 3

I asked students to do a larger illustration, with the same theme, or another of their own choice, using their personal symbol and perhaps one Miró symbol. The drawing could be created with felt-tip pens, crayons, or pencil, and students were asked to title it.

Lesson 4

This time, I asked students to create paintings on an assigned theme: their version of an Arizona desert happening. Suggested titles included "Siesta in the Sun," "Lost in the Superstitions," "Horseback at Dawn," and "Stranded on Camelback Mountain." Or, they could create an Arizona feeling with lines, colors, forms, and so on. I encouraged them to use paint or to combine paint with other materials, such as construction paper.

After the lesson, students individually showed their creations, while classmates tried to identify their secret symbols (fig. 10.36). Students thoroughly enjoyed this project.

Submitted by Miriam Chynoweth

Figure 10.35   An imaginative painting by a fourth-grader after studying Joan Miró.

Figure 10.36   Emphasis was on the use of unique "secret" symbols after studying Joan Miró.

Example 2: Second-Graders Study Paul Klee

The children in my room were grouped around me in a semicircle while I showed them pictures of paintings by Paul Klee in two books checked out from the library. As the teacher, I made no comments. The children exclaimed as I turned each page and showed different paintings. In the discussion that followed, the children commented on how well they liked the paintings, the various shapes, the brilliant colors, the nonrealistic style of the paintings, and the surrealistic quality—meaning the unreal people and places. I left the books on the table, available for the children to look at. Some looked at them alone, but most liked having their "best" friend with them to talk to about the pictures. A high level of interest was sustained. The children didn't seem to tire of looking at the books.

Every child thought that it would be a great experience to paint a picture, looking-through-the-eyes-of-Paul-Klee style. Not one child said that he or she couldn't do it—they liked the idea tremendously. Each child did his or her "own style" of Paul Klee painting.

The students had their choice of paper—colored, white, or manila drawing paper. They could select from crayons, watercolors, or combinations of materials. One

child pointed out that he would be unable to get the color effects with crayons that Paul Klee did with oil paints. I thought that was a good observation. There was no time limit. Some children continued working on their paintings for two or three days' free time.

This project was a delightful experience for the children. One of the most interesting reactions and discovery was that one could draw any way one wanted to, and it was just great! Their artwork did not have to be "real" looking. They were very enthusiastic and pleased with their drawings and paintings.

Submitted by Hazel Scott

Example 3: Third-Graders Study Marc Chagall

I wrote "Marc Chagall" on the chalkboard. Then, as a class, we looked up Chagall in the encyclopedia and discovered that he was an artist. We looked at his paintings and tried to think as he did. We looked at France and Russia on the world map to locate the areas Chagall lived in. Then we gathered a special table of clippings, photographs, and books about Chagall to be studied by students. (Note: One of my slow readers became so interested that, over the weekend, he went to the library and checked out two more books on Chagall. He proudly brought them in on Monday to add to our art table.) On the opaque projector, we studied Chagall's paintings, and

Figure 10.37   Marc Chagall, French, born Russia, 1887–1985, *White Crucifixion*, oil on canvas, 1938, 154.3 × 139.7 cm. Gift of Alfred S. Alschuler, photograph © 1995 The Art Institute of Chicago. All Rights Reserved. © 1996 Artists Rights Society (ARS), New York/ADAGP, Paris.

I presented a thumbnail sketch of the artist's life. (See Marc Chagall's *White Crucifixion*, fig. 10.37.) The children made some interesting comments: "The paintings are prettier than the windows." "Look how one thing is painted on top or inside another." "Colors are so deep." "Notice the animals, churches, couples." The class preferred the paintings of *The Juggler, The Poet, I and the Village,* and *The Birthday.*

We wrote the following words on the chalkboard and discussed them in relation to Chagall and his paintings: *contemporary, colorful, fantasy, fanciful, dreamlike, happy, poetic, life, marriage, love, death, musical.*

The students did a preliminary sketch. Then they invented ideas from their imagination in a Chagall interpretation. They used larger paper and their choice of materials. I covered the drawings with a clear plastic spray. Each child presented his or her idea in front of the class. They all enjoyed doing this project.

Submitted by Mary A. Baltz

Example 4

Lesson 1: Fifth- and Sixth-Graders Study Georgia O'Keeffe

We studied the life of Georgia O'Keeffe and looked at art reproductions of her flower paintings. We discussed form, shading, color, design, and the mood of the paintings. Calendars with large photos of flowers were used as art motivations, along with real flowers. Sixth-graders each designed a large flower and painted them; fifth-graders made pastel drawings (see fig. 10.38).

Lesson 2: Sixth-Graders Study Claude Monet

Claude Monet's *Les arceaux fleuris* (see fig. 10.5) was the motivation for the sixth grade. Color and white were added to the palette so that students would lighten up the colors. They included impressionist concepts and were involved in the landscape as space. Photographs from *Arizona Highway*

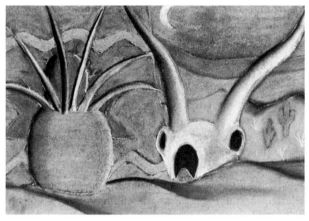

(a)

(b)

(c)

Figure 10.38   Fifth- and sixth-graders studied Georgia O'Keeffe and then interpreted her style in their own drawings. (From the classes of Pat Koepp.)

Magazine were laminated and used for the study of space: foreground, middle ground, and background. Then, students painted a landscape.

Lesson 3: Fifth- and Sixth-Graders Study Vincent van Gogh

When studying van Gogh (see fig. 8.5*b*), students discussed line direction, shape, texture, and color. Then they did their own self-portrait, using wild colors (fig. 10.39).

Lesson 4: Fifth- and Sixth-Graders Study Henri Rousseau

We combined a fine art lesson with science by studying Henri Rousseau and endangered animals. We then did murals depicting endangered animals in environments (fig. 10.40).

Figure 10.39   A student did a portrait interpretation after studying Vincent van Gogh's artworks.

Figure 10.40   After studying Henri Rousseau, students created a cut paper mural.

Lesson 5: Fourth-Graders Study Wassily Kandinsky

Fourth-grade students learned to use rulers and compasses. We discussed the fantasy, humor, and design as well as the limited color (three) in the works of Wassily Kandinsky. The students then did their own nonobjective paintings.

Submitted by Pat Koepp, art teacher,
Cartwright School District, Arizona

Example 5: Fourth- through Sixth-Graders Study Pierre Auguste Renoir

We studied Pierre Auguste Renoir in grades four through six. We looked at and discussed reproductions of his paintings showing gardens and women, portraits and still lifes. Included was information about his life (born in Paris, France), about how he had rheumatism, and about how he was a happy man and painted joyful, happy paintings. His favorite subject was women. His favorite color was blue; his least favorite, black. His edges were fuzzy, and there were few details in his works.

Then students posed like Renoir people, and we painted portraits (fig. 10.41).

Submitted by Connie Ellis, art teacher,
Cartwright School District, Arizona

Figure 10.41   Students studied Renoir women and portraits, and then drew portraits from their own models. (From the classes of Connie Ellis.)

STUDENT ARTISTS: KELLY, DAVID, AND JAMES

Kelly, age twelve, wrote, "I want to be an artist because I like art and I like making art."

David Mears, age thirteen, said:

I feel lucky that I can do artwork. It makes me feel good about my ability and at the same time, it's fun. I get my ideas from my favorite people, my favorite animals, and nature. I like creating things that are realistic and imaginable. I like sculpturing the best because it looks lifelike and it's dimensional. I wanted to make the eagle because it's my favorite bird. . . . It is important for artists to try different methods.[13]

James Baxter, a sixth-grader, said:

I make monster heads. Seems weird? Well, they look weird, too. I start with a hunk of dried clay usually made up of scraps of clay that have settled together at the bottom of the clay barrel. Then I begin to carve a monster head from the hunk. Because the clay is scrap clay, it always comes in very odd shapes. From these shapes, I figure out what the monster will look like. For example, I may imagine a huge hump as a bulging eye or a large nose, or if there is a hole at one end, it may be the start of jagged teeth. The oddly shaped scrap clay pieces are just perfect for the beginning of a monster head. . . . I thought, since I draw monsters, why not try carving them from hard clay? I tried it, and it worked![14]

How clearly these students state their view of art. For them, art is a necessary part of their thinking and life attitudes. Art is for everyone, and for everyone it should be an adventure (fig. 10.42). Art expresses your feelings to yourself as well as to others and helps others to perceive your ideas, experiences, beliefs, and values. It is interaction and feedback within yourself, which is often a source of self-motivation. It is a personal vision of your world for you to reflect back on and to provide new avenues for learning. Art tells you where you are in your perception, what skills you know, and what skills you want to pursue.

NOTES

1. "Dreamings: The Art of Aboriginal Australia," exhibition at the Asia Society Galleries, New York, October–December 1988.
2. For further information, refer to the October 1988 issue of *National Geographic*.
3. Wendy Slatkin, *Women Artists in History* (Englewood Cliffs, N.J.: Prentice-Hall, 1985).
4. Barbara Rose, "A B C Art," *Art in America*, October/November 1965.
5. Andrea Kettenmann, *Frida Kahlo* (Cologne, Germany: Benedikt Taschen, 1993), 18.
6. Patricia Hills, *Alice Neel* (New York: Harry N. Abrams, 1983).
7. "A Celebration of African-American Artistry and Vision," *Smithsonian*, November 1993, p. 136.
8. "A Celebration of African-American Artistry and Vision," *Smithsonian*, November 1993, p. 144.
9. "A Celebration of African-American Artistry and Vision," *Smithsonian*, November 1993, p. 142.
10. Paul Tillich, *The New Being* (New York: Charles Scribners Sons, 1955), 129.
11. Author's personal conversation with Ruth Weisberg.
12. Author's personal conversation with Suzanne Klotz.
13. "The Young Artist," *Arts and Activities Magazine* 81, no. 4 (November 1976): 39.
14. "The Young Artist," *Arts and Activities Magazine* 80, no. 2 (October 1976): 39.

Figure 10.42   Art is a challenging adventure, and students project their personal visions of the world in their artworks.

chapter

11

Art Analysis
Looking at and Responding to Art

I don't teach people how to paint; I teach them how to see.
Joseph Albers, Yale University

I have always felt about art that it was freedom that counted. A man must see things and say things his own way. This is his New Imagination. No artist who thinks can spend his life trying to understand another man's interest. . . . I am always very amused with people who talk about lack of subjects for painting. The great difficulty is that you cannot stop to sort them out enough. Wherever you go, they are waiting for you. The men of the docks, the children at the river edge, polo crowds, prize fights, summer evening and romance, village folk, young people, old people, the beautiful, the ugly. . . . It seems to me that an artist must be a spectator of life; a reverential, enthusiastic, emotional spectator, and then the great dramas of human nature will surge through his mind.
George Bellows

The secret to experiencing and learning about art analysis is knowing *how to see* art. If you have ever visited an art museum, you may have noticed that some people race through and see an art exhibit in fifteen minutes. Other people take hours, lingering as they walk, looking at each piece of art for several minutes. What do they look for? What do they see? Do you see the same things they see? How can you learn to see more? What should you look for? This chapter answers some of those questions. (Refer to the numerous student and artists' artworks throughout the book.)

THE ART DIALOGUE: LOOKING AND RESPONDING

To have a dialogue with an artwork means to enter into and interact with the work—to experience it by looking at it, responding to it, and comprehending it. It requires becoming familiar with the work. It requires a perception of just what *is* art (fig. 11.1).

Often, you may see an artwork and respond from a gut level: "I like it," or "No, I don't like it." We all tend to form a quick judgment of what is appealing or not appealing to us for various reasons, and this response is valid. However, in a dialogue, we want to find out *why* we like or dislike the work, to consider other opinions, and to form conclusions based on objective as well as subjective reasons.

Each individual's response to an artwork is unique and personal and is based on his or her past experiences and past artistic encounters. These experiences and encounters, in turn, are influenced by the home environment, cultural and social heritage, level of perceptual awareness, inherent art abilities, imagination, self-expressiveness, and learned art skills.

AESTHETICS

According to the National Art Education Association, **aesthetics** is a branch of philosophy that focuses on the nature of beauty, the nature and value of art, and the inquiry process associated with those topics.[1] In an article in the book *Art Education: Elementary,* Kay Alexander wrote:

> Aesthetics . . . think of it in elementary language: knowing what one likes and why. Aesthetic perception involves the

Figure 11.1   What is art? According to the nine-year-old who did this artwork: "Well, art is anything that you make up or is anything made up of the human mind. Do you think art is hard? Well, art isn't anything at all. It is as easy as learning to tie your shoe. But, even easier! I should know because I am an artist!!! Can you draw as good as me? I bet you can if you try. Art is anything at all. If you take art lessons, you should know because I have, and I learned a lot of things."

use of the senses, the emotions, and the intellect . . . to discover what is good, ugly, boring, delightful, or beautiful and precedes the formation of personal tastes. Aesthetic experiences should include responses to everyday objects as well as to fine art, architecture, furniture, clothing, and the like. . . . They [students] can consider whether standards of beauty are universal and unchanging, whether functional objects can also be artistic, whether gut reactions or an informed decision is more valid—stimulating and thought-provoking topics.[2]

ANALYZING ARTWORKS

As first outlined in chapter 2, art analysis involves inquiring into several aspects of an artwork. Experiences and the discussion process could take place step by step, or several steps may overlap at one time. In the classroom, you will want to adapt the steps and questions from simple to more complex according to the interests and abilities of your students.

The first steps—description and analysis—relate more to describing the known facts in the artwork. The following steps—interpretation, aesthetics, judgment—require greater personal and intuitive response to the artwork's meaning

and qualities. Such questions and discussions help each of us understand and form qualitative judgments and justify our decisions.

Description

Subject

Who is the artist? What is the title? What is the artwork's size? When was the artwork made? What is the image? What is the theme? What do you see? What is happening? What is the most important idea or experience in this artwork?

Materials, Processes, Techniques

What techniques, processes, and media did the artist use? Paints? Drawing tools? Clay? Wood? Metal?

Analysis

Visual Structure

What art elements and design principles—line, shape, value, color, pattern, texture, space, balance, dominance, rhythm, and contrast—are used in the artwork, and how are they brought together in a composition?

Historical Significance

What is the historical importance of the artwork? What does the artwork's subject and style tell you historically? Is this artwork part of an art movement? Does the artwork have cultural importance?

Interpretation

What is your understanding of the artwork's meaning? What is the mood and feeling of the artwork? What is the artist communicating? How does the artwork make *you* feel?

Aesthetics

Ask yourself, what is personally significant, beautiful, and of value about the artwork? Is the artwork original? Creative? Does it have value in our society? What makes it art?

Judgment (Evaluation)

What do you think of this artwork? On a scale of one to ten, with ten being your highest rating, how do you rate this artwork? Do you like it? Why?

Additional Questions

The categories and questions that follow can be used in looking at artworks and for discussions.

Description: Subject

1. What is the name of the artist, and what is the title, date, and size of the artwork?
2. What is the subject or theme represented? Is it a historical event, a portrait, a still life, a landscape, a cityscape, a zoological subject, a medical illustration, a book illustration, an architectural interior, a fantasy, a social or political commentary, a figure study, a utilitarian object, a decoration, a religious work?
3. What is happening in the artwork?
4. What is the most important idea or experience in this artwork? What is the artist saying about the ideas, beliefs, and social and cultural differences?
5. Was the artwork made recently or a long time ago? Does the imagery, such as the architecture, clothing, and vehicles, describe the time and place?
6. Does the artist's work tell you about the traditions or customs of the day? The type of people portrayed?
7. Does the subject of the artwork relate to a place or event in your own life? Is the artist's world different from or similar to yours?
8. Does the subject of the artwork show emotions? Is it mysterious? Does it tell a story, legend, or myth?
9. What is the mood of the artwork?
10. Does the work reveal creative and original vision?

Description: Materials, Processes, Techniques

1. What materials (such as watercolor, tempera, oil paint, clay, fibers, prints) did the artist use?
2. What type of art form is the final product (drawing, painting, sculpture, architectural form, ceramic, textile, collage, print, illustration, cartoon, etc.)?
3. How do the materials used play a part in helping to convey the ideas and feelings the artist intended?
4. Would the artist's idea be different if expressed in a different material?
5. What technique did the artist use? That is, how has the artist used the tools and materials in his or her own individual way to create the artwork? For example, are the tones softly blended, such as in the pencil drawings of Ingres? Or does the work reflect the linear quality of one of Rembrandt's etchings? Can you see the brush strokes? Would you describe the artist's technique as controlled, precise, splattered, poured, crosshatching, blending, spontaneous?
6. How important is the artist's technical skill to the final product?

Analysis: Visual Structure

1. How are the art elements and design principles used in the artwork? Focus on the use of lines, shapes, colors, values, space, patterns, and textures, and how they relate to balance, proportion, dominance, rhythm, harmony, unity, and contrast. How are all of these art elements and design principles structured into the final composition?
2. How are the art elements similar? What are the differences in the art elements? Does one art element dominate?
3. Is the balance symmetrical, asymmetrical, or radial?
4. Are lines straight, curved, jagged, diagonal? How do line decisions affect the final work?
5. Are shapes irregular, geometric, soft-edged, hard-edged? Which shape is closest to you? Which shape is farthest away? How do shape decisions affect the final work?
6. Are colors bright, dull, warm, cool, unlimited, limited? Do shapes come forward or recede due to their color? What is the interval between colors and shapes? Do colors move fast to your eye? How has the artist used colors and values to evoke feelings? What is the main color of the artwork? How do color decisions affect the final work?
7. Are values dark, light, blended? How do value decisions affect the final work?
8. How does the artist achieve space? Are there ground-sky relationships? Is there a foreground, middle ground, and background? Is space shallow or deep? Does it reflect overlapping perspective? How do space decisions affect the final work?

9. Are patterns created by repetition of motif? What is the order of the repetition? How do pattern decisions affect the final work?

10. Are textures rough, smooth, soft, bumpy? How do texture decisions affect the final work?

11. Is there a rhythm, movement, or beat? How does the artist achieve movement across the picture?

12. Is there one art element (line, shape, space, etc.) emphasized in the artwork?

13. Is there great variety in the art elements? Contrast?

14. Is there a feeling of harmony and unity? How is this achieved?

15. Do you feel the artist has achieved "good" composition? Describe how.

16. Considering the whole composition, what does your eye see first? Where does your eye move next? What determines this? Is it placement? Dominance? Something else?

17. In developing and creating this artwork, what four decisions did the artist make?

Analysis: Historical Significance

1. What do you know about the artist, the time period in which the artist lived, and the art movements of that particular time?

2. What is the artwork's historical importance? How does it compare to other artworks of its historical time? Is this a unique and personal statement, or is it imitative of another artist's work?

3. What style has the artist used? What period is the artwork from? Did the artist follow an artistic movement, or was he or she an innovator?

4. What does the artwork reveal about the times in which the artist lived?

5. What was the artwork's intended use? Was it a ceremonial African carving, a Russian icon, an Egyptian fresco? Where was the artwork intended to go—in a church, public building, garden, theater, museum?

6. How did culture influence the artist's work? For example, was the artist supported by a patron of the church or by royalty? Did a major historical event (such as the U.S. Depression of the 1930s) affect the art of the period?

7. How does this artwork compare to other works by the same artist? Is this piece part of a larger series? Does it indicate a change in direction for the artist?

8. If you were an art historian or an art critic, what would you say and write about the artist and the art piece?

9. Has the importance of the artwork changed over time? How significant is this artist and artwork in contemporary society?

10. Can you identify this artwork as to time? Place? Culture? Style? Movement? Technique?

11. Can you identify an artist's work by its individuality?

12. Compare your own artwork to that of a different culture and time.

Interpretation

1. What is the artist trying to communicate through the artwork? What is the most important statement? Is there a universal message? What is the point, purpose, or meaning of this work?

2. Does the artist say it in his or her own way? How is this artwork different from others? How does the artist transmit ideas and feelings? How does the artwork make you feel and why?

3. Does the artist show you new ways to see, new ways to understand life and other people, customs, cultures, and traditions, that you have never seen before?

4. If the artwork is a painting or drawing, what does the artist offer that a photograph of the same subject cannot?

5. Does the artist exaggerate certain forms or ideas? How does this affect the final artwork?

6. Does the artist include certain things and omit others? How does this affect the final artwork?

7. How does the artist demonstrate feelings, moods, or atmosphere?

8. Is the artwork a dramatization of a myth, legend, or story? Is it an allegory?

9. If any people depicted in the artwork were alive, what do you think they would say or do? Do details of the clothes, architecture, or landscape give you any clues?

10. Would you like to be in this artwork? If you were able to walk into the artwork, what would you be able to smell or hear? Where would you go, and what would you do? What are the people doing or thinking? What would you say to the people? What is happening? Would you like to live in the artwork's time and place?

11. Does the artwork have value to the society and culture?

12. Is the artist of this artwork famous? Do you think that an artwork is better when the artist is famous? If you were looking at some famous artworks and some not-so-famous artworks, do you think you could tell the difference? Why?

13. Does the title of this artwork reflect the work itself? Could you create a new title for the artwork?

Interpretation: Aesthetics

1. Would you say that there is beauty in the artwork? Why? In your opinion, what makes something beautiful? Can art be ugly?

2. How does this artwork make you feel—angry, joyful, excited, unhappy—and why?

3. Is the aesthetic quality you see in the artwork timeless? Would you enjoy viewing this artwork over and over again? Would you want to have it in your home?

4. If you were to look at this artwork in a month, do you think that you would react differently to it?

5. By whose standards do you appraise art—your own or somebody else's? Do other people consider this artwork exceptional? Does that affect how you feel about the artwork?

6. Compare this artwork with several others. Describe the outstanding qualities in each. Do the artworks have features in common?
7. What do you like and dislike in this artwork? Why?
8. What do you think the artist is trying to say in the artwork? What is the artist's message or intent?
9. What is the value of art in society? Compare art to sports, to music, to television.
10. What makes a "work of art"?
11. What is "good" art? Who makes decisions about what is good and not good?
12. Would you like to vote on the "best" painting?
13. How do you think art museum curators decide which paintings will be on exhibition in a museum?
14. What is "good taste"? Who determines good taste?
15. What makes an artist great?
16. Are students artists (fig. 11.2)?
17. Does saying you are an artist make you one? How many artworks must an artist make?
18. When someone pays a lot of money for a painting, does that make the painting more valuable than an artwork given to you by a friend?
19. Ruby, an elephant at the Phoenix Zoo, paints pictures by holding a brush in her trunk, dipping it into various colors, and applying the paint to paper (see fig. 11.3). These works are then sold in a gallery. Do you think this is art?
20. What artwork would you like to display in your classroom? In the school?
21. How do factors of time and place (such as technology, ideas, climate, resources, etc.) influence the meaning and value of a work of art?
22. Would you agree or disagree that chemical cleaning of historical, treasured artworks, such as *The Last Supper*, is beneficial?
23. Given the many social issues we have today, such as homeless people and drug abuse, where should we place the importance of art?

Judgment

Discuss and consider the issues presented in the previous lists concerning subject description, materials used, analysis of visual structure, historical importance, interpretation, and aesthetics. Try to delay forming final judgments. Then ask yourself these final questions:

1. What is the craftsmanship of the artwork? Is the degree of skill in the use of the media, techniques, and procedures outstanding to the purpose of the artwork?
2. Does the artwork convincingly express the subject, idea, or theme it is based on? Does the artwork express any of the following properties: funny, whimsical, shocking, dreamy, ethereal, quiet, joyous, aggressive, majestic, sad, depressing, strong, powerful, scary, terrifying, mysterious, exciting, dramatic?
3. Do you have a personal response to the artwork—one that you could share and talk about with others (see fig. 11.4)?
4. How original is the artwork? What degree of uniqueness, inventiveness, and imagination has the artist displayed in the artwork?

Figure 11.2 Are students expressive artists? (Photo by Heather Davenport.)

Figure 11.3 This is a painting by Ruby the elephant, who paints pictures by grasping a paintbrush with her trunk. Do you think this painting is art?

Figure 11.4 Does the artwork have a function in the student's life? Here a student paints a tee shirt.

5. What do you think of this artwork? How would you personally rank this work? Explain with specific justifications.
6. Would you buy this artwork? Would you have it in your house? Where would you put it? Would you want to donate it to an art museum? Explain your reasoning.
7. After forming a final judgment, discuss your reasons why.

GROUP DISCUSSIONS OF ARTWORKS

In an article in *Aesthetics: Issues and Inquiry*, E. Louis Lankford suggested that elementary teachers must provide art analysis activities that are concrete and limited in scope but that also spark interesting discussions:

> Given sufficient foundations, students should be encouraged to more directly engage in inquiry having to do with aesthetic topics. A good way of introducing such inquiry is through the use of vivid cases: questions, stories, and examples which capture students' attention and cause them to think about an important issue in art. A vivid case is characterized by (1) concreteness; that is, being realistic enough that the events or situations described can be readily grasped by students—they should be able to form a mental image; (2) having limited scope, so that the issue or issues are fairly easy to pick out and articulate; and (3) being tantalizing to students' imaginations, spurring them to engage in dialogue about the case.[3]

Group discussions about artworks and exhibitions of artworks in the classroom are necessary tools for learning about art. Encourage *open-ended* comments, and use positive reinforcement questions, such as "What do you like about this artwork?" Discussions about the artworks with others and exposure to others' views, perspectives, opinions, and ideas are what nurture aesthetic understanding.

According to Craig Noland, one of the authors featured in the book *Art Education: Elementary,* group discussions of artworks are the vehicle for developing critical thinking:

> Teachers can provide frequent opportunities for class dialogue and debate about various "contingent" matters in art; they are obviously beneficial when students are able to: relate the topic to their own knowledge and beliefs; rethink their initial ideas and assumptions in light of possible contradictions; explore alternative views and explanations for the same situations; and refute views expressed in class (including their own). . . . It is through such planned thinking that ordinary thinking become critical thinking.[4]

Group discussions of *student* artworks are especially meaningful as a learning technique. In such discussions, each student presents an artwork and describes the project and the method of solving it. At other times, students each contribute an art piece without revealing their identity, and the group comments on these "anonymous" works. Such group interactions and feedback provide insights that would not otherwise be possible. Exhibiting student artworks immediately upon completion builds self-esteem and acceptance and attitudes that say "What you have to say is important."

Each participant brings unique qualities to the group discussion experience. As an elementary teacher, you can be aware of and point out differences in students' perceptions. For example:

- Do students from various cultures share the same idea of what is beautiful? Ugly? Meaningful?
- Does the artwork have a function in the student's life? For example, would a student from Turkey regard a Navajo rug in the same way as a Native American?
- Do students respond to the artwork in terms of feelings?
- How do students respond to the artwork's originality?
- How do students respond to the creative intent of the artwork? For example, would a student from Africa regard a mask in the same way as a student from Boston (fig. 11.5)?
- Do students' responses differ according to where the work was made (what culture) and in what historical time frame (fig. 11.6)?
- Do subcultures result in some people caring more about some art than other art? For example, would a student from a small town in Idaho react differently to an artwork than a student from an inner-city subculture in Detroit?
- Do students use only a standard of realism to determine what is "best" art?
- Do students consider the artist's motives in creating the artwork? Was the artist trying to be as realistic as possible? To be abstract? To illustrate a religious theme or a historical story? To portray how a person looked? To

Figure 11.5 How do various students respond to creative artworks? For example, would a student from Africa regard a mask in the same way as a student from the United States?

Figure 11.6 How do students respond to art of different times and cultures?

design a record album cover? To design a table? To express personal ideas, feelings, or interests? To make a social or political comment? To create something with a functional purpose?

In review, the following additional discussion questions are relevant for analyzing all artworks:

1. Who is the artist? What is the title and date of the artwork? What is the subject matter? What materials and technique did the artist use?

2. How did the artist use line, color, shape, value, space, texture, and pattern in the artwork (see fig. 11.7)?

3. How would you analyze the artwork's composition (balance, dominance, rhythm, and contrast)? Is the artwork realistic or abstract (fig. 11.8)?

4. What is the basic feeling, mood, or idea of the artwork?

5. Do you consider the artwork to be original (see fig. 11.9), to be expressive, to demonstrate good craftsmanship?

6. What is the relationship of this artwork to history? To a certain culture?

7. What is or was the artist's purpose in creating this artwork?

8. What do you find most exciting in this artwork?

9. What is the most successful aspect of this artwork?

10. Would you change anything about this artwork?

11. Does the artist's choice of materials suit the mood or atmosphere of the artwork? Why?

12. How has the artist treated the background, foreground, and middle ground spaces?

13. Was the artist successful in presenting a concept or story idea?

14. What art elements does the artist use to unify the composition?

15. What is the center of interest?

16. Is the design flat, or does it have dimension?

17. How would you rate this artwork on a scale from one to ten, with ten indicating that you like the work very much and one indicating that you dislike it? Explain your rating.

ART RESOURCES AND THE ART MUSEUM

A large variety of art resources—for both you and your students—is available for student learning and to motivate discussion. These include:

Artists, art teachers, and art consultants (see fig. 11.10)
Art museums, docents, museum speaker's bureaus

Figure 11.8   Is this artwork realistic or abstract? Does it have flat or modeled shapes?

Figure 11.7   How did the artist use lines, shapes, and values in this artwork?

Figure 11.9   Do you think this artwork is original?

Figure 11.10 An artist talks about his art to sixth-graders at the Scottsdale Center for the Arts.

Galleries, artists' studios, art centers

Artists-in-residence programs

Local historical and cultural organizations (see fig. 11.11)

Cultural artifacts and family treasures

Guest presentations and demonstrations

Art critics and art historians

Slides, films, videos, television shows, filmstrips, multimedia presentations

Laser disks, CD-ROMs, electronic media

Original works of art, art reproductions, small study prints (post cards), photographs

Art books, art journals, art magazines

Newspapers, popular magazines (such as *Smithsonian*)

Visual displays, such as bulletin boards

Students' art galleries and exhibits

Schools' exchange exhibits

Artmobiles, traveling suitcases

Art activity centers for students to review and reinforce art learning

Audiotaped or videotaped interviews with artists

Demonstrations of art processes

Role-playing in which students pretend to be art experts, historians, art critics, or artists discussing their works

Panel discussions involving students discussing specific artists and how their works were or were not influenced by cultural, social, political powers

Perhaps the most important art resource is the art museum. The function of the art museum is twofold: First, it is a place where art objects are stored and exhibited. Second, it is an institution for educating the public about art and through art (fig. 11.12).

Art museums accomplish these goals in a variety of ways. Permanent and special exhibitions are displayed within the galleries, usually with wall charts describing the artist and works. Sometimes, interpretive material is posted. Other times, guides are available in written form or from audio headsets, tours given by **docents** (persons who lead guided tours through museums), lectures, and videotape presentations. The Metropolitan Museum of Art in New York City has an entire center where anyone can view slide presentations of collections or current exhibitions or find out about the museum's holdings and educational programs. Many museums have museum educators who organize classes and special exhibitions.

An **exhibition** at an art museum is a public showing of a collection of artworks that is intended to bring to the public a diversity of ideas, new approaches, and solutions along with the artist or artists' statement. Developing a concept for an exhibition is very much like developing a painting or sculpture. Sometimes, the concept is aesthetic; other times, it is social. An exciting exhibition ignores no direction of art but attempts to merge all directions in meaningful ways that benefit all concerned. The underlying determinant is validity based on honesty, originality, integrity, and craftsmanship.

The challenge of experiencing an exhibition program is not unlike that of an artist standing, with brush in hand, before an empty canvas. The spirit of adventure is felt from within. The often vague information concerning the exhibition limits preconceived ideas of the ultimate presentation. As elements of the exhibit unfold, the collection begins to pull together.

Appendix B lists the names and addresses of outstanding U.S. museums, and resources.

IDEAS AND MOTIVATIONS

Looking at and responding to art with elementary students can be varied and developed to accommodate students' abilities. Most of the lessons require the use of art reproductions. You can purchase large prints, or smaller art image postcards are sold in most museum art stores. Museums also sell large posters. If you wish to make your own good-quality images, cut out reproductions from art journals and other sources, such as *Artnews, Art in America, Art Education, School Arts, American Artist, Art Forum, Smithsonian, Art and Activities,* and others. Children's literature also can be good sources for art reproductions. Check especially the book illustrations of Jan Brett, Tomie de Paola, Maurice Sendak, and Chris van Allsburg.

Mount the reproductions on cardboard and laminate. Place related information as to title, artist, date, and so on, on the front or back. If information is placed on the back, students can pair up to discuss and question each other about the art piece and artist. Images can be categorized by themes, ideas, styles, art movements, art form (sculptures, paintings, architecture, and so on)—in any way that suits your objectives.

Another good idea is to provide students with a list of questions like those on pages 217–220, which they can ask themselves whenever they are looking at, responding to, researching, or discussing artworks. Providing this list on an oversized index card often makes it handier for students to hold onto and use.

(a)

(b)

(c)

(d)

(e)

Figure 11.11 Cultural artifacts and art subject matter are everywhere.

Set up art learning centers that focus on art analysis. These centers may offer opportunities for students with extra time. Also, reserve plenty of class time for viewing slides or videos on art and art issues.

Looking at Art with Your Imagination

The motivations that follow will help you to be more creative and imaginative about the way you view and respond to art and can also be used with elementary students when adapted to students' grade-level capabilities.

1. Form picture frames with your fingers, and select and focus on various interesting parts of an artwork. Discuss why these parts are interesting to you.

2. Study an artwork for one minute. Then close your eyes and describe it. Then try describing the artwork without using words—just gestures and sounds.

3. Pretend that you can jump into an artwork. How would you feel? What would you see? Where would you go?

4. Invent a new title for an artwork.

5. Invent a story or poem to go along with an artwork.

6. Study the facial expressions and gestures of figures in an artwork. Examine the movement or line direction. Imitate the gestures and expressions with your body (fig. 11.13).

7. Try to express an artwork in one movement, taste, smell, or touch.

8. Invent musical sounds, rhythms, or movements to accompany an artwork.

Figure 11.12   Children engage in various creative activities in the galleries of the Cleveland Museum of Art. (Courtesy of the Department of Art History and Education, The Cleveland Museum of Art.)

9. After studying an artwork, describe what you think the artist must have been like.
10. Describe an artwork in one word.
11. Improvise a play or skit about an artwork.
12. Pretend that there is a mystery about an artwork. Play "Detective" or "I Spy," and look for clues in the artwork to solve the mystery.
13. Describe what an artwork would be like if it were supersize or miniature.
14. Describe what an artwork would be like if it was done in a different medium.
15. Describe what you think a dream about an artwork would be like.
16. Explain how you would change an artwork if you could.
17. Describe what it would feel like to touch a particular artwork.
18. Describe what an artwork would sound like if it could make music.
19. If people are shown in an artwork, describe who and what type of people they are. If they could come alive, what would they be like or be doing? Look for the details of the hands, faces, clothing, and other items.
20. Describe what you would see if you were inside the artwork looking out.

21. If you were the person in the artwork, what would you talk about? Where are you from?
22. Invent a series of questions about an artwork. Ask others the questions, and see if they can identify the artwork from the questions.

Ways to Look at and Respond to Artworks

1. Begin each class with warm-up art words, such as *impressionism, shading, space,* and *perspective.* Write the words on the chalkboard or on index cards, and display corresponding pictures that illustrate the words. For example, under the word *space* might be a reproduction of Edward Hopper's *Night Shadows.*
2. Throughout the year, have students work together to write and illustrate a cooperative art encyclopedia that includes art terms, artists, techniques, processes, and other relevant information that comes up in class.
3. Display three art reproductions without indicating their titles. Ask students to discuss their reactions to the artworks and to give the works their own titles. Compare students' titles to those of the artists.

(a)

(b)

Figure 11.13   Study the facial expressions and gestures of figures in an artwork. Imitate them with your body.

4. Display an art reproduction. (*a*) Then distribute three 3-by-5-inch cards to each student, and ask students to write down three words prompted by the artwork (one word on each card). (*b*) Collect the cards, and with students, sort and classify them into such categories as subject matter, formal properties, and expressive qualities. (*c*) Evaluate and discuss the artwork with regard to the areas of art analysis: subject description, materials used, analysis of visual structures, historical importance, interpretation, aesthetics, and judgment. Then ask each student to write a paragraph about the artwork.

5. Display an art reproduction. Ask students to individually and quietly write a single line about the artwork. Then combine all the lines to form a group poem or story.

6. Display an art reproduction. Divide students into two teams. One team should discuss the positive attributes, the other team the negative attributes of the artwork.

7. In front of the class, have two students role-play a talk-show host interviewing an artist. The studio audience (the other students) can also ask questions of the artist.

8. Display two portraits. Draw conversational balloons above the portraits, and ask students to imagine a serious or humorous conversation between the two people in the portraits. Then ask two students to assume the personalities of the portraits and a third student to assume the part of a television reporter interviewing them.

9. Select several postcard art images, and ask students to categorize them as to style, subject matter, function (if any), technical properties (painting, etching, etc.), expressive qualities (the feeling expressed), cultural factors, and narrative (storytelling) qualities.

10. Laminate an art image from an art magazine. Create an art puzzle by cutting up the art image.

11. Display an art reproduction of a painting. Have students use the technique of "clustering" to analyze the artwork. For example, under the word *color,* list various aspects of colors used in the artwork.

12. To each student, distribute an art reproduction by a different artist, and ask students to assume the identity of the artist whose work they were given. Then ask, for example, "Where is artist Georgia O'Keeffe? Tell us about yourself—what you like to paint, what media you use. When did you create this painting? What is the subject matter? What are the most important colors, lines, shapes, and so on in your artwork?"

13. Choose an art theme for the day, such as foods, people at work, people at play, mother and child, cityscapes, the Native American culture, transportation, children in artworks, celebrations, music, dance, and many others, and have students select correlating art reproductions. Initiate a discussion about the selected images, asking, "Why do artists paint what they paint?" "Why is this art?" "Do you like this work? Why?"

14. Compare art from various times and cultures. For example, have students investigate different artifacts, such as a Greek sculpture, an African mask, an Egyptian mural, a Gothic cathedral, a Japanese kimono and a contemporary furniture design. Discussion should revolve around why each art artifact is important and meaningful to the people of the time and culture in which it was made.

15. Feature an artist of the month. Display reproductions of the artist's works, and indicate where and when each was made. Have students research the artist's life and artworks. Discuss the artist's style, subject matter, moods, and composition. Was this artist influenced by another artist?

16. Have teams of students research different artists or artistic themes. Each team then makes a presentation that includes art images in front of the class. Listening class members can award points for most informative presentation.

17. Select and display two art reproductions that are similar, and have students do in-depth comparisons. For example, if both works show people, are the figures dressed in similar or different attire? What

geographical locations, historical times, and cultures are they from? Do the images reflect any political issues—for example, are any of the figures soldiers? Do the figures appear to be poor or wealthy?

18. Select and display two art reproductions that have something in common—for example, wood sculptures from Africa, watercolor paintings, religious sculptures, or artworks by French impressionists. Have students compare and contrast the two artworks.

19. Have each student do a research project on a selected artist and then make a five-minute oral presentation to the class, using reproductions of the artist's work as visuals.

20. After students have studied an artist like Picasso, initiate a discussion about what makes (or does not make) this artist's work art and why.

21. Select images of a theme—for example, horses. Have students discuss how representations of horses have differed in various cultures and throughout history and why. (See fig. A.3.)

22. Select images of a particular art style, such as abstract art, and have students compare and contrast the artworks, discussing the main ideas, colors, shapes, and so on.

23. Display an artwork reproduction, and ask students to study it. Then have them turn away from the reproduction, and show them three other reproductions that are similar to the first one. Ask students to compare and contrast the three new reproductions with the first one shown.

24. Have each student research two artists—one contemporary artist and one artist from the past—and compare and contrast their lives and artworks. How are the artists' lives different? What would the past artist be creating today?

25. Have each student select a favorite art reproduction and then pretend to be an art critic who is evaluating the work. Students could make oral or written presentations.

26. Select an artwork, such as Vincent van Gogh's *Self-Portrait* (see fig. 8.5*b*) or *Portrait After a Costume Ball* by Edgar Degas (see fig. 11.14). Have students dress up as the characters in the painting, and ask them to express how the characters might be feeling or what they might be saying.

Figure 11.14   Edgar Degas, French, 1834–1917, *Portrait After a Costume Ball* (Portrait of Mme. Dietz-Monnin), gouache, charcoal, pastel, metallic paint and oil on canvas, 1877–79, 85.5 × 75 cm, Joseph Winterbotham Collection, photograph © 1995 The Art Institute of Chicago. All Rights Reserved.

27. Ask a student to pretend to be a museum director. As the director, the student asks class members about whether or not a certain artwork should be included in an exhibition and why.

28. Ask each student to choose a favorite artist from the past. Then have students describe how their favorite artists would be different if they were alive today.

29. Ask students: "If you could have one painting or artwork in all the world, which would it be and why?"

30. Ask students to assume the poses, gestures, and facial expressions of characters in an artwork. See if other students can then guess who the characters are. (See fig. 11.13.)

31. Place information about an artist on an index card, separate from a painting by the artist. Ask students to match the card to the painting.

NOTES

1. *National Art Education Association News* 36, no. 3 (June 1994): 10.

2. Kay Alexander, "Art Curricula by and for Art Educators," in *Art Education: Elementary* (Reston, Va.: National Art Education Association, 1992).

3. E. Louis Lankford, *Aesthetics: Issues and Inquiry* (Reston, Va.: National Art Education Association, 1992).

4. Craig Noland, "Improving Student Thinking through Elementary Art Instruction," in *Art Education: Elementary* (Reston, Va.: National Art Education Association, 1992).

Elementary Art Fundamentals

Planning and Assessment, Organizing, and Questions

chapter

12

Lesson Planning and Assessment

[We believe that] students learn best, and most integrally, from involvement in activities that take place over a significant period of time, that are anchored in meaningful production, and that build upon natural connections to perceptual, reflective, and scholastic artistic knowledge.

Howard Gardner

Chapter 2 discusses the art curriculum concepts to teach and students' capabilities in each of a number of art areas from kindergarten through sixth grade. This chapter tells you how to apply the information in chapter 2 in planning and assessing art instruction.

UNDERSTANDING THE STUDENT

Students come to school influenced by their cultural, social, and home environment; their past experiences; their inherited abilities; and their developed skills. In art lessons, they express this information, as well as their feelings, in an artistic response. As a teacher of art, you can develop, cultivate, and preserve students' feelings of success, self-worth, confidence, initiative, and responsibility in this area.

Every student's solution to an art problem is meaningful and significant. Unlike math problems, art problems have limitless solutions. The finished art product represents the way one individual expressed one solution at one specific time. It could never be exactly repeated, even if the individual tried to duplicate it.

As a teacher, you must be selective about offering a student your own ideas and solutions to the student's artwork. The student may not like or even comprehend such suggestions and may interpret them as judgment. By putting aside your personal preferences and listening carefully to what the student says, you will be able to point the student in directions that will lead him or her to relevant artistic discoveries.

Working independently in art offers students opportunities for individualized instruction. Students can research a specific area of learning that they are most interested in—for instance, specific artists, particular art movements, the development of jewelry in the Native American Navajo culture—or their assignment might be to experiment creatively with various types of water paints and to complete a certain number of paintings. To clarify an individual study area, students can state what the specific *topic* will be; list definite *objectives* to work toward; list the *materials* and *resources* to be used, such as books to be read, films to be watched, galleries and libraries to be visited, and self-instructional kits to be used; outline the *plan of operation* to complete the project; determine *how to assess* the project or research; and keep a *notebook or journal* for sketches, illustrations, notes, new information, concepts, resources, and so on, and for recording work progress.

Working in groups in art permits interchange and feedback of ideas, which helps to establish support for creative freedom, for sharing of cultural values, for verbalization of art concepts, and for opportunity for artistic discovery. Groups can establish goals to be reached together, set time limits, and determine the type of assessment techniques to be used.

Group discussions and exhibitions of student artworks can be especially meaningful as a learning strategy because they provide the student artist with the unique insights of others. In many art classes, the finished art product is exhibited immediately upon completion. Class time is planned for "Looking and Thinking about Our Work." Exhibition and discussion then become a natural part of the class experience. Group assessment discussions often include questions like those presented in chapter 11.

PLANNING ART INSTRUCTION

The areas of art growth stated in chapter 2 are defined according to age objectives and characteristics. However, keep in mind that art growth is continuous and that many stated objectives overlap. It is difficult to determine where one level starts and another stops. Also, no particular student is typical of any defined skill level. Students may indicate varying characteristics at any one time. Some students may advance quickly through a growth level; others need greater amounts of time to follow the sequence of art development.

The objectives identified in chapter 2 are only broad generalizations that imply certain art growth and that will help you to identify attainable goals for your students. Your role as a teacher is to use these characteristics and objectives as reference data to provide enriched, exciting circumstances and appropriate motivations for meaningful art experiences.

Collect art examples of the various growth levels, and keep these in chronological order as representative of the many forms of expression and symbols. Use them to observe the differences and similarities in children's art products and to monitor children's growth and development.

Common elements that flow through all developmental levels are children's natural desire to draw and paint to express themselves and their need to explore and experiment to find relationships in learning. Art learning takes place in the context of what is already known. Students understand new information when it is understood in relation to information already learned.

The process of learning about art takes place in the child's thinking. Children organize their thoughts and create artworks in ways that give clues as to the development of their thinking. Thus, a child's art products are an aid to understanding the child's total growth.

Outline for Planning Art Instruction

When planning art instruction, keep in mind that not all content objectives will occur in the same lesson. For example, art instruction may involve hands-on activities (artistic), group-related projects (perhaps art history or art analysis), individual research (intellectual—for example, studying the human body), or manipulative (skill) development.

Course content (that is, subject matter, techniques, skills, and so on) should be sequential so that knowledge can build upon itself. Establish guidelines, and convey expectations to students. This will help them to understand what is expected of them and what goals they can hope to achieve. An organized, efficient classroom with focused content avoids wasted time and unproductive student behavior.

Keep track of success rates so that students remain actively productive. Motivate students at all levels of development.

How do you assess the instructional lesson plan? How can you measure the progress made in student learning? By assessing the content and student progress, you can analyze information about what students know and can do, where each needs additional assistance, and what to change in future teaching strategies.

The following are some questions to ask yourself concerning meaningful art learning:

- Does the lesson plan directly relate to the art content, knowledge, and skills you wish the students to learn?
- Does the lesson plan focus on the art content and integrated goals, or is it directed at using media, process, and techniques?
- Is the lesson plan connected and sequential to other lessons, or is it a one-time, add-on project? Does it relate to special events?
- Does the lesson plan strengthen the student's learning in art? Should similar goals be employed in other learning areas, such as reading and science?
- Would it be of assistance for other students, teachers, parents, and administrators to discuss, plan, or have input into the plans for art learning?
- Could the art curriculum align art knowledge and skills with other areas of learning?
- Is the art learning in alignment with local art curricula in other schools, as well as with national and state standards?

Chart 12.1 presents an outline for planning art instruction.

Instruction Example: Art Presentation for Third Grade

Art Goals

1. Increase knowledge of Mexican history and artifacts.
2. Create clay figurines.

Content Objectives

As a result of the art program, each pupil should demonstrate, on a personal level, the ability to (1) perceive and understand artistic visual relationships in the environment; (2) think, feel, and act creatively with visual art materials; (3) increase manipulative skills; (4) construct clay figurines; and (5) demonstrate increased knowledge of the Mexican culture.

Motivations

The following unit is based on historical research involving relics from Teotihuacan. The unit was developed with the previously stated objectives in mind to improve students' self-concept through cultural awareness. The units are a combination of culture, social studies, and art activity.

chart   12.1
Outline for Planning Art Instruction

Lesson:
Art Goals:
A. State content objectives. Indicate what students are to learn and accomplish in the lesson. Specify the *content* objectives and what students will achieve after the instruction. In some instances, emphasis will not be on a specific objective but rather on search and experimentation, thus encouraging unique and unpredictable responses. The objectives can be stated individually, or several can be combined. Be sure to teach to the objectives.

The objectives and expectations should reflect the specific *content* area the student will investigate (fig. 12.1). Comparison of the achievement with the stated content objective then allows assessment of the learning situation. Not *all* objectives can be covered in one lesson. Objectives probably will fall into the following general categories:

1. Artistic. The student:
    a. Practices art production of line, shape, value, space, color, pattern, texture, and composition.
    b. Improves performance in drawing the human figure, portraits, still lifes, designs, landscapes, self-portraits, and imaginative compositions.

    c. Improves art production in drawing and painting techniques.
2. Perceptual. The student:
    a. Increases awareness of the self within the environment through experiences related to the senses and involving seeing, touching, feeling, hearing, tasting, moving, creating, inventing, and organizing.
3. Manipulative. The student:
    a. Improves skill in handling, experimenting with, caring for, and controlling art tools and materials.
4. Art history, art analysis, and aesthetics. The student:
    a. Studies art aesthetics and its meaning in history and cultures (fig. 12.2).
    b. Improves ability to make art judgments and decisions.
    c. Develops greater awareness of object and situation details.
    d. Develops a keener aesthetic awareness of the art elements and design principles.
    e. Has increased knowledge of artists and their artworks.
    f. Improves ability to classify artworks into styles and periods of art.
    g. Develops art values and attitudes.
    h. Has increased understanding of art terms and art language.
    i. Improves ability to know likes and dislikes.
    j. Assesses artworks using such terms as *naming, classifying, organizing, analyzing, synthesizing, describing, interpreting,* and *judgment*.
5. Intellectual. The student:
    a. Deals with concepts that involve greater observation and understanding, such as the human body (its functions and how it moves), nature, still lifes, landscapes, and the workings of machinery.
    b. Is involved with various types of thinking, such as convergent (the right answer), intuitive, divergent (multiple solutions).

Continued

Figure 12.1   In planning art instruction, it is important to state the specific content area students will investigate.

Figure 12.2   Objectives of art history and art analysis include the study of art in history and cultures. After students studied life in a Hopi community, they created this city dwelling from clay.

chart 12.1

Continued

c. Expands cognitive ability to think about such ideas as drugs, pollution, war, food, health, growth, living spaces, community spaces, and transportation.
d. Engages in self-directed and individual projects.
6. **Expressive.** The student:
   a. Improves ability to communicate ideas, feelings, emotions—what to say and how to say it.
   b. Demonstrates spontaneity, intuition, subconsciousness, automaticity, discovery, inquiry, and reflection (calls upon previous experiences).
7. **Creative.** The student:
   a. Emphasizes unique, inventive, independent, fluent, personal solutions.
B. **Plan art motivations.** Explain how to reach stated objectives and what the manner of presentation will be. How will you interact with students? Will you use any unusual experiences as part of the motivation? What action words and movements will you have? How will you involve the students? How will you involve their feelings, imaginations, interpretations? How will you verbally and nonverbally encourage questions, feedback, discussion, and interaction of ideas? Not all motivations will occur in one lesson. Possible motivations include:
1. **Skill (process) motivation.** Demonstrate and instruct in the use of different media, materials, and tools and in the execution of technical processes.
2. **Subject motivation.** Tell stories. Have students act out stories. Make up mythology.
3. **Recall motivation.** Have students recall memories, situations from past experiences.
4. **Visual observation motivation.** Provide visual models—objects, figures, landscapes, still lifes, photos, and so on.
5. Take field trips to galleries, museums, artists' studios.
6. Invent ideas. Create imaginary images.
7. Look at and discuss art examples.
8. Read and discuss a book about an artist.
9. Engage in activities that sharpen perception, educate the senses.
10. Show films, light shows, slides, art examples (such as sculptures).
C. **List materials needed.** Prepare a list of all needed tools and materials.
D. **List resources needed.** Prepare a list of all teaching aids to be used, such as teaching examples, projectors, films, slides, reproductions, television shows, videotapes, and so on.

E. **Describe instructional procedures.** Describe what you intend to present in class and how students will proceed. If an instructional process, list step by step and include:
1. **Working time.** Approximate time needed for motivation, visual aids, and process, and time needed for interaction of ideas, solutions, and evaluations.
2. **Experimentation time.** Allow time for student experimentation and new ideas. Keep select data.
3. **Changes and evaluation.** Keep select data on progress.
F. **Final resolution.** Allow students to decide when the art product is complete.
G. **Assessment of goals, objectives, achievements, progress, motivations, process.** How can objectives be improved? How can students achieve greater success with the problem? Did students learn meaningfully? Was there growth in art skills? Was time used productively?
H. **Reach conclusions.** What conclusions have you and the students arrived at from this art experience?
I. **Reflect on expanding opportunities.** Establish goals, objectives, and ideas for further lessons.
J. **Present and evaluate art products.** Provide a time for communicating and sharing through presentations, group discussions, and/or exhibitions of the art or art products and ideas (fig. 12.3). Does the art product indicate what students have learned and achieved and if the objectives have been reached?

Figure 12.3 A time for sharing ideas and sketchbooks can inspire all kinds of art impact in the classroom.

A few miles from Mexico City are the ruins of the city of Teotihuacan. The name *Teotihuacan* literally means "place of the gods." The city covers over six square miles and has two gigantic pyramids known since the time of the Aztecs as "of the sun" and "of the moon." When built, the city was composed of plazas, palaces, temples, and broad avenues. The structures were covered with white and red stucco. Clay figurines found within these structures were used to describe customs, ceremonies, and scenes of daily life.

Students will hear a brief history of Teotihuacan. Then they will be shown a number of figurines that represent those found in Teotihuacan. (See fig. 10.1 and p. 184.)

Materials Needed

1. Red, low-fire clay
2. Appropriate modeling tools: pin tool, cutting wire, wooden texture tools, or any other found objects that can be utilized
3. Water containers

4. Paper towels and sponges
5. Wedging boards
6. Nonlead, low-fire, cone .06 glazes and brushes

Resources

1. Historic information (books, slides)
2. Figurine sculptures

Process/Procedure

The teacher demonstrates the procedure first.

1. Each student should have a water container, sponge, paper towels, and a modeling tool.
2. Use cutting wire to cut 1-inch slices of clay from a bag of clay, and give one slice to each student.
3. Students should cut the slice into two or three separate pieces and work the pieces until they are not so stiff. Then they should roll the three pieces into balls.
4. Students should work one ball into the shape of a torso and use the other balls to shape arms, legs, and headdress or other body decoration.
5. In attaching one piece of clay to another, students should be sure to score (scratch) and moisten both adjoining surfaces before attaching. Cracks are likely to develop if this procedure is not followed.
6. The finished figurine should be covered with plastic for two days so that it does not dry too quickly and develop cracks. After two days, the figurine can dry uncovered at its own rate. When dry, figurines are ready to be bisque-fired and glazed.

Assessment/Achievement

Objectives were achieved. Students gained greater knowledge of Mexican history and created clay figurines.

Conclusions

More time should perhaps be allotted for this lesson. Students showed interest in further clay projects. Students organized and displayed figurines in the library, where other students viewed the exhibition with great interest.

Expanding Opportunities

Further study of other Mexican arts, such as textile weaving, and mask and jewelry making, is possible. This study also could be related to Native American culture. The lesson could then be used in fourth grade.

Presentation and Evaluation

The creation and presentation of sculptures, the exhibition, and the discussion time were successful in encouraging greater interest in Central and South American cultures and their artworks.

Submitted by David Manje, art teacher

MEASURING ACHIEVEMENT

Achievement and assessment of student learning in art is an integral part of classroom instruction. A variety of measures may be used based on specified objectives. Assessment of art learning has four purposes:

1. To provide feedback to the student
2. To record each student's achievement and progress for the student, the teacher, and the parents
3. To provide data on group performance for informed curriculum and instruction decisions, as well as data to document learning in art
4. To supply evidence of learning for reports to districts and communities

All assessment requires students' active participation. Procedures can vary in complexity, but those commonly used involve students:

1. Creating art products
2. Keeping notes, sketchbooks and journals (fig. 12.4)
3. Maintaining portfolios of artworks
4. Writing short essays
5. Answering quizzes or questionnaires

Charts 12.2 and 12.3 present a sample instruction unit and sample quiz questions.

GUIDELINES FOR ASSESSMENT

In forming guidelines for student assessment procedures, refer to the identifying characteristics and objectives listed for each age group in chapter 2. These will serve as objectives and achievements to work *toward*. Refer also to chapters 3, 4, 5, and 6 on individual art elements, which will help

Figure 12.4 Sketchbooks provide a place for students to keep their ideas and drawings together. One aspect of assessment may include students' sketchbooks.

chart 12.2

Sample Instruction Unit and Quiz

The following is a unit taught by art educator Connie Ellis to fourth-, fifth-, and sixth-graders. Students met one hour once a week.

Auguste Renoir (1841–1919), French Impressionist Painter

Auguste Renoir was born in France in 1841. His father was a poor tailor with a large family to support. As a young boy, Auguste was sent to work for a decorator of fine porcelain. He learned to paint flowers and other designs on china cups and plates. The fresh pink and blue colors Renoir used on the cups influenced the colors he would use in his paintings later in his life. As an adult, Renoir painted portraits, landscapes, figures, still-life objects, and street scenes. But Renoir's favorite subject was women. He believed that women symbolized all the warmth and beauty in the world. The women in Renoir's paintings are generic women; they do not represent an individual woman, but all women.

Renoir is well known for his impressionistic paintings. Impressionism is a style of painting that stresses the effects of light and air on a subject in an instant of time. The painter uses light, bright color and broken brush strokes to create a soft, airy impression of what he or she sees. Little attention is given to detail. Renoir sold his work and received many commissions to paint portraits in this style.

A very social man, Renoir enjoyed getting together with friends at parties and restaurants. For Renoir, living was painting. During the final years of his life, he was crippled badly with rheumatism, and he painted from a wheelchair with a paintbrush strapped to his hand. One time, a visitor asked him how he could paint beautiful pictures under such difficulties. His optimistic answer was, "One does not paint with one's hand."

From this brief history of Renoir, a questionnaire was developed:

1. Match the following terms:

   a. Generic _____ Grass, trees, mountains
   b. Portrait _____ Pink, blue, white, green
   c. Landscape _____ Short, choppy strokes of paint
   d. Impressionism _____ No name people (general)
   e. Soft, joyful colors _____ Wren-wá
   f. Renoir _____ Individual face

For each of the following sentences, circle either true (T) or false (F).

2. Renoir's favorite color was black.   T   F
3. Renoir's paintings are happy and carefree with bright colors.   T   F
4. Renoir's paintings are sad and gloomy and dark.   T   F
5. Renoir strapped a brush to his foot to paint.   T   F
6. Renoir's favorite subject to paint was animals.   T   F

---

you to establish concrete comparisons in the sections entitled "How Students Understand . . . (Line, Space, Color, etc.)." Then determine how the individual student has progressed in terms of the types of goals established in your specific art instruction plans (see chart 12.1). For example, how did the student's work progress in the history and analysis area? In the intellectual area? In the creative area? You can assess what students have learned by determining the effectiveness of your goals and by comparing initial artworks with later ones. Methods of assessment should be geared to identifying students' knowledge and progress over a period of time.

Record keeping is essential to constructive and productive student assessments. Keep index cards on all of your students—an easily referenced file that states each student's activities, accomplishments, presentations, and progress. Also keep portfolios of artworks (date the artworks) or sketchbooks to compare student self-growth and improvement.

The index cards and portfolios are helpful to both teacher and student during individual student/teacher conferences and for establishing long- and short-term goals. Hold such conferences as often as needed. During the conferences, encourage a positive success approach by calling attention to specific areas that illustrate the student's success. Remember: encouragement builds; criticism destroys. Point out where specific goals and objectives have been

reached (or not reached) to challenge and provide guidance for the student.

Student self-evaluation can be part of the assessment procedure. Such positive responsibility by the student considers (1) individual attitude, (2) interest, (3) effort, and (4) product. A self-analysis to determine a personal "grade" and identify progress can include such questions as:

"How does my artwork compare with my past art performance?'
"Can I now improve on the art piece?"
"Am I working up to my creative and artistic potential?"
"How does my work relate to the rest of the class?"

The list that follows indicates other checkpoints you may consider in art assessments of students.

POINTS TO CONSIDER IN STUDENT ACHIEVEMENT

1. Is the student self-motivating and enthusiastic?
2. Is the student willing to search out and explore new ideas?
3. Does the student pursue individual research and thoughtful reading?
4. Does the student use imaginative solutions in expressing ideas and experiences (fig. 12.5)?
5. Does the student research information concerning artists and artworks?

chart   12.3

Sample Quiz Questions

The following selected examples were taken from questionnaires and games designed to reinforce learning objectives.

1. Draw the following lines: (a) horizontal, (b) vertical, and (c) diagonal.
2. Match the following shapes:
   a. Circle   _____ Cube
   b. Rectangle   _____ Flat, one side
   c. Triangle   _____ Sphere
   d. Square   _____ Pyramid
   e. Two-dimensional   _____ Many sides
   f. Three-dimensional _____ Round
3. Draw the following three-dimensional forms: (a) cube, (b) pyramid, and (c) cylinder.

Fill in the blanks with the correct answers.

4. The lightness or darkness of a color is called _____.
5. A mark between two points is called a _____.
6. When lines connect together, it makes a _____.
7. The three primary colors are _____, _____ and _____.
8. The three secondary colors are _____, _____, and _____.
9. The complementary color of blue is _____.
10. The complementary color of red is _____.
11. A dark value of a hue (made by adding black to the color) is called a _____.
12. A light value of a hue (made by adding white to the color) is called a _____.

Mark each of the following sentences either true (T) or false (F).

13. Red and blue make green.   T   F
14. Red and orange make blue.   T   F
15. Blue and yellow make green.   T   F
16. Yellow and red make orange.   T   F
17. The "light source" can be the sun or a lamp.   T   F
18. A still life is a picture of a person holding very still.   T   F
19. Shading is blending light to dark.   T   F
20. Draw a pattern using one of the following shapes: crosses, hearts, circles, stars.
21. Symmetrical balance means that
    a. each side is different.
    b. both sides are the same.
22. Asymmetrical balance means that
    a. each side is different.
    b. both sides are the same.
23. Radial balance means that
    a. the design radiates from the center to the outside of a circle.
    b. the design is contained inside a square.
24. Match the following terms:
    a. Still life   _____ Face
    b. Landscape   _____ Most important part of picture
    c. Portrait   _____ Flat, one side
    d. Two-dimensional   _____ Trees, mountains, sky
    e. Three-dimensional   _____ Hole in a sculpture
    f. Void (negative space) _____ Many sides
    g. Center of interest   _____ Vase, flowers, fruit, plants, toys

Source: Examples are from the Cartwright School District: Coordinator Pat Jones Hunt and art educators Connie Ellis and Patricia Koepp.

Figure 12.5   In assessing art, determine if the artworks indicate progress in imaginative growth.

6. Does the student participate in group efforts?
7. Does the student practice forming opinions and making decisions and independent judgments?
8. Does the student investigate various solutions to art problems?

9. Does the student assess the art problem, self-evaluate, and then boundary-push?
10. Can the student identify similarities and differences in the art elements? Invent new shapes and textures? Learn by experimenting with colors?
11. Does the student exhibit improvement in design and composition?
12. Does the student use a working art vocabulary?
13. Is the student able to relate art learning to other learning areas?
14. Does the student demonstrate readiness to extend previously learned information into future art solutions?
15. Has the student increased his or her skill in working with art tools and materials? Has the student creatively explored and experimented with art tools and materials? Has the student's craftsmanship improved?
16. Does the student keep checklists on art procedures?
17. Does the student reach established objectives?
18. Keep in mind that some students express ideas in more realistic visual imagery, while other students express ideas with greater emotional or abstract imagery.
19. Further measuring tools include quizzes, essays, portfolios, sketchbooks, and progress file cards.

Organizing the Art Room and Materials

Drawing is the beginning to run, smile, walk. It is the starting that happens in the deepest of self, amassing the world of joy between the movement of the eye, in the hand that grasps the brain looking for the image.

Elba Damast

A well-equipped and well-organized art room benefits both you and your students—for obvious reasons: You are more able to effectively and efficiently present and demonstrate art lessons, and your students' growth and progress are not impeded by missing materials, insufficient work space, and general confusion.

Art tools and materials are exciting. Anything that will create a mark on a surface becomes a drawing instrument. A finger smeared with clay can express an idea, just as a stick dipped in ink can. At one time, artists were separated into groups, such as oil painters or watercolor painters, according to the tools they used. Today, emphasis is on the artist's *ideas,* and the artist's tools are dictated by the ideas to be expressed. The chapter explains and explores the various art tools and materials in detail.

ORGANIZING THE ART ROOM

The National Art Education Association recommends that students in grades two through six receive 100 minutes of art experiences per week throughout the school year. The association also suggests that the teacher-student ratio be no greater than one full-time art teacher to three or four hundred students.[1]

Each school should have one permanent art room equipped for group work and independent, self-directed study. A satisfactory room size is 30 feet by 60 feet, with abundant lighting. Organization of the art room will be unique, depending on the size and shape of each room, the number of students in each class, and the art curriculum. Adapt the suggestions that follow as necessary to accommodate your work space.

The art room sink should be readily accessible, with adjacent cupboards and shelves for holding painting supplies, such as paint jars, watercolor trays, brushes, and tins for holding water. Other shelving in the room can hold crayons, scissors, rulers, and other miscellaneous supplies that do not require adjacency to a sink. Stacking trays can hold artwork and paintings in the process of drying. Cupboards with drawers can hold large art reproductions and other visual support materials. All materials should be located in an easily accessed open area to facilitate easy distribution.

Brushes and pencils can be placed in large metal cans. Scissors can be stored handles up in large tin cans with holes punched in the bottom (fig. 13.1). Glue, paper scraps, crayons, and other miscellaneous supplies should be stored in small boxes or cartons. Chart 13.1 lists desired art supplies and quantities (available in art supply catalogs).

Keep the following miscellaneous art supplies on hand for exploring and experimenting:

water containers
painting surfaces (wood, fiber, or Masonite boards)
aprons, smocks, or old shirts
newspapers

Figure 13.1   Organize art tools to facilitate easy distribution.

paper towels
Popsicle sticks
tongue depressors (for mixing)
assorted papers (like wallpapers and wrapping papers)
rollers (brayers)
clothespins
exhibition areas
wires (telephone and others for sculptures)
sticks and twigs
nails
combs
sponges
shoe, cloth, root, batik, and vegetable dyes
stamp pads and stamps
soap
feathers
rags
ropes
carbon paper (various colors)
candles
cotton swabs
corks
glitter
paper doilies
masking tape
pipe cleaners
old toothbrushes
waxed paper
colored cellophane sheets
plastic wrap
sand
stones
spray bottles
squeeze bottles
old drawings and paintings for collages
copying machines
overhead projectors
computers
old jewelry
outdated film

Community sources of interesting art materials include:

1. **Newspapers.** Newspapers often have ends of rolls of newsprint left over after printing. This newsprint is ideal for large drawings with pencil, crayon, or paint. Sometimes, paper discards from a printer are available.
2. **Plastic companies.** These companies usually have discard boxes, or you can buy plastic pieces by the pound. These are good for sculpture.
3. **Leather companies.** These companies also usually have discard boxes of leather pieces.
4. **Lumber companies.** Discard piles of wood are good hunting spots for wood pieces for construction or painting projects (fig. 13.2). Also, dowel rods found at lumber companies can be sharpened in a pencil sharpener and used with ink.
5. **Local thrift stores, such as Goodwill.** In these stores, look for such items as rags and cloth (for collages), buttons, feathers, lace, old jewelry, magazines, old sweaters (unravel for the yarn), and old dolls, toys, or objects to use for still lifes.
6. **Upholstery companies.** Foam rubber and cloth materials from upholstery discard piles are good for printing and for sculpture.
7. **Mail-order companies.** Leftover or discarded Styrofoam packing can be used for art construction and printing projects.
8. **Students' homes.** Student's homes can be the sources of a wealth of art materials. Parents are often eager to donate scraps and materials to the art program, if they are invited to. A note to families might begin:

Dear Parents and Friends of [*school name*]:

> We have planned an exciting art curriculum for your child this year. The list that follows shows some of the materials we need to help with our art skills in our creative art classes. Searching for these "recycled" items can be fun (they can even be cleanup hunts!).

Figure 13.2   Scraps from the lumberyard are favorite imagination sparkers.

chart 13.1

Art Supplies for a Classroom of Thirty-Five Students

Crayons
  35 boxes of 64 colors; also, large- and small-size crayons of 8 primary colors

Powdered, liquid, or cake tempera
  The colors red, yellow, blue, white, black, magenta, turquoise, purple, ocher, orange, brown, green, and flesh in amounts appropriate to curriculum projects

Watercolor paint
  35 plastic or metal box trays with 16 colors

Brushes
  35 assorted 1-inch, ¾-inch, ½-inch, and ¼-inch long-handled bristle brushes
  35 assorted sizes of round, soft-hair brushes
  15 Japanese bamboo brushes

Paper (Note: One ream is 500 sheets)
  White drawing paper: 1 ream, 18 inches by 24 inches
  Manilla: 2 reams, 18 inches by 24 inches
  White and five or six assorted colors of kraft (butcher): 1 roll each, 36 inches wide, 100 feet long
  Assorted colored construction paper: 2 reams, 18 inches by 24 inches
  Newsprint: 2 reams, 18 inches by 24 inches, or roll ends from newspaper
  Glossy or glazed (kitchen shelf) paper for finger painting: 4 rolls

Charcoal
  35 sticks

Pastels
  15 sets of colored pastels or chalks

Erasers
  15

Drawing pencils
  35 assorted

Felt-tip markers and pens
  35 assorted-color sets, thick and thin tips (splurge on these!) or two dozen of each color, both thick and thin tips

Colored pencils
  10 assorted-color sets (12 pencils in each set)

Glue
  Wheat paste: 25 pounds (for papier-maché)
  Glue sticks: 35
  White glue (Elmer's): 2 gallons

Rubber cement: 3 medium-size jars
Liquid starch (commercial): 1 gallon

Powdered or liquid commercial detergent
  1 bottle or box

Scissors
  35

Water containers
  18 jars (pint size), cut-off milk cartons, plastic cottage cheese or margarine containers, coffee cans (water containers can be shared)

Paint containers
  Plastic squeeze jars, TV dinner trays (aluminum), 4-inch aluminum pie trays for individual colors, baby food jars, ice cube trays, muffin tins, ketchup or mustard containers (with nail in top for storage), syrup pitchers, large quart jars for storage and mixing

Glazes
  2 pints each of assorted colors

Clay
  Approximately 100 pounds of clay (in 25-pound packages) for 35 students. This will allow each student to have one to two clay experiences. A kiln is also needed for firing the clay. Kiln size will depend on your needs and budget. Approximately 10 packages of plasticine (non-hardening) modeling clay.

Printmaking tools
  For stamp printing: Sponges, cardboard, wood, and Styrofoam to cut into shapes; also, kitchen utensils, toys, and found objects for inking and printing. Tempera paint can be used for stamp printing. Water-based printing inks can be purchased from art catalogs. Brayers for inking shapes are also helpful.
  For monoprinting: Formica tables or assorted sizes of 1/8-inch plexiglass (9 inches by 12 inches is a good size) and tempera paint

Film
  For experiments. Photo shops will sometimes donate outdated film.

Weaving supplies
  Donations from community
  One dozen rolls of yarn
  Cardboard looms

Thank you for helping to make our creative art program the success it is. We need: boxes of all sizes, old jewelry, seeds, buttons, Styrofoam, wood, cloth, beads, wrapping paper, wallpaper, broken and unwanted toys, 2-inch by 2-inch slides, slide mounts, unwanted cameras, sewing remnants, rickrack, yarns, old clocks, watches, electrical objects, gears, motors, bolts, springs, screws, knobs, wheels, locks, keys, seasonal cards, posters, maps, books, magazines, local newspapers, foreign newspapers, old window shades, feathers, hats, uniforms, costumes, coffee cans, scrap wax crayons, old candle pieces, unusable musical instruments, old typewriters and parts, old radios, mannequins, wig-head stands, old bones or skulls, corn husks, gourds, large juice cans, baby food jars, egg cartons, Styrofoam trays . . . and anything else your imagination can come up with.

The art room should be furnished with movable equipment and/or separate work centers to accommodate the study of art history, art analysis, two- and three-dimensional artwork, and specialized media, such as clay, weaving, painting, drawing, and printmaking. A chalkboard is needed, as are cupboards for housing projectors, a screen for showing slides and films, a videocassette player, and a monitor for viewing videotapes.

At least one—but preferably several—display panels and possibly display cupboards for three-dimensional artworks are essential. Portable display units are also very useful and can be shared by other teachers and schools for exhibitions in hallways, libraries, cafeterias, and other places.

One area of the art room should be set aside for an art library. Many art rooms have adjoining storage rooms for art supplies and projects in progress.

Art room bulletin boards and display panels should be carefully designed and visually exciting. Mounting artworks on colored backings makes them much more interesting. Cloth materials, prints, and metallic papers add patterns and texture to the bulletin board surface area. Study store window displays for other presentation ideas.

Suggestions for making the art classroom more efficient include:

1. Arrange chairs and tables into groups in a way that makes best use of available room, floor, and hallway space. Name each group by hanging a placard with the name of an artist above it. The group of students who then sit in this area will be identified by the artist's name. Group seating aids in materials distribution and in overall class organization.
2. To get students' attention, hold up your hand and say, "Eyes and ears." Try it. It works!
3. Provide procedures for preparation of art supplies: mixing paints, thinning glues, etc. Discuss these with students.
4. Establish procedures and designate student monitors for passing out art supplies, proper use of supplies, putting supplies back, and cleaning up. Discuss these with students.
5. Assign rotating groups the responsibilities of caring for tools and supplies, distribution, pickup, and cleanup.
6. Provide positive reinforcements, such as extra credit or the title of "artist assistant."

ART TOOLS AND MATERIALS

The sections that follow give basic information about the various art tools and materials available. Whenever using new art materials, experiment with the media, both by themselves and in combination with other materials. Avoid "how-to" formulas. Restrictive directions often inhibit freedom. As an elementary teacher, demonstrate the many possibilities of each tool, and encourage your students to freely explore each material's unique properties and capabilities. In this way, the tools and materials become an important part of the lesson motivation (fig. 13.3).

Figure 13.3   Provide students with tools and materials that encourage inventive thinking and creative exploration.

Drawing Materials

Charcoal

Charcoal, a favorite tool of artists for centuries, is a black, solid residue made from burning wood in a kiln with very little air. Woods used in the past were willow, linden wood, spindle, and plum. Charcoal can also be made from bones and other vegetable residues. Today, charcoal is available in soft (soft smears the most), medium, and hard degrees, and is produced in three forms: (1) natural vine form, (2) compressed chalk form, and (3) wooden pencil.

Artists commonly use charcoal when making quick sketches, such as in gesture drawing (see chapter 3); when quick changes may be necessary, since charcoal erases easily with finger, cloth, or paper stump; and when developing tonal studies of values from dark to light because large areas showing lights and darks of a composition can be developed quickly with charcoal. Areas of tone can also be built up by using crosshatched charcoal lines. Both the sides and points of charcoal sticks are used to create a variety of textures on different types of paper surfaces. A paper towel under your unused hand can prevent smearing accidents.

Charcoal drawings are usually sprayed with a fixative when finished to prevent smudging. Common hair spray or a commercial fixative made from alcohol and shellac or plastic can be used, but do so outside.

Pencils

Over 350 different kinds of pencils are available to write on such surfaces as paper, tin, steel, iron, film, wood, plastics, glass, cloth, and even skin. One thing that all pencils have in common is that they can be used as drawing tools.

The writing pencil is made from thin slats of cedar. Eight parallel grooves are machined into a slat that is half a pencil thick. The leads are laid in, and a similarly grooved slat faced with glue is clamped on. The slats are then dried under intense heat. The grooved portions are sliced into eight pencils that are then smoothed, sanded, lacquered, imprinted, and fed into a machine that fastens on a ferrule and inserts an eraser plug. A good pencil has up to eight coats of lacquer, and the gold stamping on some pencils is real gold—to hold up under constant handling.[2]

Drawing pencils have a range of eighteen degrees, from 10H (the hardest lead), to HB (lead of medium hardness), to 7B (the softest lead). Soft leads are thicker and usually more fragile than hard leads, and they smear easily. They are preferred for freer, darker, and more spontaneous drawings. Hard leads give clear, sharp marks that do not rub off easily and are preferred for small, detailed work. Artists generally use a range of pencils from 6H to 6B. A good range for elementary classroom use is 6B, 4B, 2B, HB, 2H, and 4H. Most students prefer softer pencils, such as 6B, 4B, and 2B. The 2B pencil is the common lead pencil used in the classroom for routine schoolwork.

Pencils are used to create tonal ranges from light to dark. They are also used where more detail is desired. Combinations of pencils create interesting textures and varying feelings.

Line qualities can be changed by varying the pressure applied to a pencil: Hard pressure creates a wide, dark line, while gentle, soft pressure creates a delicate line. Varying pressure in one line indicates movement in and out. Holding the pencil in different ways will also create various lines. Colors and lines can be built one on another to create interesting forms, textures, and areas.

Elementary students like to use colored pencils. Some colored pencils are made with oil or wax and cannot be erased. Nongreasy colored pencils can be brushed with water for a watercolor texture. Grease pencils (marking pencils) are more like a crayon pencil.

Pens

A variety of pens are available for drawing. Felt- and nylon-tip pens come in a wide variety of sizes and in waterproof or water-soluble inks. They are a favorite for all school classrooms. Ballpoint pens are also available in various colors and sizes.

Artists' fountain pens come in a variety of sizes, are used with different inks, and are usually expensive. Bamboo pens are inexpensive and make a sensuous line ranging from wide to thin. Quill pens are flexible, and varying pressures create more personal and freer linear qualities. Reed pens, drawing instruments from ancient times, create bolder, blunter, more powerful lines than quill pens. Artist George Grosz used the reed pen in many of his drawings. Reed pens and quill pens used together offer a strong, visually interesting contrast.

Pen points come in a variety of shapes, widths, and flexibilities. Before the improved industrial techniques of stamping metal and forming and grinding steel were developed, pens were made from silver, brass, gold, and bronze, and were used mostly for writing. They did not hold much ink, and they tore the paper. During the 1830s, James Perry produced and patented a steel pen point that could be put in a holder. The steel pens offered longevity, flexibility, uniform quality, and a greater variety of points.

Inks

Black carbon ink, also called **India ink** or Chinese ink, is a deep, black ink and is a favorite of artists today. It was also used by the ancient Chinese and Egyptians. The carbon is made from the soot of burning oils, charcoal, wood, bones, or various seeds or stones of plants and fruits. It is ground to a fine powder and mixed with a binding media of water and glue or gum. The addition of shellac or resin to the mixture makes the ink water-resistant.

Carbon ink also comes in a stick form. When rubbed with a little water in a dish, the stick becomes liquid. The intensity of the color depends on the amount of water used.

Colored inks are also available but are usually too expensive for general use in the classroom.

Crayons

Wax crayons are made from a combination of paraffin waxes that are selected for their hardness and proper melting qualities. Paraffin wax is a residue of crude oil after gasoline, fuel oils, greases, and so on have been removed. After paraffin wax is melted, fatty acids and a substance called tallow are added. These are what give the smooth and soft feel to a crayon mark. Next, the coloring pigment (a powdered dye made insoluble with chemicals) is thoroughly stirred into the molten wax mixture. The mixture is then poured into a mold machine composed of many tubes opening onto a common flat surface, and cold water is circulated around the tubes to freeze the wax. The crayon rods are then pushed out of the tubes, taken to a labeling machine, and packed for sale.[3]

Oil-base crayons are another favorite with students because they offer a greater variety of colors and a different texture than wax crayons. In addition, the colors can be built upon each other to create new colors or blended and brushed with turpentine for new textures and colors. Artists often combine the use of oil-base crayons with a linear technique, such as pen and ink, or pencil.

Conte crayons, which are wax-base crayons used by artists, produce a line and tonal quality that is between charcoal and crayon. They are available in hard, medium, and soft, and in black, white, and brown tones.

Lithograph crayons are grease-base crayons originally intended for lithographic printing but commonly used today for drawing on paper.

Used alone or with other materials, crayons, overall, are the most popular art medium in the elementary classroom and can be used to produce a variety of effects, such as:

1. **Crayon or wax resist.** A wax design is created with crayons, candles, or by drawing into waxed paper over white paper. The design should not cover the entire paper—there should also be open paper spaces. Paint is then brushed over the paper. The waxed areas of the paper "resist" the paint and show through. Darker colors of paint are very effective over brightly colored crayon areas.
2. **Crayon etching.** The whole paper is covered with brightly colored crayon designs. The crayons are applied to the paper with hard pressure to build up brightly colored areas. When the paper is filled, the colored areas are heavily coated with black ink, crayon, or paint mixed with a little liquid soap. Then a design is etched into the black overlay color, exposing the bright colors underneath (fig. 13.4).
3. **Crayon batik.** Painted wax crayon or paraffin on cloth (similar to the crayon- or wax-resist technique described in number 1).
4. **Encaustic.** Leftover crayons are melted and then dropped into the design. Crayons can also be melted in cans or muffin tins and then painted with old brushes. A heavy cardboard backing surface is necessary for these activities, and students need proper supervision. Professional encaustic paint is made with powdered pigment added to melted beeswax.

Chalks and Pastels

Chalks and pastels blend easily and are used for tonal effects. There are many interesting ways to use chalks: For example, chalk dipped into sugar water, chalk drawn or dipped into starch, or chalk dipped in water before using produces a solid and darker line.

Pastels are ground, powdered pigment combined with water and gum tragacanth and formed into pastel sticks. Oil-base pastels have an oil and wax base and many of the same properties as the oil-base crayons discussed in the previous section.

Art Erasers

Three types of erasers are used for art:

1. Gum erasers are soft and pliable and do not tear the paper.
2. Kneaded erasers are soft and pliable, and are excellent for charcoal since they do not smudge.
3. Pink erasers are regularly used to erase marks made by pencils and graphite sticks.

Fixatives

Fixatives are binders used to prevent smudging of a finished charcoal, pastel, chalk, or pencil drawing. Common hair spray (lacquer base) can be used. In recent years, plastic sprays have become available. All labels should be read carefully, and fixative sprays should only be used outdoors.

Painting Materials

Tempera Paint

Tempera paint is opaque and water based, and is available in powder, liquid, and cake forms. The liquid form is the most commonly used. Powdered tempera mixes instantly with water and commonly comes in 1-pound cans with spouts for easy pouring. Liquid or powder detergent can be added to the paint to make it easier to remove paint stains from hands and clothing. Liquid starch can be added to the paint as an extender (to make the supply of paint go somewhat farther). This mixture also makes good finger paint. When the paint is going to be used to cover such materials as wood, plastic, or papier-maché, white glue can be added to the tempera to prevent cracking and peeling.

Liquid tempera is uniformly suspended, keeps a long time, covers easily, has brilliant color, and allows smooth brushing and blending. It is somewhat more expensive than powdered tempera but is preferred by some teachers because of its convenience and consistency. Liquid tempera comes in a variety of sizes—from 8-ounce jars to pints,

Figure 13.4   A fourth-grade student created this crayon etching.

quarts, and gallons—and is also available in unbreakable plastic squeeze bottles, which provide easier dispensing and greater convenience. Fluorescent liquid tempera is also on the market but is more expensive.

Tempera paint also comes in small, square cakes in plastic trays that offer a variety of colors or in slightly larger cakes with each color in a separate interlocking container with its own lid. The paint mixes with brush and water, never spoils, and produces strong opaque colors that can be used on wood, wax, metal, glass, plywood, rubber, plastic, foil, and cork.

During the early Renaissance (A.D. 1200–1400), before oil paint was invented, artists used a tempera paint on wooden planks. This tempera was made by adding powdered pigments to egg yolks.

Acrylic Polymer Paint and Oil Paint

Acrylic polymer paint is available in tubes as well as in jars, is more expensive, and is used primarily by professional artists. The colors are watercolor formulated with acrylic polymer plastic emulsion. This means that suspended in the formula are fine particles of colorless, synthetic resin, which forms a clear, water-resistant film when dry. The finish does not have to be treated with a varnish for permanency, but most artists cover with a final clear coating of acrylic polymer anyway. Colors are brilliant and will not change from wet to dry. Acrylic polymer paints can be used on such materials as paper, canvas, wood, and plastic.

Oil paints are also used by professional artists and are usually painted on canvas, wood, paper, or metal. Oil paints have an oil base—commonly linseed oil—and require solvents, such as turpentine, for thinning. Hog hair or bristle brushes are used. These materials are costly for classroom use.

Watercolor Paint

Transparent **watercolor paint** is made from gum arabic dissolved in water and combined with pigment. It is available in plastic (which will not rust) and metal refillable boxes of eight or sixteen colors commonly used in the classroom. Opaque watercolors, which are not as commonly used as the transparent colors, come with eight, ten, or twelve pans of color in boxes and are more expensive. For artists, a beginning palette of watercolors in tubes would include: alizarin crimson, burnt sienna, cadmium yellow, yellow ocher, Prussian blue, ultramarine blue, green, gray (Payne's gray is good for darks, rather than black), magenta, purple, turquoise, raw umber, burnt umber, white, cadmium red light, cadmium red medium, cadmium red dark, and orange. A good flesh color is a blend of yellow ocher, cadmium red light, and a little white.

Palettes

A **palette** is a surface on which to mix paint colors. Palettes can be bought commercially or improvised. Aluminum pie tins work well, as do plastic egg cartons, Styrofoam trays, ceramic dishes, plastic dishes, and cookie sheets lined with waxed paper.

Brushes

Paint brushes are either round or flat and come in a variety of sizes. Large, flat brushes are for painting large areas, while round brushes are for detailing and for lines that run thin to thick.

An **easel brush**—a flat bristle brush that will not fan out and lose its shape—is intended for large easel painting and comes in 1/4-inch, 1/2-inch, 3/4-inch, and 1-inch sizes. Another brush, made of nylon filament instead of hair or bristle, is intended for polymer painting. This brush, which comes in the same sizes as the bristle brush, is more durable and water-resistant but also somewhat more expensive. Common varnish brushes, hardware variety, or enamel brushes in 1-inch to 2-inch sizes can be trimmed to about 1 inch long and are also good for easel painting (fig. 13.5).

Watercolor brushes and **wash brushes** (a larger size of watercolor brush) are made of squirrel hair. They are full-bodied to hold a large amount of paint and to come to a fine point when dipped in water. They snap back and keep their original shape. The brush hairs must be firmly attached to the ferrule (usually made of aluminum and therefore rustproof) so that the hairs do not pull out easily. A rounded end on a plastic brush handle is safer in an elementary classroom than a pointed end. Brush numbers 2 through 14 are good selections, with 2 being the smallest and 14 the largest. Brush numbers 8, 10, and 12 are commonly used in the classroom.

Artists use sable-hair and camel-hair brushes for watercolor. These brushes are full and round, but also more expensive.

Japanese bamboo brushes come in a variety of sizes and are inexpensive, but they do not last long. They have an excellent linear quality (a thick to thin point).

All brushes should be washed thoroughly with mild soap and warm water (never hot water, as it will melt the glue in the ferrule). They should also be shaped before being stored either flat or brush-end up in jars or containers.

Papers

The texture of the paper—rough or smooth, absorbent or nonabsorbent—affects the quality of the drawing or painting. A variety of different papers allows artists to select the type of paper that best suits their intended technique, effect, or idea:

1. **Newsprint** is a very inexpensive, thin drawing paper. A heavier and better-quality newsprint is available for easel painting. A common size is 18 inches by 24 inches. It is also often available as roll ends from local newspapers.

Figure 13.5 Students enjoy using a variety of brush sizes when painting at an easel.

2. **Manila** is a cream-colored paper for painting and crayoning. A practical size is 18 inches by 24 inches. White manila drawing paper can be purchased in rolls.

3. **Bond** is a smooth-surfaced paper that is good for pencil, pen and ink, brush, and conte crayon drawings. It is available in 18-by-24-inch pads.

4. **Charcoal paper** is a rough-grained absorbent paper that is available in white, black, and tints. Tints are used by artists working with colored charcoals.

5. **Kraft paper** is inexpensive and available in large rolls of white, colored, and black. It has a good drawing and painting surface and is often used for murals.

6. **Construction paper** comes in a wide choice of colors, from bright tones to grayed shades, and is available in sheets as well as rolls. It is good for construction and collage purposes (fig. 13.6) and also for painting and for drawing with crayons and chalks.

7. Other papers for drawing and painting include 60- or 80-pound white drawing paper (commonly used in the classroom), oak tag, corrugated paper, acetate paper, tagboard, bristol board, bogus paper, poster board, tissue paper, and metallic papers. Japanese rice papers and watercolor papers are also available at a higher cost.

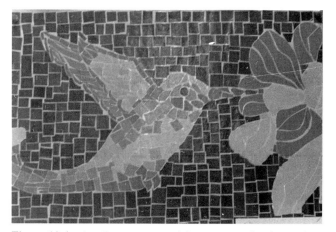

Figure 13.6 A collage constructed from papers of various colors and textures.

NOTES

1. *Purposes, Principles, and Standards* (Reston, Va.: National Art Education Association, 1994), 12.
2. Description of pencil making courtesy of the Joseph Dixon Crucible Company.
3. Description of crayon making courtesy of the American Crayon Company, a division of Joseph Dixon Crucible Company.

Good Questions Teachers Often Ask

Environments are not passive wrappings, but are, rather, active processes which are invisible.

Marshall McLuhan and Quentin Fiore,
The Medium Is the Message

For art is not in the thing itself ever, it is in you; it's your idea and your originality and the interesting way of expressing your idea.

William Glackens

The focus of this chapter is on topics for discussion and on answering basic, practical questions asked by many students and teachers of elementary art. For purposes of organization, these questions are grouped according to how they relate to art thinking, to teaching methods, or to students' art behavior.

QUESTIONS RELATED TO ART THINKING

How Can I Encourage Art Thinking?

Art thinking requires students to form a problem, develop possible alternatives, select the best alternative, and be open to reevaluation. It requires exploration and discussion of ideas. Often, questions are as important as answers, so teach by inquiry.

You can promote art thinking by encouraging students to respond openly to such questions as "How is art an important part of your everyday life?" and by initiating thoughtful, open-ended classroom discussions that share in-

formation related to problem solving and interaction of ideas. Accept each student's thinking, and make it clear that everyone's contribution is important. This will encourage students to share their ideas and thinking, feel success, and gain self-esteem within the group. Their confidence in their ability to make decisions and to be able to follow through on independent judgments—in art and also in everyday life decisions—will grow. Thus, by practicing art thinking and art decision making in the classroom, students improve their general decision-making abilities and judgments. Everyone succeeds in the classroom discussion.

What Is "Good" Art?

Certain people and institutions, such as art patrons, art critics, museums, and galleries, appear to set the standards for what is considered "good" art and what is not—standards that, like fashion, change over time. For example, in the 1950s, abstract expressionism (involving lots of slashing paint, color, and lines) was popular. In the 1960s, pop art was in fashion. Currently, artists are returning to a more figurative approach to art. New art styles are constantly appearing, while past styles seem to remain as well.

The point is that "good" art is determined by the individual, and choices are based on personal feelings, decisions, and experiences. If, as a teacher, you feel that one student does a better drawing than another, be aware that *you* are injecting personal value statements and setting the standards in your classroom and that your standards are not necessarily the only ones.

A blank piece of paper or canvas becomes alive and active the minute the first stroke of paint is applied. From then on, the artwork becomes a challenge, a puzzle to be resolved. Judgment and previous experiences decide all the corners turned, all the decisions made, and ultimately make the artwork unique. Whether or not the final product is completed, resolved, or determined to be "good" art, will, in the final analysis, be a personal decision. As an art teacher, your goal for students is to set aside personal feelings and decisions as much as possible and be open to unique art statements and artworks.

What Is Visual Literacy?

To be literate means to be able to read and write. Visual literacy, then, involves the ability to "read" art—that is, being knowledgeable of the technical and expressive qualities of an artwork, capable of analyzing the artwork critically, and able to discuss what the artwork is about and what it means to you.

What Is Talent? Who Are the Talented?

We all perceive things differently, and this is reflected in our art. Some of us exaggerate a color, others concentrate on texture, and still others are preoccupied with size relationships. Some will include many realistic details; others will fantasize and relate imaginatively.

Much of our perception is connected to what we have experienced in the past. How each of us exists in this space and time in relationship to our environment is unique. Is it any wonder, then, that each of us creates in our own individual fashion? We are all talented.

When you view a group of student artworks, however, several will probably stand out to you as extremely successful, unusually "good." Somehow, we often tend to agree on the exceptional. Even though you do not have a list of checkable measurements, such as tests, essays, or term papers, you will be able to pick out your most talented students. Objective tests can be helpful to students as self-evaluation techniques but should not be used as comparison measures to peers in art.

Some questions you might ask about student artwork are:

1. Is the artwork visually accurate? Many feel that the most realistic, photographically accurate is the best. But all approaches, such as emotional, abstract, and so on, are valid and should be encouraged.
2. Is the artwork "decorative"? That is, is it visually exciting in its use of color? Are the patterns drawn in an inventive, imaginative way? Some students seem to have a natural "talent" for using patterns and interesting details.
3. Is the artwork outstanding in its interpretation of the theme? Did the student express the idea in an unusual, unique way?
4. Is the artwork creative? Does the student use many personal and individual forms and ideas in the artwork?
5. Is this artwork what you *expected* to see? Do you only like what you look for?

Keep in mind and also communicate to students that "talent" is very often plain, hard work (fig. 14.1). The individual with great drive and many hours of practice achieves a level of skill. A high degree of motivation is also a form of talent. Encourage all students to strengthen their individual talents.

Which Is More Important—the Process or the Product?

When students are young, the process is more important than the product. The five- or six-year-old will keep repeating forms or symbols to gain confidence and sureness of achievement. Young students' attention spans are short, their motor skills are limited, and their ideas are rapid and changing. Emphasis should be on the process of creating. As students grow older, the final product gains more importance, since a satisfactory product is necessary in creative work.

When Is an Artwork Finished?

Creative people stop working on an artwork when their personal and aesthetic criteria are met. As a teacher, your focus should be on arousing students' imaginations and raising their criteria so that, as they gain mastery in working with the media, they will not be satisfied with the easiest, first, or fastest solution.

How Important Is Verbal Communication—Talking—about Art?

Any kind of verbal communication between teacher and students—when individuals are really talking and really listening to each other—is important. Not only do they share ideas and inform each other of their feelings and thoughts, but they fulfill the important need of saying something and of being heard or listened to. Whatever a student is saying that is personally meaningful is worth listening to!

This is especially true when talking about art. What each student has to say in his or her artwork or about others' artworks is important enough to be thoughtfully considered.

Figure 14.1 "Talent" almost always requires hard work.

In addition to fulfilling individuals' need to feel worthwhile and important, verbal communication about art often tends to generate new ideas and concepts. When you communicate an idea about art, you often form and structure your thoughts and classify the content. In turn, your listeners comprehend your ideas and many times embellish the thought. Through such interactions, multiple ideas tend to grow and develop.

Refer to the sections "The Art Dialogue" and "Group Discussions of Artworks" in chapter 11 for specific suggestions regarding initiating and developing classroom discussions about art.

Does Art Always Have to Be Exciting and Unusual?

Art should always be exciting to students. You, as the teacher, can make it so. New ideas are strong motivators. This does not require a massive budget but only a teacher who is committed to expanding the visual consciousness of his or her students and to presenting divergent ideas, new media, unusual stimuli, and exciting experiences to motivate students in art.

Often, simple subject matter can be explored in many unusual ways (fig. 14.2). One subject alone can spark many hours of various interpretations. Students then begin to develop a visual consciousness, with new relationships and objects in the environment viewed in new and different ways. Students also develop more intense, in-depth understanding of the subject as well as multiple possibilities for solutions (divergent thinking).

For example, many productive activities are possible with the subject of birds. The subject could be used for a drawing or observation problem, or for a relationship of shapes problem. Students could observe differences in drawing birds with various media ("Is drawing them with ink the same as drawing them with watercolor?"). Students could study bird habitats, food likes and dislikes of birds, different bird songs. Students might link birds with an in-

Figure 14.2   Eskimo artist Silas Shavings used a whale's vertebra for his sculpture.

tense emotional experience ("Did you ever see a dead bird? How did you feel?"). Drawing a bird's underlying structure would offer a different perspective of the subject.

What Is an Art Hero?

Today when we think of heroes, we think of sports, music, and movie and television personalities. But across the centuries, the artists of the time were the heroes.

An art hero is someone in the arts who was or is courageous enough to stand up for what he or she believes in, who accomplished an uplifting achievement, who transmits hopeful energy, who does something exceptionally well and shares it with others, who shines a special light through his or her art, who motivates and inspires others (fig. 14.3). Find yourself an art hero, and as a teacher, encourage your students to do likewise. Then share your heroes with each other—through reports, photographs, slides, videos, original artworks, or reproductions. Develop an art hero list that includes artists of both yesterday and today.

What Is DBAE?

The Getty Center for Education in the Arts, established in 1982, developed the concept of DBAE, which stands for **discipline-based art education.** DBAE is based on the premise that art education should be presented in a written, sequential curricula to develop students' creative abilities for (1) making art (studio art), (2) responding to and appreciating visual imagery (art criticism), (3) understanding art's cultural and historical contexts (art history), and (4) raising questions about the nature of art and making informed judgments (aesthetics).[1]

How Many Elementary Schools Have Art Teachers?

A survey by the U.S. Department of Education yielded data representing approximately 15,200 operating school districts in the United States. The survey found that:

- Twenty-six percent of elementary schools have full-time visual art specialists, 32 percent have part-time visual art specialists, and 42 percent have no art teachers.
- Sixty-seven percent of the districts with elementary schools have art curriculum guidelines that specify instructional goals in terms of student outcomes.
- Almost no districts require competency tests in the arts for promotion from one grade to the next.
- About 37 percent of elementary-level art programs use a set of required or recommended textbooks for the visual arts.[2]

Where Are the Artists Today?

When reflecting on contemporary artists, most people think of painters, sculptors, and so on. But many other art career opportunities are available for students in today's society, such as art teachers, graphic designers, craftspeople, com-

(a)

(b)

Figure 14.3 An art hero is an artist who inspires, just as professional athletes inspire. Sports activities are great motivators for art.

mercial artists, newspaper illustrators, magazine illustrators, photographers, commercial artists, medical book illustrators, clothing designers, packaging designers, costume designers, industrial designers, interior designers, architects, filmmakers, television artists, comic book artists,

Figure 14.4 The teacher can clarify art ideas by talking about art and demonstrating techniques. (Teacher: Sue Raymond.)

computer artists, stage designers, greeting card illustrators, advertising artists, furniture designers, art critics, art historians, museum directors, and museum educators.

QUESTIONS RELATED TO TEACHING METHODS
What Are Teacher Strategies?

To be effective as an art teacher, you should act as a catalyst and strive to achieve the following teaching strategies:

1. Obtain technical art knowledge of the subject being taught. You do not have to be the best artist, but you must have adequate knowledge of the subject to be an effective teacher. You also must be able to clearly present the necessary procedures for doing a particular art activity (fig. 14.4).
2. Demonstrate leadership qualities. You must be able to *plan, organize, control effectively,* and *direct.* Carefully plan and organize the art curriculum objectives and learning packages. Determine whether students have reached established art objectives.
3. Interrelate one-on-one with students. Communicate effectively. Empathize with students, and consider individual feelings and attitudes. Be warm, personal, and interested in the students.
4. Encourage students' individual ideas and artworks. Provide opportunities for students to make individual decisions. Encourage them to express their own ideas and personal statements (fig. 14.5). Allow them opportunities to work independently, as well as in groups.
5. Provide opportunities for students to realize self-esteem and self-worth through hard work, discipline, and personal responsibility for behavior.
6. Provide stimulating motivations (idea generators), as well as experiences and activities that call for thinking, problem solving, self-expression, judgment, and decision making.

Figure 14.5 Students need opportunities to express their own individual ideas and statements.

7. Respect individual differences as to range of achievement. Encourage the uncommon and unusual.
8. Encourage display and discussion of art products.
9. Initiate discussion of what has been achieved by the art experience.
10. Relate art experiences to other classroom experiences and to considerations of extended experiences.
11. Compare and contrast how artists in the past and present have solved similar art problems.

How Is the Classroom Environment Important?

The classroom is an aesthetic working environment for students' learning activities. It should not overwhelm or dominate students, but instead, should stimulate and demonstrate student participation (fig. 14.6). The classroom should reflect you and the needs, interests, attitudes, beliefs, and values of your students in the most unique, creative way possible. Environments can release imagery, visions, dramatic roles, moods, and creative thinking. Ask yourself.

- Is my classroom dynamic, vivid, electric, vital, exciting, and happy?
- Is my classroom an exciting arrangement of spaces?
- Are spaces cluttered or uncluttered, busy or simple?
- Are there spaces for messes as well as for displays?
- Is there space for producing art?
- Is there quiet space for private thinking?
- Is there adequate and flexible storage space?
- Can the spaces in my classroom be changed with space changers, such as panels, cloth, ropes, sculptures, or plastic sheeting?
- Does the color of my classroom stimulate problem solving?
- Are the walls, floor, and ceiling of my classroom inviting, exciting, and interesting?
- Is the furniture and exhibit space to scale with students?
- Is the seating arrangement flexible to different needs?
- Does the classroom have an art center?

Figure 14.6 Positive classroom environments encourage an enthusiastic student response.

- Do students help to select what is displayed? Do students help to design the display area?
- Are the spaces and exhibits child centered or teacher dominated?
- Who does most of the talking during my classes?
- When someone enters my classroom, what is their overall impression of my art curriculum?

Is Teacher Enthusiasm Important?

You, the teacher, must be the spark plug to generate excitement and enthusiasm about art! The more you know about art, the more motivated you will be. How can you teach drawing if you have never drawn? Study the area you are teaching to provide yourself with knowledge and self-confidence. If you are excited about art and appear to know what you are talking about, the students will feel your enthusiasm and catch it—it's contagious (fig. 14.7).

How Does Body Language Affect Teaching?

A good teacher knows how to capture students' imaginations by being demonstrative, by expressing emotion with

Figure 14.7 The teacher is an idea generator. Students will catch your enthusiasm. (Teacher: Flo Patrenos.)

body gestures, and by being dramatic with both voice and body. When talking to students about art, practice using dramatic voice contrasts and body language. For example, try speaking with loud/soft, quick/slow, up/down, happy/sad, busy/quiet, sharp/smooth variations. Use colorful words, storytelling information, and selectively descriptive adjectives. Change your image to play a part.

Teachers who sit behind a desk are placing an obstacle—the desk—between themselves and students.[3] In body language, the message is, "I am your superior. I am here to teach you. You must obey me." Other teachers perch on the edge of their desks and have nothing between them and their students. Some feel that this still appears to put the teacher in an elevated position and creates student resistance to the teacher. Still other teachers prefer a position in the center of the room, surrounded by students, and perhaps, sitting on top of a student's desk. Such positioning tends to communicate that the teacher is on the students' side—is one of them—while still remaining the teacher. Some teachers prefer a U-shaped arrangement of chairs. You must choose whichever approach is most effective for you.

How Can Teachers Help Students Push Creative Boundaries?

Young students are creative, alert scientists and original investigators. They solve problems and discover individual solutions for many situations that appear simple to us because we have learned a certain behavior. But to the young student, these are monumental thought discoveries.

To preserve and encourage these types of boundary-pushing discoveries, you, as a teacher, need to offer students stimulating situations that challenge the imagination and provide new and exciting possibilities and ideas. You need to share students' natural curiosity and excitement in discovery. You must exhibit and be exuberant about students' art products, and praise students in front of others for their efforts and success. Strive to inspire and to offer sincere encouragement.

One way to boundary-push in the classroom is by brainstorming. Brainstorming is a group problem-solving

or idea-generating technique that involves the spontaneous contribution of ideas from all members of the class. Brainstorming guidelines include:

1. Have students form small groups and designate one student in each group to record all of the generated ideas. Set a time limit, and indicate a minimal number of responses.
2. Present the problem.
3. Circulate among the groups as they work, encouraging spontaneity and a continuous flow of ideas, and offering suggestions for overcoming mind-set.
4. Establish a way for students to share ideas.
   a. Have all students come back together as a large group. List all of the generated ideas on the chalkboard. Categorize and consolidate all of the ideas. Evaluate and discard inappropriate responses. *OR* In a student-centered approach, have students remain in their small groups. Give them one minute to select the three best group ideas. Provide another minute for them to determine which of their three ideas is best. Then have each group share their three ideas with the rest of the class.
   b. As a large group, discuss the different ideas and then vote on the best idea.
5. Analyze and evaluate the final results as a total group and implement the chosen best idea.

Art growth should be nurtured in the home as well as in the school. Invite parents to participate and boundary-push through art. Discuss with them goals to share and how important it is for them to enjoy and appreciate their children's artworks at home. Suggest that they have a home art center for display of artworks and art collections. Ask them to provide working spaces at home for art projects and to plan interesting visits to galleries and other art-related functions.

Where Can Good Teaching Examples Be Found?

For every art project, you should show students at least two teaching examples as motivations. Whether these are drawings that you have done, a former student's artwork, photos, slides, movies, filmstrips, reproductions from art journals, magazines, postcards, or whatever, the better your examples, the better will be the resulting student product. Having more than one example provides students with more imaginative "ammunition," and they will then be less likely to try to imitate one of the examples.

Also, looking at and talking about the examples teaches students about art elements, design principles, expressive qualities, and how to use them. As a teacher, you should always encourage students' own creative expression of ideas and ways of describing their everyday personal world of subject matter.

The greatest inspirational examples you can use are from the students themselves (fig. 14.8). Students identify

Figure 14.8 Often, the best art examples come from the students themselves.

Figure 14.9 Experimenting is part of the art process.

with and relate to each other's artworks. Keep a special file for reference. Students are delighted when you ask to keep their art for your special "artists" file. Taking a photo of an individual child with his or her artwork is a special form of reward and acceptance.

Why Should the Teacher Demonstrate?

Teacher demonstrations of processes and techniques are important for clarification of desired results. You can outline the basic procedure and then let students expand on your demonstration. For example, in teaching portraits, you might want to go through the basic proportions of the head as students follow you and then move on to show students the basics of how to draw eyes, mouths, and so on. Students can then use each other as models to draw portraits. If you demonstrate the basic concepts with enthusiasm, students will catch this positive attitude and go on to improve their own skills.

When Should Materials Be Distributed?

Many teachers feel that the motivation for a particular art project (the dialogue in the classroom prior to art production) should precede the handing out of materials. This helps students to remain more focused on the teacher's presentation and to not become preoccupied with the materials they have been given. If it is more convenient to distribute materials before the motivation, you might want to have students move to another area of the room—away from the materials—before you begin your presentation. When the motivation is complete, students can then return to their seats and begin the lesson.

Should Students Have Time to Experiment?

Students who are given specific materials or tools and told exactly how to work tend to look for a prescribed procedure

and want everything explained to them. They want the authority (the teacher) to show them how to use the material or how the result should be obtained. On the other hand, when students have opportunities to be selective in their materials and are given a variety of possibilities, they demonstrate greater initiative and self-reliance.

Provide students with a choice of materials, and give them the time to experiment and explore freely (fig. 14.9). Competence and skill will automatically develop with increased manipulation and exploration of the materials. Encourage students to invent as many ways as possible to hold, use, and manipulate the tools and media. Tell them that they may discover a way to use a particular tool that no one else in the world has thought of!

Finally, whenever possible, give students the opportunity to select areas of art study that they wish to explore. Not everyone has ability or is interested in the same area of art.

Should an Art Project Ever Be Repeated?

Many artists never consider the first solution the finished product. They feel that they have to experiment and explore before discovering a satisfactory solution. In the same way, repeating an art experience is often helpful, especially if you have found ways of improving the experience. For example, you may want to change the tools or materials.

When repeating an art experience, encourage students to extend and go beyond their thinking. Suggest that they explore the details—for example, they might want to include stronger contrasts, to consider different values, to try new combinations, to accentuate the color, or to concentrate on spatial concepts.

How Often Should Students Have Art?

Students should have art as often as possible. Ideally, elementary students should have daily art experiences, but hours and scheduling will need to be flexible and will vary at grade levels. For example, one week you and your class might spend six hours on a mural for social studies or on insect drawings for science. The next week, you might spend only three hours on art-related activities. Keep in mind that, while art can be related to other areas of study, such as history, literature, drama, art appreciation, and music, it should also be studied as an independent area in itself.

Basically, it is up to you, the teacher. How many ways can you discover to have art experiences? Remember that art is a subject area that everyone can enjoy and appreciate all through life.

Should Students Be Given Patterns, Art Workbooks, or Mimeographed Sheets?

No! No! No! Some learning activities are decidedly directed. Art is not. Students should be allowed to select and decide on their ideas for themselves; they should be permitted to arrive at their own solutions. This is what makes each student's art product unique.

Some teachers rely on stereotyped, adult-oriented patterns, hectographs, mimeographed sheets, or workbooks. These are crutches and a substitute for planning for art learning. Tear up all patterned art responses; these are not the goal. Instead, the focus is to be on the individual's unique art expression and potential.

What Is Needed to Start an Art Program?

Two of the most helpful items to have when starting an art program are volunteer help and lots of materials to explore and experiment with. With regard to volunteer help, find out if there are any teacher's aides or parent volunteers who could lend you extra hands. Older students also frequently are willing to help with younger students. Or, sometimes, teachers are able to team-teach during art.

The materials necessary to start an art program will differ with different age levels. Most schools provide basic art tools, such as crayons, boxed paints, watercolors, tempera paints, brushes, and clay. In addition, many stores and industries are happy to donate discards or to sell them at cost. Refer back to chapter 13 for lists of materials needed in an art room and possible sources from which you might collect these materials at little or no charge.

What Distinguishes an Effective Teacher?

Effective teachers regularly ask themselves questions like:

1. Are specified goals being accomplished?
2. Are students gaining knowledge about and understanding of art (fig. 14.10)?
3. Are the goals and lessons appropriate to students' developmental levels and cultural backgrounds?
4. Are lessons taught in a sequential curriculum so that ideas and skills build upon one another?

Figure 14.10   Are your students gaining knowledge about art? Do they have experiences that challenge and encourage their artistic thinking?

5. Does the curriculum include artifacts and aesthetic experiences of various cultures and time periods?
6. Do students demonstrate skill development?
7. Do students have opportunities to practice dialogue and inquiry?
8. Do ideas and skills need to be reinforced?
9. What teaching strategies are most effective? Least effective? How long are motivations—more than ten minutes?
10. Do students like the class? Do they feel that they have positive experiences? Who does most of the talking?

What about Computers and Art?

Computers are becoming an integral part of daily life, including the art curriculum (see chapter 8). As an art medium, they can be used in various ways, depending on the software programs available. Animation programs, paint programs, desktop publishing programs, and word-processing programs are just a few of the types of software to consider. As a teacher, you may find database programs useful for storing lessons, supply lists, necessary materials, student progress reports, and book, slide, video, and reproduction inventories.

QUESTIONS RELATED TO STUDENTS
What about Students Who Hesitate to Draw?

Most students who have opportunities to practice their art have an endless flow of imaginative creations. They are enormously eager and excited, and are bursting with new drawing and painting ideas.

Some students, however, may resist getting involved, often because of negative previous experiences. They simply need more attention and encouragement because they feel insecure about expressing themselves. Somewhere in their previous experiences, they have probably had conflicts with their ideas. Either an adult has done the solving for the student by drawing for the child, or the student is dependent on stereotypes, such as coloring books.

Parents unknowingly hinder individual growth by rigidly controlling or criticizing what their child does—for example, "Well, Jim, that doesn't *look* like a dog." Jim was probably drawing what he knew about the dog, about how he saw and felt about the dog, but the adult didn't see the dog in the same way. If this happens several times, the child loses confidence in his or her independent thinking and feels threatened whenever asked to draw.

As the teacher, you must be sure to encourage these types of students, to praise their ideas, and to not negatively criticize. One way to show students what you consider important is by holding up students' drawings and saying things like, "See how Donna has filled her whole page?" "Do you like the way Hank has carefully drawn all the parts of the bee?"

With all of your students, and especially with the hesitant ones, it is important that you be success oriented. Remove all threats of failure. You do this by:

• Reevaluating your art goals to make sure that all students can achieve them.
• Being positive and not critical ("Tell me about your picture").
• Helping students to understand that ways to express ideas through art are unlimited.
• Always having something to say to each student that the student can understand at his or her developmental level. Discover what is important to each student.
• Being an inspiring, warm human being who is fun to talk with. Just your personal warmth and positive attitude will show your interest in the student as a person.
• Communicating the belief that art is fun, creative, meaningful, and self-motivating; that art involves seeing and discovery, and awareness of beauty and life.

Always begin at your students' level of understanding and with subjects and objects that are meaningful and relevant to your students (fig. 14.11). Boys of twelve may be much more interested in drawing cars, electronic devices, or basketball players than a bowl of fruit. Twelve-year-old girls may be more interested in drawing horses, dresses, or other girls.

The same is true in the study of art analysis. Students identify with artworks or artifacts that are of personal interest to them, that they can empathize with—perhaps because of some past experience, achievement, interest, or emotional response.

What about the Student Who Copies from Other Students?

If you become aware of one student copying others during an art project, work to involve that student more personally in the art motivation. Offer the student encouragement, and

praise him or her for inventive, independent art solutions and resourceful attitudes and ideas, whenever they occur. Try to make the student feel confident and accepted, sometimes with special privileges. For example, if you can identify a particular art area in which the student is success oriented and shows individual promise, appoint him or her as a special helper or as an "expert" in that area. Then call on your "expert" for help whenever possible You also should reexamine your goals and objectives for this student to determine if they are realistic.

Why Do Many Students Seem to Lose Their Artistic Talent As They Get Older?

Students in the early elementary grades are encouraged to express themselves openly. Much emphasis is placed on self-expression through music, language, and art. When students begin to learn to read and write, however, the emphasis changes to improving technical skills and to learning procedures. Greater rewards are given to students who can imitate correctly. For example, the student who can follow directions and demonstrate the greatest skill in forming the letters of the alphabet while staying within the ruled lines receives the highest grade. It is no mystery, then, why students' artworks and creative thinking tend to become less inspired as students progress through elementary school. Perhaps if education emphasized ways to communicate and encouraged individual expression of thoughts and ideas, instead of being overly focused on technically correct spelling, grammar, and printing, students' creativity would have a better chance to flourish.

Should Students Complete the Assigned Project?

Encourage all of your students to complete the assigned art project. When the motivation is meaningful and students are involved, they will want to express their feelings about it.

If a student hesitates to participate, provide some individual attention. Repeat the ideas discussed with the group; perhaps the student did not understand them. Ask the student about his or her feelings about the ideas. Provide approval and assistance. Encourage the student to ask questions and give answers. Then ask the student to try to complete the project. When the student finishes, reward with praise and encouragement, even if you feel that the job was not done satisfactorily.

How Important Is Exhibiting Students' Finished Artworks?

A finished artwork reflects *each student's* concerns and view of self, personal experiences, and the world, and is therefore self-revealing, fulfilling, and genuine (fig. 14.12). *All artwork* is important enough to be looked at. Exhibiting students' finished artwork:

(a)

Figure 14.11 Include themes that are relevant to students' interests when you plan subject matter for artistic expression.

(b)

Figure 14.12 "Put your best foot forward." Drawing by fourth-grade student.

- Allows the sharing of ideas and thoughts with others
- Encourages individual solutions
- Emphasizes the importance of each student's art expression
- Recognizes and respects individual completion of an idea
- Provides insights on alternative solutions
- Signifies acceptance within the group
- Provides opportunities for other teachers or parents or interested individuals to observe students' achievements
- Shows evidence of growth from previous performances
- Tells students what you feel are the best solutions in terms of the aims and objectives of the art experience
- Encourages and provides a sense of achievement to the student who has worked hard and shown progress (By displaying a student's artwork, you are telling that student: "Your artwork is significant and important, and you and I recognize this importance.")

Having students help you with the exhibit or display gives them opportunities to create and design large space areas and to learn about suggested mountings and possible combinations. Change your displays and exhibits regularly—every two to three weeks.

NOTES

1. Leilani Lattin Duke, director of the Getty Center for Education in the Arts, 1988.
2. Survey by U.S. Department of Education, Center for Education Statistics. Results published in *Bulletin*, May 1988, CS 88-417.
3. Julius Fast, *Body Language* (New York: M. Evans and Company, 1970).

appendix

Recognized Artists

The following are major historical artists students may use for art history study. Artists listed by country of origin and dates.

ITALY

Cimabue 1240–1302

Giotto 1266–1336

Simone Martini of Siena 1285–1344

Gentile da Fabriano 1360–1427

Brunelleschi 1377–1446

Ghiberti 1378–1455

Donatello 1386–1466

Fra Angelico 1387–1455

Paolo Uccelo 1397–1475

Luca della Robbia 1400–1482

Masaccio 1401–ca.1428

Alberti 1404–1472

Filippo Lippi 1406–1469

Piero Della Francesca 1416–1492

Andrea del Castagna 1423–1457

Verrocchio 1435–1488

Botticelli 1444–1510

Girolandaio 1449–1494

Leonardo da Vinci 1452–1519

Fillippino Lippi 1458–1504

Michelangelo 1475–1564

Raphael 1483–1520

Titian 1490–1576

Benvenuto Cellini 1500–1571

Tintoretto 1518–1594

Sofonisba Anguissola 1532–1625

Lucia Anguissola 1540–1565

Lavinia Fontana 1552–1614

Annibale Carracci 1560–1609

Caravaggio 1573–1610

Guido Reni 1575–1642

Artemisia Gentileschi 1593–ca.1652

Bernini 1598–1680

Giovanna Garzoni 1600–1670

Elisabetta Sirani 1638–1665

Rosalba Carriera 1675–1757

Tiepolo 1696–1770

Amedeo Modigliani 1884–1920

Giorgio de Chirico 1888–1978

FLANDERS

Jan van Eyck 1395–1441

Rogier van der Weyden 1399–1464

Hieronymus Bosch 1450–1516

Pieter Brueghel 1525–1569

Caterina van Hemessen 1528–1587

Jan Brueghel 1568–1625

Peter Paul Rubens 1577–1640

Clara Peeters 1594–1657

Anthony van Dyck 1599–1641

GERMANY

Hans Holbein, the Younger 1500–1569

Maria Sibylla Merian 1647–1717

Edvard Munch 1863–1944

Alexi van Jawlensky 1864–1941

Emil Nolde 1867–1956

Käthe Kollwitz 1867–1945

Paula Mondersohn-Becker 1876–1907

Gabrielle Munter 1877–1962

Paul Klee 1879–1940

Franz Marc 1880–1916

Ernst Ludwig Kirchner 1880–1938

Max Pechstein 1881–1955

Karl Schmidt-Rottluff 1884–1976

Max Beckmann 1884–1940

August Macke 1887–1914

Lotte Laserstein 1898–

SPAIN

El Greco 1547–1614

Jose Ribera 1588–1652

Diego Velazquez 1599–1660

Francisco Goya 1746–1828

Pablo Picasso 1881–1973

Joan Miró 1893–1983

Salvador Dalí 1904–1989

FRANCE

Georges de la Tour 1593–1652

Nicholas Poussin 1594–1665

Claude Lorrain 1600–1682

Louise Moillon 1610–1696

Antoine Watteau 1684–1721

Jean Baptiste Simeon Chardin 1699–1779

Marie Navarre 1737–1795

Angelica Kauffmann 1741–1807

Jacques-Louis David 1748–1825

Elizabeth Vigee Lebrun 1755–1842

Marguerite Gerard 1761–1837

Jean Dominique Ingres 1780–1867

Eugene Delacroix 1798–1863

Honore Daumier 1808–1879

Rosa Bonheur 1822–1899

Edouard Manet 1832–1883

Edgar Degas 1834–1917

Paul Cézanne 1839–1906

Claude Monet 1840–1926

Auguste Rodin 1840–1917

Berthe Morisot 1841–1895

Paul Gauguin 1843–1903

Camille Claudel 1856–1920

Henri de Toulouse-Lautrec 1864–1901

Suzanne Valadon 1865–1938

Pierre Bonnard 1867–1947

Edward Vuillard 1868–1940

Henri Matisse 1869–1954

Raoul Dufy 1877–1953

Maurice Utrillo 1883–1955

Marie Laurencin 1885–1956

ENGLAND

Peter Lely 1618–1680

Susan Penelope Rosse 1652–1700

William Hogarth 1697–1764

JMW Turner 1775–1851

John Constable 1776–1837

John Millais 1829–1896

Edward Burne-Jones 1833–1898

Gwen John 1876–1939

Vanessa Bell 1879–1961

Henry Moore 1898–

Barbara Hepworth 1903–1975

Lucien Freud 1922–

David Hokney 1937–

HOLLAND

Frans Hals 1580–1666

Rembrandt 1606–1669

Judith Leyster 1609–1660

Maria van Osterwych 1630–1699

Jan Vermeer 1632–1675

Jan van der Heyden 1637–1712

Rachel Ruysch 1664–1750

Vincent van Gogh 1853–1890

Piet Mondrian 1872–1944

AUSTRIA

Gustav Klimt 1862–1918

Oskar Kokoschka 1886–1980

Egon Schiele 1890–1918

UNITED STATES

John Singleton Copley 1738–1815

Benjamin West 1738–1820

Gilbert Stuart 1755–1828

Thomas Hart Benton 1782–1858

John James Audubon 1785–1851

Anna Claypoole Peale 1791–1879

George Catlin 1796–1872

Sarah Miriam Peale 1800–1885

Thomas Cole 1801–1848

Nathaniel Courier 1813–1888

Lily Martin Spencer 1822–1902

James Ives 1824–1895

George Inness 1825–1894

Frederic Church 1826–1900

Albert Bierstadt 1830–1902

James Abbott Whistler 1834–1903

Winslow Homer 1836–1910

Edmonia Lewis 1843–1911

Mary Cassatt 1844–1926

Thomas Eakins 1844–1916

Lilla Cabot Perry 1848–1935

William Merritt Chase 1849–1916

John Twachtman 1853–1902

Howard Pyle 1853–1911

Bill Traylor 1854–1947

Cecilia Beaux 1855–1942

Ellen Day Hale 1855–1940

John Singer Sargent 1856–1925

William Metcalf 1858–1925

Henry Ossawa-Tanner 1859–1937

Maurice Pendergast 1859–1924

Anna Mary Robertson (Grandma Moses) 1860–1961

Frederic Remington 1861–1909

Edmund Tarbell 1862–1938

Frank Benson 1862–1951

Cecilia Beaux 1863–1942

Charles Russell 1865–1926

Charles Dana Gibson 1867–1944

Howard Chandler Christy 1873–1952

J. C. Leyendecker 1874–1951

James Montgomery Flagg 1877–1960

Marsden Hartley 1877–1943

Joseph Stella 1877–1946

Hans Hofmann 1880–1966

George Bellows 1882–1925

Charles Demuth 1883–1935

Milton Avery 1885–1965

Georgia O'Keeffe 1887–1986

Marguerite Zorach 1887–1963

Marcel Duchamp 1887–1968

Horace Pippen 1888–1946

Alma Thomas 1891–1978

Norman Rockwell 1894–1978

John Held, Jr. 1899–1958

Alice Neel 1900–1984

Hale Woodruff 1900–1980

Louise Nevelson 1900–1988

Barbara Hepworth 1903–1975

Willem de Kooning 1904–1988

Lois Mailou-Jones 1905–

Charles Alston 1907–1977

Lee Krasner 1908–1984

Dorothea Tanning 1910–

Franz Kline 1910–1962

Jackson Pollock 1912–1956

Hughie Lee-Smith 1915–

Elizabeth Catlett 1915–

Jacob Lawrence 1917–

Charles White 1918–1979

Roy Lichtenstein 1923–

Kenneth Noland 1924–

Georgia Mills Jessup 1926–

Joan Mitchell 1926–

Helen Frankenthaler 1928–

Betye Saar 1929–

Faith Ringgold 1930–

Jasper Johns 1930–

Andy Warhol 1930–1985

Sam Gilliam 1933–

Frank Stella 1936–

Bob Thompson 1937–1966

Judy Chicago 1939–

Nancy Graves 1940–

Keith Morrison 1942–

Frederick Brown 1945–

Photographers

Mathew Brady 1823–1896

Alfred Stieglitz 1864–1946

Imogene Cunningham 1883–1976

Edward Weston 1886–1958

Man Ray 1890–1976

Paul Strand 1890–1976

Dorothea Lange 1895–1965

Ansel Adams 1902–1984

Margaret Bourke-White 1904–1971

Gordon Parks 1912–

Richard Aredon 1924–

Cindy Sherman

Architects

Louis Sullivan 1856–1924

Frank Lloyd Wright 1869–1959

Walter Gropius (German) 1883–1969

Figure A.1   Drawing by Norman Rockwell. (Courtesy of Mrs. Bruce Hamilton.)

Mies van der Rohe 1886–1969

Le Courbusier (French) 1887–1965

Buckminster Fuller 1895–1983

Philip Johnson 1906–

Sculptors

Alexander Calder 1898–1976

David Smith 1906–1965

George Segal 1924–

Duane Hansen 1925–

John Chamberlain 1927–

Edward Kienholz 1927–1994

Claes Oldenburg 1929–

Marisol 1930–

Nam June Paik

Kiki Smith

RUSSIA

Alexel Jon Jawlensky 1864–1941

Wassily Kandinsky 1866–1944

Natalia Goncharova 1881–1962

Sonia Terk Delaunay 1885–1979

Marc Chagall 1889–1985

LATIN AMERICA

José Clemente Orozco 1883–1949

Diego Rivera 1886–1957

Siqueiros 1896–1974

Rufino Tamayo 1899–1991

Maria Izquierdo 1906–1955

Frida Kahlo 1907–1954

Olga Costa 1913–1993

Lenora Carrington 1917–

José Luis Cuevas 1934–

Fernando Botero 1932–

José Maria Velasco 1840–1912

Juan O'Gorman 1905–1982

Lydia Clark 1921–

Figure A.2 *Woman with Bird Cage* by Rufino Tamayo. Oil on canvas, 43¼ inches by 33¼ inches. (Joseph Winterbotham Collection, photograph © 1995 The Art Institute of Chicago. All Rights Reserved.)

Olga Costa 1913–1993

Marina Nunez Del Prado 1910–

Mira Schendel 1919–1988

Cornelia Urueta 1908–

Remedios Varo 1908–1963

Rocio Muldonado 1951–

Ana Mercedes Hoyos 1942–

Elena Clement 1955–

Liliane Porter 1941–

Elba Damast 1944–

SELECTED CONTEMPORARY ARTISTS TO STUDY

The following lists are names of artists to study. Please refer to chapter 8, pages 111, 119, 125, 128, 142, 145, 147 for related areas. Josef Albers, Eleanor Antin, Robert Arneson, Alyce Aycock, Judith Baca, Francis Bacon, Jennifer Bartlett, Leonard Baskin, Billy Al Bengston, Joseph Beuys, Jonathon Borofsky, Anna Botsford Comstock, Louise

Figure A.3 *Ponder* by Deborah Butterfield, 1981. Sculpture of wood, wire, and steel. Approximately life size. (Courtesy of Phoenix Art Museum. Lent anonymously.)

Bourgious, Joan Brown, Deborah Butterfield, Alexander Calder, Squeak Carnwath, Marc Chagall, John Chamberlin, Barbara Chase-Riboud, Christo, Francesco Clemente, Sue Coe, Chuck Close, Robert Colescott, Joseph Cornell, Roy DeForest, Charles Demuth, Richard Diebenkorn, Arthur Dove, Rainer Fetting, Eric Fischl, Elaine Fried de Kooning, Eric Fischl, Janet Fish, Audrey Flack, Dan Flavin, Sam Francis, Mary Frank, Alberto Giacometti, Consuelo Gonzales Amezcua, Nancy Graves, Marion Greenwood, Red Grooms, Duane Hansen, Grace Hartigan, Eve Hesse, David Hockney, Jenny Holzer, Rebecca Horn, Jasper Johns, Donald Judd, Anselm Keefer, Ellsworth Kelly, Edward Kienholz, Nancy Reddin Kienholz, Willem de Kooning, Janis Kounellis, Lee Krasner, Barbara Kruger, Sol Lewitt, Carmen Lomas Garza, Robert Longo, Rene Magritte, Marisol, Agnes Martin, Mary Miss, Joan Mitchell, Piet Mondrian, Elizabeth Murray, Alice Neel, Isamu Noguchi, Claes Oldenburg, Nam June Paik, Mimmo-Paladino, Ken Price, Faith Ringgold, James Rosenquist, Susan Rothenberg, Robert Rouschenberg, Edward Ruscha, Betye Saar, David Salle, Miriam Schapiro, Julian Schnabel, George Segal, Richard Serra, Cindy Sherman, Charles Simonds, David Smith, Kiki Smith, Robert Smithson, Joan Snyder, May Stevens, Donald Sultan, Mark Di Suvero, James Turrell, Cy Twombly, Peter Voulkos

ARTISTS TO STUDY FOR PORTRAITS AND FIGURES

Ivan Albright, Milton Avery, Leonard Baskin, Jack Beal, Max Beckmann, Thomas Hart Benton, Peter Blume, Pierre Bonnard, Constantin Brancusi, Paul Cézanne, Marc Cha-

gall, William Merritt Chase, Francesco Clemente, Chuck Close, José Luis Cuevas, Salvador Dalí, Edgar Degas, Andre Derain, Richard Diebenkorn, Marcel Duchamp, Jacob Epstein, Eric Fischl, Audrey Flack, Lucien Freud, Alberto Giacometti, Vincent van Gogh, Ashile Gorky, Gustave Gourbet, Red Grooms, William Gropper, Nancy Grossman, George Grosz, Philip Guston, Marsden Hartley, David Hockney, Edward Hopper, Alexei Jawlensky, Ernst Ludwig Kirchner, Kitaj, Gustav Klimt, Oskar Kokoschka, Käthe Kollwitz, Wilhelm Lehmbruck, L. Alfred Leslie, Earl Linderman, Richard Lindner, Robert Longo, Rene Magritte, Aristide Maillol, Henri Matisse, Joan Miró, Amedeo Modigliani, Henry Moore, Edvard Munch, Alice Neel, Emil Nolde, Mimmo-Paladino, Maxfield Parrish, Philip Pearlstein, Pablo Picasso, Mel Ramos, Robert Rauschenberg, Odilon Redon, Rembrandt, Pierre Auguste Renoir, Diego Rivera, Larry Rivers, Auguste Rodin, Georges Rouault, John Singer Sargent, Egon Schiele, Fritz Scholder, George Segal, Ben Shahn, Sylvia Sleigh, John Sloan, Saul Steinberg, Wayne Thiebaud, Henri de Toulouse-Lautrec, Edouard Vuillard, Andy Warhol, Max Weber, Grant Wood, Andrew Wyeth

ARTISTS TO STUDY FOR STILL LIFE

Allen Adams, Pierre Bonnard, Georges Braque, Wendell Castle, Paul Cézanne, William Merritt Chase, Salvador Dalí, Charles Demuth, Audrey Flack, David Hockney, Alan Kessler, Edward Kienholz, Paul Klee, Fernand Leger, Rene Magritte, Henri Matisse, Joan Miró, Giorgio Morandi, Emil Nolde, Claes Oldenburg, Pablo Picasso, Stephen Posen, Joseph Raffael, Mel Ramos, James Rosenquist, Albert Pinkham Ryder, Oskar Schlemmer, Victor Spinski, Wayne Thiebaud, Edouard Vuillard, Andy Warhol

ARTISTS TO STUDY FOR LANDSCAPES

Carl Andre, Alice Aycock, Robert Bechtle, Pierre Bonnard, Georges Braque, Charles Burchfield, Deborah Butterfield, Paul Cézanne, Marc Chagall, Giorgio de Chirico, Christo, Salvador Dalí, Stuart Davis, Charles Demuth, Andre Derain, Richard Diebenkorn, Arthur G. Dove, Jean Dubuffet, Max Ernst, Richard Estes, Philip Evergood, Lyonel Feininger, Vincent van Gogh, Red Grooms, Marsden Hartley, Childe Hassam, Michael Heizer, Winslow Homer, Edward Hopper, Robert Indiana, Wassily Kandinsky, Anselm Keefer, Paul Klee, Oskar Kokoschka, Fernand Leger, Rene Magritte, Walter de Maria, John Marin, Reginald Marsh, Joan Miró, Piet Mondrian, Claude Monet, Robert Morris, Georgia O'Keeffe, Maxfield Parrish, Maurice Pendergast, Ann and Patrick Poirer, Larry Rivers, James Rosenquist, Charles Simonds, John Sloan, Robert Smithson, Chaim Soutine, Joseph Stella, Yves Tanguy, Wayne Thiebaud, Mark Tobey, Maurice de Vlaminck, Grant Wood, Andrew Wyeth

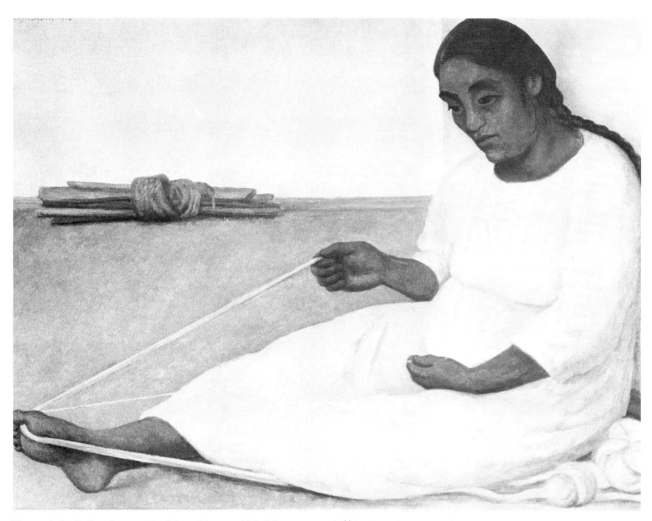

Figure A.4 *Indian Spinning* by Diego Rivera, 1936. Oil on canvas, 23½ inches × 32 inches. (Courtesy of the Phoenix Art Museum. Gift of Clare Booth Luce.)

Figure A.5 *Indian with Star Shield* By Fritz Scholder. Monoprint, 31 inches × 23 inches. (Courtesy of Marilyn Butler, Fine Art, Scottsdale, Arizona.)

Figure A.6 *Interior of a Bedroom* by Edouard Vuillard. Oil on panel, 22½ inches by 23½ inches. (Courtesy of the Phoenix Art museum. Life retention gift of Mr. and Mrs. Donald D. Harrington.)

Figure A.7 *Purple Mountains, Vence* By Marsden Hartley, 1924. Oil on canvas, 64.6 centimeters by 81.3 centimeters. (Courtesy of the Phoenix Art Museum. Gift of Mr. and Mrs. Orme Lewis.)

ARTISTS TO STUDY FOR ABSTRACT ART

Josef Albers, Karel Appel, Robert Arneson, Jean Arp, Milton Avery, Francis Bacon, Leonard Baskin, Larry Bell, Lee Bontecou, Constantin Brancusi, Georges Braque, Alexander Calder, Chuck Close, Joseph Cornell, Stuart Davis, Robert Delaney, Sonia Delaunay, Charles Demuth, Richard Diebenkorn, Jim Dine, Arthur G. Dove, Jean Dubuffet, Jacob Epstein, Max Ernst, Lyonel Feininger, Sam Francis, Helen Frankenthaler, Alberto Giacometti, Ralph Goings, Ashile Gorky, Adolph Gottlieb, Nancy Graves, Philip Guston, Marsden Hartley, Al Held, Barbara Hepworth, Hans Hofmann, Robert Indiana, Jasper Johns, Donald Judd, Wassily Kandinsky, Edward Keinholz, W. Ellsworth Kelly, Paul Klee, Franz Kline, Oskar Kokoschka, Greg Kondos, Wilhelm de Kooning, Gaston Lachaise, Suzanne Lacy, Fernand Leger, Sol LeWitt, Roy Lichtenstein, Richard Lindner, Jacque Lipchitz, Morris Louis, Kasimir Malevich, John Marin, Marino Marini, Joan Miró, Laszlo Moholy-Nagy, Piet Mondrian, Henry Moore, Robert Morris, Robert Motherwell, Louise Nevelson, Barnett Newman, Kenneth Noland, Georgia O'Keeffe, Claes Oldenburg, Jose Orozco, Pablo Picasso, Jackson Pollack, Robert Rauschenberg, Ad Reinhardt, Bridget Riley, Mark Rothko, Kurt Schwitters, Charles Sheeler, Millerd Sheets, David Smith, Saul Steinberg, Frank Stella, Joseph Stella, Clyfford Still, Mark di Suvero, Yves Tanguy, Mark Tobey, Victor Vasarely, Peter Voulkos, Tom Wesselman, William Wiley

Figure A.8 *Head(s) Improvization* by Karel Appel. Oil pastel drawing 28.25 inches by 34.25 inches. City of Scottsdale Fine Arts Collection. Courtesy of Katherine Middleton, Scottsdale Center for the Arts.

appendix

B

Museums and Other Resources

SELECTED MUSEUM PROGRAMS
The Metropolitan Museum of Art

The Metropolitan Museum of Art in New York City offers a wide assortment of interesting programs. During evening gallery talks and sketching, young students and their parents discuss and sketch different works of art in the museum's galleries. The works of specific artists as well as different themes, such as Byzantine art, French eighteenth-century painting, the French impressionists, pointillism, and cubism, have been explored in recent years. A weekend family program includes a gallery tour, sketching, and an art-related project. Topics range from "The Dance Class," "Rembrandt," and "Tranquil Landscapes," to "The Paintings and Sculptures of Edgar Degas," "Lions and Horned Creatures," and "Storm Clouds."

Guidebooks available for tours of various galleries have interesting titles, such as "A Gallery Hunt for Pacific Island Art" and "A Treasure Hunt for Pre-Columbian Art from Mexico and Peru." The books contain a floor map of the gallery, a brief historical description of the area to be focused on (for example, Pacific Island art), and instructions for following the map to find examples of this type of art in the gallery. Information about the art is provided, and related activities are suggested, such as "Can you write your age in Mayan numbers?" or "Which pot do you like best? Draw a sketch of it in the space below." The guidebooks also contain glossaries, word puzzles, and suggestions for where to see similar art.

The museum offers a program for teachers, as well as free classes for high school students devoted to understanding and exploring art. All classes are based on the museum's collections and may include gallery visits, slide presentations, sketching, and city walks.

The Museum of Contemporary Art and the Junior League of Los Angeles

In Los Angeles, the Museum of Contemporary Art (MOCA) and the Junior League of Los Angeles (JLLA) have created a student educational program in the visual arts called "Contemporary Art Start" (fig. B.1). This program is designed to introduce elementary teachers and students to the form, content, and concepts of contemporary art. At intensive workshops, the teachers work with the museum staff, docents, artists, and art directors. They receive firsthand art experience at the museum and at selected galleries and studios. The curriculum framework has developmental units focused on a variety of themes, such as contemporary sculpture, urban landscapes, environmental art, found objects, and other contemporary concepts. Within each unit, students and teachers view slides, learn and discuss art vocabulary and concepts, and address motivational questions about art.

The Baltimore Museum of Art

The Baltimore Museum of Art in Maryland has a "Materials for Teachers" program. This program loans slide sets on a variety of themes, such as "Parts of Art" (color, line, shape, and so on), "Ways and Means" (materials and techniques that artists use), and "Black Traditions" (masks and figures from Africa), to teachers for use in the classroom.

Figure B.1   As part of the Contemporary Art Start Program, fourth graders from 186th Street School use their own body movements to explore the mood and feeling of a sculpture by Joel Shapiro at The Museum of Contemporary Art, Los Angeles. Photo by Kim Kanatani.

The museum also provides a preview packet, which helps to prepare students for museum tours, and a "Muse-letter," a publication to acquaint educators with the museum's collection.

A museum guide booklet entitled *Getting to the Art of It* provides a floor map of the museum, along with information about specific artworks and motivational questions, such as "Have you ever not known what to say to a painting?" "Where do you think this painting was intended to hang?" "If you came across this spot in the wilderness, how would you get back to the waterfall?" "Could you write a story or poem to go with this work of art?" The booklet is intended to help teachers and parents explore works of art at the museum with children.

The Phoenix Art Museum

The Phoenix Art Museum provides trained museum docents to conduct group tours of the collection and changing exhibitions. Tours are available in Spanish and for those with hearing and sight disabilities. The museum's speakers bureau offers museum docents who visit school classrooms to prepare students for a museum visit or to show slide presentations that complement the classroom curricula. Exhibitions, classes, workshops, and performances are available year-round to challenge students and their families (fig. B.2).

Figure B.2   Soundingboards: An Environmental Work by Dr. Muriel Magenta, Phoenix Art Museum.

The museum also provides a masterpiece training program for school volunteers. This program includes a synopsis of art history, explanations of artists' techniques and materials, tours of the museum, and suggestions for related art projects for the classroom.

The Smithsonian Institution

The Smithsonian Institution offers a wide variety of museum exhibitions, centered around ethnic, cultural, and social themes, that can travel to different communities. Many consist of original art and artifacts complemented by wall texts. Others are photographic, supplemented with longer texts. The exhibitions are usually accompanied by related publications, guidelines, and educational materials. Titles of some of the exhibitions have been: "Black Women's Achievements Against the Odds," "Mexico As Seen by Her Children, Paintings, and Related Poetry by Children," "Power and Gold: Jewelry from Indonesia, Malaysia, and the Philippines," and "Spectacular Vernacular: Traditional Desert Architecture from West Africa and Southwest Asia." Just the titles alone are suggestive of many art themes that teachers could expand on!

The National Gallery of Art

The National Gallery of Art's extension programs are loaned free of charge to schools, libraries, and community organizations throughout the United States. Slide programs with accompanying audiocassettes, text, brochures, study prints, or posters focus on such topics as: "Introduction to Understanding Art," "The Chinese Past: 6,000 Years of Art and Culture," "The Far North: 2,000 Years of American Eskimo and Indian Art," "Treasures of Tutankhamen," "Folk Arts of the Spanish Southwest," "Textiles," and "Surveys of American Crafts and Folk Arts from the Index of American Design." Films, videocassettes, and special long-term loans of teaching packets are also available. A National Gallery of Art laser disk that contains over 16,000 works of art from the gallery's collection is available to teachers. The National Gallery of Art also offers a six-day summer study program for teachers. Write for the *National Gallery of Art Extension Program Catalogue.*

The Heard Museum

Founded in 1929, the Heard Museum is a Native American art and artifacts museum that represents both the prehistoric and living tribes of the American Southwest. The museum has more than 30,000 objects, including artifacts from Native American tribes, as well as the native cultures of South America, Asia, and Africa. Ongoing exhibitions feature modern Native American artists and craftspeople, as well as historic materials from the American Southwest. Native American artists conduct museum workshops. "Native Peoples of the Southwest" is a permanent exhibit that presents weekly video screenings on a variety of Native American subjects. Most recently, the museum, in conjunction with educational and cultural consultants, developed "Native Peoples of the Southwest: A Curriculum." Various units include class lessons in a *Teacher Guide,* color slides, audiotapes featuring native voices, overhead transparencies, classroom artifacts, and illustrated student booklets.

The Great Masterpieces Program

The Scottsdale, Arizona, Fine Arts Commission coordinates a program of art appreciation for the Scottsdale elementary schools at no cost to the school district. The "Great Masterpieces" program is totally the result of the involvement of volunteers, generous city businesses, and participating school PTAs. Each elementary school that expresses an interest in the program is encouraged to find a parent to be that school's coordinator. The coordinator, in turn, signs up parents of the schoolchildren to be "art guides."

An art guide visits the classroom twice a month, with a reproduction of a known art masterpiece and spends ten to thirty minutes talking about that reproduction. The time the guide spends in the classroom depends on the wishes of the teacher, the interest of the students, and the art guide's knowledge.

Art guides' training includes listening to five one-hour slide talks on various periods of art history, observing presentations about media and perception, learning techniques for working with children, and taking a trip to the Phoenix

Art Museum. The slide talks and many of the other presentations are provided by docents from Phoenix Art Museum's speakers bureau.

ART MUSEUMS

(Some catalogs available for slides and reproductions.)

Albright-Knox Art Gallery
Buffalo, NY 14222

Art Institute of Chicago
South Michigan and East Adams
Chicago, IL 60603

Asian Art Museum of San Francisco
Golden Gate Park
San Francisco, CA 94118

Baltimore Museum of Art
Art Museum Drive
Baltimore, MD 21218

Boston Museum of Fine Arts
P.O. Box 244
Avon, MA 02322

Buffalo Bill Historical Center
720 Sheridan Avenue
Cody, WY 82414

Carnegie Museum of Art
4400 Forbes Avenue
Pittsburgh, PA 15213

Cincinnati Art Museum
Eden Park
Cincinnati, OH 45202-1596

Contemporary Museum of Art, Los Angeles
250 S. Grand Ave. at California Plaza
Los Angeles, CA 90012

Freer Gallery of Art
Jefferson Drive at 12th Street SW
Washington, DC 20024

Frick Collection
1 East 70th Street
New York, NY 10021

J. Paul Getty Museum
17985 Pacific Coast Highway
Malibu, CA 90265

Getty Trust Publications
[Mail to: P.O. Box 2112
Santa Monica, CA 90407-2112]

Solomon R. Guggenheim Museum of Art
1071 Fifth Avenue
New York, NY 10128

Heard Museum
22 E. Monte Vista Road
Phoenix, AZ 85004

Heye Center, National Museums of the American Indian
1 Bowling Green
New York, NY 10004

Hirshhorn Museum and Sculpture Garden
Independence Avenue at 8th Street SW
Washington, DC 20560

Huntington Museum of Art
2033 McCoy Road
Huntington, WV 25701

Los Angeles County Museum of Art
5905 Wilshire Blvd.
Los Angeles, CA 90036

Metropolitan Museum of Art
1000 Fifth Ave.
New York, NY 10028

Museum of Modern Art
11 West 53rd Street
New York, NY 10019

National Gallery of Art
Sixth Street and Constitution Avenue NW
Washington, DC 20565

National Museum of African Art
National Museum of American Indian Art
Smithsonian Institution
950 Independence Avenue SW
Washington, DC 20560

National Museum for Women in the Arts
1250 New York Ave. NW
Washington, DC 20006

Oakland Museum
1000 Oak Street
Oakland, CA 94607

Oklahoma Museum of Art
7316 Nichols Road
Oklahoma City, OK 73120

Philadelphia Museum of Art
26th and Benjamin Franklin Way
Philadelphia, PA 19101

Phoenix Art Museum
1625 N. Central Ave.
Phoenix, AZ 85004

Portland Art Museum
1219 SW Park Avenue
Portland, OR 97205

Robert Miller Gallery
41 E. 57th St.
New York, NY 10022

Arthur M. Sackler Gallery
Asian and Near Eastern Art
1050 Independence Avenue SW
Washington, DC 20560

St. Louis Art Museum
Forest Park
St. Louis, MO 63110

San Francisco Museum of Modern Art
151 Third Street
San Francisco, CA 94107

Seattle Art Museum
Volunteer Park
Seattle, WA 98112

Walker Art Center
Vineland Place
Minneapolis, MN 55403

Whitney Museum of American Art
945 Madison Avenue
New York, NY 10021

Wichita Art Museum
619 Stackman Drive
Wichita, KS 67203

ART REPRODUCTIONS

(Catalogs available)

Art Education, Inc.
28 Erie Street
Blauvelt, NY 10913

Art Extension Press
P.O. Box 389
Westport, CT 06880

Complete Take 5 Program
Crystal Productions
1882 Johns Drive
P.O. Box 2159
Glenview, IL 60025

Crizmac (Prints, posters, games, videos)
3316 N. Chapel Ave.
Tucson, AZ 85716

Crystal Productions (Prints, videos)
Box 2159
Glenview, IL 60025

Davis Publications, Inc.
P.O. Box 15015
50 Portland Street
Worcester, MA 01615-0015

Fine Art Distributors (posters, postcards)
80 Kettle Creek Road
Weston, CT 06883

International Film Bureau, Inc.
332 South Michigan Avenue
Chicago, IL 61614-4382

Kisnet
6956 Eastern Avenue NW
Suite 208
Washington, DC 20012

Knowledge Unlimited
P.O. Box 52
Madison, WI 53701

New York Graphic Society, Ltd.
P.O. Box 1469
Greenwich, CT 06482

Phoenix Films and Video, Inc.
468 Park Avenue South
New York, NY 10016

Reading and O'Reilly, Inc. (filmstrips)
P.O. Box 302
Wilton, CT 06897

Dale Seymour
P.O. Box 10888
Palo Alto, CA 94303

Shorewood Reproductions (Prints, slides)
27 Glen Road
Sandy Hook, CT 06482

Starry Night Distributors, Inc.
19 North St.
Rutland, VT 05701

University Prints
21 East St.
Winchester, MA 02890

Universal Color Slide Co.
1221 Maine St., Suite 203
Weymouth, MA 02190

Roland Collection
3120 Pawtucket Road
Northbrook, IL 60062

Society for Visual Education, Inc.
Department BP
1345 Diversey Parkway
Chicago, IL 60614-1299

Yellow Ball Workshop
62 Tarbell Avenue
Lexington, MA 02173

MAGAZINES

American Artist
1515 Broadway
New York, NY 10036

American Visions: The Magazine of AfroAmerican Culture
The Visions Foundation
Frederick Douglass House—Capitol Hill
Smithsonian Institution
Washington, DC 02560

Art Education
National Art Education Association
1916 Reston Dr.
Reston, VA 22091

Art and Man
Scholastic, Inc.
351 Garver Road
P.O. Box 2700
Monroe, OH 45050-2700

Arts and Activities
591 Camino de la Reina
Suite 200
San Diego, CA 92108

Art News
48 W. 38th St.
New York, NY 10018

Art in America
575 Broadway
New York, NY 10012

Scholastic Art
Scholastic, Inc.
2931 E. McCarty St.
Jefferson City, MO 65102

School Arts
50 Portland St.
Worchester, MA 01608

A catalog of free-loan visual teaching materials is available from:

The National Gallery of Art
Department of Education Resources: Extension Programs
6th & Constitution NW
Washington, DC 20565

ART SUPPLY CATALOGS

Beckley Cardy
One E. First St.
Duluth, MN 55802
800–227–1178

Dick Blick
P.O. Box 1267
Galesburg, IL 61402
800–447–8192

Nasco
901 Janesville Ave.
Fort Atkinson, WI 53538
(or: 4825 Stoddard Road
     Modesto, CA 95356
     800–558–9595)

Sax Arts and Crafts
P.O. Box 51070
New Berlin, WI 53151–0710
800–558–6696)

Glossary

Abstract art Art that has been abstracted from nature, that describes nonrepresentational or non-naturalistic forms of expression. The forms may be simplified, geometric, identifiable, or completely unrecognizable.

Abstract expressionism An American art movement appearing in the 1940s and 1950s. Primarily a painting form characterized by large, broad brush strokes and shapes, which make the painting look as though it was done quickly and spontaneously.

Achromatic A color scheme using white, gray, and black.

Acrylic polymer paint Paint that is watercolor formulated with acrylic polymer plastic emulsion. This means that suspended in the formula are fine particles of colorless, synthetic resin, which forms a clear, water-resistant film when dry. Available in tubes as well as in jars and used primarily by professional artists.

Additive method A method of sculpting in which sculptors add parts to each other to build a form.

Aesthetics A branch of philosophy that focuses on the perception, appreciation, and beauty in art and the value of art in society.

Analogous colors Colors that are side by side on the color wheel and similar in hue, such as red, red-orange, and orange.

Analysis Looking at and responding to artworks. Involves identifying and examining separate parts (art elements and design principles) as they function independently and cooperatively in creative works.

Aperture The opening in the camera lens that permits light to enter.

Arch A construction method where an open space is bridged by a series of wedge-shaped masonry blocks that form a semicircular curve.

Architecture The study and method of designing and constructing buildings.

Arrangement Placing in an order. Organizing the art elements into a pleasing unity.

Art concepts The art elements (line, shape, value, space, color, pattern, texture) and the design principles (balance, dominance, rhythm, contrast). Within an artwork, each art concept is intertwined with and inseparable from the others so that they work together to influence the total vision.

Art criticism Describing, analyzing, and interpreting the media, processes, and structure of artworks.

Art elements The foundational tools of the artist. Consist of the visual arts components of line, value, shape, space, color, pattern, and texture.

Art experience Perceiving art through an aesthetic activity.

Art expression The presentation of perception, skills, ideas, and feelings in terms of art.

Art history A historical record of the visual arts, including information about art objects, artifacts, and artists.

Art materials Resources used in the creation and study of visual art, such as paint, clay, cardboard, canvas, film, videotape, models, watercolors, wood, and plastic.

Art media Broad categories for grouping works of visual art according to the art materials used.

Art skill The ability to perform certain actions gained through perceptions, experiences, and study.

Art therapy Treatment whose goal is to focus the individual's energies on creating artworks that promote self-actualization.

Ashcan art Art by American artists who, beginning in the early 1900s, painted city street life and experiences in American cities. Backyards, saloons, alleys, fights, and slums were often depicted in their paintings.

Assemblage An art form in which three-dimensional objects and materials are combined to form a sculpture of mixed media.

Assess To analyze and determine quality of achievement.

Asymmetrical balance The balance achieved when there is unequal distribution of forces on either side of a picture—for example, when a large object on one side of the drawing creates an overpowering feeling, a heavy weight.

Background The area of a painting or drawing represented to be farthest from the viewer.

Backlight To illuminate the object being filmed from behind.

Balance   The design principle of visual equilibrium (*harmony* or *disharmony*) achieved in an artwork. Determined by weight, directional forces, and opposing tensions. In art, balance is an illusion affected by everything happening in the artwork. For example, the design within a picture is in balance when no one part of the picture overpowers any other part, when the visual illusion created is one of equilibrium and stability.

Baroque   An ornamental, swirling style of painting that was initiated during the late sixteenth century. Characteristic are its sense of motion and grandeur. Baroque artists used light and multicurved forms and arrangement to create a romantic mysticism in their compositions. Often, baroque artists attempted to join architecture, sculpture, and painting into an entity.

Baseline concept   A drawing characteristic of young children whereby they show spatial relationships between the objects they are drawing by placing the objects on a line that represents the ground. The sky is usually indicated by a line running along the top of the page. The open space in between is "air."

Bas-relief   Describes a sculpture in low relief, projecting slightly from the background surface.

Batik   The process whereby designs are applied to cloth with candle wax or crayons and then paint is brushed over the designs.

Baud   A unit that measures the speed of electronic data transmission through a modem. The higher the number, the faster the modem operates. Often used interchangeably with bits per second, or bps, although the two terms mean different things technically.

BBS   A computer bulletin board system. Thousands exist around the world. They can be operated by anyone with the right equipment and software. Most are text-only and offer discussion areas, games, and software that can be downloaded. Some offer access to the Internet. Some charge membership fees.

Binder   A substance used to hold together pigment particles or to cause pigment to adhere to the surface to which it has been applied.

Black carbon ink   A deep, black, water-resistant ink. Also known as India ink.

Bond   A smooth-surfaced paper that is good for pencil, pen and ink, brush, and conte crayon drawings.

Calligraphic line   A line that tends to vary from thin to thick in one, quick stroke. A very light brush stroke results in a faint, thin line, while a heavy brush stroke causes a thick, dark line.

Cartoon   A preliminary drawing for solving organizational problems before beginning a painting or mural.

Cartooning   The development of one or a series of line drawings to tell a story or joke (for example, comic books, and cartoons and comic strips in newspapers and magazines), to make a statement (for example, political cartoons), or to animate (for example, Walt Disney cartoons).

Carving   A sculpture produced by taking away—cutting, chipping, or hewing wood, stone, or clay.

Casting   A sculpture process where a liquid material is poured into an open cavity (or mold) and later hardens. Often, bronze, silver, gold, polyester resins, and plaster are used.

Ceramics   The term used for the art of making earthen objects, such as pottery, which are fired in a kiln.

Charcoal   A black, solid residue made from burning wood in a kiln with very little air. Available in soft, medium, and hard degrees. Commonly used for making quick sketches.

Charcoal paper   A rough-grained absorbent paper that is available in white, black, and tints.

Chiaroscuro   A manner of creating the illusion of form with light and shade in drawing and painting.

Chroma   The brilliance or intensity of a color.

Cityscape   A painting or drawing of a city scene.

Classic   Emphasis on formal organization in terms of simplicity and clarity in taste. Often referred to in terms of Grecian concepts.

Classical   The Greek art period from 480 to 323 B.C.

Coil method (with clay)   Method of working with clay whereby rolls of clay (like snake forms) are used to build such items as large or small containers, model buildings, and animals.

Collage   Artwork in which fragments, such as paper, photographs, cloth, candy wrappers, etc., are combined and pasted to a flat surface.

Color   The perception of a light stimulus by your mind and eye. The color seen depends on the light in which the object is seen and the color that is reflected.

Color advance and recede   The effect achieved when color is sensed as being in front of or in back of another color. Warm colors advance; cool colors recede.

Color balance   The color arrangement in a design that indicates harmony or disharmony.

Color blend   The effect achieved when two similar colors are seen together as one color.

Color contrast   The effect achieved when two distinctly different colors are seen together.

Color effect   The effect achieved when a color impression is conveyed to the viewer through the use of color.

Color emphasis   The effect achieved when one color stands out from other colors through the use of contrast.

Color purity   The degree of maximum strength (or saturation) of any given color.

Color relativity   The quality of color that is dependent on the color's relationship to other colors.

Color variation   When bright colors appear to come forward and colors become more neutral as they become distant.

Color wheel   A circular chart used to study the relationships between the various colors. Primary colors are red, yellow, and blue; these are located at three equidistant points on a circle. Halfway between the primaries are the three secondary colors: green, purple, and orange.

Column   A structural vertical cylinder often found in Egyptian and Greek temple architecture.

Commercial online service   A giant BBS that charges users monthly fees for access to vast libraries of software, games, clubs, discussion groups, and information, including newspapers and magazines. Most offer colorful graphics and the ability to navigate by clicking with a mouse. The three largest services are America Online, CompuServe, and Prodigy.

Communications software   Programs that enable computers to "talk" via modems and telephone lines. Most computers running Windows already have a simple communications program, called Terminal. Others include ProComm and Crosstalk.

Complementary colors   Colors that, when used side by side, such as red next to green, offer the visual illusion of maximum contrast. On a color wheel, complementary colors are opposite one another: Red is opposite green, blue is opposite orange, and yellow is opposite violet. When opposites are mixed, colors are "grayed" or neutralized. Artists often "gray" colors this way, rather than adding black or white to a hue.

Composition   See *design*.

Conceptual art   An art style, begun in the 1960s, that focuses on the idea and process by which the artwork comes into being and that involves the spectator by actual participation. Ideas are often documented with photographs as they develop. Conceptual artists believe that the *concepts* or *ideas* behind an artwork are the real art, not the physical objects (such as paintings) that artists produce.

Construction paper   Paper that comes in a wide choice of colors, from bright tones to grayed shades, and is available in sheets as well as rolls. Good for construction and collage purposes, for painting, and for drawing with crayons and chalks.

Content   Often, the subject matter of an artwork. Can also refer to the art elements, such as line, shape, color, and so on.

Context   A set of interrelated conditions (such as social, economic, political) in the visual arts that influence and give meaning to the development and reception of thoughts, ideas, or concepts and that define specific cultures and eras.

Contour   The outside edge, the boundary. Usually, a sensitive line indicating the existence of mass in space.

Contour drawing   A drawing approach that involves looking at the object you want to draw and imagining that you are touching it with the drawing tool. In a sense, your eye becomes the drawing tool, and both your eye and the actual drawing tool move at the same time, very slowly and sensitively. In contour drawing, you do not look at your paper as you draw. Instead, you sit close to the model and look only at the point your eye and pencil are on, trying not to let your eye get ahead of your hand.

Contrast   The design principle of using opposites, unlikes, opposing elements in a composition. Example: dark against light, rough against smooth, thick against thin. Contrast adds interest and focal points. In photography, contrast is the variation between light and dark objects in a photograph that is determined by the amount, source, and direction of the light source.

Converging lines   Receding lines that appear to converge at distant points to show perspective. Examples: the receding lines in a long table, up a skyscraper, along a railroad track, or up a stairway.

Cool colors   Colors in which blue is the primary color—for example, blue, blue-green, green, blue-purple, and purple.

Crafts   A category of visual and cultural arts that includes ceramics, fibers, jewelry, enamel, wood, leather, paper, plastic, and other media.

Crayon batik   The technique whereby wax crayon or paraffin is painted on cloth. Similar to the crayon- or wax-resist technique.

Crayon etching   The technique whereby the whole paper is covered with brightly colored crayon designs, which are then heavily coated with black ink, crayon, or paint mixed with a little liquid soap. A design is then etched into the black overlay color, exposing the bright colors underneath.

Crayon-resist   The technique whereby a wax design is created with crayons or candles (or by drawing into waxed paper over white paper), with some spaces of the paper left open. When paint is then brushed over the paper, the waxed areas of the paper "resist" the paint and show through.

Creativity   The production of works of art using materials, techniques, and processes. The flexible and fluent generation of unique or elaborate ideas.

Crosshatch   The technique of suggesting modeling or shading by using crossing lines at various angles to indicate depth. Pencil or pen and ink are most often used.

CU   Close-up shot.

Cubism   An early twentieth-century art style invented by Pablo Picasso and Georges Braque in which the semiabstract image is often represented by fragmented, semitransparent shapes.

Cultural arts   Traditional expressions of ethnic groups of peoples, such as Native American forms of weaving and basketry, African masks, American quilts and handcrafted toys, and the Mexican "tree of life" sculpture. Sometimes referred to as "folk arts."

Cyberspace   A generic term used to describe the intangible "place" computer users visit when they go online.

Depth   Space that indicates three dimensions. In drawing and painting, depth is the receding space created behind the picture plane.

Design   The structure, arrangement, and organization of an artwork into a unified composition. Can also be a plan, sketch, outline, or procedure.

Design principles   Some of the fundamental characteristics in the visual arts: balance, dominance, rhythm, and contrast.

Detail   The smaller and more intricate parts of a work of art.

Detail variation   Placing the clearest detail in the foreground of a picture, while having other details become less distinct with distance.

Direction   The movement or path that leads the eye in a work of art. This movement can be created by the use of color or by any of the art elements and the relationships existing among them.

Dissolve   To fade into one picture from another or to fade out of one picture to another.

Docent   A person who leads guided tours through art galleries and museums.

Dolly   To move the camera toward or away from the object being filmed, using a wheeled platform.

Dominance   The design principle of creating a focal point of greater emphasis or stress and making it the center of interest.

Download   The process of using a modem and telephone line to copy computer files from a remote computer—such as a BBS or a commercial online service—to your computer, where they can be saved and used. Software, graphics, text, video, and even audio files can be downloaded. Opposite of *upload.*

Draftsmanship   Drawing skill.

Draping   The method of working with clay whereby clay slabs are draped over forms, such as bowls, rocks, dishes, flower holders, and so on, to achieve that particular shape.

Drawing   The fundamental process of pictorial art, emphasizing line and tone to express the artist's vision of ideas, skill, feeling, and situations.

Earth art   Art production involving altering the physical landscape by making holes, mounds, trenches, and other earth movings.

Easel brush   A flat bristle brush that will not fan out and lose its shape. Intended for large easel painting.

Eclectics   Artists who chose to incorporate elements or philosophical ideas from an era in their paintings.

Egg tempera   Pigment ground in water and mixed with egg yolk.

Elements of art   See *art elements.*

E mail   Electronic mail sent from one computer user to another. E-mail can be sent over networks, such as within an office building, or through modems and telephone lines to users on BBSs, commercial online services, or the Internet.

Emotional approach   Approach to art that involves interpreting subjects with exaggeration and distortion to emphasize an idea or express a feeling.

Emulsion   The shiny, light-sensitive coating on photographic film or paper. The coating is a gelatin substance that contains silver halide crystals.

Encaustic   The technique whereby wax colors (leftover crayons) are melted and then applied to the design.

Engraving   Making a print by forming the image cut by a hard tool into a metal plate.

Environmental arts   A category of visual and cultural arts that includes architecture, landscape design, community design, interior and furniture design, clothing and items of adornment, and product design.

Exhibition   A public showing of a collection of artworks that is intended to bring to the public a diversity of ideas, new approaches, and solutions along with the artist or artists' statement.

Exposure   The length of time light is applied to light-sensitive materials (for example, film).

Expression   A process of conveying ideas, feelings, and meanings. Refers to the artist's personal vision.

Expressionism   Art in which the artist is more concerned with expressing his or her emotional reaction to an object or situation than approaching the object or situation on a naturalistic basis. Very prevalent in German art in the twentieth century.

Expressive features   Expressions evoking affects such as joy, sadness, or anger.

Eye-level line   See *horizon line*.

Eye or station point   The concept that where you are determines your viewpoint.

Fade   To lessen the sound or brightness of the picture (such as "fade to black").

Fantasy   Describes highly imaginative and whimsical art forms.

FAQ   Frequently asked questions. New users tend to ask the same questions, so many spots in cyberspace offer FAQ files that can be read at leisure. Reading FAQs can avoid online blunders.

Fauvism   A painting movement characterized by vivid colors and free treatment of form, resulting in a vibrant and decorative effect.

Fax modem   Computer device that operates both as a modem and a fax machine, enabling users to link with remote computers via telephone lines, and to send and receive faxes.

Fine art   Art created by artists and valued for its aesthetic significance.

Fixative   A solution that is sprayed on pencil, chalk, or charcoal drawings to prevent smudging.

Fixer   A solution that fixes, or makes permanent, on film or paper the image brought out in development.

Focus   To adjust a lens so that the image it projects has maximum sharpness.

Foldover concept   A drawing characteristic of young children whereby the baseline runs horizontally across the middle of the paper, with students showing objects both above and below the baseline.

Foreground   The area of a painting or drawing represented to be nearest the viewer.

Foreshortening   A drawing technique that creates visual impact by showing an object projecting sharply toward or receding from the viewer.

Form   A shape having three dimensions: height, width, and depth.

Formal arrangement   Symmetrical and rigid organization of the art elements.

Format   The outside edges of the surface on which artists work. Could be round, long, horizontal, vertical, etc. The limited space of the format influences the various shapes drawn.

Free forms   An indefinite shape or invented form.

Freeze-frame   A static picture produced from a videotape recording.

Fresco   A water-based painting executed either on wet or dry plaster walls.

F-stop   The aperture size indicated on the camera by an F-number. The larger the opening, the smaller the number. In many cameras, the F-stop is fixed and not adjustable.

Functional   The structural elements of art used for a utilitarian purpose.

Genre   A painting of the daily activity of ordinary people.

Geometric shape   A form with straight or curved lines or both, as opposed to an organic shape, which is a form with irregular edges and surfaces.

Gesso   A white substance made of whiting (refined chalk derived from calcium carbonate), gelatin, and water, applied to a carrier as a warm liquid and used as a painting ground when dry and hard.

Gesture drawing   A drawing approach that captures the essential action or movement, a posture, what a person is doing, or the feeling of a figure or object in a very short time. It involves feeling the dynamic sensation of the form and responding to that with a scribbly or "fast" line drawing or tone that is descriptive of the action.

Glazing   Applying thin, transparent layers of color over layers of solid color, with each successive layer darker than the one beneath.

Gouache   An opaque watercolor made by mixing white with transparent watercolor.

Gradation   A gradual change from one value or color to another.

Graphic arts   Usually refers to black-and-white drawing or printmaking. The technical process of printing, printmaking, and photography.

Ground   (1) The prepared surface for painting. It is usually white. (2) The space or field around the drawing—the negative space.

Guilds   Associations of tradesmen that were formed during the Middle Ages to protect the individual and to maintain standards of performance and quality.

Harmony   The result when the structural elements are formed into a pleasing relationship.

High-angle shot   A shot taken with the camera held at a high angle.

Highlight   The lightest light in a painting, which seems to emanate from a natural (sunlight), artificial (electric light bulb), or imaginary light source within the painting.

Horizon line/eye-level line   A perspective term that refers to an imaginary line ahead of you that is level with your horizontal line of sight and on which is located the vanishing point. All edges and lines of the object pictured converge to what is called the vanishing point. Those above eye level recede down to the eye-level line, and those below eye level converge up to the eye-level line.

Hue   The classification or name of a pure color. Technically, the wavelength of light reflected from an object. When the reflected wavelength of light changes, the color changes. There are warm hues (for example, red) and cool hues (for example, blue).

Ideas   A formulated thought, opinion, or concept that can be represented in visual or verbal form.

Illumination   The amount of light reflected by an object. Illumination depends on the brightness of the light source and on the distance between the light and the receiving object.

Illustration   A picture used as a supplement to dramatize. Usually related to a story, poem, or written description.

Imaginative (abstract) approach   Highly inventive and creative approach to art that uses invented forms and ideas developed from the imagination.

Impasto   Heavy "pasty" layers of paint usually applied to the brightest areas of an oil painting.

Impressionism   An art movement begun in the 1870s and 1880s by artists from Paris whose purpose was to paint the effects of light on surfaces. These artists usually painted outdoors and with short strokes of bright colors.

Information superhighway   Term used to describe electronic networks that link people around the world. To purists, that means the Internet. Others include cable television and telephone networks. Same as *information highway*, the *infobahn*, and the *I-way*.

In relief   Describes a sculpture that has forms that project from a background.

Intensity   The strength or weakness (brightness or dullness) of a color. Sometimes called the saturation chroma, or purity of a color. A hue that is not mixed with any other color is at its maximum intensity. Mixing a color with another color lowers the hue's intensity. Bright red, for example, has greater intensity than brown or dark blue.

Internet   The worldwide computer network that links millions of computer users at schools, businesses, government institutions, military installations, and homes.

In the round   Describes a sculpture that is freestanding and that can be viewed from the front, back, or sides.

Intuitive   A type of response that is spontaneous or instinctive.

Kraft paper   Inexpensive paper that has a good drawing and painting surface and that is available in large rolls of white, colored, and black. Often used for murals.

Landscape   A painting or drawing of natural scenery.

Lens   A glass or transparent plastic material that is made with two opposing surfaces. The surfaces change the direction of light, focusing it at a place on the film. Lenses are classified on the basis of how they bend light rays.

Light   The illumination that reveals an object.

Line   A basic art element. Line is an abstract invention used to describe an outline, contour, boundary, or limit of a three-dimensional object. Line can also be a moving direction or the course in which anything moves. Sometimes, lines are used to express spatial illusions or the artist's feelings.

Low-angle shot   A shot taken with the camera held at a low angle.

LS   Long shot (full view of the background).

Manila   A cream-colored paper for painting and drawing.

MCU   Medium close-up shot.

Medium   (1) Material used for making a work of art. Examples include pencils, paints, wood, and inks. (2) The substance or liquid into which pigments are ground to make them usable as paint. Examples include oil, egg yolk, and gum arabic.

Memory drawing   A drawing approach that involves drawing from memory, without a model.

Middle Ages   A period of art history in western Europe dating from the decline of the Roman Empire to the beginning of the Renaissance, from about A.D. 476 to circa 1400.

Middle ground   The area in a picture or drawing that is between the foreground and the background.

Minimal art   Art that intentionally leaves out the traditional requirements of uniqueness, complexity, and expressive content, and takes visual simplicity to an extreme.

Mobiles   Constructions intended to move about in space, creating variations of shapes, spaces, and shadows.

Modeled drawing or modeling   (1) The representation of three-dimensional, rounded forms through the use of a variety of values and a range of tones from light to dark. Contrast is determined by the amount and source of light and the shadows created on the form. (2) Making a sculpture from pliable materials, such as clay or wax, using the hands or shaping tools.

Modem   A device that enables remote computers to be linked via telephone lines. Some are installed inside computers. Others are external, connected to computers with cables.

Monochromatic   Describes all of the shades, tints, values, and intensities of one color hue. Variations are made by adding black or white to a color, by thinning with water, or by mixing smaller amounts of color.

Monoprints   The images created by using brushes, brayer rollers, or even cotton swabs to apply paint to a nonporous surface, such as plastic or glass, and then drawing designs or images into the paint. A sheet of paper is then placed on top of the finished design, and the back of the paper is rubbed gently with the hand or the back of a spoon to transfer the paint to the paper. Artists often use an etching press to transfer the design to the paper.

Mood   An emotional feeling created by the handling of the art concepts.

Mosaic   An art form made by adhering small pieces of stone, ceramic tile, glass, etc., to a background. Used in ancient as well as contemporary art.

Motif   The dominant idea in a design.

Movement   The direction or force of relating lines, color, etc. that lead the eye over and through a work of art.

Murals   Paintings—or frescoes—that are either painted directly on a wall surface or that are fastened to a wall.

Myths   Traditional stories within a culture that attempt to explain the mysterious and unexplainable in nature or that relate to and explain practices, beliefs, and religious rites.

Negative shape   Empty space around a positive shape (the physical object or figure represented in an artwork). A design consists of the arrangement of positive and negative shapes within the boundaries of the format.

Neoclassicism   The term used to describe the art movement that followed the French Revolution (A.D. 1789 to 1815). Paintings were based on classical themes and heroic ideals. The figure was painted without feelings and with the emphasis on style, which was sophisticated, intellectual, cold, technical, and very realistic. Form was more important than light and color.

Neo-impressionism   A late nineteenth-century French method of painting in which small dabs of complementary colors, such as red and green, orange and blue, and yellow and purple, were applied side by side. The expectation was that, at a distance, the eye would fuse the colors so that they appeared to blend smoothly. Neo-impressionists expected this technique to provide more vivid coloring than that achieved by mixing the colors on the palette. Also known as pointillism.

Neutral colors   Colors such as gray that have no positive hue.

Newsprint   Inexpensive, thin drawing or painting paper. Often available as roll ends from local newspapers.

Nonobjective art   Art that has no recognizable object or subject, no reference to natural appearances. Compositional relationships, such as color, shape, and texture, are most important.

Objective art   Art that is based on the actual physical world. Tends toward naturalism.

Oil paints   Paints with an oil base—commonly linseed oil—and that require solvents, such as turpentine, for thinning. Usually used by professional artists on canvas, wood, paper, or metal.

Online   Electronically linked, as in, "I'm online with America Online." Similar to *cyberspace.*

Opaque   Describes materials, such as people and buildings, that stop light waves. Opaque objects cast shadows. With regard to color, describes thick, nontransparent color, such as that provided by tempera paint and oil paint. An opaque material is not transparent or translucent.

Op art   Art that is concerned with the optical illusions achieved with small, patterned shapes and moving visual effects.

Opposition   Contrast between colors, shapes, lines, etc.

Order   An organization or arrangement.

Organic shape   A form that has irregular edges or surfaces. Also refers to a shape existing in nature.

Outline   The line that describes the outer edges or limits of a form. Not the same as a contour line. An outline is flat and two-dimensional—a silhouette.

Overlapping   Partially covering one form with another form. The whole form that is in front of the overlapped (partially covered) form seems closer. Overlapping forms create distance.

Painting The process of creating an artwork using pigments mixed with a liquid vehicle (such as water, oil, acrylic) to a support surface (such as wood, canvas, paper).

Palette A board, tablet, or surface on which artists have their colors and on which they mix colors. May also refer to the typical color range used by a group of artists—for example, the impressionists' palette.

Pan To move the camera left or right.

Pattern Formed by intervals of repeated lines, shapes, colors, or textures that move across the surface—not into the surface. Arranged in some sequence or movement. Pattern can introduce order and unity, or contrast and variety.

Perception Visual and sensory awareness with regard to objects, images, and feelings.

Perspective (1) The illusion of representing space, depth, and volume on a two-dimensional surface so as to give them the same appearance as in nature when viewed from a given point. (2) The illusion that objects appear to get smaller as they recede from the viewer.

Picture plane The flat, two-dimensional drawing surface on which artists create three-dimensional space. Imaginary, flat vertical areas that indicate zones of distance within a painting. The three chief planes of a painting are the foreground (the area of the painting represented to be nearest the viewer), the background (the area of the painting represented to be farthest from the viewer), and the middle ground (the area between the foreground and the background).

Pigment The coloring matter that is mixed with oil, water, wax, and other substances to make paints, crayons, chalks, etc.

Pinch method (with clay) The method of working with clay whereby the thumb is inserted into a ball of clay, and the clay ball is then rotated while the thumb pushes out and "pinches" a pot shape.

Placement Placing forms lower in the picture so that they appear to come forward and placing forms higher up in the picture to cause them to appear to recede.

Plane A flat, curved, moving, two-dimensional surface of any form, such as the side of a cube.

Pointillism See *neo-impressionism.*

Point of view The position of the viewer in relationship to the scene.

Pop art Art that is a comment on the contemporary, natural environment and on commercial aspects of the culture, such as cakes, pies, and soup cans. Frequently, these objects form patterns and are repeated.

Popular art A category of visual and cultural arts that includes clothing and items of adornment, and graphic design in videos, magazines, and book illustrations.

Portrait A drawing or painting of a human model in which the artist's aim is to capture the spirit and character of the individual, as well as the person's likeness.

Positive shape The physical object or figure represented in an artwork. Empty space around the form is considered the negative shape. A design consists of the arrangement of positive and negative shapes within the boundaries of a format.

Post-impressionism The late nineteenth-century avant-garde art movement whose paintings resemble those of the impressionists in their use of bright colors. Rather than emphasizing the effects of light, the artists explored the formal structure of art and expressed their personal feelings about the image. Major post-impressionist artists are Cézanne, Gauguin, and van Gogh.

Primary colors Red, yellow, and blue. All other colors can be made by mixing these hues.

Priming Preparing the carrier with glue sizing or other materials in order to apply the ground upon which the actual painting is rendered.

Print An original work of art made from one of the printmaking processes: etching, engraving, linoleum or wood block printing, lithography, silkscreen, etc. Not to be confused with a "reproduction print" of a painting or drawing.

Printmaking The process of printing from various surfaces—for example, rubbings, stamp prints, stencil prints, and monoprints.

Process An action involving a number of methods or techniques. For example, the process of creating art, the addition and subtraction processes in sculpture, the etching and intaglio processes in printmaking, or the casting or constructing processes in making jewelry.

Proportion Relating of elements or comparing of parts as to size, quality, variety, scale, purpose, or meaning. Realistic proportions refer to "accurate" relationships of parts. In expressive works of art, the proportion may be distorted to express the idea or emotion.

Proximity The closeness of one thing to another. Also, the tension between them.

Quick-contour drawing A faster method of contour drawing that requires determining which lines are most essential to the total form. As with regular contour drawing, quick-contour drawing involves drawing without looking at the paper. The distortions and exaggerations that often result tend to add to the abstract quality or uniqueness of the drawing.

Radial balance The balance achieved when all of the art elements radiate from a central point. In nature, radial balance is exemplified in the petals of a daisy or in the cross section of a grapefruit.

Realism Art that represents actual appearances but pays little attention to detail.

Receding Describes movement into depth.

Reflection The return of light waves from a surface. On smooth or shiny surfaces, light is changed from its normal straight line and bounced off (reflected) at an angle. On uneven surfaces, light is reflected in many directions by small surfaces reflecting at various angles.

Refraction The deflection (or bending) of light waves from their normal straight path as they pass from one medium (such as air) into another (such as water). Light goes through different materials at different speeds.

Regionalists Artists who painted everyday rural life during the Depression in the Midwest. These artists included Thomas Hart Benton, Grant Wood, Charles Burchfield, and Philip Evergood.

Related colors Personal selection of colors that "go well" together.

Relief sculpture Sculpture where the forms protrude from a flat background. Sometimes called bas-relief.

Renaissance A "rebirth" of the classical art that began in the fifteenth century in Italy and spread to all of western Europe.

Rhythm The design principle of repeating a line, shape, value, color, or other art element to provide a regulated, uninterrupted flow that suggests a moving force and direction. A tempo, rhythm, or movement created in this way can be regular or irregular, pleasing or unsettling.

Rococo An eighteenth-century art style of very delicately curved ornamental shapes and forms that followed the baroque style but that was lighter in feeling and less grandiose.

Romanticism An eighteenth-century art style that was a reverberation against neoclassicism, traditional classicism, and imitative styles. Paintings stressed the emotion and personality of the individual, dramatic action, and adventure. They told thrilling stories about life and experiences. Subjects were not directly connected with realities in life. The paint quality was full of energy and movement, with open, flowing brushwork. Often, the atmosphere of the paintings took on greater significance than the naturalistic objects themselves.

Rubbings   The images made by placing paper over a raised, incised, or textured surface and then rubbing over the paper with crayons, pencils, chalk, or other colored substances.

Saturation   The purity of color from bright to dull, often referred to as intensity.

Scale   The proportional relationships of many parts to the whole. The size of a drawing in relation to the object being drawn.

Schema   A child's personally developed symbol for a person or object that is repeated again and again. For example, a child may use the same schema for the head of a man as he or she uses for the head of a child because this is what the child symbolizes for a head.

Sculpture   Three-dimensional shapes that are either modeled, cast, carved, or constructed.

Secondary colors   The colors that contain about equal amounts of two primary colors: green (made from yellow and blue), violet (made from blue and red), and orange (made from red and yellow).

Sepia   A dark-brown pigment made from secretions of cuttlefish.

Sequence   An arrangement in a series to develop a progression.

Shade   A dark value of a hue (made by adding black to the color). For example, maroon is a shade of red.

Shading   The representation of three-dimensional, rounded forms through the use of a variety of values and a range of tones from light to dark. Contrast is determined by the amount and source of light and the shadows created on the form.

Shadow   Created when rays from one or more light sources are cut off by an interposed opaque object. The object's shadows and tonal values help to reveal the object's three-dimensional form. Shadows may be sharp or diffused (scattered), depending on the light source and distance.

Shape   The contour of a form or mass—whether a real, imaginary, or abstract object—formed when a line moves through space until it meets itself and forms an enclosure. Shapes come in different proportions and sizes, in two and three dimensions. Sometimes, shapes create tension by their proximity; they can also be overlapped. Everything is composed of one or more shapes.

Shutter   The camera device for opening and closing the aperture of a lens in order to expose the film.

Silhouette   Flat, two-dimensional representation of a shape.

Size variation   Having the larger forms appear in the foreground of a picture, while having smaller forms recede with distance.

Sizing   A glue substance—usually gelatin and water—used for priming, preparation of gesso, a painting medium, and a variety of other applications.

Sketch   A quick drawing intended as an idea for a more sustained drawing.

Slab method (with clay)   The method of working with clay whereby a slab of clay is rolled out like pie dough. Then shapes are cut from the clay and joined together to form other shapes.

Soft focus   To produce an image having unsharp outlines.

Space   (1) The interval of distance between two or more objects. Where you exist in space determines your point of view. Shapes, colors, sizes, patterns, and line direction all change as you move within space because all objects in space have a position and direction relative to each other. (2) An illusion of movement into a two-dimensional picture plane. Within an artwork, space is determined by placement on the picture plane (near or far) and is created by color, value, and shape. (3) An interior. (4) An environmental space.

Spatial levels   Establishing various levels, such as foreground, middle ground, and background, to create distance and to indicate which objects are nearest, in between, and furthest away.

Spectrum   The continuum of color formed when a beam of white light is dispersed, as by passage through a prism, into red, orange, yellow, green, blue, indigo, and violet.

Stamped prints   The images made by incising designs into various materials, such as potatoes, plasticine, clay, sponges, and cardboard, and then painting or dipping the incised material into paint or ink, and pressing (stamping) onto paper or fabric.

Static   A fixed, quiet, passive quality in a work of art.

Stencils   The images created by cutting out a design or shape from a piece of cardboard or other material, thereby leaving an open shape, and then placing the stencil over a piece of paper, and filling in the design with chalks or paints.

Still life   A drawing or painting of a grouping of inanimate objects.

Stop bath   A mildly acidic solution used to check photographic development of a negative or print.

Structures   Means of organizing the components of an artwork into a cohesive whole.

Style   Refers to the artist's individual and unique manner of expression. Also refers more broadly to a characteristic of a school or period, such as the "realistic" school.

Subject matter   The object, experience, idea, or event used as the motivation for a work of art.

Subtractive method   A method of sculpting in which sculptors start with a large piece of material, such as clay, wood, or stone, and carve away the form.

Surrealism   An art movement begun in the 1920s that advocated the portrayal of the subconscious or of dream phenomena. Images vary from realistic styles to dreamlike or exotic subjects to semiabstract, often childlike styles.

Symmetrical balance   Formal balance of the art elements. The same mirror image on both sides of an artwork.

Techniques   A style or manner in which a medium is used. The artist's individual way of using the art material. Examples: cross-hatching lines, loose watercolor blends, thickly applied oil paint.

Technological arts   A category of visual and cultural arts that includes photography, Polaroid photography, film, video, computer-generated images, videodiscs, video cameras and tapes, laser disks, television, holography, copy machines, and color copiers. All of these art forms use technology and can be used in the art room.

Tempera paint   In fine art, an opaque and water-based painting medium in which the pigments are mixed with egg yolk, whether in a pure state or in emulsion. For classroom use, tempera paints are available in powder, liquid, and cake forms.

Tension   Quality of pull or strain (stress) within a composition caused by the placement and distance between forms.

Tertiary colors   Colors that are a result of mixing unequal amounts of two primary colors (for example, a green that is produced by mixing more yellow than blue) or of mixing primary and secondary colors (for example, the red-violet produced by mixing red and violet).

Texture   The illusion of an artwork's surface quality, such as rough, smooth, shiny, dull. It can be touched (tactile) and seen (visual), may be natural or synthetic.

Three-dimensional art   Artworks that have length, breadth, and depth, including sculptures of clay, metal, wood; mobiles; assemblages; neon light sculptures; and installation arts (art exhibitions using materials and objects to convey ideas).

Tie-dye   The process whereby knots are tied in cloth, such as a T-shirt, and then the cloth is dipped into liquid cloth dyes.

Tilt   To move the camera up toward the ceiling or down toward the floor.

Tint   A hue that is lightened and whose intensity is reduced by adding white. For example, pink is a tint of red.

Tone The lightness or darkness of a color. Also, the coolness or warmness of a color or painting.

Tools Instruments and equipment used to create and learn about art, such as brushes, scissors, brayers, easels, knives, kilns, and cameras.

Translucent Describes materials, such as certain plastics, that you cannot see through but that permit light waves to pass through.

Transparent Describes materials, such as glass, air, and water, that permit light to pass through them unchanged. Transparent materials do not cast shadows.

Two-dimensional art Artworks that have length and width, but not depth, including paintings, drawings, prints, and collages.

Underpainting A preliminary painting—usually in one color— applied as a beginning step in some painting techniques.

Unity A harmonious relationship of parts.

Value A quality of color that describes the amount of light (tint) or dark (shade) contained in the color on a scale ranging from black to white. Adding white to a color lightens the value. Adding black to a color darkens the value. Value can establish mood, flow, direction, and form. In a photograph, value is the variation of grays or tones.

Value scale A series of gray tones that range from white to black.

Vanishing point A perspective term that refers to the point on the horizon or eye-level line where receding parallel lines appear to converge.

Vehicle The substance or liquid mixed with previously ground pigments to make them more workable.

Viewfinder A device, such as a slide holder, for showing the area of a subject to be included in a picture. While helping to eliminate extraneous, nonessential elements from a picture, viewfinders also allow the viewer to select and "see" realistic perspective.

Visual approach Approach to art that involves seeing and representing the object as accurately as possible. A direct light source and shading are often used to represent the object realistically in space.

Visual arts A broad category of visual and cultural arts that includes the traditional fine arts, such as drawing, painting, printmaking, and sculpture; communication and design arts, such as film, television, graphics, and product design; architecture and environmental arts, such as urban, interior, and landscape design; and folk and cultural arts, which include ceramics, fibers, jewelry, and works in wood, paper, and other materials.

Visual arts problems Specific challenges based in thinking about and using visual arts components.

Volume A space or mass. The space occupied by a body. Indicated by dimensions in length, breadth, and depth.

Warm colors Red, orange, yellow—and derivatives.

Wash Describes a thin, transparent, watered-down use of paint or ink.

Wash brush A larger size of watercolor brush. See *watercolor brush*.

Watercolor brush Full-bodied brushes that hold a large amount of paint and are flat or come to a fine point when dipped in water.

Watercolor paint A transparent painting medium that uses pigment with a gum binder.

Weaving Interlacings of various materials to form a fabric, texture, or design.

Weight The perceived "heaviness" of an object or art element. Weight in a painting often depends on location, size, shape, color, and relationships to other art elements.

World Wide Web A part of the Internet that supports graphics and allows users to navigate by clicking with a mouse. It features hypertext, or words, phrases, or images usually outlined in blue that, when clicked on, send users to related files or other computer systems anywhere in the world. Also referred to as WWW or the Web.

WS Wide shot.

X-ray concept A drawing characteristic of young children whereby both inside and outside are drawn in the same picture. For example, children may draw several sides of an object, such as the front and both sides of a house, or their drawing may indicate that they can look through the walls of a house and show what is inside.

Zoom To change the focus of the lens without moving the camera (the effect of moving toward or away from the object being filmed).

Bibliography

FOUNDATION BOOKS

Alexander, Kay, and Michael Day, eds. *Discipline-Based Art Education: A Curriculum Sampler.* Los Angeles, Calif.: The Getty Center for Education in the Arts, 1991.

Amburgy, Patricia M., Donald Soucy, Mary Ann Stankiewicz, Brent Wilson, and Marjorie Wilson, eds. *History of Art Education: Proceedings from the Penn State Conference.* Reston, Va.: National Art Education Association with the assistance of the Getty Center for Education in the Arts, 1992.

Armstrong, Carmen L. *Designing Assessment in Art.* Reston, Va.: National Art Education Association, 1994.

Arnheim, Rudolf. *Art and Visual Perception.* 4th ed. Berkeley: University of California Press, 1964.

Arnheim, Rudolf. *Thoughts on Art Education.* Los Angeles, Calif.: The Getty Center for Education in the Arts, 1990.

Arnheim, R. "Learning by Looking and Thinking." *Educational Horizons* 2, no. 71 (1993): 94–98.

Art Educators of New Jersey. *Insights: Art in Special Education—Educating the Handicapped Through Art.* Reston, Va: National Art Education Association, 1990.

Art Educators of New Jersey. *Insights: Art in Special Education.* Reston, Va.: National Art Education Association, 1982.

Arts for Life. Los Angeles, Calif.: The Getty Center for Education in the Arts, 1990. Videocassette.

Aschbacher, Pamela R., and Lynn Winters. *A Practical Guide to Alternative Assessment.* Alexandria, Va.: Association for Supervision and Curriculum Development, 1992.

Blakemore, C. *Mechanics of the Mind.* New York: Cambridge University Press, 1977.

Blakeslee, T. R. *The Right Brain.* Garden City, N.Y.: Anchor Press, 1980.

Boffoly, R. L. "A Factor Analysis of Visual, Kinesthetic and Cognitive Modes of Information Handling." *Review of Research in Visual Arts Education* 8 (1978): 17–27.

Bogen, J. E. "Some Educational Aspects of Hemispheric Specialization." *U.C.L.A Educator* 17 (1975): 24–32.

Broudy, Harry S. *The Role of Imagery in Learning.* Los Angeles, Calif.: The Getty Center for Education in the Arts, 1988.

Broudy, Harry S. *The Role of Art in General Education.* Los Angeles, Calif.: The Getty Center for Education in the Arts, 1987. Videocassette.

Broudy, H. S. "A Common Curriculum in Aesthetics and Fine Arts." In *Individual Differences and the Common Curriculum.* 82nd Yearbook of the National Society for the Study of Education, Pt. 1. Edited by J. Fenstermacher and J. Goodlad, 219–247. Chicago: University of Chicago Press, 1983.

Buzan, T. *Use Both Sides of Your Brain.* New York: E. P. Dutton, 1976.

Cane, Florence. *The Artist in Each of Us.* New York: Pantheon, 1951.

Careers in the Visual Arts. Reston, Va.: National Art Education Association, 1993.

Carothers, T., and H. Gardner. "When Children's Drawings Become Art: The Emergence of Aesthetic Production and Perception." *Developmental Psychology* 15 (1979): 570–580.

Carroll, Karen Lee. "Toward A Fuller Conception of Giftedness: Art in Gifted Education and the Gifted in Art Education." Ph.D. diss., Teachers College, Columbia University, 1987.

Chapman, L. *Adventures in Art.* Worcester, Mass.: Davis Publications, 1993.

Clark, Gilbert, Enid Zimmerman, and Marilyn Zurmuelen. *Understanding Art Testing.* Reston, Va.: National Art Education Association, 1987.

Clark, Gilbert A., and Enid Zimmerman. *Resources for Educating Artistically Talented Students.* Syracuse, N.Y.: Syracuse University Press, 1987.

Clements, Claire B., and Robert D. Clements. *Art and Mainstreaming: Art Instruction for Exceptional Students in the Regular School Classroom.* Springfield, Ill.: Charles C Thomas, 1983.

Cox, M. V. "Spatial Depth Relationships in Young Children's Drawings." *Journal of Experimental Child Psychology* 26 (1978): 551–554.

Davis, William E. *Resource Guide to Special Education.* 2nd ed. Needham Heights, Mass.: Allyn & Bacon, 1986.

Day, Michael, and A. Hurwitz. *Children and Their Art.* New York: Harcourt Brace Jovanovich, 1995.

Deporter, D. A., and R. D. Kavanaugh. "Parameters of Children's Sensitivity to Painting Styles." *Studies in Art Education* 20 (1978): 43–48.

Dewey, John. *Art as Experience*. New York: Putnam, 1958.

Di Blasio, M. K. "Continuing the Translation: Further Delineations of the DBAE Format." *Studies in Art Education* 25, no. 4 (1985): 212–218.

"Discipline-Based Art Education: What Forms Will It Take?" National Invitational Conference, The Getty Center for Education in the Arts, Los Angeles, Calif., January 1987.

Dissanayake, E. "Art as a Human Behavior: Toward an Ethological View of Art." *The Journal of Aesthetics and Art Criticism* 38 (1980).

Dobbs, Stephen M. *Art Education and Back to Basics*. Reston, Va.: National Art Education Association, 1979.

Dobbs, Stephen Mark. *The DBAE Handbook: An Overview of Discipline-Based Art Education*. Los Angeles, Calif.: The Getty Center for Education in the Arts, 1992.

Doerr, S. L. "Conjugate Lateral Eye Movement, Cerebral Dominance, and the Figural Creativity Factors of Fluency, Flexibility, or Originality, and Elaboration." *Studies in Art Education* 21 (1980): 5–11.

Dorn, Charles M. *Thinking in Art: A Philosophical Approach to Art Education*. Reston, Va.: National Art Education Association, 1994.

Efland, Arthur. *History of Art Education: Intellectual and Social Currents in Teaching the Visual Arts*. New York: Teachers College Press, Columbia University, 1990.

Eisner, Elliot W. *Cognition and Curriculum: A Basis for Deciding What to Teach*. White Plains, N.Y.: Longman, 1982.

Eisner, Elliot W. *Cognition and Curriculum*. White Plains, N.Y.: K. Longman, 1982.

Eisner, Elliot W. *The Role of Discipline-Based Art Education in America's Schools*. Los Angeles, Calif.: The Getty Center for Education in the Arts, 1985.

Elementary Art Programs: A Guide for Administrators. Reston, Va.: National Art Education Association, 1992.

Erickson, Mary. *Lessons About Art in History and History in Art*. Bloomington: ERIC/Art Indiana University, 1992.

Feldman, Edmund B. *Art as Image and Idea*. Englewood Cliffs, N.J.: Prentice Hall, 1967.

Feldman, Edmund Burke. *Thinking about Art*. Englewood Cliffs, N.J.: Prentice Hall, 1985.

Feldman, Edmund Burke. *Varieties of Visual Experiences*. 3rd ed. Englewood Cliffs, N.J.: Prentice Hall, 1987.

Foster, S. "Hemisphere Dominance and the Art Process." *Art Education* 30 (1977): 28–29.

Gaitskell, Charles D., and Al Hurwitz. *Children and Their Art: Methods for the Elementary School*. 4th ed. New York: Harcourt Brace Jovanovich, 1982.

Gardner, H. "Educating for Understanding." *American School Board Journal* 7, no. 93 (1993): 35–36.

Gardner, Howard. *Multiple Intelligences: The Theory in Practice*. New York: Basic Books, 1991.

Gardner, Howard. The Getty Center for Education in the Arts, *Art Education and Human Development*. Los Angeles, Calif.: 1990.

Gardner, Howard. *Frames of Mind*. New York: Basic Books, 1985.

Gardner, Howard. *Artful Scribbles: The Significance of Children's Drawings*. New York: Basic Books, 1980.

Garrett, S. V. "Putting Our Whole Brain to Use: A Fresh Look at the Creative Process." *The Journal of Creative Behavior* 10 (1976): 239–249.

Gazzaniga, M. "The Split Brain in Man." In *Perception: Mechanisms and Modes*, edited by R. Held and W. Richards. San Francisco, Calif.: W. M. Freeman, 1972.

Gearhart, Bill R., and Mel W. Weishawn. *The Handicapped Student in the Regular Classroom*. 2nd ed. St Louis: Mosby, 1980.

Gerschwind, N. "Specializations of the Human Brain." *Scientific American* 241 (1979): 180–199.

Goldstein, E., T. Katz, J. D. Kowalchuk, and R. Saunders. *Understanding and Creating Art*. St. Paul, Minn.: West Publishing Co., 1992.

Golomb, Claire. *The Child's Creation of a Pictorial World*. Berkeley: University of California Press, 1992.

Golomb, C. "Representational Development of the Human Figure." *The Journal of Genetic Psychology* 131 (1977): 207–222.

Gombrich, Ernest H. *The Sense of Order: A Study in the Psychology of Decorative Art*. Ithaca, N.Y.: Cornell University Press, 1979.

Goodnow, J. J. "Visible Thinking: Cognitive Aspects of Change in Drawings." *Child Development* 49 (1978): 637–641.

Greer, W. D. Discipline-Based Art Education: Approaching Art as a Subject of Study. *Studies in Art Education* 25, no. 4 (1984): 212–218.

Grogg, P. "Art and Reading: Is There a Relationship?" *Reading World*, May 1978, 345–351.

Guilford, J. P. "The Nature of Creative Thinking." *American Psychology*, September 1950.

Hamblen, K. "Developing Aesthetic Literacy through Contested Concepts," *Art Education* 37, no. 5: 19–24.

Hardiman, George W., and Theodore Zernich. *Foundations for Curriculum Development and Evaluation in Art Education*. 1st ed. Champaign, Ill.: Stipes, 1981.

Harris, D. B. "The Child's Representation of Space." In *The Child's Representation of the World*, edited by G. Butterworth. New York: Plenum Press, 1977.

Hausman, Jerome J. "Computers, Video-Disks, and Art Teachers." *Art Education* 44, no. 3 (1991): 4–6.

Henley, David. *Exceptional Children/Exceptional Art: Teaching Art to Special Needs*. Worcester, Mass.: Davis Publications, 1992.

Henry, David. *Exceptional Children, Exceptional Art*. Worcester, Mass.: Davis Publications, 1992.

Herberholz, Barbara, and Lee Hanson. *Early Childhood Art*. 5th ed. Dubuque, Iowa: Brown & Benchmark, 1995.

Herberholz, Donald, and Barbara Herberholz. *Artworks for Elementary Teachers: Developing Artistic and Perceptual Awareness*. 7th ed. Dubuque, Iowa: Brown & Benchmark, 1994.

Herman, Joan L., Pamela R. Aschbacher, and Lynn Winters. *A Practical Guide to Alternative Assessment*. Alexandria, Va.: Association for Supervision and Curriculum Development, 1992.

Hewett, G. J., and J. C. Rush. "Finding Buried Treasure: Aesthetic Scanning with Children." *Art Education* 40, no. 1 (1987): 41–43.

History of Art Education: Proceedings from the Second Penn State Conference. Reston, Va.: National Art Education Association, 1992.

Hodgson, Harriet. *Artworks*. New York: Holt, Rinehart & Winston, 1990.

Hoffa, Harlan,. *Revisitations: Ten Little Pieces on Art Education*. Reston, Va.: National Art Education Association, 1994.

Hollingsworth, Patricia, and Stephen Hollingsworth. *Smart Art, Learning to Classify and Critique Art*. Tucson, Ariz.: Zephyr Press, 1989.

Hubbard, Guy. *Art in Action*. San Diego, Calif.: Coronado Publishers, 1987.

Hurwitz, Al. *The Gifted and Talented in Art: A Guide to Program Planning*. Worcester, Mass.: Davis Publications, 1983.

Ives, W., and M. Houseworth. "The Role of Standard Orientations in Children's Drawing of Interpersonal Relationships: Aspects of Graphic Feature Marking." *Child Development* 51 (1980): 591–593.

Johnson, Andra. *Art Education: Elementary.* Reston, Va.: National Art Education Association, 1992.

"Joint Statement on Integration of the Arts with Other Disciplines and with Each Other," *NAEA Advisory,* Spring, 1992.

Kaelin, Eugene. *An Aesthetics for Art Educators.* New York: Teachers College Press, 1989.

Kauppnen, Heta, and Read Diket, eds. *Trends in Art Education from Diverse Cultures.* Reston, Va.: National Art Education Association, 1995.

Kellogg, Rhoda. *Analyzing Children's Art.* Mountain View, Calif.: Mayfield Publishing, 1970.

Lanier, Vincent. *The Visual Arts and the Elementary Child.* New York: Teachers College Press, 1983.

Lankford, E. L. "A Phenomenological Methodology for Art Criticism." *Studies in Art Education,* 25, no. 3 (1984): 151–158.

Lankford, E. Louis. *Aesthetics: Issues and Inquiry.* Reston, Va.: National Art Education Association, 1992.

Lansing, Kenneth M., and Arlene E. Richards. *The Elementary Teacher's Art Handbook.* New York: Holt, Rinehart & Winston, 1981.

Lee, Sherman E. *Reflections of Reality in Japanese Art.* Bloomington: Indiana University Press, 1983.

Lewis, H. P., and N. Livson. "Cognitive Development, Personality, and Drawings: Their Interrelationships in a Longitudinal Study." *Studies in Art Education* 22 (1980): 8–11.

Light, P. H., and E. Macintosh. "Depth Relationships in Young Children's Drawings." *Journal of Experimental Child Psychology* 30 (1980): 79–87.

Logan, Fred. *Growth of Art in American Schools.* New York: Harper & Row, 1955.

Lowenfeld, Viktor. *Creative and Mental Growth.* 1st ed. New York: Macmillan, 1947.

Lowenfeld, Viktor, and W. Lambert Brittain. *Creative and Mental Growth.* New York: Macmillan Publishing Co., Inc., 1987.

Madega, Stanley S. *Arts & Aesthetics: An Agenda for the Future.* New Brunswick, N.J.: Transaction Books, 1978.

Madeja, Stanley. *Gifted and Talented in Art Education.* Reston, Va.: National Art Education Association, 1983.

"Mainstreaming Art for the Handicapped Child: Resources for Teacher Preparation." *Art Education,* November, 1984.

Marantz, K. "The Importance of Being Language: The Passion of Political Possibilities." *Studies in Art Education* 29, no. 2 (1988): 67–71.

Marantz, K. *The Arts, Cognition & Basic Skills.* 1st ed. New Brunswick, N.J.: Transaction Books, 1977.

McCallum, R. S., and S. M. Glynn. "The Hemispheric Specialization Construct: Developmental and Instructional Considerations for Creative Behavior." Paper read at the meeting of the National Association of School Psychologists, San Diego, Calif., 1979.

Mitchelmore, M. C. "Developmental Stages in Children's Representation of Regular Solid Figures." *Journal of Genetic Psychology* 133 (1978): 229–239.

Mittler, Gene A. *Art in Focus.* Mission Hills, Calif.: Glencoe Publishing Co., 1989.

Moody, William J. *Artistic Intelligences: Implications for Education.* 3rd ed. New York: Teachers College Press, 1990.

Moore, Ronald, ed. *Aesthetics for Young People.* Reston, Va.: National Art Education Association, 1995.

"National Assessment of Art." *Design and Drawing Skills.* Washington, D.C.: U.S. Government Printing Office, 1977.

Nicki, R. M., and A. Gale. "EEG, Measures of Complexity, and Preference for Nonrepresentational Works of Art." *Perception* 6 (1977): 281–286.

Ocvirk, Otto G., Robert O. Bone, Robert E. Stinson, and Philip R. Wigg. *Art Fundamentals: Theory and Practice.* 7th ed. Madison, Wisc.: Brown & Benchmark, 1996.

Ornstein, R. E. *The Psychology of Consciousness.* 2nd ed. New York: Harcourt Brace Jovanovich, 1977.

Parsons, M. J. *How We Understand Art: A Cognitive Developmental Account of Aesthetic Experience.* New York: Cambridge University Press, 1987.

Payne, Ruth. *Exceptional Children in Focus.* 4th ed. Columbus, Ohio: Merrill, 1989.

Pekarick, Andrew. *Behind the Scenes.* Series. New York: Hyperion Books for Children, 1992. (*Painting Behind the Scenes, Sculpture Behind the Scenes*)

Pritchard, M. *Philosophical Adventures with Children.* Lanham, Md.: University Press of America, 1985.

Purposes, Principles, and Standards For School Art Programs. Rev. ed. Reston, Va.: National Art Education Association, 1994.

Raudsepp, Eugene. *More Creative Growth Games.* New York: G. P. Putnam's Sons, 1980.

Read, Herbert. *Education Through Art.* Rev. ed. New York: Pantheon Books, 1958.

Read, Herbert. *The Meaning of Art.* London: Faber and Faber, 1931.

"Research Readings For Discipline-Based Art Education: A Journey Beyond Creating." Stephen M. Dobbs, editor. Reston, Va.: National Art Education Association, 1988.

Rollins, Jeanne. *The National Visual Art Standards.* Reston, Va.: National Art Education Association, 1994.

Rubin, Judith. "Growing Through Art with the Multiple Handicapped." *Viewpoints: Dialogue in Art Education,* 1976.

Rush, J. C. "Components of Tutored Images Within a Studio Art Lesson." Paper presented at National Art Education Association meeting, Los Angeles, Calif., 1988.

School Art Programs: A Guide for School Board Members and Superintendents. Reston, Va.: National Art Education Association, 1992.

Schwartz, Bernard. "The Power and Potential of Laser Video-disk Technology for Art Education in the 90s." *Art Education* 44, no. 3 (1991): 8–17.

Semrau, Penelope, and Barbara A. Boyer. *Using Interactive Video in Education.* Needham Heights, Mass.: Allyn & Bacon, 1994.

Sevigny, M. J. "Discipline-Based Art Education and Teacher Education." *Journal of Aesthetic Education,* 21, no. 2: 95–126.

Sharer, J. "Children's Inquiry into Aesthetics." Paper delivered at the National Art Education Association Convention, New Orleans, 1986.

Smith, Ralph A., ed. *Discipline-Based Art Education: Origins, Meaning, and Development.* Champaign: University of Illinois Press, 1989.

Smith, Ralph. *Excellence II: The Continuing Quest in Art Education.* Reston, Va.: National Art Education Association, 1995.

Soucy, Donald, and Mary Ann Stankiewicz, eds. *Framing the Past: Essays on Art Education.* Reston, Va.: National Art Education Association, 1990.

Susi, Frank. *Student Behaviors in Art Classrooms: The Dynamics of Discipline.* Reston, Va.: National Art Education Association, 1995.

Tauton, M. "The Influence of Age on Preferences for Subject Matter, Realism, and Spatial Depth in Painting Reproductions." *Studies in Art Education* 21 (1980): 40–52.

Thompson, Christine, ed. *The Visual Arts and Early Childhood Learning*. Reston, Va.: National Art Education Association, 1995.

Thorne, Joye H. "Mainstreaming and Procedures: Eligibility and Placement." *NAEA Advisory*, Spring, 1990.

Uhlin, Donald. *Art For Exceptional Children*. Dubuque, Iowa: Wm. C. Brown, 1972.

Verhelst, Wilbert. *Sculpture: Tools, Materials and Techniques*. 2nd ed. Englewood Cliffs, N.J.: Prentice Hall, 1988.

Viktor Lowenfeld Speaks on Art and Creativity. Reston, Va.: National Art Education Association, 1968.

Visual Arts Education Reform Handbook. Reston, Va.: National Art Education Association, 1995.

Wachowiak, Frank. *Emphasis Art*. 4th ed. New York: Harper & Row, 1985.

Wigg, Philip R., Jean Hasselschwert, and Willard F. Wankelman. *A Handbook of Arts and Crafts*. 9th ed. Dubuque, Iowa: Brown & Benchmark, 1997.

Willats, J. "How Children Learn to Draw Realistic Pictures." *Journal of Experimental Psychology* 29 (1977): 367–382.

Winner, E. *Invented Worlds, The Psychology of the Arts*. Cambridge: Harvard University Press, 1982.

Wittrock, M. C., et al. *The Human Brain*. Englewood Cliffs, N.J.: Prentice Hall, Inc., 1977.

Young, Bernard, ed. *Art, Culture and Ethnicity*. Reston, Va.: National Art Education Association, 1990.

Youngblood, M. S. "The Hemispherality Wagon Leaves Laterality Station at 12:45 for Art Superiority Land." *Studies in Art Education* 21 (1979: 44–49.

Zimmerman, Enid. "Assessing Students' Progress and Achievements in Art Education." *Art Education* 45, no. 6 (1992): 16.

ART BOOKS

Adams, Laurie Schneider. *A History of Western Art*. Dubuque, Iowa: Brown & Benchmark, 1994.

Ades, Dawn. *Art in Latin America*. New Haven, Conn.: Yale University Press, 1989.

"A Framework for Multicultural Education." *NAEA Advisory*, Fall, 1991.

Alcorn, Johnny. *Rembrandt's Beret*. New York: William Morrow, 1991.

Alva, Walter, and Christopher Donan. *Royal Tombs of Sipan*. Los Angeles: University of California, 1993. (History of the Moche people of ancient Peru.)

Artists of Contemporary Mexican Painting. Organized by the American Society, New York, 1990.

Aukerman, Ruth. *Move Over, Picasso! A Young Painter's Primer*. New Windsor, Md.: Pat Depke Books, 1994.

A Weekend With _____ . Series. New York: Rizzoli International Publications, 1991. (*Degas* by Rosabianca Skira-Venturi; *Picasso* by Florian Rodari; *Rembrandt* by Pascal Bonafoux; *Renoir* by Rosabianca Skira-Venturi.)

Barrett, Terry. *Criticizing Art: Understanding the Contemporary*. Mountain View, Calif.: Mayfield Publishing Co., 1994.

Barrez, Bonnie, executive editor. *ARTnews for Students*, 48 West 38th Street, New York, NY 10018. Magazine for students 9–15. New in 1995.

Battin, Margaret, John Fisher, Ronald Moore, and Anita Silvers. *Puzzles About Art: An Aesthetic Casebook*. New York: St. Martin's Press, 1989.

Betti, Claudia W., and Teel Sale. *Drawing: A Contemporary Approach*. 2nd ed. New York: Holt, Rinehart & Winston, 1986.

Biller, Geraldine P. *Latin American Women Artists 1915–1995*. Milwaukee, Wis.: Milwaukee Art Museum, 1995.

Birren, Faber. *History of Color in Painting*. New York: Van Nostrand Reinhold, 1980.

Bober, Natalie S. *Marc Chagall, Painter of Dreams*. Philadelphia: The Jewish Publications Society, 1991.

Boddeley, Oriana, and Valerie Fraser. *Drawing the Line*. New York: Verso, 1989.

Bridgman, George. *Constructive Anatomy*. New York: Dover Publications, Inc., 1960.

Bro, Lu. *Drawing: A Studio Guide*. New York: W. W. Norton & Co., 1985.

Brommer, Gerald F. *Discovering Art History*. 3rd ed. Worcester, Mass.: Davis Publications, 1996.

Brommer, Gerald F., and Nancy K. Kinne. *Exploring Painting*. Worcester, Mass.: Davis Publications, 1995.

Brommer, G. F. *Discovering Art History*. Worcester, Mass.: Davis Publications, 1996.

Brown, Osa. *The Metropolitan Museum of Art Activity Book*. New York: Harry N. Abrams, 1990.

Chaet, Bernard. *An Artist's Notebook: Techniques and Materials*. New York: Harcourt Brace College Publishers, 1979.

Chaet, Bernard. *The Art of Drawing*. 3rd ed. New York: Harcourt Brace College Publishers, 1983.

Children's Atlas of Native Americans. Chicago, Ill.: Rand McNally, 1992.

Clark, Kenneth. *What is a Masterpiece?* New York: Thames & Hudson, 1979.

Colle, Marie-Purre. *Latin American Artists in Their Studios*. New York: Vendome Press, 1994.

Computer Artist. Pennwell Publication, P.O. Box 3188, Tulsa, OK.

Computer Graphics World. Pennwell Publication, Tulsa, OK.

Computer Pictures. Montage Publication, Inc. P.O. Box 16926, North Hollywood, CA 91615.

Cooper, Mario. *Painting with Watercolor*. New York: Van Nostrand Reinhold, 1981.

Cotton, Bob. *Cyberspace Lexicon*. London: Interactive Media, 1994.

Craven, Wayne. *American Art: History and Culture*. Dubuque, Iowa: Brown & Benchmark, 1994.

D'Alelio, Jane. *I Know That Building: Discovering Architecture With Activities and Games*. Washington, D.C.: The Preservation Press, 1989.

Diebenkorn, Richard. *Etchings and Drypoints 1949–1980*. Houston, Tex.: Houston Fine Arts Press, 1981.

Du Moulin, Yvonne. *Creating Watercolor Techniques*. New York: Van Nostrand Reinhold, 1982.

Dubelaar, Thea, and Ruud Bruijn. *Looking for Vincent*. New York: Checkerboard Press, 1992.

Edwards, Betty. *Drawing on the Right Side of the Brain*. Los Angeles: J. P. Tarcher, Inc., 1979.

Ellinger, Richard G. *Color Structure and Design*. New York: Van Nostrand Reinhold, 1980.

Finn, David. *How to Visit a Museum*. New York: Harry N. Abrams, 1985.

First Impressions: Introductions to Art. Series. New York: Harry N. Abrams, 1990/92.

Fitzpatrick, Virginia L. *Art History: A Contextual Inquiry Course*. Reston, Va.: National Art Education Association, 1992.

Florian, Douglas. *A Potter*. New York: William Morrow, 1991.

Foster, Richard, and Pamela Tudor-Craig. *The Secret Life of Paintings*. New York: St. Martin's Press, 1986.

Gardner, Helen. *Art Through the Ages*. Revised by Horst de la Croix and Richard G. Tansey. New York: Harcourt Brace Jovanovich, 1991.

Gelman, Woody. *The Best of Charles Dana Gibson*. New York: Crown Publishers, Inc., 1969.

Gilbert, Rita, and William McCarter. *Living with Art*. New York: Alfred A. Knopf, Inc., 1988.

Gilbert, Rita, and William McCarter. *Living With Art*. New York: Alfred A. Knopf, 1995.

Glubok, Shirley. *Art of _____* Series. New York: Macmillan, 1988. (*Colonial America, New American Nation, Old West, Southwest Indians, Northwest Coast Indians, North American Indians, Plains Indians, Spanish in the U.S.* and *Puerto Rico, China, India, Japan, Africa, America in the Gilded Age, photography, Peru, Ancient Rome, Etruscans, Vikings,* etc.)

Goldsmith, Lawrence C. *Watercolor Bold and Free*. New York: Watson-Guptill Publications, 1980.

Gombrich, Ernest H. *The Story of Art*. 5th ed. Englewood Cliffs, N.J.: Prentice Hall, 1989.

Gombrich, E. H. *Art and Illustration*. Bollington series. Princeton, N.J.: Princeton University Press, 1960.

Goodman, Cynthia. *Digital Visions, Computers and Art*. New York: Harry N. Abrams, 1987.

Goodwin, MacArthur. *Design Standards for School Art Facilities*. Reston, Va.: National Art Education Association, 1993.

Greh, Deborah. *Computers in the Artroom: A Handbook for Teachers*. Worcester, Mass.: Davis Publications, 1990.

Heller, Nancy G. *Women Artists: An Illustrated History*. New York: Abbeville Press, 1987.

Herbert, Robert L. *Modern Artists on Art*. Englewood Cliffs, N.J.: Prentice Hall, Inc., 1964.

Hoban, Tana. *Spirals, Curves, Fanshapes & Lines*. New York: Greenwillow Books, 1992.

Hogarth, Burne. *Dynamic Figure Drawing*. New York: Watson-Guptill Publications, 1980.

Janson, H. W. *History of Art for Young People*, 4th ed. New York: Abrams, 1992.

Janson, H. W. *History of Art*, 5th ed. New York: Abrams, 1994.

Jenkins, Jessica. *Thinking About Colors*. New York: Dutton Children's Books, 1992.

Johns, Arthur F. *Introduction to Art*. New York: HarperCollins, 1992.

Kaplan, Janet. *Unexpected Journeys: The Art and Life of Remedios Varo*. New York: Abbeville Press, 1994.

Kissick, John. *Art: Context and Criticism*. 2nd ed. Dubuque, Iowa: Brown & Benchmark, 1996.

Lahti, N. E. *Plain Talk about Art*. Brooklyn, N.Y.: York Books, 1989.

Lamm, Robert C. *The Humanities in Western Culture: Volumes 1 & 2*. Dubuque, Iowa: Brown & Benchmark, 1996.

Lee, Sherman E. *Reflections of Reality in Japanese Art*. Bloomington: Indiana University Press, 1983.

Lerner, Sharon. *The _____ in Art*. Series. Minneapolis, Minn.: Lerner Publications, 1970. (*Self-portrait, Portraits, Circus and Fairs, Farms and Farmers, Kings and Queens,* etc.)

Lippard, Lucy. *Mixed Blessings: New Art in a Multicultural America*. New York: Pantheon Books, 1990.

Loumaye, Jacqueline. *Art for Children*. Series. New York: Chelsea House, 1994. (*Brueghel, Chagall, daVinci, Degas, Gauguin, The Impressionists, Matisse, Miró, Picasso, The Renaissance, Rousseau, Van Gogh*.)

Loveless, Richard, ed. *The Computer Revolution and the Arts*. Tampa: University of South Florida Press, 1989.

Lowery, Pat. *I am an Artist*. Brookfield, Conn.: Millbrook Press, 1992.

Lucie-Smith, Edward. *Art in the Seventies*. Ithaca, N.Y.: Cornell University Press, 1980.

Lucie-Smith, Edward, *Latin American Art of the 20th Century*. New York: Thames & Hudson, 1993.

Matthews, Sarach. *Young Discovery Library Series*. Ossining, N.Y.: Young Discovery Library, 1988/89.

McKissack, Patricia. *Aztec Indians*. Chicago, Ill.: Children's Press, 1985.

Micklethwait, Lucy. *I Spy: An Alphabet in Art*. New York: Greenwillow Books, 1992.

Muhlberger, Richard. *What Makes a Degas a Degas?* New York: Viking, 1993. (Also *Monet, Brueghel, Raphael, Rembrandt,* and *Van Gogh*.)

Museum Colors, Museum Numbers, Museum Shapes. Boston: Museum of Fine Arts, 1993.

National Museum of African Art. *The Art of West African Kingdoms*. Washington, D.C.: Smithsonian Institution Press, 1987.

Native Peoples of the Southwest. Susan Shaffer Heard Museum, 1987.

Nemett, Barry. *Images, Objects and Ideas: Viewing the Visual Arts*. Dubuque, Iowa: Brown & Benchmark, 1992.

Nicolaides, Kimon. *The Natural Way to Draw*. Boston, Mass.: Houghton Mifflin, 1941.

Ocvirk, Otto G., Robert E. Stinson, Phillip R. Wigg, Robert O. Bone, and David L. Cayton. *Art Fundamentals: Theory & Practice*. 7th ed. Dubuque, Iowa: Brown & Benchmark, 1994.

Pepper, Frank. *Art of the Electronic Age*. New York: Harry N. Abrams, 1993.

Piper, David. *Looking at Art*. New York: Random House, 1984.

Ragans, R. *Art Talk*. Mission Hills, Calif.: Glencoe Publishing Co., 1988.

Richmond, Robin. *Children in Art: The Story in a Picture*. Nashville, Tenn.: Ideals Children's Books, 1992.

Richmond, Robin. *Introducing Michaelangelo*. Boston: Little Brown, 1991.

Roalf, Peggy. *Looking at Paintings*. Series. New York: Hyperion Books for Children, 1992. (Dancers, Landscapes, Families)

Rosen, Randy, et al. *Making Their Mark: Women Artists Move Into the Mainstream*. Edited by Catherine Brawer. New York: Abbeville Press, 1991.

Rubenstein, Charlotte Streifer. *American Women Artists*. Boston: G. K. Hall & Co., 1982.

Russell, Stella Pandell. *Art in the World*. 3rd ed. New York: Holt, Rinehart & Winston, Inc., 1989.

Russell, Stella Pandell. *Art in the World*. New York: Holt, Rinehart & Winston, 1989.

Schwartz, Lillian F. *The Computer Artist's Handbook*. New York: W. W. Norton & Co., 1992.

Selz, Peter. *Art in Our Times*. New York: Harry N. Abrams, 1981.

Sewell, Darrel, Dewey Mosby, and R. A. Minter. *Henry Ossawa Tanner*. New York: Rizzoli International Publications, 1991.

Slatkin, Wendy. *Women Artists in History: From Antiquity to the Twentieth Century*. Englewood Cliffs, N.J.: Prentice Hall, 1990.

Smeets, Rene. *Signs, Symbols & Ornaments*. New York: Van Nostrand Reinhold, 1982.

Sproccati, D. Sandro, ed. *A Guide to Art*. New York: Harry N. Abrams, 1992.

Stofflet, Mary. *Latin American Drawings Today*. Seattle: University of Washington Press, 1991.

Szabo, Zoltan. *Creative Watercolor Techniques*. New York: Watson-Guptill Publications, 1980.

The Graywolf Annual Five: Multi-Cultural Literacy. Saint Paul, Minn.: Graywolf Press, 1988.

The National Museum of the American Indian, Smithsonian Institution and others. *Native Peoples*. Phoenix, Ariz.: Media Concepts Group, Inc.

Vanderpoel, John H. *The Human Figure*. New York: Dover Publications, Inc., 1958.

What Every Young American Should Know and Be Able to Do in the Arts. Reston, Va.: National Standards for Arts Education, 1994.

Wilson, Forrest. *What it Feels Like to be a Building.* Washington, D.C.: The Preservation Press, 1988.

Winn, Peter. *Americas.* New York: Pantheon Books, 1992.

Woolf, Felicity. *Picture This: A First Introduction to Paintings.* New York: Doubleday, 1989.

Woolf, Felicity. *Picture This Century.* New York: Bantam Doubleday Dell, 1993.

Yenawine, Philip. *Shapes, Lines, Colors, Stories.* Series. New York: Bantam Doubleday Dell, 1991.

Yenawine, Philip. *How to Look at Modern Art.* New York: Harry N. Abrams, 1991.

Index